Analyses of the ecology, biology and society of past and present-day hunter-gatherers are at the core of this interdisciplinary volume. Since the seminal work of *Man the Hunter* in 1968, new research in these three areas has become increasingly specialised, and the lines of communication between academic disciplines have all but broken down. This volume aims to re-establish an interdisciplinary debate, presenting critical issues commanding an ongoing interest in hunter–gatherer research, covering evolution and history, demography and biology, technology, social organisation, art and language of diverse groups. As a reference text, this book will be useful to scholars and students of cultural and social anthropology, archaeology, biological anthropology and human sciences.

CATHERINE PANTER-BRICK is Reader in Anthropology at the University of Durham. Her research interests focus on health and reproduction, human biology and ecology She has also edited *Biosocial Perspectives on Children* (1998), and co-edited *Hormones, Health and Behavior* (1999) and *Abandoned Children* (2000).

ROBERT H. LAYTON is Professor of Anthropology at the University of Durham. His interests lie in social change and social evolution, and he is author of several books including *The Anthropology of Art* (1981/1991), *Australian Rock Art* (1992) and *An Introduction to Theory in Anthropology* (1997).

PETER ROWLEY-CONWY is Reader in Archaeology at the University of Durham. His main research interest is the archaeology of anatomically modern hunter-gatherers, their patterns of land use and resource exploitation, and the ways in which they developed or adopted agriculture. He is editor of *Mesolithic Northwest Europe* (1987), *Whither Environmental Archaeology?* (1994) and *Animal Bones, Human Societies* (2000).

D1354670

THE BIOSOCIAL SOCIETY SYMPOSIUM SERIES
Series editor: Dr Catherine Panter-Brick, University of Durham

The aim of the Biosocial Society is to examine topics and issues of biological and social importance and to promote studies of biosocial matters. By examining various contemporary issues and phenomena, which clearly have dimensions in both the social and biological sciences, the Society hopes to foster the integration and inter-relationships of these dimensions.

Previously published volumes

Volumes 1–8 are available from Oxford University Press.

Hunter–gatherers:
an interdisciplinary perspective

Edited by

CATHERINE PANTER-BRICK,
ROBERT H. LAYTON and
PETER ROWLEY-CONWY
University of Durham

CAMBRIDGE
UNIVERSITY PRESS

PUBLISHED BY THE PRESS SYNDICATE OF THE UNIVERSITY OF
CAMBRIDGE
The Pitt Building, Trumpington Street, Cambridge, United Kingdom

CAMBRIDGE UNIVERSITY PRESS
The Edinburgh Building, Cambridge CB2 2RU, UK
40 West 20th Street, New York, NY 10011–4211, USA
10 Stamford Road, Oakleigh, VIC 3166, Australia
Ruiz de Alarcón 13, 28014 Madrid, Spain
Dock House, The Waterfront, Cape Town 8001, South Africa

http://www.cambridge.org

First published 2001

Printed in the United Kingdom at the University Press, Cambridge

Typeface Baskerville 11.5/14pt   *System* 3B2   [CE]

A catalogue record for this book is available from the British Library

Library of Congress Cataloguing in Publication data

Hunter–gatherers: an interdisciplinary perspective/edited by
Catherine Panter-Brick, Robert H. Layton & Peter Rowley-Conwy.
    p.   cm. – (The Biosocial Society symposium series)
Includes bibliographical references.
ISBN 0 521 77210 9 – ISBN 0 521 77672 4 (pb)
1. Hunting and gathering societies – Research.
I. Panter-Brick, Catherine, 1959– .
II. Layton, Robert, 1944– .
III. Rowley-Conwy, P., 1951– .   IV. Series.
GN388.H865   2001
306.3′64–dc21   00–058511

ISBN 0 521 77210 9 hardback
ISBN 0 521 77672 4 paperback

Contents

Contributors

M.W. CONKEY
Department of Anthropology, University of
California–Berkeley
Berkeley, California 94720–3710, USA

A. FROMENT
Laboratoire ERMES, ORSTOM, 5 rue du Carbone,
45072 Orleans Cedex 2, France

M.R. JENIKE
Department of Sociology and Anthropology, Pomona College,
420 N. Harvard Avenue, Claremont, California 91711–6397,
USA

S.L. KUHN
Department of Anthropology, Emil W. Haury Building,
University of Arizona, Tucson, Arizona 85721, USA

R.H. LAYTON
Department of Anthropology, University of Durham,
43 Old Elvet, Durham DH1 3HN, UK

P. MCCONVELL
Australian Institute of Aboriginal and Torres Strait Islander
Studies, Canberra ACT 2601, Australia

C. PANTER-BRICK
Department of Anthropology, University of Durham,
43 Old Elvet, Durham DH1 3HN, UK

R. PENNINGTON
  Department of Anthropology, University of Utah,
  Salt Lake City, Utah 84112, USA

P. ROWLEY-CONWY
  Department of Archaeology, Science Site, South Road,
  University of Durham, Durham DH1 3LE, UK

M.C. STINER
  Department of Anthropology, University of Arizona,
  Tucson, Arizona 85721, USA

R. TORRENCE
  Division of Anthropology, Australian Museum,
  6 College Street, Sydney NSW 2010, Australia

B. WINTERHALDER
  Department of Anthropology, University of North Carolina,
  Chapel Hill, North Carolina 27599, USA

1

Lines of enquiry

CATHERINE PANTER-BRICK, ROBERT H. LAYTON
AND PETER ROWLEY-CONWY

Areas of research

Analyses of the ecology, biology, and society of past and present-day hunter–gatherers are at the core of this interdisciplinary volume. A great deal of new research has been published in these three areas since *Man the Hunter* (Lee and DeVore 1968), but almost invariably in separate works rather than in a single volume. Consequently, hunter–gatherer studies have become increasingly specialised, the common forum provided by *Man the Hunter* and the lines of communication between academic disciplines having all but broken down.

The recent *Cambridge Encyclopedia of Hunters and Gatherers* (Lee and Daly 1999) presents the ethnographies of 53 groups world-wide and reviews the history and culture, the indigenous world-views, and the emergence of hunter–gatherers in wider public and political discourses. However, in contending that recent concerns have 'moved relatively far from evolutionary and ecological preoccupations' (p. 11), it includes little coverage of important issues in the field of biological anthropology and human ecology. Most other publications on hunter–gatherers either exclude biology and consider almost entirely present-day groups (Ingold *et al.* 1988, Burch and Ellana 1994), or conversely focus on evolutionary ecology (Bettinger, 1991, Kelly 1995), exclusively archaeological populations (Soffer and Gamble 1990), or a single group or region (Hill and Hurtado, 1996, Biesbrouck *et al.* 1999).

The present volume brings together several contributions in archaeology, social anthropology and biological anthropology. What issues are raised that command a continuing interest in these areas of research? There is, first and foremost, recognition that the diversity of hunter–gatherer groups requires satisfactory analysis. Given this diversity, there are three major questions to address: Is 'hunter–gatherer' a meaningful category? How have hunter–gatherers been characterised by previous research? How do we approach hunter–gatherer variability? This chapter reviews the first two questions briefly, then considers the last by way of introducing the other chapters in this volume.

Is 'hunter–gatherer' a meaningful category?

Lee and Daly (1999: 3) define foraging (a term used synonymously with hunting and gathering) as 'subsistence based on hunting of wild animals, gathering of wild plant foods, and fishing, with no domestication of plants, and no domesticated animals except the dog'. This provides a 'minimal' definition, a starting-point on which to graft a more nuanced understanding of hunter–gatherers. It is important, however, to begin with a useful 'working definition'.

Hunters and gatherers rely upon a mode of subsistence charac-terised by the *absence of direct human control* over the reproduction of exploited species, and little or no control over other aspects of population ecology such as the behaviour and distribution of food resources. In essence, hunter–gatherers exercise no deliberate al-teration of the *gene pool* of exploited resources, in contrast to people who rely in the main upon an agricultural or pastoralist subsistence base. There will always be problematic cases with such a working definition. Thus contemporary foragers often practise a mixed subsistence – for example, gardening in tropical South America, reindeer herding in northern Asia, trading in south and southeast Asia and parts of Africa (Lee and Daly, 1999: 3). There are also ambiguous practices – such as the fine line between 'wild' and 'cultivated' sago palms in Indonesia (Ellen 1988) or 'wild' and 'domestic' pigs in highland Papua New Guinea (Rosman and Rubel 1989), where the 'cultivation' or 'domestication' of resources does not (as expected) entail their genetic alteration. Such problematic cases do not however detract from the general utility of a 'working definition' which focuses on the distinctive characteristics of hunter–gatherer subsistence activities.

The distinction between subsistence practices has empirical support, even though people who rely solely on hunting and gathering are fairly rare in the ethnographic record. Indeed most subsistence communities engage in a number of different economic activities – such as foraging, herding, or cultivation – but they do so in different proportions. One type of activity tends to predominate: there is not a continuous range of proportions, such that most societies do fall at one end or the other of a range of possibilities. As demonstrated by Hunn and Williams (1982), there is a hiatus between non-agricultural and agricultural subsistence practices. These authors plotted the percentage dependence on one particular activity such as hunting, gathering, fishing, herding, and agriculture for a sample of 200 societies drawn from the *Ethnographic Atlas* (Murdoch 1967). Some societies depend upon cultivated products for less than 5% of their diet; many others depend upon them for more than 45%. Remarkably few groups depend upon cultivation for between 5% and 45% of their subsistence. The data are limited in referring only to contemporary or recent societies, who have all been influenced by Euro-American colonialism, and they do not include archaeological populations. None the less, they indicate that the distinction between 'hunter–gatherers' and 'agriculturalists' has empirical utility at least in economic terms.

This 'working definition', which identifies hunting and gathering as subsistence activities entailing negligible control over the gene pool of food resources, has the virtue of simplicity. Yet it is useful, particularly in providing a distinction between hunter–gatherers and other populations.

How have hunter–gatherers been characterised?

An impetus for recent research has been to explore the tremendous diversity of population groups known as hunter–gatherers, groups manifestly successful in an impressive range of habitats. Of course an appreciation of hunter–gatherers involves more than the examination of the features of a given subsistence economy across different environments. Lee and Daly (1999: 3) emphasised that 'subsistence is one part of a multi-faceted definition of hunter–gatherers: social organisation forms a second major area . . . , and cosmology and world-view a third'. For these authors, the common characteristics of (contemporary) foragers are thus their type of economy, social organisation, and ideology. They also mention a number of significant divergences, such as the degree of violence and warfare, the status of women, and the distinction between 'simple' versus 'complex' organisation and associated notion of immediate or delayed return (elaborated by Kelly 1995).

Many researchers have tried to identify hunter–gatherers in terms of a 'package' of characteristics (e.g. economic, ecological, socio-cultural and ideological traits). The nature of the 'glue' they thought might hold the package together is of great interest. Should one identify hunting and gathering as a cultural and technological 'stage' of human history or evolution, concerning oneself with categories and 'levels' of social organisation? Or should one follow a Marxist interpretation which identifies the 'mode of production' as primarily holding the socio-cultural package together? Is there such a thing as a hunter–gatherer 'ethos' and is it related to resource acquisition? Or should one focus attention on the variability within and between hunter–gatherer groups? Is this variability best understood within an ecological framework, one which examines behaviour in terms of adaptive strategies coping with environmental, technological or socio-demographic constraints? Or is there room for a more interpretative view of changes in the social or political organisation of different groups and sub-groups over time? Are there any ethnographic cases of 'pure' hunter–gatherers or are all influenced by contact with farmers, herders or traders? These are some of the many different ways in which hunter–gatherers have been charac-terised by previous research. In sum, what do we make of the category 'hunter–gatherers' and its diversity?

European scholars traditionally stressed the homogeneity of the category for reasons that were often overtly political. In the seven-teenth century, hunter–gatherers were typecast by Hobbes (1651) as the primeval state of humanity, living lives he famously described as 'solitary, poor, nasty, brutish, and short'. By contrast, his contemporary John Dryden (1670) depicted them as living in a state of grace from which the rest of humanity had fallen, coining the equally famous phrase 'the noble savage' to describe them. These perspectives used hunter–gatherers for opposing political purposes, but both depicted them as a unitary type, timeless and ahistorical. They are one representation of the 'glue' portraying hunter–gatherers as a distinct and separate human category.

An emphasis on distinct categories of human organisation continued into much more recent times, for example in the concept of the single 'hunter–gatherer mode of production' put forward by Marxist scholars (see discussion in Lee 1988). The concept of a mode of production posits necessary relations between property, labour and exchange, all of which are uniquely human constructs (Leacock and Lee 1982: 61). For Marx and Engels, the unique feature of human subsistence was the conscious character of its productive activities, instilled through the experience of living in society (Ingold *et al.* 1988: 270). The concept of a hunter–gatherer mode of production is however a political rather than an ecological one; while clearly more sophisticated than its predecessors, it still presents a single ahistorical category whose coherence is explained through a single theoretical framework. Echoes of the same notion appear in Sahlins's 'original affluent society' (Sahlins 1968 1974) and Woodburn's 'immediate return' systems (Woodburn 1982). Even if two hunter–gatherer modes of production are recognised (such as immediate return/egalitarian and delayed return/inegalitarian), the diversity of hunter–gatherer social formations is poorly represented by such categories.

More recent attempts to identify a complex or 'package' of traits characteristic of hunter–gatherers have been concerned with the 'evolution' of this way of life. These take a diachronic, rather than synchronic, view of a set of behaviours which cohere over a span of time. It is often said that 99% of the evolutionary history of humans has been spent in a hunter–gathering mode of subsistence. This approach seeks to establish what demarcated hunting and gathering from earlier means of food procurement, such as scavenging, enabling 'foragers' to be successful over a very long period of human evolutionary history. It is also known that humans and chimpanzees share a high degree of genetic resemblance (98% to 99% of DNA and the products of coding genes are identical; King and Wilson 1975; Neel 1999, p. 3). Given that apes hunt small animals, and also spend much of the day gathering vegetable plants and fruit, what differentiates hunting and gathering in humans from that of apes? Few definitive answers have been forthcoming, but propositions about exchanges of food, division of labour and provisioning of children in hominids have been extensively debated (Hawkes *et al.* 1997). Another line of enquiry, which raises some fundamental questions discussed in this volume, concerns the comparison between anatomically modern hunter–gatherers in the archaeological record, other hominids such as the Neanderthals, and present-day populations studied ethno-graphically.

In considering what 'package' of behaviours made the evolutionary strategy of foragers so successful, it is essential to examine what continuities persisted over past and present populations, and how long or short-term changes in given practices can be explained. Because of the diversity of habitats and modes of exploitation, these issues can only be addressed by adopting a very fine-grained analysis of the 'ecology' of hunter–gatherer populations, namely of the usage people made of their environments and the impact that environments – often unpropitious and therefore eliciting appropriate responses – had on human behaviour and biology. In this scheme, it is the *range of behaviours* and the *flexibility* of human groups, not uniformity, which deserves emphasis. We see this range of behaviours as arising both through responses to different environments and through the trajectory of different cultural traditions.

Diversity of approaches: hunter–gatherer variability

The field of hunter–gatherer research is obviously vibrant enough to have generated and accommodated many different approaches and a diversity of theoretical interests. The chapters in this volume present a number of these approaches, summarising relevant issues and current knowledge with respect to a particular field of interest. Some of the main issues debated in this volume have been raised above, but it is instructive to outline here the concerns and theoretical interests of particular chapters.

Consider first of all the issue of hunter–gatherer variability. Is diversity in usage of habitat and technology, in diet, physical attributes and reproductive histories, in range of languages and social organisation, a matter of local responses to environmental constraints, of increasing 'sophistication' through time, or of differential contact with 'outsiders'? Several contributors address the issues of evolution, history, and change among present and past hunter–gatherers, seeking to portray the flexibility of hunter–gatherer groups. Winterhalder shows that many aspects of the society and economy of contemporary hunter–gatherers are usefully considered from the perspective of behavioural ecology. Practices such as food storage and associated hierarchies are likely to occur in environments where storage is a major adaptive strategy for survival. The optimal foraging models detailed in this chapter are designed to explore how flexible are such traits or lifestyle attributes and how quickly they might respond to change. Rowley-Conwy addresses the same issue of flexibility in social organisation, while adding a time dimension, revisiting the common assumption that 'simple' egalitarian (or immediate return) hunter–gatherers form a baseline from which 'complex' groups later developed. If the variability documented by Winterhalder among contemporary hunter–gatherer groups is at least partly a response to environmental conditions, the same variability should be visible in the past.

Torrence shows that many aspects of technology vary according to the resources they are designed to procure. If resources are varied and continuously available, a generalised technology capable of a variety of functions is preferred. On the other hand, if resources are concentrated and only temporarily available, technology is specialised, dedicated to maximising returns in a short time. Kuhn and Stiner consider this technological flexibility through time rather than across space, comparing modern and pre-modern humans. They conclude that modern humans in Europe and southwest Asia display the same flexibility that is documented by Torrence among contemporary groups, probably as far back as the Early Upper Palaeolithic some 30 000 years ago. The Neanderthals do not: their technology is relatively sophisticated, but remains relatively static in the face of environmental changes.

As Kuhn and Stiner add a time dimension to the contemporary variability discussed by Torrence, so Rowley-Conwy extends the principles outlined by Winterhalder to past hunter–gatherer societies. The flexibility seen in present-day groups is also a characteristic of the archaeological record of modern humans, even though this record is flawed, coarse-grained and open to various interpretations.

Two other chapters have less recourse to the imperfect archaeological database, but also argue that present flexibility is likely to extend into the past. McConvell considers language 'shift' among hunter–gatherers, using mostly present-day linguistic distributions to reconstruct movements and changes in the past. There are indications of rapid linguistic changes at certain times and places, and some supporting evidence from the archaeological record of at least Australia. Pennington shows that there has been substantial variability in the reproductive histories of contemporary groups for whom demographic histories have been properly documented. Rapid population increase may be possible when new areas are colonised, but elsewhere her life-table models show that population seems to have remained stable or static for long periods. Pennington also re-evaluates some of the hypotheses advanced to explain the reduced fertility of hunter–gatherer populations, highlighting sexually transmitted diseases as an important variable affecting demography.

As further emphasised by Jenike and Froment, hunter–gatherer populations are not a 'biological entity' with recognisable health or morphological profiles in contrast to the characteristics of farmers and industrialist populations. Yet too often we have adopted a uniform view – or normative model – of hunter–gatherer diets, levels of physical activity, exposures to infection, body morphologies and genetic differentiation. Both authors argue in favour of a more informed understanding of the sources of variation in hunter–gatherer subsistence ecology. Their data lead to consideration of quite flexible adaptive responses to ecological constraints, and of their application to archaeological populations.

The next papers follow a more 'humanist' approach towards issues of agency among hunter–gatherers. Conkey explores the socially constructed meaning of hunter–gatherer art forms. This is clearly not a subject that can be directly addressed by means of environmental context, even though it does have a temporal dimension that some other chapters are unable to address, since art survives from the remote hunter–gatherer past in a variety of places. This testifies once again to the flexibility of hunter–gatherers in the past as well as the present, even if we may never be able to comprehend the socially constructed meanings that underlie the art. As mentioned by Torrence in her chapter, even technology has a socially constructed dimension, less closely linked to the procurement of resources. Layton, for his part, handles an emotive issue, namely the history of hunter–gatherer interaction with farmers, herders and the Nation State. He shows how some of the Western 'myths' concerning hunter–gatherers and their environment have influenced state policy. He also discusses political issues such as land rights, which sometimes involve contemporary dramas like court cases and demonstrations, as well as the affirmation of hunter–gatherer identities by the (sometimes deliberate) adoption of material symbols in direct opposition to those of colonial or national regimes. The future of hunter–gatherers in contact with other groups is also highlighted as an important issue by Froment, who forecasts that a collapse in their ways of life could lead, paradoxically, to significant improvements in terms of health.

This volume aims to provide undergraduate and postgraduate students with a set of accessible and balanced reviews of topics which excite the current interest of a large number of researchers working with hunter–gatherers. In tackling ecological, biological and cultural issues from prehistory to the present-day, it provides an overview of this important way of life. We now have a large body of evidence documenting fine-grained behavioural variability in hunter–gatherers. Current research has moved on to formulate a number of principles, testable hypotheses, even competing theoretical approaches, to evaluate against the ethnographic and archaeological data. The myths about 'pristine' hunter–gatherer groups being separate from the rest of humanity and not sharing its concerns have long been exploded. This was illustrated by an anecdote reported in *The Economist* (19 October 1996: 145): while deep in the Kalahari, an elderly hunter putting poison on his arrows turned to a Westerner visiting the campsite and asked whether he believed O.J. Simpson (then on trial for murder in the USA) was guilty.

References

Bettinger, R.L. (1991). *Hunter–Gatherers: Archaeological and Evolutionary Theory.* New York: Plenum.

Biesbrouck, K., Elders, S. and Rossel, G. (1999). *Central African Hunter–Gatherers in a Multidisciplinary Perspective: Challenging Elusiveness.* Leiden: Research School CNWS Publications.

Burch, and Ellana, (1994). *Key Issues in Hunter–Gatherer Research.* Oxford: Berg.

Ellen, R. (1988). Foraging, starch extraction and the sedentary life style in the lowland rainforest of central Seram. In *Hunters and Gatherers: History, Evolution and Social change,* vol. 1, ed. T. Ingold, D. Riches and J. Woodburn, pp. 117–134. Oxford: Berg.

Hawkes, K., O'Connell, J.F. and Rogers, L. (1997). The behavioural ecology of modern hunter–gatherers, and human evolution. *Trends in Ecology and Evolution* **12**: 1–42.

Hill, K. and Hurtado, A.M. (1999). *Ache Life History: The Ecology and Demography of a Foraging People.* New York: Aldine de Gruyter.

Hunn, E.S. and Williams, N.M. (1982). Introduction. In *Resource Managers: North American and Australian Hunter-Gatherers,* ed. N.M. Williams and E.S. Hunn, pp. 1–16. Canberra: Australian Institute of Aboriginal Studies.

Ingold, T., Riches, D. and Woodburn, J. (eds.) (1988). *Hunters and Gatherers: History, Evolution and Social Change,* vol. 1 and 2. Oxford: Berg.

Kelly, R.L. (1995). *The Foraging Spectrum: Diversity in Hunter–Gatherer Lifeways.* Washington DC: Smithsonian Institution Press.

King, M.-C. and Wilson, A.C. (1975). Evolution at two levels in humans and chimpanzees. *Science* 188 (no. 4184): 107–188.

Lee, R.B. (1988). Reflections on primitive communalism. In *Hunters and Gatherers: History, Evolution and Social Change,* ed. T. Ingold, D. Riches and J. Woodburn, pp. 252–268. Oxford: Berg.

Lee, R.B. and Daly, R. (1999). Foragers and others. In *The Cambridge Encyclopedia of Hunters and Gatherers* ed. Lee, R. B. and Daly, R., pp. 1–19. Cambridge: Cambridge University Press.

Lee, R.B. and DeVore, I. (eds.) (1968). *Man the Hunter*. Chicago: Aldine.

Murdoch, G.P. (1967). *Ethnographic Atlas*. Pittsburgh: University of Pittsburgh Press.

Neel, J.V. (1999). When some fine old genes meet a 'new' environment. In *Evolutionary Aspects of Nutrition and Health: Diet, Exercise, Genetics and Chronic Disease*, ed. A.P. Simopoulos, pp. 1–18. Basel: Karger.

Rosman, A. and Rubel, P.G. (1989). Stalking the wild pig: hunting and horticulture in Papua New Guinea. In *Farmers as Hunters*, ed. S. Kent, pp. 27–36. Cambridge: Cambridge University Press.

Sahlins, M. (1968). Notes on the original affluent society. In *Man the Hunter*, ed. R.B. Lee and I. DeVore, pp. 85–89. Chicago: Aldine.

Sahlins, M. (1972). Stone Age Economics. Chicago: Aldine.

Soffer, O. and Gamble, G. (eds.) (1990). *The World at 18,000 BP*; vol 1, *High Latitudes*; vol 2, *Low Latitudes*. London: Unwin Hyman.

Woodburn, J. (1982) Egalitarian societies. *Man* (N.S.) **17**: 431–451.

2

The behavioural ecology of hunter–gatherers

BRUCE WINTERHALDER

Ethnographic variability and behavioural ecology

In behavioural terms, hunter–gatherers are defined to large extent by their economy. Forager subsistence (food, fuel, fibre, etc.) is derived from non-domesticated resources, species not actively managed by themselves or by other human beings. Foragers are those peoples who gain their livelihood fully or predominantly by some combination of gathering, collecting, hunting, fishing, trapping, or scavenging the resources available in the plant and animal communities around them. By this definition, key properties of this form of economy are ecological in nature. While there are different and sometimes more precise definitions of hunter–gatherers, this one has the advantage of simplicity. It does not confuse primary with derivative and more variable features of this lifeway, such as 'band-level' social organisation or an egalitarian social ethic.

While views have shifted dramatically over time on the important features of this *mode of production* – compare Lee and DeVore (1968) with Dahlberg (1981) – nearly everyone looks to hunter–gatherers for foundational insights into the origins of human capacities and inclinations. Foragers are a primary testing ground for broader anthropological theory. In this chapter, I describe recent *behavioural ecology* work on foraging and I examine some implications of this work for our understanding of the foraging economy. I avoid as much as is possible duplicating material covered in other recent reviews of hunter–gatherer studies (e.g. Barnard 1983, Meyers 1988, Bettinger 1991, Kelly 1995).

Although we can define and delimit a category – the hunter–

gatherer form of economy – we must immediately add that the societies so encompassed are highly diverse. Although the number of these societies and the populations they represent had dwindled by the beginning of their ethnographic documentation, foragers are known from most continents and from a variety of habitats. The Shoshoni of the Great Basin, the Australian Aborigines, the arctic Inuit, the Aka of the Philippines, the Mbuti, Hadza, and Ju/!Hoansi of Africa, and the Ache of Paraguay are but a few of the well-known examples. They vary along every imaginable dimension of socio-economic comparison (Kelly 1995): in the diversity and types of food and other resources consumed, in degree of task group and residential mobility, in forms of intra- and inter-group exchange and land tenure, in group size and structure, in male and female role differentiation, and along a spectrum of egalitarian to more strati-fied social organisation. The variety is so great that some anthro-pologists (although not behavioural ecologists) despair of clear definition, robust generalities or coherent, encompassing theoretical explanations of hunter–gatherer lifeways. Presumably the diversity that existed in prehistoric times was significantly greater (Kuhn and Stiner, this volume).

Despite considerable variety, the comparative ethnographic study of hunter–gatherers provides four generalisations that require ex-planation. Despite exceptions, these features stand out as common patterns. They are: (1) apparent under-production, and a general lack of material accumulation; (2) routine food sharing; (3) egalitar-ianism; and (4) despite number 3, a routine division of labour between the foraging activities of males and females: men more commonly hunt while women more commonly gather. Behavioural ecology analyses offer insights on all of these patterns.

Models and applications

In the last two decades, behavioural ecology models have been central to the analysis of the foraging economy (Winterhalder and Smith 1981, Smith and Winterhalder 1992). This approach makes the assumption that hunters are proficient and skilled, and it applies that assumption through the methodology of *constrained optimisation* (Foley 1985, Torrence, this volume). In this respect, it draws on concepts and techniques used in micro-economics and evolutionary biology. The approach is also self-consciously *reductionist*. It relies on very simple models that focus their analytical gaze one-at-a-time on quite specific elements of the foraging economy.

In both respects, behavioural ecologists adopt scientific styles of analysis that cause unease among some anthropologists (e.g. Ingold 1996), especially those who cherish holism, relativism, and a focus on human uniqueness above all. Behavioural ecologists acknowledge that hunter–gatherer behaviour surely is complex and multi-causal in origin, but they also insist that until we know the effects of causes taken separately, there is little possibility of understanding their action taken together. In somewhat broader terms, interdisciplinary volumes such as this one exemplify this same point.

Clues to the origins of the four patterns cited earlier are found in models focused on (a) resource selection and the location and movement of foragers with respect to resources, and (b) intra-group transfer of resources.

Resource selection and the use of patches

It is worth reflecting that we owe our current capacity to consume and enjoy a great variety of foodstuffs to the wide-ranging omnivory of our primate ancestors. Were we the immediate descendants of pandas, eating would be monotonous and a lot duller. That same omnivory implies that hominid foragers have consistently faced multiple choices in the subsistence quest. All environments contain more species that are edible to humans than can be effectively harvested by them. Resource selection models attempt to analyse this situation by asking what environmental features most directly affect the evolution of foraging behaviour, and what resource species a proficient forager will seek to harvest.

Resource selection (also called diet choice) models were among the first developed in behavioural ecology. In the *encounter-contingent model*, a searching forager randomly comes upon edible resources. Each encounter provokes this choice: take the time to harvest this

Table 2.1. *Encounter-contingent resource selection and optimal harvest set*[a]

Ranked resource types, R_i	Profitability for each type, R_i (MJ/hr)	Harvest sets (those resources pursued upon encounter)	Foraging efficiency (E_f, or NAR) for harvest sets (MJ/hr)
R_C	13.240	(R_C)	4.039
R_D	8.012	(R_{CD})	4.450
R_A	6.576	(R_{CDA})	4.877
R_B	5.701	(R_{CDAB})	>> 5.065 <<
R_F	4.115	(R_{CDABF})	4.856
R_E	2.533	(R_{CDABFE})	4.521
R_H	1.720	($R_{CDABFEH}$)	4.123
R_G	0.812	($R_{CDABFEHG}$)	3.010

[a] Hypothetical resource types (R_i) are ranked by their profitability (their pursuit and handling efficiency) and the overall foraging efficiency (E_f) or net acquisition rate (NAR) is calculated for stepwise additions of items to the set that will be harvested when encountered. Each addition reduces search costs to an encounter with an item that will be pursued, but takes up less and less profitable resources. Foraging efficiency increases so long as the profitability of the item added is greater than the NAR of the resource set without it (compare the profitability of an item to the efficiency of the harvest set one row up). The double inequalities (>> <<) show the optimal harvest set. Despite the potential savings in search costs of adding item R_F, its low profitability and hence the opportunity cost of its harvest eliminates it (and all subsequent items of lesser rank) from the best choice set.

item, or continue searching in the hope of finding something more desirable to harvest. Typically each item is a species and we measure desirability by the *net acquisition rate* (NAR) of energy. The trade-off posed here invokes a standard micro-economic concept: that of *opportunity costs*. Pursuing the found item precludes seeking and obtaining something else. It is the best choice only if the foregone opportunity, the something else, is less valuable than the opportunity at hand. A hypothetical illustration of the mathematical procedure, or algorithm, for finding the optimal set of resources is shown in Table 2.1.

We can use this model to predict changes in resource selectivity as a function of changes in the environment or in the forager's capacities. For instance, decreasing encounter rates with highly ranked items already within the optimal set lowers overall foraging efficiency and causes resource selection to expand. Conversely, increasing encounter rates with highly ranked resources progressively narrows the range of resources selected. If a resource is outside of the optimal set, an increase in its encounter rate will not move it into that set. Pennies in a field of sufficient dollars will be ignored whatever their numbers. However, increasing the profitability of a resource that is outside of the selected set may move it into the diet.

In my work with Cree foragers living in the boreal forest of northern Ontario, I wanted to predict how resource use might have changed with the introduction of traps, snares, and rifles. These technologies all elevated profitability, and should have expanded the variety of species harvested. By contrast, the later introduction of snowmobiles, a technology that greatly increased the rate of encountering items, should have narrowed it. These shifts can be verified from historical data (Winterhalder 1983). More generally, both ethnographers (e.g. of the Ache, Hill et al. 1987; the Etolo, Dwyer 1985; the Hadza, Hawkes et al. 1991; the Inuit, Smith 1991) and archaeologists (e.g. Broughton and Grayson 1993) have used this encounter-contingent model to analyse hunter–gatherer resource selectivity, with good success. Hunting and gathering has its modern analogues. Gray and Lowery (1998) use foraging theory to analyse variance in the alliance behaviour of lobbyists, who must decide whether to forage alone or in a 'flock' for legislative policy proposals favourable to their constituencies. And, in aid of contemporary foragers of a different sort, designers of search algorithms for the world wide web base some of their models on foraging theory (Pirolli and Card 1995). We can only lament not having a behavioural ecology study of the foraging strategies of London taxi drivers prior to centralised, radio-telephone dispatchers.

The encounter-contingent model identifies the constellation of costs and benefits which must be estimated or measured in order to predict resource selectivity. Because these factors vary by locality, society, and technology, the model potentially has the capacity to explain much of the subsistence diversity observed among foragers.

Resource species might also be localised in discrete *patches*, with intervening spaces empty of desirable items. This situation is addressed by models of patch choice and patch residence time. Within a patch, the rate at which food can be harvested declines as a function of the time the forager spends there. The most accessible and dense clusters of ripe fruit are harvested before moving to more difficult and less attractive ones. The first shot at a flock of birds takes by surprise the most vulnerable; subsequent shots must be placed among the ever more wary and evasive of those that linger. This is a common situation for foragers, and it raises two questions: Which patch types will be included in the set harvested? How much time should be dedicated to each patch before moving on to a fresh one?

The first question is answered by use of an algorithm like that for selecting resource items, with patches ranked by their initial NAR. The second question is answered by the *marginal value theorem*, or MVT (Charnov 1976), shown in Figure 2.1. An optimal forager abandons a patch when its declining *marginal* rate of return equals the NAR of foraging averaged over visits to many patches. In- creasing encounter rates (lessened travel time) raise foraging effi- ciency and reduce patch residence time; lessened search costs have the same effect. As patches become richer or as harvest costs within the patch diminish, residence time also decreases. A forager moves more quickly through an environment dense with rich patches, taking less from each one encountered, than through an environ- ment with fewer and/or lower-quality patches. A forager nearly always will depart a patch before it has been fully depleted of resources. As an incidental consequence of this pattern, the forager leaves behind the breeding stock that will allow the patch to recover.

Although human and primate behavioural ecologists report anecdotal observations that are qualitatively consistent with predic- tions of the marginal value theorem, I do not know of quantitative, anthropological tests of the model. For instance, McGrew (personal communication) observes that each 'dip' of the twig used by termite-fishing chimpanzees returns fewer of the edible insects. When yield drops sufficiently, the chimp will leave and travel the distance to a new mound to begin anew. How closely chimpanzees

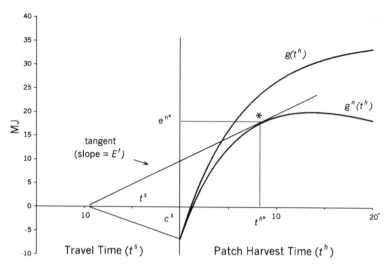

Figure 2.1. The marginal value theorem for one patch type. The forager expends time (t_s) and incurs energy costs (c_s) travelling between patches in search of a favourable patch to exploit. Within such a patch, its *gross* rate of resource gain – $g(t_h)$ – diminishes as a function of time. This gain function is offset downward by c_s to cover travel costs. The slope of the forager's *net* gain function – $g_n(t_h)$ – gives the instantaneous net rate of return. This rate becomes negative if the rate of gross intake falls sufficiently that it fails to cover metabolic expenditures. The optimal patch residence time (t_{h*}) is found by drawing a line from the x-axis travel cost (here, $t_s = 9$ hrs) that is tangent (*) to the net gain curve, $g_n(t_h)$. The slope of this line gives the best possible net acquisition rate or efficiency (E_f) of foraging [$E_f = e_{n*}/(t_s + t_{h*})$]. This establishes the general rule that an optimal forager abandons a patch when its declining *marginal* rate of return equals the average efficiency of foraging. Beyond t_{h*} the forager's rate of resource acquisition would be below what it can achieve by locating and harvesting additional patches. Other predictions about patch residence are derived by manipulating the variables represented in the graph (e.g. travel time, t_t) or the shape of the resource gain function. A simple extension of the model will handle multiple patch types (Charnov 1976).

match the optimum departure point is unknown, but the general pattern is consistent with the MVT.

The MVT introduces a second concept borrowed from micro-economics and essential to the analysis of foraging and other types of economy: *marginal analysis*. The value of many economic choices or activities changes as a function of their magnitude or duration.

The quantity of a good accumulated, the duration of a productive task, and the time since an activity has been performed are examples. A decision to stop consumption or to cease one activity in preference for another is made by comparing the value of the last unit gained to the alternative. Thus the *marginal* value of the current patch is compared to the average value of moving on. In the encounter-contingent model, the value of the next ranked resource is compared to the marginal value of the resource set without it (Table 2.1).

Habitats and the use of space

Patches are discrete, localised concentrations of resources, on a spatial scale such that a forager might encounter several in the course of a day. A covey of quail or a cluster of fruit trees are examples. By contrast, *habitats* are regional features, environmental zones that are relatively homogeneous in the resources they offer a forager and distinguishable from other zones at a similar scale. Alpine and adjacent valley zones in the Great Basin of the western United States are one example, coastal and interior arctic habitats another. Movement among habitats most likely involves a change of residence.

The *ideal free distribution* (IFD) attempts to represent the basic logic of habitat selection and migration (Fretwell and Lucas 1970). The IFD assumes that habitat quality is a function of population density. In turn, habitat quality determines the equilibrium distribution of the foragers. Although very simple, this model contains a host of interesting implications (Figure 2.2). They can be discovered by playing with the form or position of the elements that constitute the graphical representation. The model behaves somewhat differently if settlers are able to inhibit competition from newcomers, through territoriality or other barriers. Fretwell (1970) calls this an 'ideal despotic distribution'.

Whitehead and Hope (1991) find partial support for the IFD in the distribution and movement of sperm whaling ships off the coast of the Galapagos and in the north Pacific during the mid-nineteenth century. It would provide an excellent perspective for examining

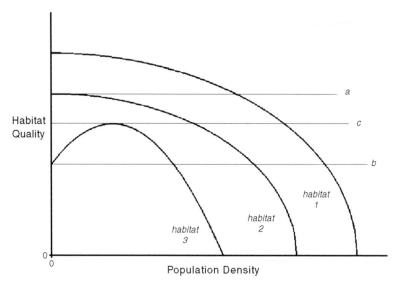

Figure 2.2. The ideal free distribution. Foragers in a region are presumed to settle first in the best habitat available, *habitat 1*. As their numbers grow and density increases, they experience a decline in the quality of *habitat 1*, due to increasing competition for resources. When the marginal quality of *habitat 1* has dropped to the point (horizontal line *a*) that it equals the quality of *habitat 2*, continued settlement will be spread into both. The equilibrium distribution over habitats is set when all individuals experience the same habitat quality, i.e. when relative habitat densities are such that no one gains by relocating. Predictions from this model are based on hypothesised changes in the shape and position of the curves, or the conditions that govern movement between habitats (Fretwell and Lucas 1970). For instance, increasing population density initially improves the quality of *habitat 3* (for instance, partial clearing by human immigrants improves browse for game animals). Migrants will not move there until the experienced quality of *habitats 1* and *2* has dropped to horizontal line *b*. Once begun, relocation to *habitat 3* will lead to depopulation of *habitats 1* and *2* because each migrant makes *habitat 3* more attractive to the next (up to horizontal line *c*). The depopulation stabilises only when further population growth must be allocated to declining portions of the respective curves.

episodes of general habitat expansion by hominid foragers, from the earliest migrations within and out of Africa to the late Pleistocene colonisation by *Homo sapiens* of nearly every habitat on the globe (Kuhn and Stiner, this volume). To my knowledge the IFD has not been applied to this type of question.

Comparative ethnographic study shows that residential relocation is quite common among hunter–gatherers. The frequency of moves is highly variable, ranging from 0 or just a few up to 60 moves per year. The distance is most commonly in the 5 to 10 km range, occasionally 60 or 70 km (Kelly 1995: Table 4–1). What foraging dynamics produce this mobility and what are the factors contributing to its diversity?

Many hunter–gatherers are *central place foragers* (CPF). Whether on day trips or longer hunting and gathering expeditions, individuals or small groups radiate from and return to a central site. We expect this site to be located adjacent to a critical resource if that resource is rare and bulky (e.g. water), or more generally at the acquisitional centre of gravity of resources such as water, fuel, and food. From this central place, nearby resources are exploited first, in a process that produces a gradient of resource availability. Depletion diminishes with distance from the home base. And, having located with respect to a small set of critical resources, the group may find that some necessary foodstuffs or material goods are found only in distant habitats. These geographical constraints raise two questions: When and how often should camps move? Does travel in order to forage in a distant habitat alter the resource set that should be pursued there?

A variation on the marginal value theorem offers one entry to the first problem. Local depletion and the travel costs of reaching more distant and less depleted zones lower foraging efficiency. NAR falls with duration of settlement, but it does so at a decreasing rate because total resources (potential area to be exploited) increase rapidly with radial distance from the camp. The net yield of foraging as a function of residence time measured in days or weeks will look something like the lower curve in Figure 2.1. The average number of foraging days lost to a relocation can be represented as was travel time in the MVT. The tangent gives the overall NAR and establishes the optimum residence time.

Manipulation of this model shows that camps will move more often if (1) relocation costs are low, (2) depletion (or depression) of zones immediately around the occupied camp is rapid, and/or (3) alternative residential sites offer high initial rates of return. Seasonal changes in resource availability will modify the return curves independently of exploitation, and may produce relocation apart from, or in interaction with, depletion. Kelly (1995) uses a somewhat different model to arrive at similar predictions. He argues that environmental conditions in post-Pleistocene North America led to especially rapid residential moves by foraging bands, a situation explaining the very rapid colonisation of the continent by the big-game hunters.

Our central place forager may need to travel through non-productive territory in order to reach a distant habitat containing a selection of potential resources. Whatever is harvested there is carried back to the residential site to be processed and consumed or stored, either by the forager or dependents. This raises the question: Do the travel costs between the living site and distant habitat in which foraging occurs modify the hunter–gatherer's best selection of resources in that habitat? The key model for this situation was originally developed by biologists (Orians and Pearson 1979) for the study of colonial nesting birds, most of which are constrained to use the same physical apparatus (e.g. beak or claws) to capture and carry prey. For a red-winged blackbird, capture and delivery of one item precludes or seriously handicaps capture of another on the same trip. With this constraint and the need to amortise NAR over two-way travel costs, CPF models show that it is better to return with something large than small, even if the latter was more easily located and caught.

Although quite important in biology, the *direct* applicability of this model to modern human foragers is quite limited. Once hominids had carrying devices such as net bags (Lee 1979) and butchery tools, they could harvest and accumulate multiple small items or cut-up large ones, thereby avoiding the need to bias their best-choice resource selection based on loading constraints. It is easily shown that these technologies greatly increase the efficiency of foraging from a central place. They also may have been instrumental in the evolution of residential bases.

Metcalfe and Barlow (1992; see also Bettinger *et al.* 1997) have adapted the CPF model so that it will predict when a resource will undergo *field processing* to remove low-utility portions prior to its transport back to a camp. Their model treats the unprocessed and processed form as if they were two different resources. The unprocessed form takes less handling time in the field and allows for more round trips, but incurs the cost that a portion of the transported load has little or no value. By contrast, field processing takes time and lessens the number of round trips possible, but the load carried is made up of high-value materials only. Given estimated load capacities, processing costs, and the utilities of high- and low-value portions (Barlow and Metcalfe 1996), the model will predict the travel distance at which field processing becomes the best option for a particular resource. Potential examples are ubiquitous. Besides separating nut meats or shellfish from their shells, they include freeing edible animal tissues from low-utility skin, bone, carapace, hooves and the like, and separating high-grade stone tool material from its low-quality matrix at a quarry.

Zeanah (2000) has developed a mathematical model that determines when central place hunters who travel from their residence *A* to a distant site *B* to gather resources logistically should reverse the pattern and relocate to that second site, making logistic foraging trips back to *A* (Figure 2.3). For instance, in the Owens Valley pre-1350 BP, foraging bands faced a seasonal trade-off. They could reside in the valleys, near to low-return plant and small game resources while logistically hunting limited numbers of high value mountain sheep. Or, they could reside in the nearby alpine habitat of those mountain sheep, if they were sufficiently abundant.

In 1964 Brown argued that *territorial behaviour* would be expected only if the benefits of exclusive use outweighed the costs of resource defence. He predicted that the cost : benefit ratio would be favourable to territoriality only when resources were moderate in density, evenly distributed, and predictable in their location. By contrast, if resources existed only at very low densities or were clumped together in unpredictable locations, then the area required to provide a sufficient or reliable quantity of food would be too large to patrol and defend economically. Likewise, at densities high enough to saturate the needs of the local foraging population, exclusive use would gain no benefit over shared use, thus would not recover the high cost of defending an attractive hoard. Brown demonstrated

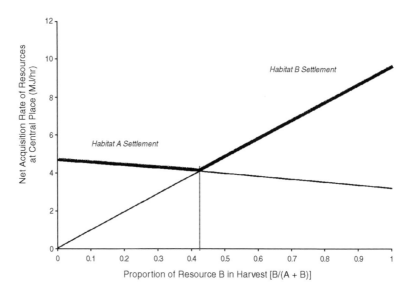

Figure 2.3. Residential and logistic procurement. A foraging band can locate residentially in habitat A or B. If it locates in A, members on average make 2-hr round trips to locations where they harvest resource A at a rate of 7.786 MJ/hr. However, from a habitat A residence, band members must make a 12-hr (round trip) logistic trek to reach locations where they can harvest habitat B resources, at a rate of 14.065 MJ/hr. Should they settle residentially in habitat B, the converse situation applies: 2-hr round trips to resource B and a 12-hr (logistic) round trip to resource A. Given differing ratios of demand for resources A and B, the optimal mix of residential and logistic procurement is indicated by the shaded line segments. If A and B are perfect substitutes and both are bountiful, the clear choice is settle in habitat B and harvest only resource B. However, if the geographically separated resources are complementary (e.g. plant foods versus game, water versus wood for fuel), meaning that some of each is needed or desired, or if the more desired of the two is in exceptionally short supply, then logistic and residential procurement must be mixed. Given the specific parameters of this treatment, residence in habitat B remains optimal, with logistic travel to procure resource A, provided that resource B makes up at least 42% of the harvest. If B is less than 42%, residence should shift to habitat A with logistic procurement of resource B (Zeanah, 2000).

that alternative tactics such as home ranges and mobility could be related to similar environmental parameters.

Dyson-Hudson and Smith (1978) show that this model accurately predicts the land tenure regimes of selected hunter–gatherer populations. Steward's (1938) classic Great Basin study provides two contrasting cases. Living in an arid environment of sparse and unpredictable foodstuffs, Western Shoshoni bands occupied ranges that shifted and sometimes overlapped from year to year. They lacked defended territories. By contrast, the Owens Valley Paiute lived surrounded by more salubrious habitats. Their denser and more predictable resource base encouraged permanent settlement of bands within villages that claimed and defended delimited territories. Cashdan (1983), on the other hand, found that San (Kalahari) foragers are most territorial in the areas of *lowest* resource density. On the face of it, this is a contradiction of the model's prediction. However, Cashdan suggests that Brown's model must be modified to better reflect human communication skills and the lowered costs of defence by social means. Any sighting of an intruder can be communicated to all band members, and the San need not patrol a perimeter in order to actively monitor and socially defend a space.

Brown's behavioural ecology approach to the question of territoriality had two especially attractive features, found generally in behavioural ecology models. It circumvented some of the liabilities of functionalist interpretations by requiring a clear analysis of the environmental circumstances, as well as the costs and benefits, in which a specific range of behaviours might evolve. And it showed that land use options, from territorial defence through home ranges to nomadism, were facultative and highly contingent on shifting resource distributions. In a similar analysis, Kummer (1991) has examined the evolutionary origins of respect for possession and the distribution of this trait among the primates.

Food transfers

The models examined so far are concerned with production. They analyse the selection of resources and how this is affected by factors such as their value, density and predictability, as well as their local and regional patterns of spatial distribution and defense (Cashdan 1992). Behavioural ecologists also have developed a series of models that address questions of distribution. These intra-group *transfers* of resources include behaviours described variously as sharing, exchange, and trade (Winterhalder 1996*a*,*b*).

All behavioural ecology models of distribution begin with two assumptions. (1) The individuals forage as a group, or, if they forage separately, they come together as a group to consume at least part of the catch, perhaps at a central place. This condition, *social foraging*, is very likely to be true of hominids and certainly is true of ethnographically known foragers. (2) They harvest one or more resources in the form of a packet, a natural unit larger than can be immediately consumed by the individual that acquires it. The small game animal, clutch of eggs, or large melon found by an australopithecine are examples of packets. Encounter with such packets is likely to be fairly rare and unpredictable. Day by day, some individuals succeed and others fail to locate packets. Due to stochastic factors, they are unequally successful in the food quest.

Certain selective pressures come into play when some individuals in the group find themselves holding more than their fill and others find themselves with less. Among the most basic of these is *tolerated theft* (Blurton Jones 1987), better described as *scrounging* (Vickery *et al.* 1991). Food transfers occur because it pays individuals with a deficit to contest the holdings of those with a surfeit. Those with surplus will relinquish their extra portions because they gain little or no advantage in defending them. Portions will transfer among individuals until the marginal value of their holdings equalises (Winterhalder 1996c). Scrounging is probably a dominant mechanism generating food transfers among those primate species occasionally observed to hunt other vertebrates. Examples include chimpanzees (Stanford 1995) and capuchin monkeys (Rose 1997). It probably is one element among several in the food transfers occurring in human societies (see below).

Reciprocity is a second route for food transfers. In reciprocity, an individual with surplus food transfers portions to an individual who has less, in the expectation that the favour later will be returned when their circumstances are reversed. Because reciprocity is subject to cheating (an individual will be tempted to profit by accepting but not fully returning the benefits of generosity), the conditions for it to evolve are more restricted than those for scrounging. Participants must remain in contact, role reversals between giver and taker must be balanced and frequent, and the group must be able to recognise and sanction cheaters. A large body of game theory is devoted to understanding the circumstances under which reciprocity is a viable and stable tactic in a group.

Among the benefits of food transfer reciprocity is protection from unpredictable food shortfalls. Winterhalder (1990) has shown that the pooling and division of resources acquired from just a few unsynchronised sources is highly effective in reducing risk from daily fluctuations in success of the food quest. An example is foragers returning to a central place from independent hunting and gathering trips.

Food transfers within a group may also be analysed as *exchange*, in which edible resources move against other goods or services, usually without the delay implied in reciprocity. Kaplan and Hill (1985*a*) propose that Ache men who contribute more food to sharing networks than they or their families receive from them are benefiting indirectly through receipt of sexual access to females or alliance support from community members.

Hawkes (1993) has proposed a fourth mechanism for food transfers, the *show-off model*. It is a form of transfer based in sexual selection theory and the differing fitness opportunities of males and females. Her proposal means to explain the common ethnographic observation that men are more often the hunters, specialising on the largest and least predictable of resource species, even though in some cases foraging for other resources would generate calories more efficiently. In addition, the game obtained by men is shared more widely within the group. Women are typically gatherers who specialise on dependable foods, such as plants, which are commonly consumed within their family unit. Hawkes argues that men have the reproductive option of seeking unpredictable but highly desired protein-rich foods. Men benefit from the enhanced social prestige and perhaps the mating opportunities that follow from providing occasional subsistence bonanzas. Women, by contrast, are constrained to produce relatively few offspring and reliably provision them with gathered foods.

While the empirical evidence for the show-off hypothesis is

understandably limited, the idea is attractive for its explanatory reach. At present, Hill and Kaplan (1993) offer one compelling, alternative explanation for the same observations. They propose that the constraints of female childcare and selection for enhanced maternal attention to developing offspring are more compatible with gathering than with hunting. In their view, this is sufficient to explain the widespread hunter–gatherer division of labour and associated food transfers. A second alternative explanation is based on the concept of *costly-signalling* (see Smith and Bliege Bird, 2000), whereby males engage in risky and attention-getting displays of public provisioning because it conveys honest information about their economic and social prowess, information that benefits them and recipients. While costly signalling generates net benefits for the signaller, it does not require reciprocity.

Given social foraging and the unsynchronised acquisition of food-stuffs in packets, intra-group food transfers are likely to result from some combination of scrounging, reciprocity, risk minimisation, exchange, showing off, and costly signalling. This is an embarrass-ment of difficult-to-separate causal possibilities. Although there have been many fine ethnographic studies of food sharing, most did not record the detailed, quantitative information needed to assess the relative importance of these overlapping hypotheses.

A few recent studies have tried to do so, with partial success. Among the Ache, subtropical forest foragers living in Paraguay, Kaplan and Hill (1985*a,b*) found that widespread, intra-group transfers are common for the more highly valued resources (e.g. meat, honey) acquired asynchronously and in the form of packets. Transfer patterns are consistent with reciprocity and risk-minimisa-tion. They do not appear to be directed preferentially along lines of biological relatedness. Moreover, some hunters produce and give more to food transfer networks than they receive in return. Kaplan and Hill suggest that these highly productive hunters possibly are receiving delayed exchange benefits in the form of subtle social or covert reproductive benefits. On the Pacific island of Ifaluk (Western Carolines), Betzig and Turke (1986) found that foodstuffs derived from fishing and horticulture are routinely passed among house-holds. Their research was limited to a test of kin selection, and they found that food transfers follow theoretical expectations based on cost : benefit ratios and degree of biological relatedness. In a third example, distribution of turtle meat among the Meriam of the Torres Strait is consistent with scrounging and with male exchange of meat for socio-political or reproductive benefits (Bliege Bird and Bird 1997). Turtle-meat transfers also have certain features that are consistent with the costly-signalling hypothesis (Smith and Bliege Bird, 2000). By contrast, Hames (2000) attributes inter-household exchange of foodstuffs among the Yanomamo of lowland Venezuela to reciprocity and risk reduction.

Dwyer and Minnegal (1993) were unable to find evidence supportive of the show-off hypothesis in a study of Kubo foragers. They suggest that individual Kubo hunters achieve significant advantages by specialising on certain species and environmental zones. They then reduce consumption variance by pooling and distributing the catch, a form of risk minimisation. In a final example, Ziker (1998) documents and analyses the increased importance of localised reciprocity among aboriginal Siberians following the collapse of state socialism in the Soviet Union. In decreasing order of influence, inter-household transfers of subsistence production gained from hunting, fishing, and trapping appear to be patterned by reciprocity among community members, obligations to kin, the value attached to reduced daily consumption variance (risk minimisation) and, to a lesser degree, the desire to avoid a reputation for stinginess or hoarding, such as would occur if scrounging were too often rebuffed.

The range of models developed on intra-group food distribution highlights an advantage to the reductionist methodology of behavioural ecology: it has produced a set of analytical tools that appear capable of explaining both the complexity and especially the diversity of transfer behaviours in hunter–gatherer societies. Much of the inter-societal variation that characterises the term sharing likely can be explained by differing degrees of influence from scrounging, reciprocity, risk minimisation, exchange, showing off, costly signalling, and perhaps by mechanisms yet to be discovered. It probably is significant that most case studies find that more than one cause is operating and also differ on which is assigned greatest importance. Peterson's (1993) concept of *demand sharing* is just what one would expect from this overlapping mix of causes and motivations. He observes that among Australian Aborigines, food 'sharing' is rife with social tension. Givers are often reluctant, and respond only when pressured by supplicants; the generosity of sharing is demanded, and individuals with food sometimes avoid those without. It is also known that in the right socio-environmental circumstances, a wide variety of species engages in intra-group food transfers (review in Winterhalder, 2001). Sharing occurs opportunistically across a wide variety of taxa, and it cannot be invoked as a late-occurring feature in a progressivist treatment of hominid evolution (Rowley-Conwy, this volume).

Key features of foraging economies

How do behavioural ecology models such as these help explain regular features of foraging economies? *Under-production* has been attributed to a high degree of residential mobility (e.g. Sahlins 1972). The reason is simple: material accumulation is unattractive to those who must move frequently and carry their property with them. Mobility requires portability. The marginal value theorem, central place foraging models, and the ideal free distribution underwrite this insight by showing why, how, and to what degree mobility is a result of resource distribution patterns, including localised depletion. Because residential but not logistic mobility limits accumulation, it is important that we be able to predict which of these forms of movement is most likely, a capacity afforded by the Zeanah model. Further, while mobility may suppress the desire for property, transfer behaviours also can act to discourage excess production. For instance, virtually all discussions of scrounging point out that it limits individual incentives to produce. Because of such features, foraging economies typically discourage ambitious production.

No fewer than six models address the intra-group *resource transfers* known generally as 'sharing.' Transfers arise in response to a mix of ecological (intermediate-sized resources, subsistence risk) and social (showing off, costly signalling) factors. Because of unique socio-ecological circumstances, the causal effectiveness of these mechanisms will vary among populations. As a result, transfer behaviours are likely to be ubiquitous, but their form and extent will be diverse. Behavioural ecology shows that sharing may be much more heterogeneous than it has seemed from standard ethnographic accounts.

Social anthropologists have argued that *egalitarianism* is a consequence of two features of hunter–gatherer life: (1) the very limited degree to which individual hunter–gatherers sequester resources with concepts of private property, and (2) the very high degree to which they value reciprocity and, with it, a general disdain for material routes to status. Evolutionary models focused on territoriality and respect for possession help us to understand the former feature. With respect to the latter, models of transfer behaviour suggest that reciprocity may be only a minor element among the mechanisms equalising material wealth in hunter–gatherer societies. Those models that do envision ambitious producers have them dispersing goods as widely as possible in exchange for social prestige (showing off) or as a means of validating prowess (costly signalling). Both tend to forestall differential material accumulation.

Anthropology generally has lacked compelling explanations for the routine *male–female division of labour* found in foraging societies. Explanations based on differing physical capabilities are empirically weak and have the taint of chauvinism about them; socio-cultural explanations that cite symbolic causes have not managed to evade circularity. Behavioural ecology models deriving from sexual selection theory, including selection for maternal parental investment, showing off and costly signalling, show promise. However, these models are too novel and recent to have had extensive empirical assessment.

The assumption of constrained optimisation

The basic methodology of behavioural ecology analysis has been well described (citations in Smith and Winterhalder 1992). An assumption of this approach – constrained optimisation – is troubling to some anthropologists. Why expect subsistence efficiency of foragers? After all, they are not factory labourers whose work is governed by time-and-efficiency experts or the demands of a competitive market for commoditised labour. There are at least four possible responses to this question.

First, there are ultimate or evolutionary reasons for this expectation. Neo-Darwinian selection persistently eliminates variants that do not efficiently acquire resources for survival and reproduction. A tendency toward optimisation is built into the evolutionary process, even if optimality as such is rarely achieved. Because many hunter–gatherers have long co-evolutionary histories with resource species, their procurement skills have had to keep pace with the constant selection pressure they and other harvesters place on the evasive capacities of their living resources. With every generation, co-evolution raises the stakes on hunter–gatherer proficiency. The lengthy duration of this mode of livelihood itself is an indication of its effectiveness, as is the evidence of prehistoric colonisation by hunter–gatherers of the most varied and demanding of global habitats.

Second, a proximate response would focus on how individual foragers gain and apply the cognitive and physical skills needed for success in the food quest. Rational choice is part of the answer. Some hunting and gathering behaviour is carefully calculated. On discovering moose tracks, Cree hunters carefully study their age and condition for what they reveal about the animal's size, movements, and intentions. They survey surrounding forage for evidence that the animal would be tempted to linger nearby for browse. They evaluate the temperature, wind, and snow conditions to appraise the likelihood it was in an especially wary frame of mind. These and other factors are carefully appraised in reaching a decision like that envisioned by the encounter-contingent model: pursue the trail of this moose, or continue searching for a better pursuit opportunity.

But rational choice is only part of the answer. An evolutionary approach opens up other possibilities. Many foraging decisions probably are guided by rules of thumb (e.g. large size is a good indicator of profitability) arrived at through various selective mechanisms acting on cultural inheritance (reviewed in Durham 1990). Or, they are guided by tacit skills gained as young foragers follow the lead of experienced adult mentors and then augment that experience on their own. Unfortunately, we know very little about the proximate, cognitive psychology of foraging decisions, or its development in apprentice foragers.

Third, methodology is an important consideration. To reduce the danger of ethnocentrism anthropologists prefer to begin their investigations with the assumption that the economic actions of foragers are sensible and effective in context. Constrained optimisation gives this ethical commitment an operational quality: it makes analytical work possible.

Finally, the ethnographic literature on foragers is replete with empirical testimony to their ecological acumen and economic skills. If behavioural ecology models were to mislead the detailed analysis of this record, this would be revealed through ethnographic study and hypothesis testing. We start with the expectation of constrained optimisation because it is the best way to test understanding of the goals and constraints that shape foraging behaviour. Studies like those cited above show that this assumption has proven quite useful.

Conclusions: the foraging mode of production

Attempts to understand foragers in broad theoretical terms have drawn upon a variety of perspectives, well described in historical terms by Bettinger (1991). Whether described as a culture core, as in Steward's (1955) cultural ecology, or mode of production, as in Marxist analysis (Elster 1985), most scholars have assumed that the basic economic features of hunter–gatherers influence their social, political, and other cultural behaviours. Behavioural ecology provides us an understanding of the micro-ecological foundations (cf. Elster 1985) for those basic features, as they manifest themselves in the variety of foraging societies. It offers a unitary approach that takes diversity seriously by moving from categorical statements such as, 'Hunter–gatherers under-produce', to analytical claims of the form, 'We can predict that the level of hunter–gatherer production will vary as a function of socio-ecological variables x, y and z.'

Among the alternative perspectives available, Marx has provided us one of the most enduring, instructive, and problematic of tools for thinking about foragers, the *mode of production* concept (Lee 1981). A mode of production has two components: the forces of production (land, labour, skills, and tools or technology), and the relations of production (the property rights that govern access to resources and their distribution). The concept is important for its broad, comparative potential of the range of economic systems found through human history. However, because Marx developed and exemplified the idea primarily in the context of capitalist societies, there has been ongoing debate about how closely and usefully it applies to other economic formations, such as foragers.

The features of foraging societies that behavioural ecology is able to help explain correspond more or less directly to the forces (e.g. resource selection) and the relations (e.g. transfers, egalitarianism, division of labour) of production. Behavioural ecology thus provides micro-ecological foundations for the analysis of the foraging mode (cf. Layton 1999 for a similar effort to find common ground between Darwinian and Marxian analysis). Put differently, ecological context must be made a prominent analytical element in the mode of production concept if it is to be useful in the analysis of foragers. The density and profitability, location, reliability, and response to exploitation of natural resources are just as important to hunter–gatherer economics as capital, commodities, and equilibrium-setting markets to the capitalist mode. Likewise, analysis using the mode of production concept must be willing to make selective use of micro-economic concepts such as marginal analysis and opportunity costs (cf. Elster 1985). Behavioural ecology demonstrates the critical role of such concepts in understanding economic and social features of hunter–gatherer populations.

Behavioural ecology analysis supplies reasons to think that foraging constitutes an identifiable mode of production (Lee 1981). By extension, hunter–gatherers exist as a defensible analytical category (Panter-Brick *et al.*, this volume). Seen in their ethnographically modal configurations, foragers and pastoralists have high degrees of logistic and residential mobility, but foragers lack cargo-bearing domesticates. This feature has profound implications for material accumulation. Foragers also are virtually unique in having evolved very limited forms of property with respect to essential resources and foraging range. And they are unusual in the variety of mechanisms that produce widespread and generally equitable distribution of food and other resources within social groups. All of these features arise to significant degree from properties of the ecological setting of forager subsistence.

Behavioural ecology analysis accommodates our intuition that foraging economies are profoundly different while it simultaneously insists that forager behaviour can be understood by the same analytical tools applied to other societies. In effect, we need not despair of clear definition, robust generalities or coherent, encompassing theoretical explanation of hunter–gatherers despite their variety and their difference from our own economic experience.

References

Barlow, K.R. and Metcalfe, D. (1996). Plant utility indices: two Great Basin examples. *Journal of Archaeological Science* **23**: 351–371.

Barnard, A. (1983). Contemporary hunter–gatherers: current theoretical issues in ecology and social organisation. *Annual Review of Anthropology* **12**: 193–214.

Bettinger, R.L. (1991). *Hunter-Gatherers: Archaeological and Evolutionary Theory.* New York: Plenum Press.

Bettinger, R.L, Malhi, R. and McCarthy, H. (1997). Central place models of acorn and mussel processing. *Journal of Archaeological Science* **24**: 887–899.

Betzig, L.L. and Turke, P.W. (1986). Food sharing on Ifaluk. *Current Anthropology* **27**: 397–400.

Bliege Bird, R.L. and Bird, D.W. (1997). Delayed reciprocity and tolerated theft: the behavioural ecology of food-sharing strategies. *Current Anthropology* **38**: 49–78.

Blurton Jones, N.G. (1987). Tolerated theft, suggestions about the ecology and evolution of sharing, hoarding and scrounging. *Social Science Information* **26**: 31–54.

Broughton, J.M. and Grayson, D.K. (1993). Diet breadth, adaptive change, and the White Mountains faunas. *Journal of Archaeological Science* **20**: 331–336.

Brown, J.L. (1964). The evolution of diversity in avian territorial systems. *The Wilson Bulletin* **76**: 160–169.

Cashdan, E. (1983). Territoriality among human foragers: ecological models and an application to four Bushman groups. *Current Anthropology* **24**: 47–66.

Cashdan, E. (1992). Spatial organisation and habitat use. In *Evolutionary Ecology and Human Behavior*, E. A. Smith and B. Winterhalder, pp. 237–266. New York: Aldine de Gruyter.

Charnov, E.L. (1976). Optimal foraging, the marginal value theorem. *Theoretical Population Biology* **9**: 129–136.

Dahlberg, F. (ed.) (1981). *Woman the Gatherer*. New Haven: Yale University Press.

Durham, W.H. (1990). Advances in evolutionary culture theory. *Annual Review of Anthropology* **19**: 187–210.

Dwyer, P.D. (1985). A hunt in New Guinea: some difficulties for optimal foraging theory. *Man* (N.S.) **20**: 243–253.

Dwyer, P.D. and Minnegal, M. (1993). Are Kubo hunters 'show offs'? *Ethology and Sociobiology* **14**: 53–70.

Dyson-Hudson, R. and Smith, E.A. (1978). Human territoriality: an ecological reassessment. *American Anthropologist* **80**: 21–41.

Elster, J. (1985). *Making Sense of Marx*. Cambridge: Cambridge University Press.

Foley, R. (1985). Optimality theory in anthropology. *Man* (N.S.) **20**: 222–242.

Fretwell, S.D. and Lucas, H.L. Jr. (1970). On territorial behaviour and other factors influencing habitat distribution in birds. I. Theoretical development. *Acta Biotheoretica* **19**: 16–36.

Gray, V. and Lowery, D. (1998). To lobby alone or in a flock: foraging behavior among organised interests. *American Politics Quarterly* **26**: 5–34.

Hames, R. (2000). Reciprocal altruism in Yanomamo food exchange. In *Adaptation and Human Behavior: An Anthropological Perspective*. N. Chagnon, L. Cronk, and W. Irons, pp. 397–416. Hawthorne, NY: Aldine de Gruyter.

Hawkes, K. (1993). Why hunter–gatherers work: an ancient version of the problem of public goods. *Current Anthropology* **34**: 341–361.

Hawkes, K., O'Connell, J.F. and Blurton Jones, N.G. (1991). Hunting income patterns among the Hadza: big game, common goods, foraging goals and the evolution of the human diet. *Philosophical Transactions of the Royal Society of London, B* **334**: 243–251.

Hill, K. and Kaplan, H. (1993). On why male foragers hunt and share food. *Current Anthropology* **34**: 701–706.

Hill, K., Kaplan, H., Hawkes, K. and Magdalena Hurtado, A. (1987). Foraging decisions among Aché hunter–gatherers: new data and implications for optimal foraging models. *Ethology and Sociobiology* **8**: 1–36.

Ingold, T. (1996). The optimal forager and economic man. In *Nature and Society: Anthropological Perspectives*, ed. P. Descola and G. Palsson, pp. 25–44. London: Routledge.

Kaplan, H. and Hill, K. (1985a). Hunting ability and reproductive success among male Ache foragers: preliminary results. *Current Anthropology* **26**: 131–133.

Kaplan, H. and Hill, K. (1985b). Food sharing among Ache foragers: tests of explanatory hypotheses. *Current Anthropology* **26**: 223–246.

Kelly, R.L. (1995). *The Foraging Spectrum: Diversity in Hunter-Gatherer Lifeways*. Washington DC: Smithsonian Institution Press.

Kummer, H. (1991). Evolutionary transformations of possessive behavior. In *To Have Possessions: A Handbook on Ownership and Property*, ed. R.W. Rudmin, pp. 75–83. Corte Madera CA: Select Press.

Layton, R. (1999). Exploitation after Marx. In *The Anthropology of Power: Empowerment and Disempowerment in Changing Structures*, ed. A. Cheater, pp. 133–148. London: Routledge.

Lee, R.B. (1979). *The !Kung San: Men, Women, and Work in a Foraging Society*. Cambridge: Cambridge University Press.

Lee, R.B. (1981). Is there a foraging mode of production? *Canadian Journal of Anthropology* **2**: 13–19.

Lee, R.B., and DeVore, I. (eds.) (1968). *Man the Hunter*. Chicago: Aldine.

Metcalfe, D. and Barlow, K.R. (1992). A model for exploring the optimal trade-off between field processing and transport. *American Anthropologist* **94**: 340–356.

Meyers, F.R. (1988). Critical trends in the study of hunter–gatherers. *Annual Review of Anthropology* **17**: 261–282.

Orians, G.H. and Pearson, N.E. (1979). On the theory of central place foraging. In *Analysis of Ecological Systems*, ed. D.J. Horn, G.R. Stairs, and R.D. Mitchell, pp. 155–177. Columbus: Ohio State University Press.

Peterson, N. (1993). Demand sharing: reciprocity and the pressure for generosity among foragers. *American Anthropologist* **95**: 860–874.

Pirolli, P. and Card, S. (1995). Information foraging in information access environments. Association for Computing Machinery, Special Interest Group on Computer-Human Interaction. URL: http://www.acm.org/sigchi/chi95/proceedings/papers/ppp_bdy.htm

Rose, L.M. (1997). Vertebrate predation and food sharing in *Cebus* and *Pan*. *International Journal of Primatology* **18**: 727–765.

Sahlins, M. (1972). *Stone Age Economics*. Chicago: Aldine.

Smith, E.A. (1991). *Inujjuamiut Foraging Strategies*. New York: Aldine de Gruyter.

Smith, E.A. and Bliege Bird, R.L. (2000). Turtle hunting and tombstone opening: public generosity as costly signaling. *Evolution and Human Behavior* **21**: 223–244.

Smith, E.A. and Winterhalder, B. (eds.) (1992). *Evolutionary Ecology and Human Behavior*. New York: Aldine de Gruyter.

Stanford, C.B. (1995). Chimpanzee hunting behavior and human evolution. *American Scientist* **83**: 256–261.

Steward, J.H. (1938). *Basin-Plateau Aboriginal Sociopolitical Groups*, Bulletin 120. Washington DC: Bureau of American Ethnology.

Steward, J.H. 1955. The concept and method of cultural ecology. In *Theory of Cultural Change: The Methodology of Multilinear Evolution*, ed. J.H. Steward, pp. 30–42. Urbana: University of Illinois Press.

Vickery, W.L., Giraldeau, L.-A., Templeton, J.J., Kramer, D.L. and Chapman, C.A. (1991). Producers, scroungers, and group foraging. *American Naturalist* **137**: 847–863.

Whitehead, H. and Hope, P. (1991). Sperm whalers off the Galapagos Islands and in the Western North Pacific, 1830–1850: ideal free whalers? *Ethology and Sociobiology* **12**: 147–161.

Winterhalder, B. (1983). Boreal foraging strategies. In *Boreal Forest Adaptations: The Northern Algonkians*, ed. A. Theodore Steegmann, Jr., pp. 201–241. New York: Plenum Press.

Winterhalder, B. (1990). Open field, common pot: Harvest variability and risk avoidance in agricultural and foraging societies. In *Risk and Uncertainty in Tribal and Peasant Economies*, ed. Elisabeth Cashdan, pp. 67–87. Boulder CO: Westview Press.

Winterhalder, B. (1996a). Social foraging and the behavioral ecology of intragroup resource transfers. *Evolutionary Anthropology* **5**: 46–57.

Winterhalder, B. (1996b). Gifts given, gifts taken: the behavioural ecology of nonmarket, intragroup exchange. *Journal of Archaeological Research* **5**: 121–168.

Winterhalder, B. (1996c). A marginal model of tolerated theft. *Ethology and Sociobiology* **17**: 37–53.

Winterhalder, B. (2001). Intra-group transfers of resources and their implications for hominid evolution. In *Meat Eating and Human Evolution*, ed. C.B. Stanford and H.T. Bunn, Oxford: Oxford University Press.

Winterhalder, B. and Smith, E.A. (eds.) (1981). *Hunter–Gatherer Foraging Strategies: Ethnographic and Archaeological Analyses*. Chicago: University of Chicago Press.

Zeanah, D.W. (2000). Transport costs, central-place foraging, and hunter–gatherer alpine land-use strategies. In *Intermountain Archaeology* ed. D.B. Madsen and M.D. Metcalfe, pp. 1–14. Salt Lake City: University of Utah Press.

Ziker, J.P. (1998). Kinship and exchange among the Dolgan and Nganasan of northern Siberia. *Research in Economic Anthropology* **19**: 191–238

3

Time, change and the archaeology of hunter–gatherers: how original is the 'Original Affluent Society'?

PETER ROWLEY-CONWY

The Original Affluent Society

This highly evocative phrase first appeared in *Man the Hunter* (Lee and DeVore 1968*a*), used by Marshall Sahlins to describe hunter–gatherers:

> This was, when you come to think of it, the original affluent society. By common understanding an affluent society is one in which all the people's wants are easily satisfied . . . [but] wants are 'easily satisfied' either by producing much or desiring little, and there are, accordingly, two possible roads to affluence. The Galbraithian course makes assumptions peculiarly appropriate to market economies . . . But there is also a Zen solution to scarcity and affluence, beginning from premises opposite from our own, that human material ends are few and finite and technical means unchanging but on the whole adequate. Adopting the Zen strategy, a people can enjoy an unparalleled material plenty, though perhaps only a low standard of living. (Sahlins 1968: 85)

These concepts were developed in *Stone Age Economics* (Sahlins 1972), the first chapter of which was entitled 'The Original Affluent Society'. Sahlins rooted the Zen concept of 'want not, lack not' (p. 11) in the mobility of hunter–gatherers. Most groups carry with them all their material possessions, which must thus be kept to a minimum. In a word, 'mobility and property are in contradiction' (p. 12).

Sahlins's formulation sprang directly from the definition of hunter–gatherers provided by Lee and DeVore in *Man the Hunter*: 'we make two basic assumptions about hunters and gatherers: (1) they live in small groups and (2) they move around a lot' (Lee and

DeVore 1968*b*: 11). Five outcomes of this were responsible for shaping hunter–gatherer society: (a) little personal property and an egalitarian social system; (b) sporadic gatherings of bands, and much mobility of individuals between bands; (c) a fluid organisation involving no territorial rights; (d) no food storage; and (e) no group strongly attached to a particular area (Lee and DeVore 1968*b*: 12). This was the Original Affluent Society (OAS) in a nutshell, and provided a clear vision of what hunter–gatherers were like.

Hunter–gatherer variability

The OAS was so powerful a concept that hunter–gatherer variability received little consideration until 12 years after *Man the Hunter*. Binford (1980) and Woodburn (1980) then each created a typology of hunter–gatherers in which one type conformed to, while the other type diverged from, the OAS model.

Binford (1980) distinguished between 'foragers' and 'collectors' (Figure 3.1). Foragers correspond to the OAS: they move relatively often, and individuals return to the residential base each day. Collectors however move less often, and are found in environments in which resource availability varies in both time and space. Resource storage helps counteract temporal variation: food collected in a season of plenty may be stored for later use. Resource transport helps counteract spatial variation: special-purpose field camps are used to procure and process resources which are then transported back to the base camp. Binford termed this a 'logistic strategy'.

Woodburn (1980) coined the term 'immediate return' for groups corresponding to the OAS because food collected on a particular day is consumed almost immediately: the return upon labour is immediate. In 'delayed return' societies on the other hand consumption is delayed. Resources may be stored for later consumption, and/or work may be expended on complex items like fish traps before the relevant resource becomes available. Woodburn explored two further corollaries. First, a fish trap involves considerable labour, and the trap and its catch will therefore belong to those who constructed it. Individuals or groups thus own territories. Second,

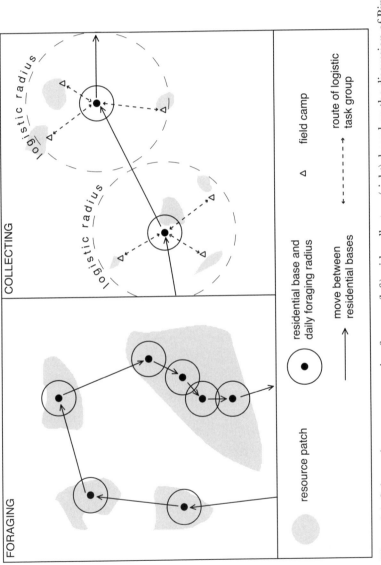

Figure 3.1. Schematic maps contrasting foragers (left) with collectors (right), based on the discussion of Binford (1980). Each shows the same proportion of hypothetical annual rounds, so that foragers' residential bases are occupied for shorter periods than those of collectors.

the ownership of both territories and stored food represents unequal access to wealth. Food is not shared throughout the group, so society tends to be hierarchical. Territoriality and social hierarchy are both in flat contradiction to the OAS.

These two typologies produce similar but not identical classifications. Inuit store food and are logistically organised, although most are not territorial or hierarchical. Australian Aborigines do not store food, but are to an extent territorial. Layton (1986) resolved these anomalies: Inuit are obliged to store food due to seasonal variation in resources, but unpredictable inter-annual and spatial variations make territoriality unviable. Aborigines are territorial mainly with regard to water: ritual knowledge about water sources is jealously guarded while in other respects they practise an immediate return strategy. This allows us to construct a four-fold typology of hunter–gatherers (Rowley-Conwy 1999):

1. The OAS: groups with little or no logistic movement of resources or food storage. These are mostly found in tropical regions (e.g. the Aborigines), although some occur in higher latitude areas where resources are available throughout the year; people can move from one resource to the next, exploiting them in sequence without the need for much storage.
2. Logistic groups that do not defend territories, such as most Inuit.
3. Logistic groups that do defend territories – many of Woodburn's delayed return groups.
4. Sedentary groups who invariably defend territories and store resources, forming a continuation from type 3.

This typology applies to ethnographically known groups. Archaeology was similarly challenging the assumption that all hunter–gatherers conformed to the OAS, but identifying divergent groups was more difficult because of the problems of interpreting the archaeological record. Sedentism, which could be identified, did not conform to the OAS (Price 1981, Rowley-Conwy 1983). Archaeologists use the term 'complex' to describe non-OAS groups, perhaps unfortunate because it means that 'simple' is sometimes used to describe OAS groups, but it will be followed here. Applying this terminology to the four-fold typology, type 1 or OAS groups are non-complex, the rest forming a continuum towards the most complex type 4 groups.

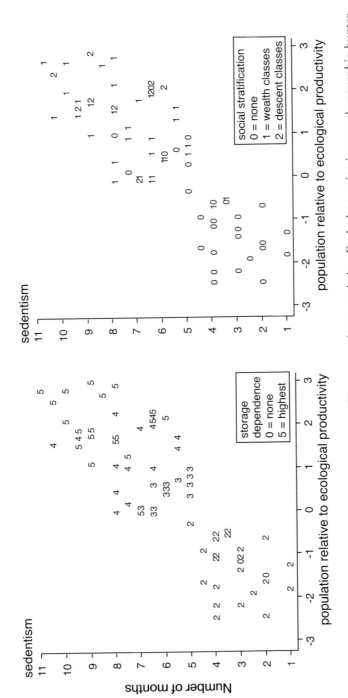

Figure 3.2. Correlations between various attributes of hunter–gatherer societies. Each data point is one ethnographic hunter–gatherer group. Sedentism is the number of months for which the winter settlement is occupied. Population relative to ecological productivity is calculated by Keeley (1988, p. 385). Societies with wealth classes are those where individuals can acquire high status during their lives; societies with descent classes are those in which status is inherited. (Redrawn from Keeley 1991, Figs. 17.1 and 17.6.)

Anthropological work on variability has been taken further in several ways. For example, territoriality has been linked to environmental factors: if an important resource appears in predictable concentrations, then that area is likely to be the exclusive territory of an individual or group; while if resources are unpredictable, flexibility is a better response (Dyson-Hudson and Smith 1978). Archaeology gains an unexpected bonus here because territorial hunter–gatherers sometimes bury their dead in cemeteries whereas non-territorial ones do not. An archaeological cemetery thus probably indicates a territorial group (Saxe 1970, Pardoe 1988). Technology becomes more specialised when maximum resources have to be procured in a short period (Torrence, this volume). The major cross-cultural surveys of Keeley (1988, 1991) demonstrate that population density and sedentism are linked (Figure 3.2); so is dependence on storage, and social factors: territorial descent classes characterise the sedentary groups with most storage. A hierarchical society is thus linked to economic factors. This is a further bonus for archaeology: if we can demonstrate a degree of sedentism or locate a cemetery, other aspects of complexity, harder to see archaeologically, may be confidently predicted.

Progressivist views of complexity

Anthropology in recent years has usually presented variability as synchronic, occurring across space, in a largely adaptive context. Archaeology tends to approach it very differently, often presenting it as diachronic, developing through time, in a largely progressive context. More often than not this is done implicitly. While Brown and Price (1985: 436) eschew the band/tribe/chiefdom/state progressivist typology of Service (1962), their volume is entitled *Prehistoric Hunter-Gatherers: The Emergence of Cultural Complexity* (Price and Brown 1985). The search for an 'emergence' of complexity, reflected in so many article and chapter titles, signals an implicit belief that there was a time *before* complexity emerged; a time, therefore, of universal simplicity.

These two views cannot both be right. Either variability is a response to local conditions, or it is time-dependant and tending towards complexity. This chapter argues in favour of local responses and local historical trajectories, and against any progressive trend, by challenging the one aspect of the OAS that is usually accepted without question: its originality.

Progressivist views of the emergence of complexity are usually couched in one of two ways. Both involve intensification, namely an increase in the productivity (or production) of resources. However, demographic viewpoints see population increase as the prime mover, while social viewpoints see increasing social obligations as causing increased production.

The demographic view holds that hunter–gatherer populations increase as a matter of course, so groups must intensify, i.e. produce more food from a given area. A particularly clear statement comes from Zvelebil (1995), reproduced as Figure 3.3. Each time population catches up with resources it 'bounces' productivity upwards, firstly via greater mobility and diversification (OAS strategies), then specialisation (a type 2 logistic strategy), storage (types 3 or 4), and ultimately husbandry and domestication. The problem lies in the time-scale: complexity is the endpoint of a long trajectory. Figure 3.3 covers only the late Mesolithic of Zvelebil's region (the Baltic). This implies that during the previous 5000 years since postglacial colonisation, population was below environmental carrying capacity. Population must therefore have been growing very slowly. In areas like Portugal, continuously occupied since the arrival of modern humans, the time lag would be 30 000 years.

Would population density remain below capacity for so long? This is widely debated, the Australian terminology being the most explicit: 'fast-trackers' suggest fast population increase up to carrying capacity, 'slow-trackers' that it remains low for a long period (Mulvaney and Kamminga 1999: 132–3). Human populations might well grow very fast. Discussing the hunter–gatherer occupation of North America, Diamond (1987) states that an annual growth rate of 1.4% will turn 100 people into 1 000 000 people *in one thousand years*. Birdsell (1957) calculates that a founder population of 25 people could saturate Australasia with 300 000 hunter–gatherers in 2204 years. Pennington (this volume) documents much

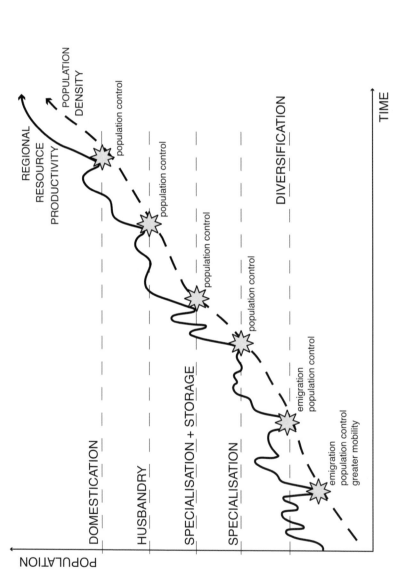

Figure 3.3. Population density, resource productivity, and resource-use strategies. (Redrawn from Zvelebil 1995, Fig. 2.)

variety in growth rate even within the small remaining sample of hunter–gatherers. Groups colonising new areas like the Baltic would probably have had rates of increase at or above the highest levels observed recently.

Faced with such figures, slow-trackers must explain why hunter–gatherer populations should increase only very slowly. Voluntary population control is usually suggested (Hayden 1972): people perceive that increased population means increased work, and therefore choose to keep their population well below carrying capacity by means of infanticide, etc. There are two difficulties with this. First, it is difficult to establish whether infanticide really has been very important among recent hunter–gatherers (Kelly 1995: 232ff.). Second, the suggestion runs counter to biological theory by treating the group rather than the individual as the unit of selection, by invoking 'cultural controls' as the means of decision-making. Individuals who ignored the 'controls' would however gain an evolutionary benefit by filling the underpopulated landscape with their descendants. Non-hierarchical OAS groups exercise little control over individuals and would not be able to police a slow-track demographic policy.

Social obligations are the other pressure sometimes invoked for increased production. Bender (1978) states that developing alliance networks are crucial; there is 'a direct link between evolving social institutions and increasing pressure on production' (1978: 213). This can transform an OAS group into a type 4 society: 'Surplus production involves delayed return: in response to the requirements of the alliance and leadership seasonally abundant foodstuffs and other material items will accumulate in quantities over and above immediate requirements' (ibid.). Under these circumstances 'clearly there is a pay-off in staying put and creating permanent storage facilities' (ibid.).

Directional and incremental change in social institutions is assumed, but there is no reason why alliances should become more complex and demanding through time. OAS groups in fact maintain some of the most complex alliance networks known to anthropology, and these are satisfactorily serviced without departure from OAS behaviour. The !Kung of Botswana maintain numerous partners up to 200 km away in the exchange system known as *hxaro* (Wiessner 1982). In southeastern Australia people travelled hundreds of kilometres to attend gatherings at points of temporary resource abundance (McBryde 1984). Such activities fit well with the flexible organisation of these OAS groups and do not appear to cause directional change away from this. Social intensification *per se* does not therefore account for when and why some societies should become complex and others should not.

Hunter–gatherer complexity: the archaeological record

It has been argued above that the theoretical underpinnings of the progressivist view are not solid. The archaeological record of anatomically modern humans is now examined. There are six assumptions, often implicit, involved in the progressivist view, which are discussed in turn.

Assumption 1: There is a trend from simple to complex

It is often argued that aquatic resources are a late addition to the human diet. Binford (1991) states that 'Pleistocene people . . . , it is well known, favoured terrestrial resources' (p. 134); at the Pleistocene/Holocene boundary there was an 'aquatic resource revolution'; the appearance of logistic (type 2 or 3) strategies was dependent on this revolution, and on the development of transport technologies such as water transport and pack animals (p. 138).

Pleistocene marine strategies are hard to examine because the sea has risen >100 m since the last glacial maximum and has flooded most coastlines, but work in various areas has revealed aquatic interests. New Ireland (northeast of New Guinea) was occupied by 33 000 BP, requiring a sea crossing of *c.* 50 km (Allen *et al.* 1988). The Solomon Islands were occupied before 28 000 BP, requiring a voyage of over 130 km, involving sailing out of sight of land (Wickler and Spriggs 1988). Several sites have produced marine fish and molluscs; these are in steep areas where the sea was never far away. The evident use of watercraft removes one of Binford's objections, and at 19 000 BP live marsupials were transported to New Ireland and released to found populations which could be hunted (Flannery and White 1991) – a delayed-return activity if ever there was one! On the Australian mainland marine evidence is available from at least 25 000 BP (Morse 1988), and it has even been suggested that the entire first occupation of Australia was coastally oriented (Bowdler 1977). In southern Africa marine resources were exploited still earlier. The shell midden at Herolds Bay is 125 000 years old (Brink and Deacon 1982). Many others are known, and marine foods may have played an important role in the evolution of modern humans (Parkington in press).

Binford's statement was heavily based on Europe, where evidence of marine exploitation is indeed concentrated in the post-glacial. However, some hints from the glacial period are found in areas of steep topography. Thousands of Upper Palaeolithic limpets come from the northern Spanish sites of El Juyo (Madariaga de la Campa and Fernández Pato 1985) and La Riera (Ortea 1986). Seal bones have been recovered from Nerja (Morales *et al.* 1998), Gorham's Cave and Altamira (Cleyet-Merle 1990), all in Spain. Bones of tunny were recovered from the Grimaldi caves in northwestern Italy, which suggests offshore boating, and occasional marine fish turn up elsewhere (ibid.). Artistic representations of marine fauna include the famous baton from Montgaudier, an inland site in southern France, which shows two seals (Figure 3.4). Seals may occasionally swim up rivers and be seen inland, but the Montgaudier specimens are well depicted and clearly engraved by someone who knew seals well. Under the nose of the leading seal is what is sometimes described as a salmon, but this is more likely to be a whale as it appears to have a spout above its head. Fish depictions are generally difficult to identify, but flatfish are exclusively marine and are shown at Mas d'Azil and Altxerri in the Pyrenees.

These cases do not of course demonstrate logistic strategies, but it is hard to see how hunter–gatherers could have survived in ice-age

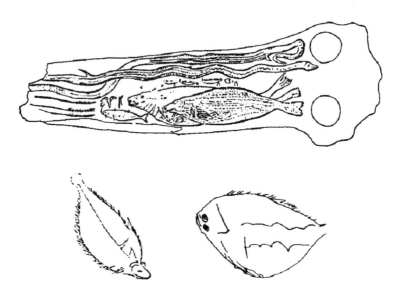

Figure 3.4. The Montgaudier baton (top), and the flatfish from Altxerri (left) and Mas d'Azil (right). (Redrawn from Cleyet-Merle 1990.)

Europe without them. Reindeer and salmon were the major terrestrial and aquatic resources, and ethnographically they are classic targets of logistic strategies. What could have prevented Upper Palaeolithic people from developing maritime adaptations? Specialised multi-component technology for hunting land mammals appeared by 30 000 BP (Knecht 1993), and recent dates on art reveal a complex ritual system just as early (Clottes 1999), so technological and ideological flexibility were evidently not lacking. There are some hints of coastal specialisation. Clustering of art sites along the north Spanish coast may indicate territorial groupings (Layton 1987), and marine shell ornaments predominate at Riparo Mochi in northwestern Italy but hardly penetrate inland (Stiner 1999). These examples suggest communities oriented towards the sea – but of whose territories we can only see a small part. Coastlines dating from the Pleistocene/Holocene boundary are above water in western Sweden and Norway due to isostatic rebound, and they have evidence of settlement. Neither the sites in Sweden (Schmitt 1995) nor those in Norway, some of which are large and lie north of the Arctic Circle (Thommessen 1996), have preserved fauna, but they must be coastally oriented. Most of Norway was still under ice, with only islands and headlands available for settlement. This Arctic maritime adaptation must have been logistically organised.

This evidence is sufficient to indicate the likelihood of maritime adaptations during the Upper Palaeolithic, and the nature of the resources makes type 3 or even type 4 groups most probable. The only time we can examine a relevant coast (Norway and Sweden), settlement is demonstrated – and most glacial Atlantic and Mediterranean coasts would have been less demanding than this because of the presence of hinterland resources not available in Norway due to glacial coverage.

The postglacial however remains the accepted time that complexity emerged, in particular the later Mesolithic. Cemeteries are often late Mesolithic, and it has been argued that 'some sort of demographic threshold was crossed in some parts of western Europe at around 6500 years ago' (Clark and Neeley 1987: 124). Most cemeteries are however near the coasts, which is where we should expect them: the territorial groups that use cemeteries would appear in productive and reliable resource areas, which mostly means the coasts. Because earlier coasts are now under the sea, any earlier Mesolithic cemeteries would remain inaccessible. Europe does have one terminal Pleistocene cemetery, at Arene Candide in northwestern Italy, containing 20 individuals (Cardini 1980); this is an area where topography means that the shoreline has not moved far, and as at nearby Riparo Mochi there are many shell ornaments. This is a strong indication that complex groups may have existed elsewhere as well.

The hypothesis that cemeteries result from demographic increase must be examined against evidence in other areas. In the Murray Valley in southeastern Australia cemeteries are known as early as 13 000 BP (Pardoe 1988) – some 40 000 years after the first colonisation of Australia. In North Africa a series of late glacial cemeteries (Wendorf 1968, Lubell *et al.* 1984) postdates modern human occupation by maybe 100 000 years. In the Mississippi Valley however the logistically organised Dalton culture used cemeteries as early as

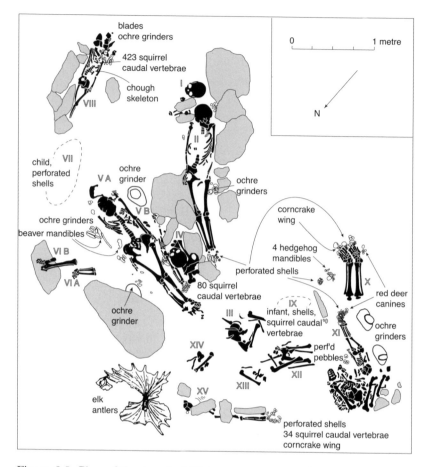

Figure 3.5. Plan of the terminal Pleistocene cemetery from Arene Candide, Liguria, Italy. Positions of some grave goods marked. (Redrawn from Cardini 1980, Fig. 2.) (Published by kind permission of the Istituto Italiano di Paleontologia Umana.)

10 750 BP – just 750 years after the first occupation of the region (Morse *et al.* 1996). Such hugely diverse time-lags argue strongly against the demographic steamroller.

This evidence from around the world demonstrates much Pleistocene interest in marine resources (contra Binford, above). Much evidence is distorted by coastal loss, but enough remains from Norway to New Ireland to make the case for type 3 groups in many areas (see also Kuhn and Stiner, this volume). There is no archaeological evidence that hunter–gatherers display an inherent trend from simple to complex.

Assumption 2: Only simple groups were present among early anatomically modern humans

This assumption is virtually ubiquitous, but caution is suggested by the arguments based on Mesolithic cemeteries. Skhul and Qafzeh caves in Israel, both around 90 000 years old, contain 10 and 18 skeletons of modern humans respectively. If they are cemeteries their implications for territoriality should not be ignored because of their antiquity.

Gargett (1999) has argued that the Qafzeh assemblage is a natural accumulation of skeletons rather than deliberate burials, because the skeletons are fragmentary, incomplete and disarticulated, and there are no clearcut grave pits. However, the number of individuals is more than could accumulate by chance, and Gargett does not consider whether these anatomically modern people might also have been behaviourally modern. Disarticulation and breakage are common in cave cemeteries, and grave pits are often unnecessary. At Arene Candide, Cardini states that:

> Some of the inhumations were inserted directly into modest natural depressions formed between the tumbled blocks from the overlying deposits, others appeared to be protected both by these same blocks already present in the deposits and by the deliberate placing of other lumps or slabs of limestone, which in a few cases encircled the inhumation and in others partially covered it. Many graves were disturbed or completely destroyed by the placing of subsequent burials, with the consequent dispersal of the bones. Only in a few cases . . . do we observe a deliberate placing, something like a secondary deposition of groups of bones coming from previous disturbed inhumations. (1980: 13, my translation)

This disturbance appears similar to that at Qafzeh, but Arene Candide is an indubitable cemetery replete with grave goods and ochre (Figure 3.5); utilised ochre was also found associated with one of the Qafzeh skeletons (Vandermeersch 1969).

Much more information is needed regarding the behaviour of early modern humans. In the meantime we cannot dismiss the possibility of complexity merely because it is 'too early'; this should be investigated, not assumed in advance.

Assumption 3. Change towards complexity occurs slowly

Archaeologists often assume that a trend towards complexity occurs slowly over the long term, perhaps millennia. Archaeological evidence however suggests that such changes can take place much faster when the opportunity arises.

A good example comes from southern Scandinavia. Late Mesolithic coastal settlements have long been taken to indicate complexity (Rowley-Conwy 1983), but the middle Mesolithic was little known because sea level rise had flooded contemporary coastlines. Underwater archaeologists have recently examined these coastlines and put archaeological developments into ecological context. The rising sea crossed the -27 m threshold into the present waterways at 7000 BC (Figure 3.6), and due to flat topography much land was then flooded very rapidly. As soon as sea levels began to stabilise, indications of complexity appeared in the form of large semi-sedentary settlements, cemeteries and large fish traps. The chronology of these (Figure 3.6) shows no time-lag; within the limits of dating resolution they appear immediately.

Other examples have already been mentioned. The Dalton culture in the Mississippi Valley was logistically organised and used cemeteries less than a millennium after people first arrived in the area (Morse et al. 1996). The rapid logistically organised occupation of the Norwegian coast occurred as soon as the retreating glaciers had exposed the islands and headlands (Thommessen 1996). Thus complexity may appear rapidly in response to environmental opportunities. This does not support the suggestion that complexity emerges slowly as the endpoint of internal development.

How rapid can responses be? These archaeological examples suffer from the imprecision of our dating methods – uncertain by at least the standard deviation of a radiocarbon date. Various anthropological studies have provided tighter resolution. The Mbaka of central Africa, formerly OAS-type hunter–gatherers, settled down to become farmers and rapidly developed a hierarchical wealth-

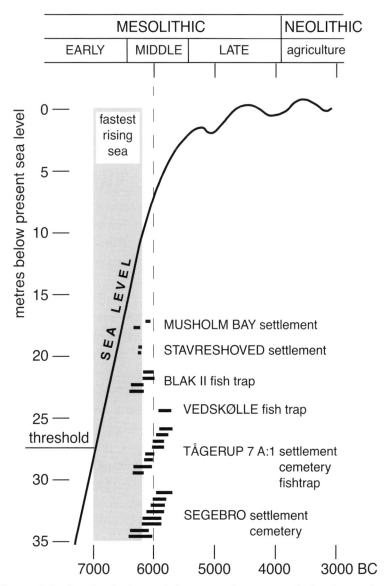

Figure 3.6. Sea level rise and hunter–gatherer complexity in southern Scandinavia; black bars are calibrated radiocarbon ages. The −27 m threshold is the level at which the southern Scandinavian waterways began to be flooded. (Sea level curve from Christensen *et al.* 1997, Fig. 2; Musholm Bay from Fischer and Malm 1997; Stavreshoved from Fischer 1997*a*; Blak II from Sørensen 1996; Vedskølle from Fischer 1997*b*; Tågerup from Andersson and Knarrström 1997; Segebro from Larsson 1982.)

based society – 'not due to imitative processes, but to the requirements of their new activities' (Meillassoux 1973: 197). Aboriginal
groups near Lake Eyre oscillated between type 3 territoriality and
storage in productive years, and OAS-type sharing and flexibility in
lean years (Layton *et al.* 1991: 258–9). This suggests that archaeologists should not view 'social factors' as rigid and inhibitors of
change, particularly among hunter–gatherers.

Assumption 4. Change towards complexity is irreversible

The progressivist view that complex groups appear towards the end
of hunter–gatherer history carries with it the assumption (often
implicit) that agriculture is the next 'stage' of directional development. From this perspective, change towards simplicity is unexpected – but it is far from uncommon.

A good example comes from Labrador, Canada. The Maritime
Archaic tradition began about 7500 BP. Numerous settlements are
known, such as Aillik (Figure 3.7). The Aillik sequence starts at 6000
BP with structures 6 and 7, and ends at 4300–3600 BP with structure
2, a 28-metre longhouse. This is by no means the largest: Nulliak
Cove has 27 longhouses, some measuring 100 metres in length –
though all were not occupied at once. The Aillik specimen has seven
or more compartments each of a size appropriate for a nuclear
family, and about 10 stone-lined storage pits around it; this may
indicate storage by the individual families (Fitzhugh 1984). These
longhouses were probably foundations for tents, suggesting seasonal
occupation in summer. The large aggregation size means that 'some
kind of social mechanisms for organizing large groups (for example,
leadership hierarchies) may have been in operation' (Hood 1993:
170). This level of social integration disappeared at the end of the
Maritime Archaic tradition, which overlaps chronologically with the
immigrant Paleoeskimo responsible for structure 1 at Aillik (Figure
3.7).

The demise of other apparently complex adaptations is also
documented. Late Palaeolithic occupants of the lower Nile Valley
may have smoked and stored large numbers of catfish; the environment was stable and productive and sites quite large (Vermeersch *et*

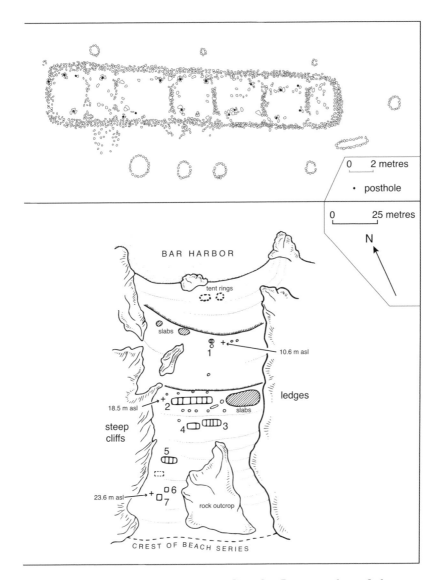

Figure 3.7. Aillik, Labrador, eastern Canada. Bottom: plan of the cove, showing the raised beaches and structures (m asl = metres above sea level). Top: enlarged plan of structure 2. (Redrawn from Fitzhugh 1984, Figs. 1 and 2.)

al. 1989: 111). The 'Wild Nile', a period of high and violent floods starting at 11 500 BP, brought this to a close, and the valley was apparently abandoned until 8000 BP. Thus 'for the inhabitants of the lower Nile Valley, the Pleistocene–Holocene transition would seem to have been an unmitigated disaster' (Close 1996: 54). In the Mississippi Valley, the cemeteries and logistic adaptation of the Dalton culture ended at 10 000 BP, to be followed by an OAS group (Morse *et al.* 1996).

Archaeology therefore provides sufficient examples to demonstrate that change can go either way: simple to complex, or complex to simple. Directional change towards incremental complexity is not supported by the empirical record.

Assumption 5. Change towards complexity is a step towards agriculture

This assumption is often explicit. An argument that complex hunter–gatherers in southern Sweden at 4400 BC were not developing towards agriculture (Rowley-Conwy 1998) has been criticised by the editors of the volume in which it appeared! 'Rowley-Conwy is wrong . . . Even though the movement of agriculture across central Europe at 4400 BC was a coincidence unrelated at that point to the lives of south Scandinavian hunter–gatherers, *they were soon to feel its impact . . .*' (Zvelebil *et al.* 1998: 2, added emphasis). This endows the hunter–gatherers with 20–20 foresight, as well as a curious desire to 'get ready' for the arrival of farming on the opposite side of the Baltic Sea – over 100 km away. Farming did not actually appear in southern Sweden until 1500 years later. Another clear statement comes from Hodder (1990), who argues that a major step towards agriculture was the 'domestication of society'. This was essentially the appearance of a hierarchical delayed-return organisation that Hodder terms 'the domus' (from the Latin word meaning 'home'). After this, domestication occurred: 'it was through the domus that the origins of agriculture were thought about and conceived . . . The domus became the conceptual and practical locus for the transformation of wild into cultural . . . [and]

provided a way of thinking about the control of the wild . . .'
(Hodder 1990: 38–9).

To what extent are complex hunter–gatherers potential agriculturalists? In both northern Europe and eastern Turkey, such groups
were probably sedentary and collected nuts; wild cereals grew in
neither area. Domestication claims are based on pigs: there are
many juveniles in the archaeological assemblages, and this is
believed to result from domestic culling patterns (Zvelebil 1995,
Hongo and Meadow 1998, Rosenberg *et al.* 1998). But is a juvenile
age structure likely to indicate domestication? Large sedentary
hunter–gatherer groups would increase hunting pressure, and this
can lead to a more juvenile kill without any domestication being
involved (Elder 1965). The hunting of juveniles can markedly *increase*
the wild population, even though this seems counter-intuitive to
Western notions of sportsmanship. This is shown for moose in
Figure 3.8. (Grenier 1979). The effect will be even more marked in
pigs because of their multitudinous offspring. Many juveniles in an
archaeological pig population is probably not about domestication;
it is simply about hunting more pigs.

It is refreshing to examine the best-researched complex hunter–
gatherer tradition known to archaeology, and see how it has dealt
with agriculture. The Jomon of Japan comprises mainly type 3 or
4 groups which lasted from the late Pleistocene until the first
millennium BC (Imamura 1996). Many large sites are known,
including coastal shell middens and inland villages, and houses are
substantial (D and E in Figure 3.9). Sedentary occupation has
been demonstrated via shellfish (Koike 1980) and fish (Akazawa
1981). Salmon was a major quarry, involving a logistic strategy
and storage (Matsui 1996). In the interior, storage pits for nuts are
large and common (Imamura 1996 pp. 104–6). Some still contain
nuts; the oldest of these is from Higashi-Kurotsuchida, dated to
11 300±130 BP (Miyaji 1999). There are many cemeteries, and
society may have been hierarchical (Kobayashi 1992). This led to
early suggestions of agriculture (e.g. Kamikawana 1968), but a
great deal of subsequent work has demolished this claim; suitable
plants are in fact absent (Imamura 1996: 106–9). Agriculture

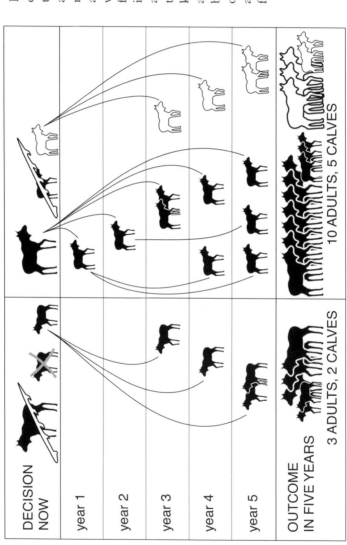

Figure 3.8. Effect of hunting choice on a moose population. Encountering a female and two calves, a hunter may kill the adult; on average one calf will die without the protective female, while the other and its progeny total five animals after five years. Alternatively the hunter may kill a calf, in which case the adult female continues to breed, as does the other calf, producing 15 animals after five years. (Modified from Grenier 1979, Fig. 2.)

DECISION NOW

year 1

year 2

year 3

year 4

year 5

OUTCOME IN FIVE YEARS

3 ADULTS, 2 CALVES

10 ADULTS, 5 CALVES

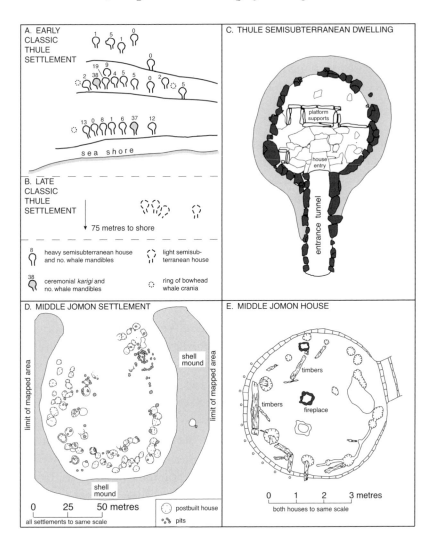

Figure 3.9. Settlements and houses. A–B: Early and late Classic Thule Inuit settlements at Creswell Bay, northern Canada. (Redrawn from Savelle 1987, Figs. 87 and 90b). C: Early Classic Thule winter house. (Redrawn from Dumond 1977, Fig. 111). D: Middle Jomon shell midden at Takane-Kido. (Redrawn from Barnes 1993, Fig. 28). E: Middle Jomon house from Idojiri. (Redrawn from Aikens and Higuchi 1982, Fig. 3.31). In A, B and D not all houses need have been occupied at the same time; four building phases are represented in D.

arrived from the Asian mainland in the first millennium BC, when domestic pigs appear (Nishimoto 1994). The Jomon was not 'getting ready' for this to occur; in most areas of Japan population was decreasing in the period before this. Only in the northeast, the last area to go agricultural, was population increasing (Koyama 1978).

Eight thousand years of complexity did not lead to an indigenous Jomon agriculture. Jomon studies have freed themselves from this predestination, so groups can be examined for their own sake – not for what they might become.

Assumption 6. The most interesting hunter–gatherers are those who became farmers

Natufian type 3 or 4 groups inhabited the Near East for 3000 years before the emergence of agriculture. They collected wild grass seeds. The idea that this activity is a prelude to agriculture is widespread. Arguing for autochthonous intensification in Australia, Lourandos (1983: 92) describes 'the process being nipped in the bud by the coming of the Europeans'; but as grass seeds were being collected there before 25 000 BP (McConnell and O'Connor 1997) one may ask how much longer one would have had to wait. Harlan (1989) argued that modern African seed collection with beating baskets was a prelude to domestication, but this collection method causes no genetic change in the grass (Hillman and Davies 1992); wild sorghum has been collected in Africa since at least 8500 BP (Magid 1995), so collection evidently need not lead to domestication. The belief that seed collectors were proto-agriculturalists led to the Wadi Kubbaniya fiasco, where domestic barley, lentils and chickpeas in contexts dated to 18 000 BP were uncritically accepted as evidence of Palaeolithic agriculture (Wendorf et al. 1982). These items all proved to be misidentifications or recent contaminants (Hillman et al. 1989).

So was the Natufian in any sense pregnant with agriculture? Claims of Natufian domesticated cereals have proved groundless (Legge 1986), and the collection of wild cereals at Abu Hureyra *decreased* through time (Hillman *et al.* 1989). Wild wheat and barley were collected by 19 000 BP in the Near East (Kislev *et al.* 1992), so here too there was a very long lead-in time. Wild grass seed collection is by no means restricted to complex groups. In Keeley's (1992) survey of 93 ethnographic hunter–gatherer societies, complexity and wild grass seed collection revealed no correlation whatsoever.

There was therefore nothing about the Natufian that made agriculture inevitable. Agriculture appears to have resulted from the meshing of a series of unrelated factors of which the Natufian delayed-return economy was only one; climatic change and plant genetics were just as crucial (Hillman 1996). Had these factors not all come together, the Natufian might have continued hunting and gathering indefinitely.

The Arctic is the area that all hunter–gatherer archaeologists should know about. The impossibility of agriculture in the Arctic is an antidote to theories of its inevitability elsewhere. Groups may use ceramics and ground stone (Gusev *et al.* 1999) without being suspected of Neolithic activities. Thule Eskimo in the central Canadian Arctic were presented with a remarkable opportunity around AD 1000: a warming climatic trend meant less sea ice, and an increase in bowhead whales. Thule Eskimo actively hunted these; even juveniles weighed up to 10 tons (Savelle and McCartney 1991). This practice led to the construction of villages as large and as sedentary as those of the Natufian (Figure 3.9A), consisting of many heavy semisubterranean houses built of whalebones, stone and turf and equipped with a coldtrap entrance tunnel (Figure 3.9C) – though not all houses need have been occupied at once. Ceremonial *karigi* houses and circles of whale crania appear. Sites are quite far apart, with smaller camps and storage locations in between them, indicating a logistic strategy with a large logistic radius (cf. Figure 3.1) (Savelle 1987; Savelle and McCartney 1988). Of all the type 3 and 4 groups described here, this is probably the most remarkable. A cooling trend from AD 1200 decreased bowhead whale availability; settlements became smaller, houses less permanent, and *karigi* and whale skull circles ceased being constructed

(Figure 3.9B). After AD 1600 further cooling decreased whale availability even more. At European contact the Netsilik people in the area used many short-lived settlements to exploit sequentially available resources. They were among the least storage-dependent of any Inuit groups (Balikci 1970) and so most closely approached the OAS.

Agriculture could never have been an outcome of Thule complexity; but had such a spectacular archaeological manifestation occurred anywhere else in the world it would surely have been suggested.

Conclusions

There is no directional trend among hunter–gatherer societies. Numerous examples reveal complexity coming and going frequently as a result of adaptive necessities. The adaptationist view cannot be reconciled with progressivist theories, whether demographically or socially based, but is in stark opposition to them. Most hunter–gatherers who became farmers have done so as the result of stimuli from agricultural neighbours. Hunter–gatherers with no agricultural neighbours originated agriculture very rarely, perhaps only three or four times – empirical evidence for the low likelihood of such an event occurring. Most hunter–gatherer historical trajectories would never have resulted in agriculture had that way of life not impinged on them from the outside.

In 10 000 years agriculture and its outcomes have come to dominate the world. Agricultural economies, despite catastrophes and reversals, can usually be intensified: new animals can be domesticated, ploughs can be made more effective, locally adapted crops such as oats can be added, animals can provide traction and other secondary products, transport and redistribution systems can be improved, pests controlled, industrial fertilisers produced, and crops genetically modified. Hunter–gatherer economies were not like this. Salmon, nuts, reindeer or grass seeds cannot be intensified indefinitely; the limits to growth will be reached unless domestication follows.

If the Original Affluent Society is not 'original', what is it? Archaeologists have often regarded terroriality, rigid group membership and social hierarchy as stepping stones from the OAS towards ourselves, but these features are all found among chimpanzees. From this perspective the flexibility, mobility and social equality of the Original Affluent Society may be the most remarkable and specialised social form that humans have ever evolved. It has no claim to be the original human condition.

Acknowledgements

Thanks to Tim Murray, David Frankel and the Department of Archaeology at La Trobe University in Melbourne where this chapter was written, to Mary Stiner and John Parkington for unpublished work, to Pamela Rose, Phil Edwards and Roberto Maggi for literature, and to Alessandra Buonfino for checking my Italian translation. An early version was delivered as the Meyerstein Lecture in Oxford in 1997; thanks to Helena Hamerow.

References

Aikens, C.M. and Higuchi, T. (1982). *Prehistory of Japan*. New York: Academic Press.

Akazawa, T. (1981). Maritime adaptation of prehistoric hunter–gatherers and their transition to agriculture in Japan. *Senri Ethnological Studies* 9, 213–258.

Allen, J., Gosden, C., Jones, R. and White, J.P. (1988). Pleistocene dates for the human occupation of New Ireland, northern Melanesia. *Nature* **331**: 707–709.

Andersson, M. and Knarrström, B. (1997). Plats 7A: 1 – ett mesolitisk boplatskomplex vid sammanflödet Braån-Saxån. In *Skåne, Malmöhus Län, Järnvägan Västkustbanan, Avsnittet Landskrona-KävlinGe 1996–1997, Arkeologisk Förundersökning*, (vol. 1), ed. M. Svensson and P. Karsten, 75–99. Lund: Riksantikvarieämbetet.

Balikci, A. (1970). *The Netsilik Eskimo*. New York: Natural History Press.

Barnes, G. (1993). *China, Korea and Japan: the Rise of Civilisation in East Asia*. London: Thames and Hudson.

Bender, B. (1978). Gatherer-hunter to farmer: a social perspective. *World Archaeology*, **10**: 204–222.

Binford, L.R. (1980). Willow smoke and dogs' tails: hunter–gatherer settlement systems and archaeological site formation. *American Antiquity* **45**: 4–20.

Binford, L.R. (1991). Mobility, housing, and environment: a comparative study. *Journal of Anthropological Research* **46**: 119–152.

Birdsell, J.B. (1957). Some population problems involving Pleistocene man. *Cold Spring Harbor Symposia on Quantitative Biology* **22**: 47–69.

Bowdler, S. (1977). The coastal colonisation of Australia. In *Sunda and Sahul*, ed. J. Allen, J. Golson and R. Jones, pp. 205–246. London: Academic Press.

Brink, J.S. and Deacon, H.J. (1982). A study of a last interglacial shell midden and bone accumulation at Herolds Bay, Cape Province, South Africa. In *Proceedings of the VIth Biennial Conference held at the Transvaal Museum, Pretoria, 26–29 May 1981*, ed. J.C. Vogel, E.A. Voigt and T.C. Partridge, pp. 31–39. Rotterdam: A.A. Balkema.

Brown, J.A. and Price, T.D. (1985). Complex hunter–gatherers: retrospect and prospect. In *Prehistoric Hunter-Gatherers. The Emergence of Cultural Complexity*, ed. T.D. Price and J.A. Brown, pp. 435–442. New York: Academic Press.

Cardini, L. (1980). La necropoli mesolitica delle Arene Candide (Liguria). *Memorie dell'Istituto Italiano di Paleontologia Umana* **3**: 9–31.

Christensen, C., Fischer, A. and Mathiassen, D.R.1. (1997). The great sea rise in the Storebælt. In *The Danish Storebælt since the Ice Age*, ed. L. Pedersen, A. Fischer and B. Aaby, pp. 45–54. Copenhagen: A/S Storebælt Fixed Link.

Clark, G.A. and Neeley, M. (1987). Social differentiation in European mesolithic burial data. In *Mesolithic Northwest Europe: Recent Trends*, ed. P. Rowley-Conwy, M. Zvelebil and H.P. Blankholm, pp. 121–127. Sheffield: University of Sheffield, Department of Archaeology and Prehistory.

Cleyet-Merle, J.-J. (1990). *La Préhistoire de la Pêche*. Paris: Editions Errance.

Close, A.E. (1996). Plus ça change: the Pleistocene–Holocene transition in northeast Africa. In *Humans at the End of the Ice Age*, ed. L.G. Straus, B.V. Eriksen, J.M. Erlandson and D.R. Yesner, pp. 43–60. New York: Plenum Press.

Clottes, J. (1999). Twenty thousand years of palaeolithic cave art in southern France. In *World Prehistory. Studies in Memory of Grahame Clark*, ed. J. Coles, R. Bewley and P. Mellars, pp. 161–175. Oxford: Oxford University Press. (Proceedings of the British Academy 99).

Diamond, J.M. (1987). Who were the first Americans? *Nature* **329**: 580–581.

Dumond, D. (1977). *The Eskimos and Aleuts*. London: Thames and Hudson.

Dyson-Hudson, R. and Smith, E.A. (1978). Human territoriality: an ecological reassessment. *American Anthropologist* **80**: 21–41.

Elder, W.H. (1965). Primeval deer hunting pressures revealed by remains from American Indian middens. *Journal of Wildlife Management* **29**: 366–370.

Fischer, A. (1997*a*). People and the sea – settlement and fishing along the mesolithic coasts. In *The Danish Storebælt since the Ice Age*, ed. L. Pedersen, A. Fischer and B. Aaby, pp. 63–77. Copenhagen: A/S Storebælt Fixed Link.

Fischer, A. (1997*b*). *Marinearkæologiske forundersøgelser forud for etablering af en fast Øresundsforbindelse*, vol. 2. Copenhagen: Miljø- og Energiministeriet, Skov- og Naturstyrelsen.

Fischer, A. and Malm, T. (1997). The settlement in the submerged forest in Musholm Bay. In *The Danish Storebælt since the Ice Age*, ed. L. Pedersen, A. Fischer and B. Aaby, pp. 78–86. Copenhagen: A/S Storebælt Fixed Link.

Fitzhugh, W. (1984). Residence pattern development in the Labrador Maritime Archaic: longhouse models and 1983 surveys. In *Archaeology in Newfoundland and Labrador – 1983*, ed. J.S. Thomson and C. Thomson, pp. 6–41. St. John's, Newfoundland: Historic Resources Division, Department of Culture, Recreation and Youth.

Flannery, T.F. and White, J.P. (1991). Animal translocation. *National Geographic Research and Exploration* **7**: 96–113.

Gargett, R. (1999). Middle palaeolithic burial is not a dead issue: the view from Qafzeh, Saint-Césaire, Kebara, Amud, and Dederiyeh. *Journal of Human Evolution* **37**: 27–90.

Grenier, P. 1979. New regulations on moose hunting in Quebec. *Canadian Wildlife Administration* **4**: 28–31.

Gusev, S.V., Zagoroulko, A.V. and Porotov, A.V. (1999). Sea mammal hunters of Chukotka, Bering Strait: recent archaeological results and problems. *World Archaeology* **30**: 354–369.

Harlan, J.R. (1989). Wild-grass seed harvesting in the Sahara and Sub-Sahara of Africa. In *Foraging and Farming*, ed. D.R. Harris and G.C. Hillman, pp. 79–98. London: Unwin Hyman.

Hayden, B. (1972). Population control among hunter–gatherers. *World Archaeology* **4**: 205–221.

Hillman, G.C. (1996). Late Pleistocene changes in wild plant-foods available to hunter–gatherers of the northern Fertile Crescent: possible preludes to cereal domestication. In D.R. Harris (ed) *The Origins and Spread of Agriculture and Pastoralism in Eurasia*, 159–203. London: UCL Press.

Hillman, G.C. and Davis, M.S. (1992). Domestication rate in wild wheats and barley under primitive cultivation: preliminary results and archaeological implications of field measurements of selection coefficient. In *Préhistoire de l'Agriculture: Nouvelles Approches Expérimentales et Ethnographiques*. Centre de Recherches Archéologiques Monographe 6, ed. P.C. Anderson, pp. 113–158. Paris: CNRS.

Hillman, G.C. Colledge, S.M. and Harris, D.R. (1989). Plant-food economy during the epipalaeolithic period at Tell Abu Hureyra, Syria: dietary diversity, seasonality and modes of exploitation. In *Foraging and Farming*, ed. D.R. Harris and G.C. Hillman, pp. 240–268. London: Unwin Hyman.

Hillman, G.C., Madeyska, E. and Hather, J. (1989). Wild plant foods and diet at late palaeolithic Wadi Kubbaniya: the evidence from charred remains. In *The Prehistory of Wadi Kubbaniya*, vol. 2, *Stratigraphy, Paleoeconomy and Environment*, ed. F. Wendorf, R. Schild and A.E. Close, pp. 162–242. Dallas: Southern Methodist University Press.

Hodder, I. (1990). *The Domestication of Europe*. Oxford: Blackwell.

Hongo, H. and Meadow, R.H. (1998). Pig exploitation at neolithic Çayönü Tepesi (southeastern Anatolia). *MASCA Research Papers in Science and Archaeology* **15**: 77–98.

Hood, B. (1993). The Maritime Archaic Indians of Labrador: investigating prehistoric social organisation. *Newfoundland Studies* **9**: 163–184.

Imamura, K. (1996). *Prehistoric Japan*. London: UCL Press.

Kamikawana, A. (1968). Sites in middle Yamanashi-ken and Middle Jomon agriculture. *Asian Perspectives* **11**: 53–68.

Keeley, L.H. (1988). Hunter–gatherer economic complexity and 'population pressure': a cross-cultural analysis. *Journal of Anthropological Archaeology* **7**: 373–411.

Keeley, L.H. (1991). Ethnographic models for late glacial hunter–gatherers. In *The Late Glacial in Northwest Europe*, ed. N. Barton, A.J. Roberts and D.A. Roe, pp. 179–190. London: Council for British Archaeology.

Keeley, L.H. (1992). The use of plant foods among hunter–gatherers: a cross-cultural survey. In *Préhistoire de l'Agriculture. Nouvelles Approches Expérimentales er Ethnographiques* Centre de Recherches Archéologiques Monographe 6, ed. P.C. Anderson, pp. 29–38. Paris: CNRS.

Kelly, R.L. (1995). *The Foraging Spectrum: Diversity in Hunter-Gatherer Lifeways*. Washington DC: Smithsonian Institution Press.

Kislev, M.E., Nadel, D. and Carmi, I. (1992). Epipalaeolithic (19 000 BP) cereal and fruit diet at Ohalo II, Sea of Galilee, Israel. *Review of Palaeobotany and Palynology* **73**: 161–166.

Knecht, H. (1993). Early Upper Palaeolithic approaches to bone and antler projectile technology. In *Hunting and Animal Exploitation in the Later Palaeolithic and Mesolithic of Eurasia*, ed. G.L. Peterkin, H. Bricker and P. Mellars, pp. 33–47. Archaeological Papers of the American Anthropological Association 4.

Kobayashi, T. (1992). Patterns and levels of social complexity in Jomon Japan. In *Pacific Northeast Asia in Prehistory*, ed. C.M. Aikens and S.N. Rhee, pp. 91–96. Pullman: Washington State University Press.

Koike, H. (1980). *Seasonal Dating by Growth-Line Counting of the Clam*, Meretrix lusoria. Tokyo: University Museum, University of Tokyo.

Koyama, S. (1978). Jomon subsistence and population. *Senri Ethnological Studies* **2**: 1–65.

Larsson, L. (1982). *Segebro: En Tidigatlantisk Boplats vid Sege Ås Mynning.* Malmö: Malmö Museum.

Layton, R. (1986). Political and territorial structures among hunter–gatherers. *Man* (N.S.) **21**: 18–33.

Layton, R. (1987). The use of ethnographic parallels in interpreting upper palaeolithic rock art. In *Comparative Anthropology*, ed. L. Holy, pp. 210–239. Oxford: Blackwell.

Layton, R. Foley, R. and Williams, E. (1991). The transition between hunting and gathering and the specialised husbandry of resources. *Current Anthropology* **32**: 255–263.

Lee, R.B. and DeVore, I. (eds.) (1968a). *Man the Hunter.* Chicago: Aldine.

Lee, R.B. and DeVore, I. (1968b). Problems in the study of hunters and gatherers. In *Man the Hunter*, ed. R.B. Lee and I. DeVore, pp. 3–12. Chicago: Aldine.

Legge, A.J. (1986). Seeds of discontent: accelerator dates on some charred plant remains from the Kebaran and Natufian cultures. In *Archaeological Results from Accelerator Dating*, ed. J.A.J. Gowlett and R.E.M. Hedges, pp. 13–21. Oxford: Oxford University Committee for Archaeology.

Lourandos, H. (1983). Intensification: a late Pleistocene–Holocene archaeological sequence from southwestern Australia. *Archaeology in Oceania* **18**: 81–94.

Lubell, D., Sheppard, P. and Jackes, M. (1984). Continuity in the epipalaeolithic of North Africa with emphasis on the Maghreb. *Advances in World Archaeology* **3**: 143–191.

Madariaga de la Campa, B. and Fernández Pato, C.A. (1985). Estudio malacologico de la cueva 'El Juyo'. In *Excavaciones en la Cueva del Juyo*, ed. I. Barandiarán, L.G. Freeman, J.G. Echegaray and R.G. Klein, pp. 75–95. Madrid: Ministerio del Cultura.

Magid, A.A. (1995). Plant remains from the sites of Aneibis, Abu Darbein and El Damer and their implications. In *Aqualithic Sites along the Rivers Nile and Atbara, Sudan*, ed. R. Haaland and A.A. Magid, pp. 147–177. Bergen: Alma Mater.

Matsui, A. (1996). Archaeological investigations of anadromous salmonid fishing in Japan. *World Archaeology* **27**: 444–460.

McBryde, I. (1984). Kulin greenstone quarries: the social contexts of production and distribution for the Mt William site. *World Archaeology* **16**: 267–285.

McConnell, K. and O'Connor, S. (1997). 40 000 year record of food plants in the Southern Kimberley Ranges, Western Australia. *Australian Archaeology* **45**: 20–31.

Meillassoux, C. (1973). On the mode of production of the hunting band. In

French Perspectives in African Studies, ed. P. Alexandre, pp. 187–203. Oxford: Oxford University Press.

Miyaji, A. (1999). Storage pits and the development of plant food management in Japan during the Jomon period. In *Bog Bodies, Sacred Sites and Wetland Archaeology*, ed. B. Coles, J. Coles and M. Schou-Hansen, pp. 165–170. Exeter: Department of Archaeology.

Morales, A., Roselló, E. and Hernández, F. (1998). Late upper palaeolithic subsistence strategies in southern Iberia: tardiglacial faunas from Cueva de Nerja (Málaga, Spain). *European Journal of Archaeology* **1**: 9–50.

Morse, D.F. Anderson, D.G. and Goodyear, A.C. (1996). The Pleistocene–Holocene transition in the eastern United States. In *Humans the the End of the Ice Age*, ed. L.G. Straus, B.V. Eriksen, J.M. Erlandson and D.R. Yesner, pp. 319–338. New York: Plenum Press.

Morse, K. (1988). Mandu Mandu Creek rockshelter: Pleistocene human coastal occupation of North West Cape, Western Australia. *Archaeology in Oceania* **23**: 81–88.

Mulvaney, D.J. and Kamminga, J. (1999). *Prehistory of Australia*. St. Leonards, NSW: Allen and Unwin.

Nishimoto, T. (1994). Domesticated pigs in the early agricultural period in Japan. *Archæozoologia* **6**: 57–70.

Ortea, J. (1986). The malacology of La Riera cave. In *La Riera Cave* Anthropological Research Papers 36, ed. L.G. Straus and G.A. Clark, pp. 289–313. Tempe: Arizona State University.

Pardoe, C. (1988). The cemetery as symbol. The distribution of prehistoric Aboriginal burial grounds in southeastern Australia. *Archaeology in Oceania* **23**: 1–16.

Parkington, J. (in press). The impact of the systematic exploitation of marine foods on human evolution. *Proceedings of the Dual Congress, Sun City 1998*.

Price, T.D. (1981). Complexity in 'non-complex' societies. In *Archaeological Approaches to the Study of Complexity*, ed. S.E.van der Leeuw, pp. 55–97. Amsterdam: University Press.

Price, T.D. and Brown, J.A. (eds.) (1985). *Prehistoric Hunter-Gatherers: The Emergence of Cultural Complexity*. New York: Academic Press.

Rosenberg, M., Nesbitt, R., Redding, R.W. and Peasnall, B.L. (1998). Hallan Çemi, pig husbandry, and post-Pleistocene adaptations along the Taurus-Zagros arc (Turkey). *Paléorient* **24**: 25–41.

Rowley-Conwy, P. (1983). Sedentary hunters: the Ertebølle example. In *Hunter-Gatherer Economy in Prehistory*, ed. G.N. Bailey, pp. 111–126. Cambridge: Cambridge University Press.

Rowley-Conwy, P. (1998). Cemeteries, seasonality and complexity in the Ertebølle of southern Scandinavia. In *Harvesting the Sea, Farming the Forest*, ed. M. Zvelebil, L. Domanska and R. Dennell, pp. 193–202, Sheffield: Sheffield Academic Press.

Rowley-Conwy, P. (1999). Economic prehistory in southern Scandinavia. In *World Prehistory: Studies in Memory of Grahame Clark, Proceedings of the British Academy*, ed. J.M. Coles, R.M. Bewley and P.A. Mellars, pp. 99, 125–159.

Sahlins, M. (1968). Notes on the original affluent society. In *Man the Hunter*, ed. R.B. Lee and I. DeVore, pp. 85–89. Chicago: Aldine.

Sahlins, M. (1972). *Stone Age Economics*. Chicago: Aldine.

Savelle, J. (1987). *Collectors and Foragers: Subsistence-Settlement System Change in the Central Canadian Arctic, A.D. 1000–1960*. Oxford: British Archaeological Reports.

Savelle, J.M. and McCartney, A.P. (1988). Geographical and temporal variation in Thule Eskimo subsistence economies: a model. *Research in Economic Anthropology* **10**: 21–72.

Savelle, J.M. and McCartney, A.P. (1991). Thule Eskimo bowhead whale procurement and selection. In *Human Predators and Prey Mortality*, ed. M. Stiner, pp. 201–216. Boulder: Westview Press.

Saxe, A. (1970). Social dimensions of mortuary practices. Unpublished PhD thesis, University of Michigan.

Schmitt, L. (1995). The West Swedish Hensbacka: a maritime adaptation and a seasonal expression of the North-Central European Ahrensburgian. In *Man and Sea in the Mesolithic*, Oxbow Monograph 53, ed. A. Fischer, pp. 161–70. Oxford: Oxbow Books.

Service, E.R. (1962). *Primitive Social Organisation: An Evolutionary Perspective*. New York: Random House.

Sørensen, S.A. (1996). *Kongemosekulturen i Sydskandinavien*. Jægerspris: Egnsmuseet Færgegården.

Stiner, M.C. (1999). Palaeolithic mollusc exploitation at Riparo Mochi (Balzi Rossi, Italy): food and ornaments from the Aurignacian through Epigravettian. *Antiquity* **73**: 735–754.

Thommessen, T. (1996). The early settlement of northern Norway. In *The Earliest Settlement of Scandinavia*, ed. L. Larsson, pp. 235–240. Stockholm: Almqvist and Wiksell. (Acta Archaeologica Lundensia, Series in 8°, 24)

Vandermeersch, B. (1969). Découverte d'un objet en ocre avec traces d'utilisation dans le Moustérien de Qafzeh (Israël). *Bulletin de la Société Préhistorique Française* **66**: 157–158.

Vermeersch, P.M., Paulissen, E. and Van Neer, W. (1989). The late palaeolithic Makhadma sites (Egypt): environment and subsistence. In *Late Prehistory of the Nile Basin and the Sahara*, ed. L. Krzyzaniak and M. Kobusiewicz, pp. 87–114. Poznan: Archaeological Museum.

Wendorf, F. (1968). *The Prehistory of Nubia*. Dallas: Southern Methodist University Press.

Wendorf, F., Schild, R. and Close, A.E. (1982). An ancient harvest on the Nile. *Science* **82**: 68–73.

Wickler, S. and Spriggs, M. (1988). Pleistocene human occupation of the Solomon Islands, Melanesia. *Antiquity* **62**: 703–706.

Wiessner, P. (1982). Risk, reciprocity and social influences on !Kung San economics. In *Politics and History in Band Societies*, ed. E. Leacock and R.B. Lee, pp. 61–84. Cambridge: Cambridge University Press.

Woodburn, J. (1980). Hunters and gatherers today and reconstruction of the past. In *Soviet and Western Anthropology*, ed. E. Gellner, pp. 95–117. London: Duckworth.

Zvelebil, M. (1995). Hunting, gathering, or husbandry? Management of food resources by the late Mesolithic communities of temperate Europe. *MASCA Research Papers in Science and Archaeology*, **12** (Supplement): 79–104.

Zvelebil, M. Domanska, L. and Dennell, R. (1998). Introduction: the Baltic and the transition to farming. In *Harvesting the Sea, Farming the Forest*, ed. M. Zvelebil, L. Domanska and R. Dennell, p. 1–7. Sheffield: Sheffield Academic Press.

4

Hunter–gatherer technology: macro- and microscale approaches

ROBIN TORRENCE

Scales of analysis

The study of technology is essential for understanding what humans are all about. Tool-using has often been cited as a quintessential quality of being human and the contemporary world puts more faith in technology to achieve goals than in any other means. Since changes in material culture played a major role in discredited theories which envisage the evolution of culture as one of increasing sophistication and complexity, anthropologists have shied away from technology. Fortunately, new theoretical developments are providing original insights into understanding the role of tools in societies and these can be profitably applied to explaining the vast differences among the technologies of current and past hunter–gatherers.

Archaeological theory has largely been pitched at *macroscale* analyses which produce a 'Big Picture' of how variability in technology is structured. Inspiration from evolutionary ecology has encouraged the development of models which predict the basic outlines of an optimal technology (Torrence 1989*a*). The recognition that risk is a key factor in shaping hunter–gatherer food-getting technology (Torrence 1989*b*; Bleed 1996; Bamforth and Bleed 1997) has played a particularly important role in new approaches. An understanding of patterning on a global level is a major outcome of macroscale theory, but the concepts can also be used to understand major changes in technology, particularly for the long time periods appropriate to prehistoric archaeology. In contrast, theory mainly inspired from ethnographic research has concentrated on processes that take place at the level of a local group, household or individual (Dobres and Hoffman 1994). Analysis focused on this *microscale* generally concentrates on how technology is meaningfully and socially constituted and how it can transform social life. Although there are important philosophical disagreements among users of macro- and microscale theory, their results are complementary and a full understanding of hunter–gatherer technology requires the application of both approaches.

Regardless of theoretical orientation, scholars agree that technology is not simply tools and their applications. Technology is defined as comprising physical actions by knowledgeable actors who use carefully chosen materials to produce a desired outcome. It is also recognised that it is constructed and constrained by the specific social, symbolic and historical context in which it takes place (Lemonnier 1993; Dobres and Hoffman 1994; Bleed 1997). The key elements of technology are physical setting, social context, actors, knowledge, energy sources, raw materials, tools, actions and outcomes. Although the two approaches accept this general definition, they vary in the degree to which the variables are given preference. Macroscale theories use a *comparative approach* and emphasise environmental context, energy, raw materials and tools, whereas microscale theories normally focus on *particular cases* and concentrate on social context, actors and knowledge. For both approaches technology is distinguished from other forms of behaviour because it uses physical actions to achieve material outcomes.

Macroscale approaches

The technological solutions we observe in hunter–gatherer societies past and present are the particular outcomes of decisions which have sought optimal outcomes to goals identified by the actors. These goals were derived from and mediated by the perceived social and physical environments and do not necessarily involve maximisation of some property such as energy or reproductive success. In my view the desired outcome as defined by the users is the most important factor in determining the choice of tools and actions

(Torrence 1989*b*: 58; Bamforth and Bleed 1997: 111), although technology must also be adjusted to fit competing goals and constraints posed by the social and physical environments.

My approach focuses on the organisation of an assemblage of tools rather than on the design of individual tools (cf. Bamforth and Bleed 1997: 111–12; contra Hayden *et al.* 1996: 10). As noted by Shott (1986: 15–16), many archaeological attempts to theorise technology have overemphasised the functional characteristics of tools in terms of specific tasks (i.e. tool size, weight, form, profile, angle of the working edge) and have failed to consider the basic organisation of tool-using and its relationship to other aspects of behaviour. In contrast, the macroscale approach attempts to elucidate the general processes that determine the overall character of hunter–gatherer tool-kits and the way they are manufactured and used.

Strategies for optimising risk and other currencies have been successfully modelled by archaeologists. The technological solutions summarised in this chapter provide the frameworks for understanding macroscale variability among hunter–gatherer technologies past and present. To illustrate how optimal modelling of technology works on the macroscale, I will focus on the tools used by hunter–gatherers to obtain food. Considered on a global level, there is enormous variation among recent hunter–gatherers (Table 4.1). Using concepts like more or less 'evolved' or 'advanced' to explain the differences is irrelevant. Instead, one should try to understand why different choices were made.

I begin with some basic principles. First, it is important to recognise that in most situations the range of equally suitable technological solutions to a particular problem is quite large. Consequently, prediction of technological behaviour is most amenable to situations where environmental constraints, and most particularly the climate of risk, are quite strict and where a restricted range of solutions is viable (Torrence 1989*a*: 4; Bamforth and Bleed 1997: 111). Technology is not, however, isolated from the wider cultural setting. People pursue a range of goals simultaneously and juggle their priorities and find compromises between their competing aims and their social and physical environments.

Table 4.1. *Global variation in food-getting technology among recent hunter–gatherer groups*

Hunter–gatherer group	Latitude	Tool type							
		Instruments		Weapons		Tended facilities		Untended facilities	
		No.[a]	TU[b]	No.	TU	No.	TU	No.	TU
Tiwi (Australia)	12	3	6	6	6	2	2	0	0
Andamanese (Indian Ocean)	12	4	8	4	31	3	12	0	0
Ingura (Australia)	14	3	3	6	19	3	8	1	2
Chenchu (India)	16	7	13	7	26	6	16	0	0
Naron Bushman (Namibia)	19	2	5	5	19	3	5	2	11
Aranda (Australia)	24	4	7	4	21	7	10	1	4
Owens Valley Paiute (N. America)	37	4	9	9	44	10	30	5	24
Surprise Valley Paiute (N. America)	42	7	15	9	27	19	41	4	14
Tasmanian (Australia)	42	3	3	3	3	4	8	1	1
Klamath (N. America)	43	9	18	7	35	22	70	5	28
Twana (N. America)	48	4	7	12	70	19	96	13	64
Tlingit (N. America)	58	4	7	8	25	8	34	8	55
Tanaina (N. America)	60	7	13	16	83	3	17	14	111
Ingalik (N. America)	62	6	14	13	64	15	61	21	157
Nabesna (N. America)	63	1	1	8	36	8	23	8	45
Caribou (N. America)	63	3	12	10	39	13	37	8	30
Angmaksalik (N. America)	66	4	18	18	151	9	20	2	13
Iglulik (N. America)	69	3	8	20	142	8	27	11	48
Copper (N. America)	70	4	16	8	11	36	4	17	27
Taremiut (N. America)	71	1	3	18	133	10	41	6	28

[a] No. is number of types. [b] TU is number of technounits.
Source: Based on Oswalt 1976, tables 8.1, 9.1.

Second, when modelling an optimal technology, it is important to recognise the conditions under which technology is necessary and beneficial. Tools that are only powered by human labour have a very limited capacity for maximising energy returns. For example, Hill and Hawkes (1983: 165) note that Ache hunters captured only half their prey using bow and arrows; the rest was obtained simply with hands or clubs. Furthermore, they estimate that the foraging rate (measured in kilos obtained per hour) could have been raised considerably if the hunters placed all their efforts on capturing game that could be taken by hand. In contrast to *processing* energy efficiently, the greatest benefit of hunter–gatherer tools used in subsistence is to *manage the availability* of energy in time and space. This is achieved by reducing the distance between the predator and prey and/or by attracting, capturing and holding resources (Torrence 1983, p. 16). These tools reduce the risk of not getting enough food.

Archaeologists have considered raw material, energy, time, risk and information as currencies which might be optimised by technology, but risk has been shown to be the most useful. As defined here, risk is made up both of the probability of not meeting dietary requirements and the costs of such a failure (Torrence 1989*b*: 58–60, Bamforth and Bleed 1997). Wiessner (1982: 172–3) identified four general kinds of behaviour that reduce risk: prevention of loss; transfer of loss; storage; and pooling of resources. Technology plays a major role in the prevention of loss and is sometimes used in storage, whereas social strategies, such as exchange relationships, are better equipped for transferring loss and pooling resources. Most of the strategies which Wiessner describes involve the reduction of risks which occur on relatively long time-scales, as for example over weeks, seasons or years. In contrast, tools are most effective for coping with problems that must be solved in a short time-scale, such as minutes or hours, and they may not be useful in other contexts. This point is especially important for trying to understand the variability in the way hunter–gatherers reduce risk. Tools are chosen for their ability to capture prey that is only accessible for short periods of time. For longer-term tasks, hunter–gatherers use other methods to prevent the loss of resources, such as the acquisition, sharing and passing on of knowledge about resource distributions, methods for tracking game, moving around, etc.

For hunter–gatherers, Weissner's first component of risk – namely the probability of failing to procure dietary requirements – is faced whenever a potential resource is encountered. The consequences of failing to acquire adequate supplies of food, variously labelled the 'severity of the risk' (Torrence 1989b: 59) or 'failure costs' (Bamforth and Bleed 1997) determine whether a group will respond. When the risk is significant, as measured by the availability of alternative food sources, technology will be employed to avoid it.

The tools and actions used by hunter–gatherers to obtain food are devised to reduce the probability of failure in cases where the costs of not doing so are high. If the probability of loss is encountered frequently, the tools and techniques used to reduce risk will be highly structured (Wiessner 1982). More importantly, the amount of energy invested into producing and maintaining an effective technology will be directly related to the size of the failure costs (Cashdan 1985). In general, the choice of action and tool type is linked to risk defined as the probability of loss, whereas strategies for the procurement, manufacture, design and use of tools are caused by the severity of the risk.

Tool assemblage structure

Tool assemblage structure is described in terms of the particular mix of tool types (*composition*); number of types (*diversity*); and number of parts of each tool (Torrence 1983) or the average number of parts per tool in an assemblage (*complexity*) (Bousman 1993, Bamforth and Bleed 1997). To illustrate how the climate of risk affects tool assemblage structure, I will use Oswalt's typology of food-getting tools and his measure of technounits as the number of parts of tools.

Oswalt (1976: 64) defines instruments as tools 'used to impinge on masses incapable of significant motion and relatively harmless to people': e.g. digging sticks, probes and some clubs. Weapons, such as spears, bows and arrows, harpoons and fish hooks, are defined as tools which apply energy directly to mobile prey. In contrast, the definition of facilities is that they use energy indirectly to control an animal's movement by attracting, directing or holding it (Oswalt 1976: 105). Facilities may be tended by one or more individuals or left to operate on their own. Hunting blinds and game surrounds are good examples of tended facilities, whereas most traps and snares are untended facilities which hold game until the hunter arrives.

Since Oswalt's different tool classes vary in how they can counter the probability of loss and reduce failure costs, they are found in different contexts. The choice between weapons and instruments depends on the nature of the prey, whereas facilities are added because of the level of failure costs rather than their specific functions. As defined above, instruments are suitable for acquiring plants or immobile animals and so they are found in all hunter–gatherer assemblages, but comprise the largest proportion when these resources comprise the bulk of the diet (Torrence 1983: Table 3.2). In contrast, weapons are best designed to reduce the time and energy input into the pursuit of mobile prey by reducing the distance between the place a prey is spotted and where it is captured. Weapons are also commonly used by hunter–gatherers, but the relative contribution to the tool-kit depends on the abundance of facilities, whose distribution is more restricted. Tended facilities, such as fish dams, hunting blinds or constructed hunting drives and surrounds, are a useful add-on which increase the effectiveness of weapons by restricting the mobility of the prey so that the hunter can get closer to it, but they are most useful when the resources are aggregated and multiple kills can be achieved. Finally, untended facilities reduce search time for resources, since they work while the hunter is somewhere else carrying out independent searches. Untended facilities are also particularly important in contexts where search time is high.

Failure costs, and therefore the level of risk, increase toward the poles because the availability of food decreases with longer winters and there are fewer alternative resources because species diversity has an inverse relationship with latitude. Latitude is therefore a useful proxy measure for severity of risk with higher latitudes having higher risks. Table 4.1 shows that as one moves away from the

Equator into zones of higher risk, tended facilities are increasingly added to weapons in assemblages. Untended facilities play almost no role in low latitude technologies, but are extremely important among northern groups, especially those dependent on terrestrial or freshwater resources. The type of tool used to procure animals also responds to increasing failure costs as monitored by latitude. Near the Equator small mammals are mainly hunted with instruments and weapons, but in the far north untended facilities such as traps are more common (Torrence 1983: Table 3.4). Similarly, tended facilities are used in the hunting of large terrestrial mammals to a greater degree in the riskier northern environments than among low-latitude groups.

When failure costs rise, additional inputs are made. The diversity of tools increases because special-purpose tools are the most effective at reducing the probability of risk. Complexity of tools also increases because adding extra parts can decrease time spent hunting and add to the reliability of the tool. For example, the Australian Aranda, who live in an aseasonal environment with many alternative plant and animal resources, use very few tools (Oswalt 1976: 237) and failure costs are ameliorated largely through mobility. In direct contrast are the Angmagsalik Inuit, who have few alternative sources of food, especially in the winter when they depend almost entirely on seals. They depend on a very diverse and complex assemblage in which there are many different harpoon forms: for example, one type of harpoon comprises 26 parts (Oswalt 1976: 294). Both the diversity and complexity of assemblages is positively correlated with latitude, and by inference with failure costs (Figures 4.1, 4.2). Tools used to exploit aquatic species are in general more complex than land-based gear because there is a greater risk of losing the prey, but within the class of aquatic tools, complexity is determined by the severity of the risk and varies with latitude (Bousman 1993: 73, Bamforth and Bleed 1997: 120–1).

Storage

Technology is most effective at controlling subsistence risk by preventing the loss of resources in the first place. Storage is another

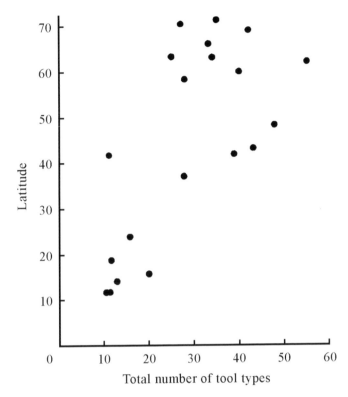

Figure 4.1. Assemblage diversity increases directly with higher levels of risk which is monitored by latitude (in degrees). Based on data in Table 4.1.

option used to varying degrees by most hunter–gatherers (e.g. Binford 1980, Rowley-Conwy and Zvelebil 1989) because it increases the time and, in the case of preservation, the space over which resources can be used. The level of investment into storage technology depends on the frequency with which the probability of loss, i.e. degree of risk, is met. Where failure costs are high, sophisticated techniques and facilities for storage are utilised, as among Northwest Coast Indians who developed complex ways to smoke and store salmon on which their subsistence is heavily dependent for the entire winter (Testart 1988). Nunamiut Eskimos can find food throughout the year, although the supplies fluctuate, so their storage technology is much simpler (Binford 1978). Groups with low risk, such as the !Kung Bushman (Wiessner 1982: 65) or

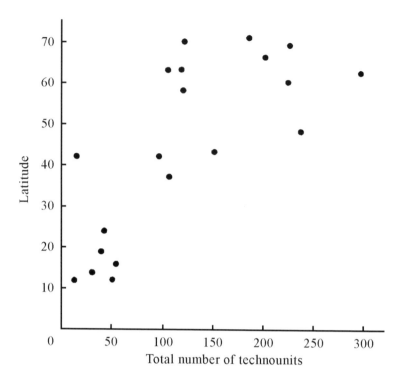

Figure 4.2. Assemblage complexity increases with the degree of risk as measured by latitude (in degrees). Based on data in Table 4.1.

Australian Aborigines (Blainey 1975), store very little food and have little special technology to do so. As with assemblage complexity, the degree of storage has a global pattern with levels increasing toward the poles with a particularly high incidence in northern temperate zones and a slight decrease in the polar regions (Testart 1982).

Design systems

The analysis of design systems (Table 4.1), defined by Nelson (1991: 57) as 'the selection and integration of strategies for making, using, transporting, and discarding tools and the materials needed for their manufacture and maintenance', has proved to be an extremely provocative way to understand technological organisation. Relia-bility and maintainability (Bleed 1986) are the most important for understanding variability in hunter–gatherer technology. Since they solve different problems, they should be considered as variables rather than optional types of systems (Bleed 1986: 740, Torrence 1989*b*: 63) and elements of both designs can be incorporated into a single technology depending on the timing and the severity of risk.

Reliable designs prevent failure so that the technology 'always works when it is needed' (Nelson 1991: 66). They operate below capacity, the equipment is overdesigned, well constructed and sturdy, and tools are composed of numerous redundant parts which can function as a backup so that the system keeps running even if some of the parts wear out or break. The resulting assemblage will therefore contain both diverse and complex tools. Procurement of raw materials, manufacture, use and repair are carefully scheduled so as not to conflict with the periods when the equipment is required. To cope with the demands of manufacturing a reliable tool-kit, specialist technicians with much knowledge and skill may also be necessary. Good examples of reliable designs and technology are found among Eskimo assemblages. In these cases there are numerous strong, well-constructed, complex tools such as the Angmagsalik harpoons mentioned earlier which have many components. A large battery of specialised tools was also employed to reduce the probability of failure: e.g. hole probes, seal indicators, harpoon rests, wound plugs, drag lines (Bleed 1986: 743).

Reliability is costly since it demands high levels of raw material, time, energy and skills. Consequently, a reliable system has to return high benefits. The degree to which a technology is reliable is positively correlated to the cost of failure (i.e. severity of risk) (Torrence 1989*b*: 63, Myers 1989) whereas Bleed's (1986) second design option, maintainability, solves the problem that tools have to work whenever needed. Maintainability is a response to the need for either continuous or unpredictable use. To ensure tool-use is interrupted as little as possible, maintainable tools are made of modular parts which can be replaced easily and these are arranged in a series so if one fails, the tool can still be used. Unlike the scheduling in reliable technologies, manufacture and repair is continuous to avoid potentially risky down time. Tools and/or parts are replaced before they wear out to prevent failure while in use. The level of investment into a maintainable technology will depend as usual on the level of failure costs of not having the technology up and running.

Maintainability is the major characteristic of low-latitude foragers, such as the !Kung San described by Bleed (1986: 742), who carried multiple arrows as backups, so that a tool would always be ready for use, and also a number of spare parts and partially finished tools which could be made ready quite quickly. Most hunters need maintainable tool-kits because they cannot predict exactly when they will encounter game. Inuit technologies incorporate maintainable options as well as reliable ones because the timing of the task is unpredictable and failure costs are high. For example harpoons are composed of serial parts that can be repaired quickly and multiple tools are usually carried on hunting trips to serve as backups in case of failure (Torrence 1989b: 63).

Nelson (1991: 70–3) has divided maintainable designs into those which are *flexible* and change their form for different functions, as for example by reworking and recycling, and those which are *versatile* and require no change in form to carry out a number of tasks: i.e. multi-purpose tools (Hayden *et al.* 1996: 13). Flexibility and versatility are planned strategies that are intended to cope with a wide range of anticipated tasks whose distribution in time is difficult to predict. These can be contrasted with *opportunistic* technological behaviour in which people respond immediately to unintended conditions (Nelson 1991: 65). One would expect the degree of opportunism also to be negatively correlated with failure costs.

Curation is risk-averse behaviour which takes place as part of a maintainable design strategy. As initially described by Binford (1977), a curated technology is one in which tools are made in advance of anticipated use, are carried around in anticipation of use, and whose lives are prolonged so as to be continually ready for use. Unlike other authors (e.g. Hayden *et al.* 1996: 10, 14), I distinguish between curation and longevity, because the former is a very specific strategy, whereas the latter is a response to any one of a number of different problems. Differentiating curation from other forms of longevity in the archaeological record is not straightforward (Bamforth 1986, Nelson 1991: 62–63, Odell 1996).

The opposite of curation is an expedient strategy in which tools are made when needed, used on the spot, and then discarded immediately (Binford 1977). Nelson (1991: 64) has argued that expediency is not unorganised behaviour or the absence of curation. It is used when tasks and raw materials are expected to occur at the same location and where there is sufficient time to carry out the intended tasks. In opposition to curation, expediency is negatively correlated with the severity of risk.

The adoption of risk-averse behaviour for creating and maintaining an effective technology can create costs that may have to be overcome by further strategies. For instance, reliability and maintainability can make demands on the nature of raw material resources, time and energy. Binford (1979) noted that the Nunamiut Eskimo embed the procurement of stone within other activities. If they are in the vicinity of a stone source and have some spare time, they will collect raw material, rather than return home empty-handed. If trips to stone sources cannot fit in with other needs, the group may need to prolong the use-lives of their tools. To cope with the need for many complex and diverse tools, Eskimos schedule special times of the year specifically for gearing up their equipment (Torrence 1989*b*: 5), but Bamforth and Bleed (1977: 124) point out that living off stored foods is not always an option.

Constraints on technology

Constraints on technological options caused by the physical and social environment can also play a significant role. Raw material availability, mobility and knowledge (including skill) are frequently considered by archaeologists, however their importance has often been inflated. Concentrating on constraints implies an assumption that people will attempt to minimise inputs (e.g. time, energy and raw materials) simply for the sake of doing so. In contrast, the optimising approach assumes that technologies are solutions to problems identified by their users and not necessarily the result of maximising a currency of some type (Torrence 1989*a*: 4).

Two of Nelson's (1991: 73–6) design options, transportability and longevity, are responses to constraints. Mobile hunter–gatherers, such as the Bushman (Bleed 1986: 742) benefit if they can build portability into their technological designs (Shott 1986) and this is carried out using smaller tools (Ebert 1979, Kuhn 1994), lighter weight material, and/or adopting multi-purpose (i.e. versatile) tools to the degree that failure costs tolerate these. Shott (1986) found a strong negative correlation between the number of residential moves per year and assemblage diversity. In contrast, complexity of tools was not significantly correlated with mobility. Unfortunately, he did not have adequate data for high-latitude groups, who have considerable levels of diversity and complexity because they must cope with high levels of risk. We can conclude, then, that where possible hunter–gatherers optimise portability by adopting general-ised tool-kits. In situations where the need for reliable tool-kits leads to highly diverse and complex assemblages, as for example among Eskimos, portability is difficult to achieve. In these situations strate-gies for transporting the gear have been devised: i.e. large boats (umiaks) or dogs with packs or sleds.

Reasons for prolonging the longevity of tools has been debated at length by archaeologists (e.g. Hayden *et al.* 1996, Odell 1996). The problem is that longevity is a plausible response to a number of different causes including energy minimisation (Bousman 1993: 77), timing of tasks (Binford 1977, 1979, Torrence 1983), severity of risks (Torrence 1989b), production costs (Bousman 1993, Bamforth and Bleed 1997), shortages of raw materials caused by limited distribu-tion in the physical environment (e.g. Bamforth 1986, Andrefsky 1994), lack of access due to mobility patterns (e.g. Kuhn 1994, Odell 1996, Parry and Kelly 1987) or social restrictions (Jeske 1992). Most of these 'causes', however, are in fact responses to other problems faced by hunter–gatherers. Because of the degree of equifinality about longevity, it is most productively studied within a wider study of technological design options, rather than as an independent variable.

A third constraint, knowledge (and therefore skill), is important. All groups which have survived have obviously met minimal condi-tions. People may not be aware of every kind of technology and once one has been chosen, it may condition and limit further choices. For example, the emphasis on blades as blank forms in the

Old World and on bifaces in the New World were probably arbitrary choices. Once made, however, people worked within the bounds of the technology to solve the various problems they faced.

Optimal technology

The 'Big Picture' macroscale theoretical framework describes the general properties of hunter–gatherer tool-use in terms of the composition, complexity and diversity of tool-kits and outlines a number of design strategies for the procurement, manufacture and use of tools. Style as an active way to encode and process information has also been modelled in this way by Wiessner (1983, 1984). Constructing the basic outline of an optimal technology is valuable because it provides a good basis for understanding the solutions adopted by various people and for explaining change, but it is not comprehensive. Predicting tool assemblage structure using risk as a currency is a productive modelling approach only in situations for which the costs of failure are very severe. In other cases, individual choice has a broader scope because many technical options can satisfy goals and constraining factors such as raw material availability may be quite important.

Even when macroscale predictions are appropriate because failure costs significantly affect survival, the Big Picture is only just a general description of assemblage structure and design options. There is much leeway for individual creativity because a number of different tool forms or methods of manufacture can solve the same design mandates. The approach is not always easy and straightforward to use (Hayden *et al.* 1996) because social factors, such as knowledge of alternatives, concepts of proper behaviour, social constructions of the labour force, etc., will condition the choices that are made at a particular time and place (Torrence 1989b, Lemonnier 1993). Technology is devised to suit a task, but the exact details are culturally conditioned. Everyone is unlikely to be aware of every option and once one has been chosen, it may condition and limit further options.

Given the limitations of the macroscale approach, it is fascinating that it explains variability in hunter–gatherer tool-kits so well and has proved a very useful tool for archaeology. As Oswalt's data show, where risk is low, recent hunter–gatherers have not created elaborate subsistence technologies, although they could have chosen to do so, but they have instead minimised energy inputs by selecting as few simple tools as possible and by increasing their portability and longevity. The evidence demonstrates that where possible hunter–gatherers have chosen to invest their time and energy in other activities, which we can assume had higher pay-offs. Since the choices exhibited appear to have been so consistent, limited, and directed to achieving a technology that minimises exposure to risks, then the scope to use the Big Picture approach is much larger than one might have expected on theoretical grounds alone. This is very good news for archaeologists who are largely forced to observe behaviour on the macroscale.

A wide range of archaeological case studies which have modelled technological change in terms of optimal models using risk has now been undertaken and many have had excellent results (Bamforth and Bleed 1997). For instance, changes in the nature of risk have helped understand why there is a wide-scale decrease in the complexity and sophistication of stone tool technology with the adoption of domesticated resources and sedentism (Parry and Kelly 1987, Torrence 1989b, Odell 1996). Short-term risk is no longer a factor in these cases and so locally available raw materials can be procured whenever it is convenient, tools made as needed, and there is no requirement to prolong the use-lives of tools. The archaeological record then shows a marked change from a curated technology using highly distinctive tools to expedient behaviour and an emphasis on unretouched tools.

Another good example of the importance of risk in prehistoric technologies are the changes that took place during the Mesolithic of Europe. In separate studies Myers (1989), Jochim (1989) and Eerkens (1998) have shown that differences in the emphasis on microlithic components of composite tools is caused by changes in the availability of game. Reliable tools made in advance were important when hunting was based on the intercept of large numbers of game at particular localities. In contrast, when game was dispersed and unpredictable, the tool-kit had to be maintainable as well. The response was to increase the number of stone points on the arrows so that at any time some would be useable, to use small insets that could easily be replaced and tools that could be repaired easily and quickly.

Microscale approaches

To understand the variety in hunter–gatherer technology that cannot be explained by macroscale theory, one needs to turn to theory which focuses explicitly on how choices are made when the costs of failing to complete a task are minimal. Although it seems that hunter–gatherers take a minimising view toward subsistence technology, it is unlikely that this will apply to all aspects of technology. In these cases the specific historical and social context is crucial. Microscale theory is essential because it helps flesh out the generalised Big Picture drawn using the optimising approach described above.

The microscale approach has been heavily influenced by French anthropology and has only recently become popular among English-speaking archaeologists. Using insights from Leroi-Gourhan (1993), Lemonnier (1993) argued that technology is a fundamentally social activity in which the knowledge, techniques and organisation of labour employed as well as the tools themselves are socially produced and have symbolic meaning. These ideas are beginning to have an important and profound impact on the study of hunter–gatherer technology (e.g. Schlanger and Sinclair 1990, Gamble 1998).

The description of the kinds and order of actions involved in the manufacture and use stone tools, the *chaîne opératoire* (operational sequence) (Lemonnier 1992, pp. 25–50), has been mainly used by French archaeologists studying Palaeolithic hunter–gatherers to reveal the concepts and cognitive processes embedded within the technological practices they describe (e.g. Schlanger and Sinclair 1990, Perlès 1992). The potential of the approach is illustrated by an important study of social relations at the site of Etiolles in the Paris Basin by Pigeot and her colleagues (Dobres and Hoffman, 1994:

237–9). An analysis of the *chaîne opératoire* using extensive refitting of stone artefacts showed that there were differences in the competence of the knappers who made tools in discrete areas at the site. These were interpreted as evidence for the presence of skilled and apprentice stoneworkers which the archaeologists suggest represent different age groups.

The French school has been criticised for putting too much emphasis on *descriptions* of activities rather than an attempt to understand underlying *processes* (Dobres and Hoffman 1994: 213, 219, 237, Edmonds 1990: 58). Dobres and Hoffman (1994) propose that in addition to the detailed descriptions of social context, social theory is required. They propose practice theory in which individuals use their social knowledge to carry out actions. The process of using tools, however, also has an effect on how people conceive of their world and can lead to unintended consequences. In this view technology both exhibits world views and contributes to their construction. Rather than look for external causes, as in macroscale theories, microscale approaches focus on individual choice carried out within a particular social milieu and concentrate on how people determine the technologies which they use and also how their reflexive properties feed back to create their social world. Often the emphasis is on daily social action by individuals and how this articulates with the wider society. The role of power and the organisation of labour with respect to how technologies are made and used are also favoured topics for microscale analyses.

Microscale approaches have yet to be widely applied to the study of hunter–gatherer technology, but they are extremely important because we know too little about how technology is socially created and conditioned, how it is used to create, reaffirm and modify social processes, and what role these processes have played in the evolution of human societies. Additional studies emphasising choice by individual actors and focusing on the organisation of labour in terms of age, sex and status would contribute a great deal to our overall understanding of hunter–gatherer technology. Given the growing importance of various branches of 'practice theory' and the new emphases on subjects such as gender, symbolism and perception in archaeology, it seems likely that microscale analyses will have a greater role to place in future studies of hunter–gatherer technology.

Gender, symbolism and style

The organisation of labour in terms of gender, the symbolic proper-ties of artefacts, the use of material items and the stylistic traits of objects which communicate information are among the many properties of technology that have been considered from both micro and macroscale perspectives. It is important to recognise the role of technology in the social and ideational spheres as well as in mundane daily life and to demonstrate that even ordinary, everyday tools carry many levels of meaning for their users.

The gendering of hunter–gatherer stone technology has until recently been considered to be relatively unproblematic: men have been assumed to be the major, if not the only, makers and users of stone artefacts. Gero (1991) and Bird (1993) have demonstrated that this assumption has been based on a long history of androcentrism and ignorance. Since women make and use many of their own tools (including flaked and ground stone tools) in most recent hunter–gatherer societies, it would not be surprising if that were the case in the past as well.

Graves-Brown (1996) begins with Gero's (1991) suggestion that unmodified flakes were made by women, but shaped, retouched tools were the products of men. He uses this principle to discover when the separate foraging roles of men and women became complementary and entwined. Using distinctive retouched tools and the clear division of assemblages into 'tools' and 'debitage,' he argues that the interdependence of males and females dates to the Upper Palaeolithic in Europe. In contrast, Binford and Binford (1969: 81–2) proposed gender differences were present in the Middle Palaeolithic. They suggested that women utilised locally available stones for processing plant materials at the Jabrud cave site in Syria, whereas the hunting tools, which were manufactured from flint obtained from distant sources had been manufactured by men who ranged over larger areas.

Since technology plays a meaningul role in social life, it is not surprising that stone tools have symbolic meanings in hunter–gatherer societies. For example, in Australia both the sources of stone and the artefacts themselves carry powerful meanings because they are associated with Ancestral Beings from the Dreamtime (e.g. Cane 1988, Jones and White 1988, Taçon 1991). Access to certain quarries is restricted to particular initiated men who must behave in proper ways to protect themselves from these very powerful places (Taçon 1991: 199, Jones and White 1988). Artefacts made from stone obtained from these quarries also have symbolic significance which imbues their users with special powers. This, in turn, reinforces the power of the males who could procure, make and use the tools. Taçon (1991) has suggested that quartz and quartzite were especially valued as raw materials because they are shiny and irridescent, properties often associated with Ancestral Beings. The Australian examples show that the choice of raw material is not always based on purely technical criteria: symbolic meaning and related social factors such as restricted access and power may also be quite important.

Artefacts carry information about their makers and users and these can be used in various social strategies (Wobst 1977, Gero 1989). Wiessner's (1983, 1984, 1997) studies of the use of style by Bushman groups provides a good example. She argues that style is a non-verbal way of communicating personal and social identity which has evolved among humans because it carries out a number of functions. Artefacts:

> (a) express information about identity and its positive correlates, such competence, strength or worth;
> (b) provide indicators of similarity that modify physical differences;
> (c) help establish homogeneity between individuals in different groups and hence facilitate the expansion of kinship networks;
> (d) attract mates from other groups to forge the ties necessary for expanding socially defined kinship networks. (Wiessner 1997: 159)

Her case studies of projectile points and bead working among the !Kung San (Ju/'hoansi) Bushman of the Kalahari Desert have shown that style is actively used to express personal and ethnic differences and one's position within society (Wiessner 1983, 1984).

She also argued that the maintenance of difference was an important to *hxaro* exchange systems involving projectile points and beadwork. These helped reduce risks through enabling partners to make demands when needed.

Wiessner (1997) has also demonstrated that artefacts can lose their power to transmit information, if their role in society becomes diminished. Changes over 20 years in beadwork show that the Bushman makers illustrate their position with regard to others in terms of style. Furthermore, the use of traditional designs to decorate modern material culture demonstrates how they have attempted to preserve principles of equality and reciprocity which have formed the basis of mutual support systems. Wiessner's studies demonstrate that the study of style to express identity has enormous potential for understanding how hunter–gatherer societies are coming to terms with their incorporation within the modern world economic system.

A synthesis

Although they derive from conflicting theories of human social action, macroscale and microscale analyses of technology are both necessary and useful because they complement each other. The tension between them is productive because it forces scholars to examine all aspects of technology and to consider the insights from both theoretical viewpoints. It cannot be assumed that changes in technology are inevitably the result of either external, physical or internal, social factors. One or another may be more or less relevant in different settings. Neither school of technology has yet to adequately considered how people use technology to mediate the complex interactions between their physical and social environments. A synthesis of both views is required.

Gamble (1998) has made a productive start in bringing together macro- and microscale theories on hunter–gatherer technology. His work looks at the critical role that the daily making and use of tools played in the development of extended social networks in Palaeolithic societies. He has argued that individuals and things can be linked conceptually through action. Since objects can symbolise people who use them, they have the potential, particularly through various types of exchange, to extend 'social life beyond the practical limits set on co-presence interaction by time, the body and space' (Gamble 1986: 432).

The technology of hunter–gatherers living in the modern world has been ignored by anthropologists. This is a pity since microscale studies of everyday, technical practices could lead to important insights concerning the process of change in these contexts, as illustrated by Wiessner's (1997) analysis of style, and such studies could be profitably expanded to take in the comparative, macroscale level. For archaeology, continued efforts to improve and use both macro- and microscale approaches to hunter–gatherer technology are essential because the consequences of tool-making and using provide the majority of the evidence available for understanding the evolution of and changes in human behaviour.

One of the greatest difficulties in understanding variability in human behaviour is that many variations in technology are suited to the same circumstances. This greatly compounds the difficulty of understanding changes in the archaeological record. Are the differences we observe the result of environmental changes which have set up new problems to be solved, new goals invented by the users, difference choices undertaken by individual actors, or a better solution to the same goals? The optimising approach is helpful in addressing these questions, but only when combined with detailed microscale studies concerned with how choices are made will we be able to sort out the alternatives. Many more case studies are needed that begin by appreciating the relative contributions of both macro- and microscale theory as they stand currently and then move beyond them.

Acknowledgements

This research was supported by an Australian Research Council Senior Fellowship at the Australian Museum. Discussions with Huw

Barton, Peter Bleed, Clive Gamble, Brian Hayden, Peter Hiscock, and Peter White have been extremely helpful.

References

Andrefsky, W. (1994). Raw material availability and the organisation of technology. *American Antiquity* **59**: 21–35.

Bamforth, D.B. (1986). Technological efficiency and tool curation. *American Antiquity* **51**: 38–50.

Bamforth, D.B. and Bleed, P. 1997. Technology, flaked stone technology, and risk. In *Rediscovering Darwin: Evolutionary Theory in Archaeological Explanation*, Archaeological Papers of the American Anthropological Association 7, ed. C.M. Barton and B.A. Clark, pp. 109–140. Arlington MA: American Anthropological Association.

Binford, L. (1977). Forty-seven trips. In *Stone Tools as Cultural Markers*, ed. R.V.S. Wright, pp. 24–36. Canberra: Australian Institute of Aboriginal Studies.

Binford, L. (1978). *Nunamiut Ethnoarchaeology.* New York: Academic Press.

Binford, L. (1979). Organisation and formation processes: looking at curated technologies. *Journal of Anthropological Research* **35**: 255–273.

Binford, L. (1980). Willow smoke and dogs' tails: hunter–gatherer settlement systems and archaeological site formation. *American Antiquity* **45**: 4–20.

Binford, L. and Binford, S. (1969). Stone tools and human behaviour. *Scientific American* 220: 70–84.

Bird, C.F.M. (1993). Woman the toolmaker: evidence for women's use and manufacture of flaked stone tools in Australia and New Guinea. In *Women in Archaeology: A Feminist Critique*, Occasional Papers in Prehistory 23, ed. H. du Cros and L. Smith, pp 22–30. Canberra: Research School of Pacific and Asian Studies, Australian National University.

Blainey, G. (1975). *Triumph of the Nomads: A History of Ancient Australia.* South Melbourne: Macmillan.

Bleed, P. 1986. The optimal design of hunting weapons: maintainability or reliability? *American Antiquity* **56**: 19–35.

Bleed, P. (1996). Risk and cost in Japanese microblade technology. *Lithic Technology* **21**: 95–107.

Bleed, P. (1997). Content as variability, result as selection: toward a behavioural definition of technology. In *Rediscovering Darwin: Evolutionary Theory and Archaeological Explanation*, Archaeological Papers of the American Anthropological Association 7, ed. C.M. Barton and G.A. Clark, pp. 95–104. Arlington MA: American Anthropological Association.

Bousman, C.B. (1993). Hunter–gatherer adaptations, economic risk and tool design. *Lithic Technology* **18**: 59–86.

Cane, S. (1988). Written on stone: a discussion on ethnographic and Aboriginal perspection of stone tools. In *Archaeology with Ethnography: An Australian Perspective*, ed. B. Meehan and R. Jones, pp. 88–93. Canberra: Highland Press.

Cashdan, E. (1985). Coping with risk reciprocity among the Basara of northern Botswana. *Man* (N.S.) **20**: 222–242.

Dobres, M. and Hoffman, C.R. (1994). Social agency and the dynamics of prehistoric technology. *Journal of Archaeological Method and Theory* **1**: 211–258.

Ebert, J. (1979). An ethnoarchaeological approach to reassessing the meaning of variability in stone tool assemblages. In *Ethnoarchaeology: Implications of Ethnography for Archaeology*, ed. C. Kramer, pp. 59–74. New York: Columbia University Press.

Edmonds, M. (1990). Description, understanding, and the *chaîne opératoire*. *Archaeological Review from Cambridge* **9**: 55–70.

Eerkens, J. (1998). Reliable and maintainable technologies: artefact standardisation and the early to later Mesolithic transition in northern England. *Lithic Technology* **23**: 42–53.

Gamble, C. (1998). Palaeolithic society and the release from proximity: a network approach to intimate relations. *World Archaeology* **29**: 426–449.

Gero, J.M. (1989). Assessing social information in material objects: how well do lithics measure up? In *Time, Energy and Stone Tools*, ed. R. Torrence, pp. 92–105. Cambridge: Cambridge University Press.

Gero, J.M. (1991). Genderlithics: women's roles in stone tool production. In *Engendering Archaeology: Women and Prehistory*, ed. J.M. Gero and M.W. Conkey pp. 163–193. Oxford: Basil Blackwell.

Graves-Brown, P. (1996). Their commonwealths are not as we supposed: sex, gender and material culture in human evolution. In *The Archaeology of Human Ancestry: Power, Sex and Tradition*, ed. J. Steele and S. Shennan, pp. 347–360. London: Routledge.

Hayden, B., Franco, N. and Spafford, J. (1996). Evaluating lithic strategies and design criteria. In *Stone Tools: Theoretical Insights into Human Prehistory*, ed. G. Odell, pp. 9–51. New York: Plenum Press.

Hill, K. and Hawkes, K. (1983). Neotropical hunting among the Aché of eastern Paraguay. In *Adaptive Responses of Native Amazonians*, ed. R.P. Hames and W.T. Vickers, pp. 139–188. New York: Academic Press.

Jeske, R. (1992). Energetic efficiency and lithic technology: an upper Mississippian example. *American Antiquity* **57**: 467–481.

Jochim, M.A. (1989). Optimisation and stone tool studies: problems and potential. In *Time, Energy and Stone Tools*, ed. R. Torrence, pp. 106–111. Cambridge: Cambridge University Press.

Jones, R. and White, N. (1988). Point blank: stone tools manufacture at the Ngilipitji Quarry, Arnhem Land, 1981. In *Archaeology with Ethnography: an*

Australian Perspective, ed. B. Meehan and R. Jones, pp 51–87. Canberra: Highland Press.

Kuhn, S. (1994). A formal approach to the design and assembly of mobile toolkits. *American Antiquity* **59**: 426–442.

Lemonnier, P. (1992). *Elements for an Anthropology of Technology*, Anthropological Papers no. 88. Ann Arbor: Museum of Anthropology, University of Michigan.

Lemonnier, P. (1993). Introduction. In *Technological Choices: Transformations in Material Culture since the Neolithic*, ed. P. Lemonnier, pp. 1–35. London: Routledge.

Leroi-Gourhan, A. (1993). *Gesture and Speech*. Cambridge: Massachusetts Institute of Technology Press.

Myers, A. (1989). Reliable and maintainable technological strategies in the Mesolithic of mainland Britain. In *Time, Energy and Stone Tools*, ed. R. Torrence, pp. 78–91. Cambridge: Cambridge University Press.

Nelson, M. (1991). The study of technological organisation. *Archaeological Method and Theory* **3**: 57–100.

Odell, G. (1996). Economizing behaviour and the concept of 'curation.' In *Stone Tools: Theoretical Insights into Human Prehistory*, ed. G. Odell, pp. 51–80. New York: Plenum, Press.

Ortner, S. (1984). Theory in anthropology since the sixties. *Comparative Studies in Society and History* **26**: 126–166.

Oswalt, W.H. (1976). *An Anthropological Analysis of Food-Getting Technology*. New York: Wiley.

Parry, W. and R. Kelly (1987). Expedient core technology and sedentism. In *The Organisation of Core Technology*, ed. J. Johnson and C. Morrow, pp. 285–308.

Perlès, C. (1992). In search of lithic strategies: a cognitive approach to prehistoric chipped stone assemblages. In *Representations in Archaeology*, ed. J.-C. Gardin and C. Peebles, pp. 223–247. Bloomington: Indiana University Press.

Rowley-Conwy, P. and Zvelebil, M. (1989). Saving it for later: storage by prehistoric hunter–gatherers in Europe. In *Bad Year Economics: Cultural Responses to Risk and Uncertainty*, ed. P. Halstead and J. O'Shea, pp. 40–56. Cambridge: Cambridge University Press.

Schlanger, N. and Sinclair, A. (eds.) (1990). Technology in the humanities. *Archaeological Review from Cambridge* **9**(1).

Shott, M. (1986). Technological organisation and settlement mobility: an ethnographic examination. *Journal of Anthropological Research* **42**: 15–51.

Taçon, P. (1991). The power of stone: symbolic aspects of stone use and tool development in western Arnhem Land, Australia. *Antiquity* **65**: 192–207.

Testart, A. (1982). The significance of food storage among hunter–gatherers: residence patterns, population densities, and social inequalities. *Current Anthropology* **23**: 523–37.

Testart, A. (1988). Food storage among hunter–gatherers: more or less security in the way of life? In *Coping with Uncertainty in Food Supply*, ed. I. de Grain and G. Hearson, pp. 170–174. Oxford: Clarendon Press.

Torrence, R. (1983). Time-budgeting and hunter–gatherer technology. In *Prehistoric Hunters and Gatherers in Europe*, ed. G.M. Bailey, pp. 11–22. Cambridge: Cambridge University Press.

Torrence, R. (1989*a*). Tools as optimal solutions. In *Time, Energy and Stone Tools*, ed. R. Torrence, pp. 1–6. Cambridge: Cambridge University Press.

Torrence, R. (1989*b*). Re-tooling: towards a behavioural theory of stone tools. In *Time, Energy and Stone Tools*, ed. R. Torrence, pp. 57–66. Cambridge: Cambridge University Press.

Wiessner, P. (1982). Beyond willow smoke and dogs' tails: a comment on Binford's analysis of hunter–gather settlement systems. *American Antiquity* **47**: 171–178.

Wiessner, P. (1983). Style and social information in Kalahari San projectile points. *American Antiquity* **48**: 253–276.

Wiessner, P. (1984). Reconsidering the behavioural basis for style: a case study among the Kalahari San. *Journal of Anthropological Archaeology* **3**: 190–234.

Wiessner, P. (1997). Seeking guidelines through an evolutionary approach: style revisited among the !Kung San (ju/'Hoansi) of the 1990s. In *Rediscovering Darwin: Evolutionary Theory and Archaeological Explanation*, Archaeological Papers of the American Anthropological Association 7, ed. C. Barton and G. Clark, pp. 157–176. Arlington MA: American Anthropological Association.

Wobst, M. (1977). Stylistic behaviour and information exchange. In *Papers for the Director: Research Essays in Honour of James B. Griffin*, Museum of Anthropology Anthropological Papers 61, ed. C. Cleland, pp. 317–342. Ann Arbor: Museum of Anthropology, University of Michigan.

5

The antiquity of hunter–gatherers

STEVEN L. KUHN AND MARY C. STINER

Introduction

It is often said that humans have lived by hunting and gathering for more than 99% of our evolutionary history, but there is something more to being a hunter–gatherer than just eating non-domesticated plants and animals. This chapter examines resemblances and differences between modern hunter–gatherers and earlier Pleistocene humans in Europe and Western Eurasia, and explores some general explanations for observable variation.

In comparing modern and ancient foragers, it is not sufficient to use one or two modern hunter–gatherer groups as 'model foragers'. The strategy adopted here is to characterise the limits of variation in the economies, technologies, and social arrangements of recent hunter–gatherers, and to use these observations as a baseline for assessing behavioural variation in the remote past. If ancient human groups showed similar ranges of variation to modern foragers, then the basic structure of modern human hunter–gatherer adaptations was probably in place long ago. If the expected patterns of variation are not manifest archaeologically, we are dealing with a very different sort of hunting and gathering hominid.

This chapter concentrates on two fundamental dimensions of recent forager behaviour – subsistence and technology – both of which have robust archaeological consequences. It encompasses cases from the Middle and the Late Upper Palaeolithic of Europe and western Asia, spanning environments from the arid subtropics to the periglacial steppes, and attributable to both modern (*Homo sapiens sapiens*) and archaic humans (e.g., Neanderthals, *H. heidelberg-*

ensis). We focus on Pleistocene Eurasia in particular because of its high density of archaeological data, diverse environments, and appreciable climatic and latitudinal gradient.

Hunters of the recent and remote past

We reserve the term 'recent' hunter–gatherers for Holocene foragers that coexisted with agricultural societies, especially for groups documented over the past 150 years. 'Ancient' hunter–gatherers refers to all Pleistocene humans, regardless of taxonomic or cultural status.

Obviously, recent and ancient foragers inhabited very different worlds. The natural environments of the last 150 years of the Holocene are especially different from those of most Palaeolithic groups. Environments are variable over time and across space, however, making impossible broad generalisations about how conditions differ today from those 'back then'. Ecological factors thus are more profitably approached by considering known clines or other physical gradients period by period. A more general difference between recent and ancient hunter–gatherers concerns demography: modern populations are several orders of magnitude larger (Groube 1996, Pennington, this volume). Moreover, the world is no longer occupied exclusively by foragers. Even at first contact with colonial societies, hunter–gatherers lived in regular and sometimes close proximity with agriculturalists, pastoralists, or merchants (Layton, this volume). Surviving hunter–gatherers have been part of 'world systems' for as long as Western scholars have known about them (e.g. Bird-David 1991, Woodburn 1991).

This has led some scholars to question the relevance of ethnographic accounts to understanding human life in the remote past (Spielmann and Eder 1994). However, we are better served by seeking to understand the factors that moulded the diversity of recent foraging adaptations. Uncovering predictable relations among a few key variables in the modern world would provide a sound basis for recognising and ultimately accounting for unexpected patterns in ancient foragers. It is particularly important to emphasise patterns that cross-cut groups with very different histories (see also Layton, this volume) to minimise the influences of the post-Neolithic world.

Variation in recent hunter–gatherer diet and technology

Researchers have identified a number of robust patterns of variation in subsistence, technology, land use, and social life among ethnographically documented hunter–gatherer groups. There is clear environmentally linked variation in the range and importance of food sources. Humans have exploited a vast array of wild foods. A convenient way of classifying them is to rank them in terms of their net 'cost' to foragers, and whether they are primarily sources of food energy (e.g. fats and carbohydrates) or nutrients essential to physical growth and maintenance (e.g. protein) (Speth and Spielmann 1983). A high-rank resource provides a rich nutritional return relative to the costs of locating, procuring, and processing it. Lower-ranked resources provide less food value, are more costly to obtain, or both.

Experimental and ethnographic studies of wild food collection are summarised in Table 5.1. Several conclusions can be drawn despite some obvious limitations of the data. In general, efficiency follows nutritional values, with meat providing the greatest food value per unit weight, foliage the lowest. Large game animals rank highest because of their size, and tubers, seeds and nuts rank lowest because of yield per unit time or cost of procurement and processing. Small to medium-sized animals (reptiles, small mammals, birds) have intermediate rankings. Few data are available for marine foods, fruits, and insects, but some of them provide exceptional returns in some environments (Dufour 1987, Hayden 1981*a*).

The relation between gross yields (kJ/kg) and net productivity (kJ/hr) is important for small animals, and for seeds and nuts. Meat from small animals is as nourishing per kilogram as large game, yet procurement of smaller species often is less efficient. This is because efficiency is measured in terms of net yields. Considerably more energy may be needed to catch a deer than a rabbit, but a large

Table 5.1. *Net (kJ/hr) and gross (kJ/kg) energy yields of various resource classes for human forager groups.*

	Number of cases	kJ/hr			kJ/kg	
		Mean	Min.	Max.	Mean	SD.
Large game	4	63 398[a]	36 000[a]	75 115[a]	6980[b]	1383[b]
Small mammals	14	16 034[a]	1672[a]	56 317[a]	6980[b]	1383[b]
Reptiles	3	15 850[a]	17 556[a]	12 435[a]	4489[b]	715[b]
Birds	3	4472	961[a]	8255[a]	(no data)	
Roots and tubers	14	6120[a]	418[a]	26 133[a]	2926[c]	1680[c]
Roots and tubers	9	10 412[d]	3695[d]	23 333[d]	2926[c]	1680[c]
Seeds and nuts	34	3520[a]	380[a]	18 538[a]	13 188[c]	9334[c]
Seeds and nuts	9	6508[d]	1203[d]	24 933[d]	13 188[c]	9334[c]
Foliage	–		(no data)		1250[c]	819[c]
Fruits	–		(no data)		2403[c]	1463[c]

[a] Data from Kelly 1995, Table 3.3. [b] Data from Hawkes *et al.* 1982, Hurtado and Hill 1987. [c] Data from Pennington 1989. [d] Data from Wright 1994, Table 2.

animal provides a much greater amount of food. Small animals must be obtained and processed in large numbers to equal the food provided by one modestly-sized ungulate (Gamble 1986: 113, Bailey 1978). Small prey may be attractive for other reasons, such as their more consistent availability, and certain reptiles and shellfish may be unusually desirable simply because they can be collected with little effort. Seeds and nuts are remarkably concentrated sources of nourishment, exceeding on average the caloric value of wild game. Their ranking based on net returns is relatively low because processing seeds by grinding or pounding is very labour-intensive (Hawkes and O'Connell 1985, Simms 1987, Stahl 1989, Wright 1994). The nutritional figures in Table 5.1 are for cooked grains; their yield would be far less if they were not fully processed.

The relative ranking of resource classes also seems to be inversely correlated their general abundance or absolute productivity per unit land (Winterhalder, this volume). Large game animals tend to be dispersed and mobile, while smaller game exist at higher densities. Grass seeds and nuts may be the most abundant and concentrated of all (Pianka 1978: 278–83). The link between the relative yield and spatial concentration of a resource influences the mobility of human foragers. If high-ranked resources are not aggregated, as with salmon runs or caribou migrations, it is impossible to depend on them year-round without extensive mobility (Kelly 1995: 130–31).

Theory predicts that consumers will rely on resources that provide the best return for effort in whichever currency is most limited, turning to lower-ranked resources only when the cost of searching for the higher-ranked foods becomes excessive (see Winterhalder, this volume). Addition of a new resource to the diet depends not so much on its natural abundance, but on the availability of the next highest-ranked food. These ideas inform the study of environmentally linked variation in forager diet.

Some of the clearest patterns of variation in modern hunter–gatherer diets follow latitude. The degree of dependence on vegetable foods declines away from the Equator as a simple function of primary environmental productivity. They are 'replaced' in the north by terrestrial game or aquatic resources, depending on the proximity of coastlines, lakes, and marshes (Lee 1968, Hayden 1981*a*, Keeley 1995); in the far north, meat may constitute almost 100% of the diet. Closer to the equator there is greater variation in dietary composition as a consequence of higher diversity and abundance of birds, small mammals and reptiles (Pianka 1978: 291–6, Rosenzweig 1996: 25). Because the returns from small and medium-sized animals generally are higher than those for plants, we would expect foragers to exploit such animals in preference to seeds or tubers, if the former are available. None the less, many low-latitude hunter–gatherers rely extensively on vegetable foods, especially in arid regions.

Table 5.2 shows that as reliance on vegetable foods increases, seeds, the very resources that require most processing and yield the lowest returns, become more important. Thus a heavy dependence on vegetable foods in lower latitudes is not simply explained by the presence of easily obtained plant foods. Instead, it reflects situations in which access to higher-ranked foods is limited, or in which human populations have grown so far that they can no longer be sustained on the least costly resources. In some environments large animals and other high-ranked food types are highly dispersed and thus unreliable. Unfortunately, we have few clues as to what the natural abundance of game should have been in most places.

Of course hunter–gatherers do not collect and process food without tools. Durable elements of technology provide direct and indirect clues about economic adaptations. Projectile tips, spear points, arrow heads, harpoons, and the like are the more obvious material correlates of hunting and fishing. Grinding stones, mortars and pestles, querns, mullers, and similar objects are good indicators of a heavy reliance on wild seeds and nuts. Their relative abundance in archaeological assemblages should reflect the extent to which human groups depended on vegetable resources with high processing requirements. Simple ratios of hunting weapons to grinding tools cannot be used to reconstruct dietary emphases, however, as these artefact classes have very different use lives and discard patterns. None the less, seed-grinding implements are valuable relative indicators of diet.

Torrence (1983, 1989, this volume) and others (Shott 1986,

Table 5.2. *Relationship between dependence on plant foods and types of staples among ethnographically documented foraging societies*

Percentage plants in diet	Number of plant staples	Foliage	Fruit	Fruit, and roots	Roots	Fruit, roots and nuts	Nuts	Fruit, roots nuts and seeds	Seeds
0–5	6	1	4						
6–15		2	14	2					
16–25			4	7	1				
26–35			1	2	5	4	10		
36–45			1	1	2	3		1	
46–55			2			2	4	2	2
56–65				1		1	3	2	3
66–75									1
76–85							1		

Source: After Keeley 1995, Table 9.2.

Oswalt 1976, Binford 1977, 1979, Bousman 1993) have observed that the complexity, variety, and degree of labour investment in artefact production and maintenance all are closely connected to how the food quest is organised. Most notably, the elaboration of hunter–gatherer technologies, measured in terms of the number of distinct artefact forms and the number of individual elements combined to form single artefacts, increases with latitude and with the degree of dependence on fish or game (Oswalt 1976, Torrence 1983, Bousman 1993). As technological complexity increases, the amount of time and energy expended in making and mending artefacts also increases. Torrence sees latitudinal trends in artefact complexity as by-products of hunter–gatherers' strategies for risk reduction, responses to the discontinuous availability of resources and a focus on mobile elusive prey. Narrow windows of opportunity for getting game place a premium on optimal tool performance, achieved primarily through the use of elaborate, 'overdesigned' and highly specialised equipment (Bleed 1986, Bousman 1993). Human mobility can be a complicating factor, however, as frequent residential moves tend to promote lightweight tool-kits (Kuhn 1994, Shott 1986).

No aspects of human behaviour are so consistently documented in the archaeological literature as diet and technology, although there are other interesting and potentially significant axes of variability. One strategy of risk reduction typical of many recent foragers has distinct archaeological consequences: residential mobility is a common solution to local fluctuations in food availability, as it allows hunter–gatherer groups to 'map on' to fluctuating resource distributions (Binford 1980, Kelly 1983). Uninhibited residential mobility is only feasible in a relatively empty environment, however. If many foraging groups have an interest in the same set of resources, access must be co-ordinated or selectively restricted in order to avoid conflict. Virtually all documented foraging groups thus possess norms of land tenure or preferential access to resources.

Dyson-Hudson and Smith (1978) and Kelly (1995: 198) conclude that systems of social boundary defence develop where one group experiences a surplus of food while another is experiencing a shortage. In this case access to land is regulated socially rather than through active defence: permission is required to use an area or to establish rights of access via kinship, friendships, or partnerships (Peterson 1975, Cashdan 1983). Non-kin relationships are often maintained by the exchange of goods (Wiessner 1982, Cashdan 1985, Burch 1988). Archaeologically, the movement of exotic items can be a signature of this form of territorial organisation. The value of having access to another individual's territory lies in the likelihood that it will contain desirable resources when foods are scarce in one's own home range, so relationships with far-away individuals may be more important than with close neighbours. In some environments it is even expected that hunter–gatherers will exclude adjacent groups from their lands, while using social mechanisms to promote access to more distant territories (Kelly 1995: 198). Here long-distance exchange may be especially significant.

To summarise, variation among recent foragers provides a number of general expectations for Pleistocene foragers. Most obviously, the degree of dependence on hunting and/or marine resources should increase to the north, and also within a given area as conditions become colder during glacial/interglacial cycles. Conversely, dependence on vegetable resources should be higher nearest to the Equator, or as conditions became warmer and drier over time. Plant remains seldom survive in Palaeolithic sites, and their role in early diets is difficult to assess. Fortunately, the ethnographic record indicates that any substantial dependence on vegetable foods normally entails a focus on seeds and nuts and requires non-perishable processing equipment. We should also expect to find a greater variety of complex technologies in northern parts of the human range, or during colder climatic intervals. Finally, evidence for the exchange of exotic goods in connection with territorial organisation and strategies for managing resource risk should be manifest widely.

The Pleistocene evidence: cultural geography in the Palaeolithic

In applying expectations derived from modern foragers to Pleistocene archaeological data, we focus only on general tendencies.

Deviations from our expectations are of greatest interest, as they signal a different set of foraging behaviours, even a fundamentally different kind of forager. We focus on the later Upper Palaeolithic and Middle Palaeolithic of Europe and southwest Asia (the Near East), where the density of data is sufficient to evaluate the trends and patterns summarised in the previous section. The Middle and Late Stone Ages of sub-Saharan Africa have also yielded abundant evidence, but the climatic gradient is not steep enough for our purposes.

The Late Upper Palaeolithic and Epipalaeolithic

The Late Upper Palaeolithic and Epipalaeolithic are the most recent Pleistocene cultures, and it is no surprise that they display the greatest behavioural affinity to modern hunter–gatherers. The Late Upper Palaeolithic (LUP) in Europe and the Epipalaeolithic in western Asia lasted from approximately 20 000 (uncalibrated radiocarbon) years ago to the end of the Pleistocene, roughly 10 000 years ago. It is in the LUP that one first gets a strong sense that the human world was structured according to fine-grained cultural differences as much as physical geography (Gamble 1986, Byrd 1994, Goring-Morris and Belfer-Cohen 1998). In Europe, the LUP subsumes a number of technocomplexes, including late Gravettian, Solutrean, Magdalenian, Epigravettian, and Azilian (Gamble 1986). In southwestern Asia it includes Kebaran, Geometric Kebaran, Natufian, and Mushabian in the Levant, and Zarzian in the Tauros/Zagros region (Bar-Yosef 1981, Madeyska 1990, Goring-Morris 1995, Henry 1995). The LUP spans both the Last Glacial Maximum and subsequent climatic amelioration, which are some of the most extreme and rapidly fluctuating environmental conditions of the Pleistocene. The LUP is characterised by a rich and well-studied archaeological record (Gamble and Soffer 1990a, Soffer and Gamble 1990) and was exclusively the product of anatomically modern humans (*Homo sapiens sapiens*).

Several technological constants typify this period. One is the tendency toward microlithisation – many tiny retouched tools occurring in lithic assemblages. Microliths are widely presumed to have served as the edges, points, and barbs of composite tools. By and large, microlithic and larger tools are made on small elongated blanks known as blades and bladelets, although production techniques vary considerably. Some LUP toolmakers also employed a variety of durable organic materials such as bone, antler, and ivory. Ornaments, exotic materials (shell, amber, rare pigments) and art are present in most regions and in some, but not all, assemblages.

Although LUP cultures shared a number of general features, they vary greatly in their details. A large component of this variation fits well with the trends described for recent hunter–gatherers by Torrence (1983, 1989 and this volume) and Oswalt (1976). Projectile weapons are a case in point. The LUP arsenal of northern Europe includes a vast range, from stone points to plain, unbarbed bone or antler *saggaie*, to organic armatures equipped with stone cutting edges, to barbed harpoons (Figure 5.1). These preserved parts may represent only the tip of the technological iceberg – some of the durable elements must have formed the cutting edges, tips, and barbs for an even wider variety of implement types whose organic parts are no longer preserved.

The full range of tool forms known for the LUP is never represented within a single industry or phase (e.g. Straus 1993, Knecht 1997). Some specialised forms, such as Magdalenian and Azilian barbed harpoons, are found in only a limited area (Julien 1982). The greatest diversity in LUP weaponry, including the stone, bone, and antler components, is found in northern and alpine Europe (Gamble 1986: 225–6). Sites on the Russian plain (Borziyak 1993, Grigor'ev 1993: 55) have yielded especially large and varied assemblages of bone, antler, and ivory implements, and several Magdalenian sites in Germany have yielded collections of more than 50 osseous projectile points (Weniger 1987). In contrast, the northern Mediterranean is characterised by a narrower variety of bone and stone weapons (Gamble 1986, Bietti 1990, Mussi 1990). In the Near East bone and antler points are even more scarce compared with northern Europe (Bar-Yosef 1981, 1990, Goring-Morris 1995). The Near Eastern artefacts tend to be relatively simple sharpened bone splinters (Newcomer 1974, Campana 1989) (Figure 5.2). Only at the end of the Epipalaeolithic, during the

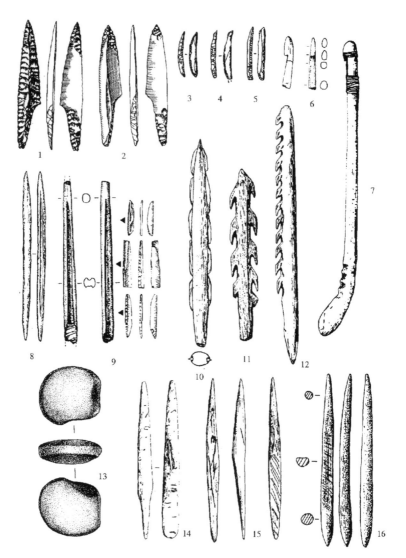

Figure 5.1. Examples of foraging technology of high-latitude European Late Upper Palaeolithic hunter–gatherers. (From Laville *et al.* 1980, Strauss and Clark 1986, Geneste and Maury 1987, Borziyak 1993, Geneste and Plisson 1993, Pokines and Krupa 1997.)

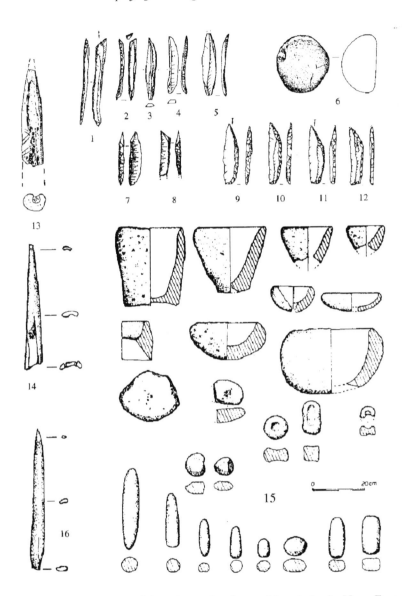

Figure 5.2. Examples of foraging technology of low-latitude Near Eastern Late Upper Palaeolithic hunter–gatherers. (From Copeland and Hours 1977, Goring-Morris 1995, Henry 1995.)

Natufian period, do substantial and diverse bone artefact assemblages appear, and even then projectile components continue to be fairly scarce (Campana 1989).

Of course, foraging tool-kits of the Near Eastern Epipalaeolithic may have emphasised stone and perishable wood materials rather than bone and antler. Still, such raw materials have important implications concerning manufacturing investment. The production of bone, antler, or ivory artefacts is particularly labour- and time-intensive compared to the manufacture of stone tools (Knecht 1997: 200). Replication experiments suggest that even the simplest bone or antler points require a minimum of three production stages, involving a combination of abrasion, carving, and other labourious techniques (Newcomer 1977, Julien 1982, Campana 1989, McComb 1989). Elabourate harpoon barbs or hafting elements entail several more steps (e.g. Julien 1982: 127–35.) Thus, even if wooden armatures were common in southern Eurasia during the LUP, the use of bone and antler in high-latitude regions shows that there was both greater variety of and greater investment in the production of artefacts in the north.

Geographic patterning in technology for plant use is the opposite of that of hunting equipment. The Epipalaeolithic of southern Eurasia is not simply an impoverished version of the northern LUP. A variety of implements for the exploitation of vegetable foods, including grinding slabs, querns, and mortars and pestles, is found in early Epipalaeolithic sites of the Near East (Bar-Yosef 1987, 1990, Byrd and Garrard 1990, Wright 1994, Goring-Morris and Belfer-Cohen 1998) and North Africa (Wendorf and Schild 1980). Their frequency increases over the final 10 000 years of the Pleistocene, but even the early specimens were relatively well made (Wright 1994) (Figure 5.2). Remarkable preservation at the waterlogged site of Ohalo II in Israel provides a rare glimpse of highly diversified plant-food diets from the Last Glacial Maximum (Kislev et al. 1992). Farther south, in the Nile Valley, early grindstones are found in the LUP Kubbaniyan culture, where they seem to have been used to process the bulbs and rhizomes of wetland plants (Hillman et al. 1989, Close and Wendorf 1990). The early importance of grinding equipment in southwest Asia indicates late Pleistocene foragers in low latitude, arid regions were not only making use of concentrated but relatively low-yield foodstuffs, but also relying on these foods heavily enough to warrant elabourate processing. In northern Europe, by contrast, grinding stones are far less visible in the late Palaeolithic or even Mesolithic (Jochim 1998: 148). Grinding stones suitable for processing plants do occur sporadically in Upper Palaeolithic layers in some northern sites (de Beaune 1993, Borziyak 1993), but their functions are difficult to ascertain. Many of them may have been used to pulverise bone for grease rendering or for grinding pigments (e.g. Soffer 1985, de Beaune 1993).

Most discussions of LUP and Epipalaeolithic diet and subsistence behaviour focus on larger prey, especially ungulates. Exploitation of megafauna (mammoths, mastodons, rhinoceri) occurred only in a limited range of conditions, and it is not clear that healthy individuals were regularly hunted anywhere (Soffer 1990 1993, Abramova 1993). Ungulates were the main focus of large game hunting during the Palaeolithic everywhere except Australia. Eurasia is particularly rich in ungulate species (Diamond 1994) and nearly all of them were hunted to some degree. Monospecific or nearly monospecific ungulate faunas are reported for LUP sites in several regions of the Old World, and include assemblages dominated by barbary sheep in North Africa (Close and Wendorf 1990), gazelle in the Levant (Legge 1972, Davis 1982), reindeer, horse, bison or ibex in northerly or highland areas (Audouze 1987, Weniger 1987, Straus 1990*b*, Krotovna and Belan 1993). These cases have sometimes been taken as evidence for 'specialised hunting' and intentional restriction of diet breadth. For the most part, faunas dominated by a single ungulate species can be explained more simply in terms of climate- or latitude-driven shifts in mammalian communities, or hunting opportunities mediated by prey behaviour and biogeography (Garrard 1980, Bailey 1983, Davidson 1983, Simek and Snyder 1988, Stiner 1990 1994, Bar-Oz *et al.* 1998).

Human hunting of artiodactyls during the LUP and Epipalaeolithic followed the long-established theme of prime-dominated harvesting, irrespective of climate or latitude (Stiner 1990). Subtle reductions in the mean age at death in artiodactyl death assemblages indicate nearly continuous harvesting pressure in some regions of Eurasia (Stiner 1994). The diversification of foraging technology characteristic of the LUP and Epipalaeolithic further suggests increasing specialisation in hunting techniques, and by implication, increases in harvesting efficiency. Concentrated seasonal harvesting in colder areas may also have become more common at this time (Audouze 1987, Weniger 1987). Methods for maximising the food value of carcasses, including grease rendering via boiling as done by some modern hunting peoples (Binford 1978), probably evolved in the LUP. The thick litter of fire-cracked stones in some Magdalenian sites in France and Germany (Audouze 1987, Weniger 1987), for example, could result from the extraction, concentration, and storage of bone grease.

Important shifts in the use of small game also occurred during the Upper Palaeolithic. In addition to the longer-standing reliance on slow-moving, easily collected reptiles, molluscs, and eggs in low-latitude regions during earlier periods (discussed in greater detail below), a variety of elusive prey was increasingly emphasised from the Early Upper Palaeolithic onward. The first of these were birds such as fast-reproducing partridges (Stiner et al. 1999, 2000). Heavy use of lagomorphs, particularly hares, tends to appear somewhat later, mainly after the Last Glacial Maximum. This later shift was widespread, including areas of the northern interior and arid lands to the south. Hares became an important component of the diet by LUP times in southern Europe (Davidson 1983, Clark 1987, Straus 1990b, Zilhão 1990, Stiner et al. 1999), western Europe (Berke 1984), Moravia (Svoboda 1990), the Central Russian Plain (Soffer 1990) and in the Dnestr region (Borziyak 1993). A surge in lagomorph exploitation occurs by roughly the same time in western Asia (Byrd and Garrard 1990, Munro 1999, Stiner et al. 2000), but apparently a good deal later in North Africa (Smith 1998). Environmental changes brought on by global warming may have expanded the habitats favoured by lagomorphs and thus their numbers in Eurasia. However, early wolf den faunas reveal that lagomorphs were locally abundant yet largely ignored by humans prior to the Upper Palaeolithic in some areas (Stiner 1994).

While shellfish had been a part of human subsistence since the Middle Palaeolithic (Klein and Scott 1986, Stiner 1993), they began to suffer population declines from overexploitation during the Late Upper Palaeolithic and Epipalaeolithic. Economically important taxa along the Mediterranean and Atlantic shores included mussels, limpets, and turbans (e.g. Bailey 1978, 1983, Clark and Straus 1983), all of which could be gathered from the littoral zone. Over-harvesting by humans caused significant shell size diminution in limpet populations in Italy by 23 000 BP (Stiner *et al.* 1999), and by the late Magdalenian and Azilian (12 000–10 000 BP) at La Riera on the Atlantic coast of Spain (Clark and Straus 1983). Substantial exploitation of fish came very late to the north, however. There is evidence for limited use of salmon beginning with the Solutrean or Magdalenian at the earliest (Mellars 1985, Hayden *et al.* 1987, Zilhão 1990, Jochim 1998), but evidence for substantial dependence on fish is common only in the Mesolithic (e.g. Straus and Clark 1986, see Rowley-Conwy, this volume). Intensive fresh-water fish exploitation occurred as early as 18 000 BP in some arid southern regions, such as the Jordan and Nile Valleys (Close and Wendorf 1990, Nadel 1991, Nadel and Hershkovitz 1991). In the Maghreb of North Africa, land snails were extensively used from Last Glacial Maximum onward, their shells forming dense middens in some sites (Close and Wendorf 1990).

Small-scale exchange of goods was virtually ubiquitous in the LUP. Although the production of art is often considered a hallmark of the period, most, though not all, art objects come from northern Europe (Gamble and Soffer 1990*b*: 16). On the other hand, most LUP populations, whether in southern Europe (Bahn 1982, Bietti 1990, Mussi 1990, Straus 1990*b*: 203), northern Europe (e.g. Gamble 1986: 222, 332–8, Weniger 1987 1990), or the Near East (e.g. Bar-Yosef 1987, 1990, Goring-Morris and Belfer-Cohen 1998), found some use for unusual objects or raw materials, usually modified for suspension. A minor but significant proportion of the ornaments from LUP sites was made of raw materials that could only be obtained from distant sources. For example, Kebaran (early Epipalaeolithic) sites in the Levant contain marine shells obtained from sources up to 300 km away (Bar-Yosef 1990: 66, Byrd and Garrard 1990: 90–2). Baltic amber is found in continental sites of northeastern Europe in later phases of the LUP (Soffer 1985). Lithic raw materials of exceptional quality were also sometimes moved considerable distances, presumably via trade and exchange. The quantities of exotic items vary from region to region (e.g. Straus 1990*b*), and the uneven reporting makes it difficult to test for geographic clines in the amount of long-distance transfer of goods. It none the less appears that exchange of raw materials was especially common in northern and central Europe (Schild 1976, Weniger 1990, Svoboda *et al.* 1996: 153, Jochim 1998: 219–20). Some sort of long-distance exchange was practised by most LUP populations, and the differences among these societies were largely a matter of degree. More research is needed on this question, but the kinds of socially-mediated options for managing resource risk associated with trading networks among recent hunter–gatherers seem to have been quite widespread during the LUP and Epipalaeolithic.

The last 10 000 years of the Pleistocene represents an exceptionally dynamic period in terms of global climate and the organisation of human lifeways. Many of the general features of the LUP and Epipalaeolithic described above became more strongly expressed with time. For example, proportions of microlithic artefacts increased throughout Eurasia. In coastal northern Europe, shellfish and fish took on ever greater dietary roles toward the end of the Palaeolithic and the Mesolithic (Gamble 1986, Clark 1987), the same may be said for lagomorph exploitation in many regions of Eurasia. In the Near East, people came to rely more and more on seeds, nuts, and other wild vegetable foods, culminating in the Natufian and other culture complexes (Henry 1989, Belfer-Cohen 1991, Byrd 1994). This apparent directionality of change suggests that people were increasingly locked into new routines, with fewer and fewer options to return to the prior conditions and ways of living.

The Middle Palaeolithic

Chronologically and environmentally, the Middle Palaeolithic (a.k.a. Mousterian) covers much more than the LUP. Mousterian assemblages were first produced roughly 250 000 years ago in the Near East (Mercier *et al.* 1995), slightly later in Europe (Mellars

1996). Middle Palaeolithic technologies lasted as late as 30 000 years ago in southwestern Europe (Straus 1996, D'Errico *et al.* 1998). The Middle Palaeolithic of Eurasia spans at least two major glacial maxima and two warm intervals, and many shorter oscillations (Van Andel and Tzedakis 1996). Mousterian industries are most commonly associated with the Neanderthals (*Homo neanderthalensis* or *H. sapiens neanderthalensis*), but the remains of anatomically modern humans (*H. sapiens sapiens*) have been found in Mousterian layers at the sites of Skhul and Qafzeh in the Levant (Vandermeersch 1981, Bar-Yosef 1992).

The Middle Palaeolithic is often described as being comparatively homogeneous across vast stretches of the Old World (e.g. Foley 1991). However, calling the Mousterian monotonous disguises a great deal of diversity in certain dimensions of material culture, and thus noteworthy complexity of some aspects of human behaviour. Mousterian assemblages embody a startling array of techniques for reducing stone into flakes and blanks, including but not limited to the many varieties of Levallois technology (Boëda *et al.* 1990, Boëda 1991, Kuhn 1995, Hovers 1998). Even prismatic blades, generally associated with the Upper Palaeolithic, are common in some Middle Palaeolithic sites (Marks and Monigal 1995, Révillion 1995, Bar-Yosef and Kuhn 1999). Some of these methods of stone-working are more difficult to execute than the techniques commonly used by modern hunter–gatherers in the Americas or Australia. Researchers debate the reasons for this technological diversity in the Mousterian, citing functional or economic variables, limitations imposed by raw materials, and socially encoded traditions of flint-working (reviewed in Hovers 1998). Regardless of its causes, the existence of such varied lithic technologies contradicts the common view of the Middle Palaeolithic as monotonous.

Other archaeological data also testify to considerable behavioural flexibility and even sophistication on the part of Mousterian hominids. These hominids flourished in a great range of environments, from desert margins to the edges of continental glaciers. What is more, artefacts were sometimes transported over distances well in excess of a single day's foraging radius (Geneste 1986, Roebroeks *et al.* 1988, Féblot-Augustins 1993, 1997), indicating that Mousterian tool-makers sometimes thought well ahead about their needs for tools. Variable strategies of raw material consumption and artefact resharpening also indicate flexible responses to the challenges of keeping mobile groups supplied with tools and raw materials (e.g. Wengler 1990, Kuhn 1992, 1995, Féblot-Augustins 1993, 1997, Henry 1995). Subsistence data likewise suggest that Middle Palaeolithic hominids were resourceful foragers, capable and willing to take anything from clams to wild cattle and bison, and perhaps some even larger animals as well.

What seems to be missing from the Mousterian, and primarily responsible for its reputation for monotony, are the predictable geographic *trends* in material culture typical of both the ethnographic record of recent foragers and the archaeological record of LUP hunter–gatherers. In contrast to the LUP, it is difficult to find consistent links between environmental variables and the preserved elements of Mousterian technology that might be related to food procurement. Most Middle Palaeolithic assemblages contain pointed artefacts, either unretouched Levallois points or retouched Mousterian points, which some investigators believe were used as projectile tips (Shea 1989, 1998) (Figure 5.3). Microwear studies suggest that these artefacts were multi-functional (Beyries 1988, Shea 1989, Anderson-Gerfaud 1990), however, so not all 'points' were specifically made to serve as projectile tips. Shea (1998) argues that the frequencies of points in assemblages from the Levant vary with local environment and reflect the relative importance of large-game hunting. However, the same basic range of forms appears throughout the vast temporal and geographic range of the Mousterian.

Globally, there is no evidence that the diversity or degree of elaboration in potential weapon tips increases as one moves from the Near East into northern Europe, a marked contrast to the LUP. Variation in the sizes and shapes of Levallois or Mousterian points generally are more closely linked to limitations imposed by raw materials or to methods of production than to functional differences. There are rare departures from the basic theme of the Levallois/Mousterian point in Eurasia, including uni- or bifacially worked 'leaf points' in Middle Palaeolithic assemblages stretching from

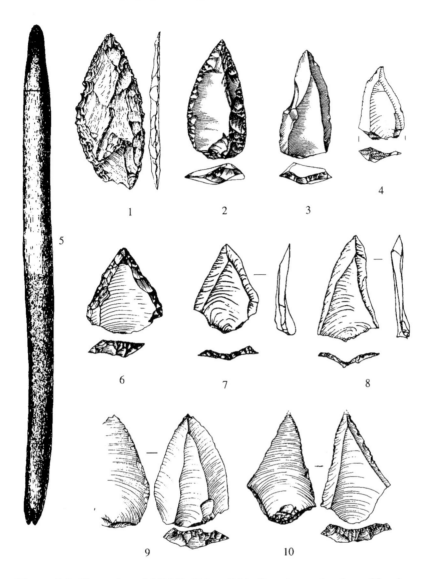

Figure 5.3. Examples of Middle Palaeolithic foraging technology. Numbers 1–5 are from Europe, numbers 6–10 are from the Near East. (From Crew 1976, Ronen 1984, Juffreau 1984, Müller-Beck 1988, Rigaud 1989, Henry 1995, Kuhn 1995, Gaudzinski 1999.)

Greece to Belgium (Mellars 1996: 130), and the so-called 'backed points' on thick blades from Tönchesberg, an early Middle Palaeolithic site in Germany (Conard 1992). Even the bifacial points are essentially the same kind of artefact as Mousterian and Levallois points – namely large, pointed stone tools, which, if hafted at all, were probably fitted to heavy thrusting weapons. Similarly, there is no evidence that the complexity and diversity of Mousterian hunting weapons waxed or waned with climate. In southwest France, for example, the Quina Mousterian variant is most consistently associated with cold conditions (Mellars 1996: 188–9), when humans' need for meat and animal fat would have been great. However, Quina-type assemblages are known for their large, heavily modified sidescrapers, and certainly not for the abundance or elaboration of potential projectile points (Bordes 1961, 1972).

Overall, the Middle Palaeolithic tool-kit shows a remarkably low level of investment per implement across Eurasia. Aside from the wooden spears or spear shafts thought to have been used, nothing in the classic Mousterian repertoire would require more than about 20 minutes' work to produce. In the LUP, and among recent foragers, high levels of technological elabouration and labour investment are manifest in certain tools as well as in the exploitation of durable but difficult-to-work organic substances such as bone and antler. Mousterian hominids sometimes used these materials, but much less frequently than their LUP counterparts; moreover, they were generally either employed 'as is' or minimally modified (Vincent 1989, Gaudzinski 1999). Of the few organic artefacts that survive, only the wooden spear from Lehringen (Adam 1951), and much older examples from Schoeningen (Thieme 1997), seem to be directly related to hunting (but see Gamble 1987). Most of the other items are of ambiguous function, or, in the case of large mammal ribs pointed at one end (e.g. Gaudzinski 1999, Vincent 1989) (Figure 5.3), could have been 'digging sticks'.

The lack of elaborate hunting technology should not be taken to imply that Mousterian foragers were ineffective predators. Hominids have been hunters of large game for a very long time with a rather limited range of technological aids. The contents of many

Middle Palaeolithic sites are dominated by hominid-generated bone debris, including abundant remains of ungulates. As early as the later Middle Pleistocene, some game selection is biased toward prime adult prey (Gaudzinski 1995, Stiner and Tchernov 1998), a feature distinguishing human habits from those of all large non-human predators (Stiner 1990 1994). In Europe and the Near East, human-caused damage to the bones (cut marks, percussion fractures, and burning), as well as relatively complete body-part representation indicate that Middle Palaeolithic humans enjoyed uninhibited access to large game (e.g. Chase 1986, David and Poulain 1990, Hoffecker *et al.* 1991, Farizy and David 1992, Stiner 1994, Rabinovitch and Tchernov 1995). The products of foraging were deliberately aggregated in some later sites, where they were processed and consumed by multiple individuals, creating thick refuse accumulations (e.g. Speth and Tchernov 1998). Other sites appear to represent individual kills (e.g. Conard 1992) or even loci of repeated kills of one or several animals (e.g. Jaubert *et al.* 1990, Debénath and Jelinek 1998). Other aspects of Middle Palaeolithic foraging behaviour are not easy to reconcile with the practices of recent hunter–gatherers. In some instances, hominids left artefacts in sites where the majority of faunal remains are attributable to large carnivores (Lindly 1988, Brugal and Jaubert 1991, Stiner 1994, Stiner *et al.* 1996). In others, occasional scavenging, primarily of ungulate head parts in spring, is associated with small-game use (Stiner 1994).

Perhaps the most striking feature of Middle Palaeolithic game use is the dominance of high-ranked prey, regardless of latitude. Common prey species included large and medium-sized ungulates (Chase 1986, David and Poulain 1990, Jaubert *et al.* 1990, Stiner 1990, 1994, Hoffecker *et al.* 1991, Bar-Yosef *et al.* 1992, Gaudzinski 1995, Speth and Tchernov 1998, Stiner and Tchernov 1998). The only small animals regularly exploited had very low costs of capture (Stiner *et al.* 1999, 2000). Shellfish were collected, albeit in small quantities, throughout the Mediterranean region (Klein and Scott 1986, Stiner 1993 1994), as were tortoises in low-latitude areas (Stiner and Tchernov 1998, Stiner *et al.* 1999). Rare are the remains of agile small prey such as rabbits and birds (Stiner *et al.* 1999,

2000), species that are difficult to catch without special equipment. For assemblages whose taphonomic histories have been examined systematically – an essential qualifier to any comparison – data on Middle Palaeolithic game use fulfill the ecological expectation of declining prey species diversity with increasing latitude. Small animals were relatively more important to Middle Palaeolithic diets at lower latitudes than in the north, where preserved faunas consist almost exclusively of ungulate remains.

Direct evidence for the use of plant resources is sparse in the Middle Palaeolithic, at least partly because of preservation biases. A few unusual sites have limited evidence for plant exploitation. Kebara cave in Israel yielded burned seeds of wild legumes (Bar-Yosef et al. 1992: 530), presumably collected by hominids. Mousterian levels at Gorham's Cave, on Gibraltar, preserve burned remains of pine nuts and wild olives (Barton et al. 1999) in association with battered beach cobbles. Interestingly, the technological components necessary for intensive processing are uncommon or absent. Aside from hammerstones, which served a range of purposes, artefacts that could have been used to process vegetable foods are seldom if ever reported in Mousterian sites, whether in the southern Levant or in northern Europe. We should not be surprised to learn that Mousterian foragers consumed seeds and other vegetable foods, but it is clear that they did not go to any great lengths to process them. These high-cost, high-yield resources thus were not key dietary staples.

Finally, there is the question of how Middle Palaeolithic groups coped with resource risk via social relations. Ornaments and long-distance movement of shell and other raw materials, ubiquitous features of LUP and Epipalaeolithic cultures, are remarkably rare in the Middle Palaeolithic. Lithic raw materials were sometimes moved considerable distances (Féblot-Augustins 1997), but this may reflect no more than the normal transport of artefacts in the course of foraging and residential movement (Kuhn 1992). Unusual objects such as crystals and fossils are known for the Middle Palaeolithic, but they are very rare and seldom came from distant sources. Potential ornaments from Mousterian sites are limited to a few pierced animal teeth spread over thousands of square kilometres

(Chase and Dibble 1987, Mellars 1989*a,b*, 1996: 369–75, Davidson and Noble 1989, Hayden 1993), and all date to the late Middle Palaeolithic. The exchange of exotic items, whatever their social or symbolic value, was not a regular or frequent part of the Mousterian behavioural repertoire.

Humans with a difference

The records of the LUP and the Middle Palaeolithic both reveal considerable variability across time and space. However, neither the range of variation nor the trends across environmental gradients is the same for the two periods. The differences can highlight the question of the antiquity of the hunter–gatherer lifeways as we know them from ethnographic and historical accounts.

LUP and Epipalaeolithic peoples were distributed from the tropics to the subarctic. Variation across environmental gradients in subsistence and technology is much like that observed among ethnographically documented hunter–gatherers, with good evidence for greater dependence on hunted and/or fished foods in northern Eurasia, and earlier, intensive use of plant foods in southern areas such as the Levant. Diversity, elaboration, and relative investment in foraging technology, especially hunting gear, appear to increase with latitude. Low-volume, long-distance exchange, taken as evidence for broad networks of alliances, is ubiquitous. Of course it is impossible to find complete recent analogues for LUP groups, so Pleistocene evidence thus actually expands the range of known hunter–gatherer adaptations. None the less, the picture of broad-scale variability in the LUP is not unfamiliar to anthropologists who study modern hunter–gatherers.

In contrast, the Middle Palaeolithic world seems to have been populated by very different sorts of foragers. Human behaviour of this period certainly varied from one context to the next, but global variation in the archaeological evidence does not fit the expectations based on recent or LUP hunter–gatherers. At least three major differences can be identified. First, technological and faunal evidence for the Middle Palaeolithic suggests rather limited variation in subsistence with latitude, beyond that governed by prey distributions. Second, the labour invested in subsistence technology shows no relation to climatic gradients. Wherever they lived, Mousterian foragers employed a fairly similar tool-kit, at least from stone, and seldom elabourated the production of artefacts. Interestingly, the ways in which tools were made and raw materials obtained show considerable flexibility – it is only the end-products that are so similar. Third, it appears that Mousterian groups had little need for durable symbols of group membership and individual identity, and they seldom exchanged distinctive, durable goods to maintain relationships across territorial boundaries.

These particular features of the Middle Palaeolithic record are not in themselves unexpected. Even in the recent past *some* foragers might have subsisted almost exclusively on high-ranked foods, used relatively unelabourated technologies, or practised little exchange with their neighbours. What is surprising is that such a pattern persisted for so long over such a broad area for the Mousterian, from full glacials to prolonged interglacial periods and from the central Russian steppes to the deserts of North Africa. Clearly, one can not explain the shared characteristics of Middle Palaeolithic artefact and faunal assemblages by reference to a particular set of ecological conditions.

Since the Middle Palaeolithic archaeological evidence does not fit with expectations based on modern hunter–gatherers, what sort of adaptations does it represent? Middle Palaeolithic (and earlier) foraging groups seem to have been very 'light on the landscape'. They consistently targeted high-return, highly-ranked resources in most circumstances, expending little effort on small game and vegetable foods. Because high-ranked foods are most susceptible to over-harvesting, this would imply that human population densities remained very low. Nor did Mousterian hominids substantially affect the size/age distributions of slow-growing, slow-reproducing small animals (Stiner *et al.* 1999, 2000). We can further infer that group sizes were small or that larger aggregations were uncommon. Just how small Mousterian groups were is not clear, but even the widely cited minimum hunter–gatherer band size of 25 (see discussion in Kelly 1995: 205–13) could be an overestimate. The evidence also suggests that individuals did not participate in broader alliance networks of the types documented among recent hunter–gatherers and perhaps that residence patterns and group affiliation were even more fluid than they were among recent foragers (Gamble 1986: 384–6).

If Middle Palaeolithic regional populations were small and sub-divided into essentially autonomous foraging groups, some of the other departures from expected modern hunter–gatherer behaviours make more sense. Small, independent foraging groups naturally limit the scope of consumer and food-sharing networks. It can be argued that much of the pay-off for technological innovation among modern hunter–gatherers stems from (a) the sizes of co-operating consumer groups, and (b) the social benefits obtained by successful and generous providers (e.g. Hawkes 1991). If there were few individuals partaking in the fruits of foraging during the Middle Palaeolithic, the social and energetic benefits of increasing foraging efficiency by investing in elabourate technology would have been minimal (Kuhn and Stiner 1998a). Moreover, the pressure for dietary and technological diversification would also have been weak, because levels of intra-specific competition would have been relatively low. Higher population densities in the LUP produced the opposite effect.

The notion that Mousterian hominid populations were thinly distributed could therefore explain aspects of resource use and technological evolution. However, this begs the question of why population levels remained low for so long. Taken at face value, hominids seem to have manifest exceptionally slow population growth rates over the long term (Groube 1996: 101, Pennington, this volume). A lack of evidence for regular long-distance exchange implies that the sorts of alliance networks that allowed more recent foragers to cope with severe fluctuations in the food supply (Wiessner 1982, Cashdan 1985, Smith 1988) simply did not exist in the Middle Palaeolithic. Mousterian populations may have responded to environmental stress demographically, whereas Late Upper Palaeolithic populations elaborated tools to process costly resources more efficiently and employed social mechanisms for buffering risk in addition to demographic responses.

What about the Early Upper Palaeolithic?

The Early Upper Palaeolithic (EUP) (ca. 45 000 to 20 000 BP) is central to debates about the origin and spread of anatomically modern humans. Up to this point we have explicitly distanced our discussion from the thorny topic of modern human origins, in order to separate the idea of 'modern' hunter–gatherer adaptations from considerations of the taxonomic status of Palaeolithic populations. Researching patterns of geographic variation for the EUP is complicated by ambiguities with dating, particularly as one approaches the limits of the radiocarbon method. Moreover, the demographic situation may have been unusually complex, with two human (sub)species – Neanderthals and anatomically modern *Homo sapiens* – coexisting for several thousand years. Any interactions between these populations should have had profound consequences for the formation of archaeological records. These reservations notwithstanding, it is worth briefly considering the EUP evidence for variation in light of the discussions above.

Some aspects of the EUP fit well with the tendencies described for the LUP. There is some evidence for greater elaboration of technology in northern Eurasia. The Aurignacian, the most widely-distributed EUP complex in Europe, is associated with a variety of distinctive bone and antler artefacts, especially points (e.g. Hahn 1977, Delporte 1991). Relatively 'costly' weapon types are known from EUP assemblages of the Near East but are comparatively rare; at Hayonim Cave (Israel), the Levantine Aurignacian assemblage of layer D included typical bone or antler points (Belfer and Bar-Yosef 1981). However, the more widely distributed Ahmarian complex is associated with a limited bone and antler technology (Bar-Yosef and Belfer-Cohen 1988, Gilead 1991, Schyle 1992). The Castelperronian and the Uluzzian, the former of which at least was produced by Neanderthals, also contain a few simple bone points and other bone artefacts (reviewed in D'Errico *et al.* 1998).

In Europe at least, the EUP also marks the abrupt appearance of ornaments, as well as the exchange of exotic materials over long distances (Hahn 1972, Soffer 1985, Mellars 1989*a,b*, White 1989 1993, Taborin 1993*a,b*, Fiocchi 1996–7, Kuhn and Stiner 1998*b*).

Both of these qualities suggest that the social mechanisms for maintaining relationships between distant groups or individuals were already established in Europe. Some EUP assemblages of western Asia also contain modest numbers of shell ornaments (e.g. Rust 1950, Schyle 1992), but the data are sparser, perhaps due to preservational factors. Information about long-distance transport of lithic raw materials in the EUP is ambiguous. EUP assemblages contain more exotic flints than do Mousterian assemblages in some places (Kuhn 1995, Svoboda *et al.* 1996: 120–6, Turq 1996), but in other areas Mousterian and EUP raw material exploitation patterns are similar (Geneste 1986, Roebroeks *et al.* 1988).

Subsistence data suggest that intensification in resource use, particularly the exploitation of birds, began with the EUP in Eurasia (Stiner *et al.* 1999, 2000), but that artefacts associated with the processing of vegetable foods remained quite limited (de Beaune 1993, Wright 1994). There seems to have been some pressure on EUP populations to intensify the means for hunting animals, but not enough to foster heavy reliance on seeds and nuts. However, the EUP dates to a period of relatively cold climatic conditions, while the LUP and the longer Middle Palaeolithic include both warm and cold intervals. For this reason, we cannot rule out the possibility that the scarcity of evidence for plant food exploitation is due simply to the scarcity of suitable plant foods.

In the long run we suspect that most of the trends in human variation during the EUP will prove similar to those observed in the Late Upper Palaeolithic. Problems with chronology and the demographic complexities of the EUP are sufficient grounds for withholding judgement at present. We also emphasise that the question of the taxonomic status is more often a source of distraction than clarification for questions of the evolution of behaviour.

Conclusion

Modern hunter–gatherer adaptations in diet and technology were globally established by the LUP (20 000 BP), perhaps even by the EUP (ca. 45 000 BP). While the lifeways of particular Upper

Palaeolithic groups were unlike those of recent foragers, LUP hunter–gatherers responded to ecological and demographic factors in ways similar to modern foraging societies. By contrast, the archaeological record of the Middle Palaeolithic represents a different – albeit quite successful – range of behaviours. Mousterian foragers dealt with environmental variation in some unexpected ways, and their potential for population growth may have been lower as a consequence. While Middle Palaeolithic hominids hunted and gathered, they were a different kind of hunter–gatherer from any presently known.

If Mousterian hominids did not behave in quite the same ways as modern hunter–gatherers, it is likely that earlier humans probably did not either. None the less, one should not simply divide prehistory into pre-Upper Palaeolithic foraging groups and Upper Palaeolithic hunter–gatherers. So-called modern hunter–gatherer adaptations did not appear suddenly as a complete package. Many profound evolutionary changes in hominid adaptations occurred prior to the Upper Palaeolithic in Eurasia, and some of these remain essential to definitions of what it is to be human. The foragers of the Upper Palaeolithic and recent ethnographic past are distinguished by greater technological investment in response to seasonal or unpre-dictable food supplies. They also exhibited unique capacities to pack landscapes with people and to manipulate social ties in ways that buffered the most serious risks of a foraging lifestyle. Nevertheless, they represent just a few late chapters in a long and complicated evolutionary story that began more than 2.5 million years ago.

Important evolutionary events are not necessarily manifest where we first search for them. Paleoanthropologists have focused atten-tion on evidence for the exploitation of large mammals, and consider the emergence of 'Man the (Big Game) Hunter' a great milestone in human evolutionary history. But hominids have hunted large game since at least the late Middle Pleistocene, well before the appearance and spread of anatomically modern humans or Upper Palaeolithic technology. Unexpectedly, the exploitation of small game and plants shows much more interesting trends.

A number of technological changes must have accompanied the trends in small-game exploitation. The early success of hominids as large-game predators was not accompanied initially by major advances in hunting technology; the use of wooden spears goes back at least 500 000 years (Thieme 1997) and the only major change in hunting weapons prior to the Upper Palaeolithic would have been the lashing of a pointed stone flake to the end of a wooden shaft. There is, on the other hand, a clear association in time between increases in human diet breadth and rapid radiations in the formal elements of Upper Palaeolithic technology in the late Pleistocene. A variety of new artefact forms, ranging from harpoons to traps and nets – to use Hayden's (1981*b*) felicitous term, 'gadget technologies' – were probably necessary to make the collection of many kinds of small animals worthwhile (Hayden 1981*b*, Soffer 1985: 313, Holliday 1998). Milling equipment would have been needed to make the most of seeds and nuts. While these kinds of tools may enhance the overall efficiency or reliability of foraging, they are sometimes costly to manufacture, and their appearance and proliferation may mark fundamental changes in land use and the allocation of time and labour among foragers. Traps, nets, and grindstones are also not items that normally attract the attention of Palaeolithic archaeologists, partly because they are difficult to identify in archaeological contexts, but they are extraordinarily important from an evolutionary perspective.

Acknowledgements

We thank Jeff Brantingham, Natalie Munro, Kate Sarther, Todd Surovell, and Bonnie Pitblado, and the other participants in a hunter–gatherer seminar for sharpening our understanding of many of the issues discussed here.

References

Abramova, Z.A. (1993). Two examples of terminal Palaeolithic adaptations. In *From Kostenki to Clovis: Paleoindian and Upper Paleolithic Adaptations*, ed. O. Soffer and N. Praslov (eds.) 85–100. New York: Plenum Press.

Adam, K. (1951). Der Waldelefant von Lehringen, ein jagdbeute des diluvialen menschen. *Quartär* 79–92.

Anderson-Gerfaud, P. (1990). Aspects of behaviour in the Middle Palaeolithic: functional analysis of stone tools from southwest France. In *The Emergence of Modern Humans: An Archaeological Perspective*, ed. P. Mellars, pp. 389–418. Edinburgh: Edinburgh University Press.

Audouze, F. (1987). The Paris Basin in Magdalenian times. In *The Pleistocene Old World: Regional Perspectives*, ed. O. Soffer, pp. 183–200. New York: Plenum Press.

Bahn, P. (1982). Inter-site and inter-regional links during the Upper Palaeolithic: the Pyranean evidence. *Oxford Journal of Archaeology* 1: 247–268.

Bailey, G. (1978). Shell middens as indicators of postglacial economies: a territorial perspective. In *The Early Postglacial Settlement of Northern Europe*, ed. P. Mellars, pp. 37–64. London: Duckworth.

Bailey, G. (1983). Economic change in late Pleistocene Cantabria. In *Hunter–Gatherer Economy in Prehistory: A European Perspective*, ed. G.N. Bailey, pp. 149–165. Cambridge: Cambridge University Press.

Bailey, G. (ed.) (1983). *Hunter–Gatherer Economy in Prehistory: A European Perspective*. Cambridge: Cambridge University Press.

Bar-Oz, G., Dayan, T. and Kaufman, D. (1999). The Epipalaeolithic faunal sequence of Israel: a view from Neve David. *Journal of Archaeological Science* 26: 67–82.

Bar-Yosef, O. (1981). The Epi-Palaeolithic complexes in the southern Levant. In *Préhistoire du Levant*, ed. J. Cauvin and P. Sanlaville, pp. 389–408. Paris: Editions du CNRS.

Bar-Yosef, O. (1987). Late Pleistocene adaptations in the Levant. In *The Pleistocene Old World: Regional Perspectives*, ed. O. Soffer, pp. 219–236. New York: Plenum Press.

Bar-Yosef, O. (1990). The Last Glacial Maximum in the Mediterranean Levant. In *The World at 18,000 BP*, vol. 2, *Low Latitudes*, ed. C. Gamble and O. Soffer, pp. 58–77. New York: Plenum Press.

Bar-Yosef, O. (1992). The role of western Asia in modern human origins. In *The Origin of Modern Humans and the Impact of Chronometric Dating*, ed. M. Aitken, C. Stringer and P. Mellars, pp. 193–200. London: The Royal Society.

Bar-Yosef, O. and Belfer-Cohen, A. (1988). The Early Upper Palaeolithic in Levantine caves. In *The Early Upper Palaeolithic: Evidence from Europe and the Near East*, ed. J. Hoffecker and C. Wolf, B.A.R. International Series 437, pp. 23–41. Oxford: British Archaeological Reports.

Bar-Yosef, O. and Kuhn, S. (1999). The big deal about blades: laminar technologies and human evolution. *American Anthropologist* 101: 322–338.

Bar-Yosef, O., Vandermeersch, B., Arensburg, B., Belfer-Cohen, A., Goldberg, P., Laville, H., Meignen, L., Rak, Y., Speth, J., Tchernov, E., Tillier,

A.-M. and Weiner, S. (1992). The excavations in Kebara Cave. Mt. Carmel. *Current Anthropology* **33**: 497–550.

Barton, R.N.E., Currant, A., Fernandez-Jalvo, Y., Finlayson, J.C., Goldberg, P., Macphail, R., Pettit, P. and Stringer, C. (1999). Gibraltar Neanderthals and results of recent excavations in Gorham's, Vangard and Ibex Caves. *Antiquity* **73**: 13–24.

de Beaune, S. (1993). Nonflint stone tools of the Early Upper Palaeolithic. In *Before Lascaux: The Complex Record of the Early Upper Palaeolithic*, ed. H. Knecht, A. Pike-Tay and R. White, pp. 163–192. Boca Raton: CRC Press.

Belfer-Cohen, A. (1991). The Natufian of the Levant. *Annual Review of Anthropology* **20**: 167–186.

Belfer, A. and Bar-Yosef, O. (1981). Aurignacian at Hayonim Cave. *Paléorient* **7**: 19–42.

Berke, H. (1984). The distributions of bones from large mammals at Petersfels. In *Upper Palaeolithic Settlement Patterns in Europe*, ed. H. Berke, J. Hahn, and C.-J. Kind, pp. 103–108. Tübingen: Verlag Archaeologica Venatoria, Institut für Urgeschichte der Universität Tübingen.

Beyries, S. (1988). Functional variability in lithic sets in the Middle Palaeolithic. In *Upper Pleistocene Prehistory of Western Eurasia*, ed. H. Dibble and A. Montet-White, pp. 213–224. Philadelphia: University Museum Monograph 4.

Bietti, A. (1990). The late Upper Palaeolithic in Italy: an overview. *Journal of World Prehistory* **4**: 95–155.

Binford, L. (1968). Post-Pleistocene adaptations. In *New Perspectives in Archaeology*, ed. S. Binford and L. Binford, pp. 313–341. Chicago: Aldine.

Binford, L. (1977). Forty-seven trips. In *Stone Tools as Cultural Markers*, ed. R.V.S. Wright, pp. 24–36. Canberra: Australian Institude of Aboriginal Studies.

Binford, L. (1978). *Nunamiut Ethnoarchaeology.* New York: Academic Press.

Binford, L. (1979). Organisation and formation processes: looking at curated technologies. *Journal of Anthropological Research* **35**: 255–273.

Binford, L. (1980). Willow smoke and dogs' tails: hunter–gatherer settlement systems and archaeological site formation. *American Antiquity* **45**: 4–20.

Bird-David, N. (1991). Hunter–gatherers and other people: a re-examination. In *Hunter–Gatherers*, vol. 1, *History, Evolution and Social change*, ed. T. Ingold, D. Riches and J. Woodburn, pp. 17–30. New York: Berg.

Bleed, P. (1986). The optimal design of hunting weapons. *American Antiquity* **51**: 737–747.

Boëda, E. 1991. Approche de la variabilité des systèmes de production lithique des industries du Paléolithique inférieur et moyen: chronique d'une variabilité attendue. *Techniques et Culture* **17–18**: 37–79.

Boëda, E., Geneste, J.-M. and Meignen, L. (1990). Identification de chaînes opératoires lithiques du Paléolithique ancien et moyen. *Paleo* **2**: 43–80.

Bordes, F. (1961). Mousterian cultures in France. *Science* **134**: 803–810.

Bordes, F. (1972). *A Tale of Two Caves*. New York: Harper and Row.

Borziyak, I.A. (1993). Subsistence practices of late Palaeolithic groups along the Dneister River and its tributaries. In *From Kostenki to Clovis: Paleoindian and Upper Paleolithic Adaptations*, ed. O. Soffer and N. Praslov, pp. 67–84. New York, Plenum Press.

Bousman, B. (1993). Hunter–gatherer adaptations, economic risk, and tool design. *Lithic Technology* **18**: 59–86.

Brugal, J.-P. and Jaubert, J. (1991). Les gisements paléontologiques Pleisto-cènes a indices de fréquentation humaine: un nouveau type de comporte-ment de predation? *Paleo* **3**: 15–41.

Burch, E. (1988). Modes of exchange in north-west Alaska. In *Hunters and Gatherers*, vol 2, *Property, Power and Ideology*, ed. T. Ingold, D. Riches, and J. Woodburn, pp. 95–109. New York: Berg.

Byrd, B.F. (1994). From early humans to farmers and herders – recent progress on key transitions in southwest Asia. *Journal of Archaeological Research* **2**: 221–253.

Byrd, B. and Garrard, A. (1990). The Last Glacial Maximum in the Jordanian desert. In *The World at 18,000 BP*, vol. 2, *Low Latitutdes*, ed. C. Gamble and O. Soffer, pp. 78–96. New York: Plenum Press.

Campana, D. (1989). *Natufian and Protoneolithic Bone Tools: The Manufacture and Use of Bone Implements in the Zagros and the Levant*. BAR International Series 494. Oxford: British Archaeological Reports.

Cashdan, E. (1983). Territoriality among human foragers: ecological models and an application to four Bushman groups. *Current Anthropology* **24**: 47–66.

Cashdan, E. (1985). Coping with risk: reciprocity among the Basarwa of northern Botswana. *Man* (N.S.) **20**: 454–474.

Chase, P. (1986). *The Hunters of Combe Grenal: Approaches to Middle Palaeolithic Subsistence in Europe*, BAR International Series 286. Oxford: British Archae-ological Reports.

Chase, P. and Dibble, H. (1987). Middle Palaeolithic symbolism: a review of current evidence and interpretations. *Journal of Anthropological Archaeology* **6**: 263–296.

Clark, G.A. (1987). From the Mousterian to the Metal Ages: longterm change in the human diet of northern Spain. InThe Pleistocene Old World: Regional Perspectives, ed. O. Soffer, pp. 293–316. New York: Plenum Press.

Clark, G.A. and Straus, L.G. (1983). Late Pleistocene hunter–gatherer adapta-tions in Cantabrian Spain. In *Hunter–Gatherer Economy in Prehistory: A European Perspective*, ed. G. Bailey, pp. 131–148. Cambridge: Cambridge University Press.

Close, A. and Wendorf, F. (1990). North Africa at 18,000 BP. In *The World at 18,000 BP*, vol. 2, *Low Latitutdes*, ed. C. Gamble and O. Soffer, pp. 41–57. New York: Plenum Press.

Copeland, L. and Hours, F. (1977). Carved and plain bone tools from Jiita (Lebanon) and their early Kebaran Context. *Proceedings of the Prehistoric Society* **43**: 295–301.

Conard, N. (1992). *Tönchesberg and its Position in the Palaeolithic Prehistory of Northern Europe.* Bonn: Dr Rudolf Habelt.

Crew, H. (1976). The Mousterian site of Rosh ein Mor. In *Prehistory and Paleoenvironments in the Central Negev, Israel,* vol. 1, *The Avdat/Aqev Area,* ed. A.E. Marks, pp. 75–112. Dallas: Southern Methodist University.

David, F. and Poulain, T. (1990). La faune de grands mammifères des niveaux XI et XC de la Grotte du Renne à Arcy-sur-Cure (Yonne): étude préliminaire. In *Paléolithique Moyen Récent et Paleolithique Supérieur Ancien en Europe,* ed. C. Farizy, pp. 319–323. Ile de France: Mémoires du Musée de Préhistoire 3.

Davidson, I. (1983). Site variability and prehistoric economy in Levante. In *Hunter–Gatherer Economy in Prehistory: A European Perspective,* ed. G. Bailey, pp. 79–95. Cambridge: Cambridge University Press.

Davidson, I. and Noble, W. (1989). The archaeology of perception: traces of depiction and language. *Current Anthropology* **30**: 125–155.

Davis, S. (1982). Climatic change and the advent of domestication: the succession of ruminant artiodactles in the late PleistoceneHolocene in the Israel region. *Paléorient* **8**: 5–14.

Debénath, A. and Jelinek, A. (1998). Nouvelles fouilles à La Quina (Charente). Résultats préliminaires. *Gallia Préhistoire* **40**: 29–74.

Delporte, H. (1991). La séquence aurignacienne et périgordienne sur la base des travaux récents réalisés en Périgord. *Bulletin de la Société Préhistorique Française* **88**: 243–256.

D'Errico, F., Zilhão, J., Julien, M., Baffier, D. and Pelegrin, J. (1998). Neanderthal acculturation in western Europe? A cricitcal review of the evidence and its interpretation. *Current Anthropology* **39** (Supplement): S1–S44.

Diamond, J. (1994). Zebras and the Anna Karenina Principle. *Natural History* **103**: 4–10.

Dufour, D. (1987). Insects as food: a case study from the northwest Amazon. *American Anthropologist* **89**: 383–397.

Dyson-Hudson, R. and Smith, E. (1978). Human territoriality: an ecological reassessment. *American Anthropologist* **80**: 21–41.

Farizy, C. and David, F. (1992). Subsistence and behavioural patterns of some Middle Palaeolithic local groups. In *The Middle Palaeolithic: Adaptation, Behaviour, and Variability,* ed. H. Dibble and P. Mellars, pp. 87–96. Philadelphia: University Museum Monographs 72.

Féblot-Augustins, J. (1993). Mobility strategies in the late Middle Palaeolithic of Central Europe and Western Europe: elements of stability and variability. *Journal of Anthropological Archaeology* **12**: 211–265.

Féblot-Augustins, J. (1997). La Circulation des Matières Premières au Paléolithique. ERAUL 75. Liège: Université de Liège.

Fiocchi, C. (1996–7). Le conchiglie marine provenienti dalla Grotta di Fumane (Monti Lessini-Verona). Atti dell' Istituto Veneto di Scienze, Lettere ed Arti **155**: 1–22.

Foley, R. (1991). Hominids, humans and hunter–gatherers: an evolutionary perspective. In *Hunters and Gatherers*, vol. 1, *History, Evlution and Social Change*, ed. T. Ingold, D. Riches and J. Woodburn, pp. 207–221. New York: Berg.

Gamble, C. (1986). *The Palaeolithic Settlement of Europe*. Cambridge: Cambridge University Press.

Gamble, C. (1987). Man the shoveler: alternative models for Middle Pleistocene colonisation and occupation in northern latitudes. In *The Pleistocene Old World: Regional Perspectives*, ed. O. Soffer, pp. 81–98.

Gamble, C. and Soffer, O. (eds.) (1990a). *The World at 18,000 BP*, vol. 2, *Low Latitudes*. New York: Plenum Press.

Gamble, C. and Soffer, O. (1990b). Pleistocene polyphony: the diversity of human adaptations at the Last Glacial Maximum. In O. Soffer and C. Gamble, pp. 1–23. New York: Plenum Press.

Garrard, A. (1980). Man–animal–plant relationships during the Upper Pleistocene and Early Holocene of the Levant. Unpublished PhD, University of Cambridge.

Gaudzinski, S. (1995). Wallertheim revisited: a re-analysis of the fauna from the Middle Palaeolithic site of Wallertheim (Rheinhessen/Germany). *Journal of Archaeological Science* **22**: 51–66.

Gaudzinski, S. (1999). Middle Palaeolithic bone tools from the open-air site Salzgitter-Lebenstedt (Germany). *Journal of Archaeological Science* **26**: 125–142.

Geneste, J.-M. (1986). Systèmes d'approvisionnement en matières premières au Paléolithique moyen et au Paléolithique supérieur en Aquitaine. In *L'Homme de Néandertal*, vol. 8, *La Technique*, ed. M. Otte, pp. 61–70. Liège: ERAUL 35.

Geneste, J.-M. and Maury, S. (1997). Contributions of multidisciplinary experimentation ot the study of Upper Palaeolithic projectile points. In *Projectile Technology*, ed. H. Knecht, pp. 165–189. New York: Plenum Press.

Geneste, J.-M. and Plisson, H. (1993). Hunting technologies and human behaviour: lithic analysis of Solutran shouldered points. In *Before Lascaux: The complex Record of the Early Upper Paleolithic*, ed. H. Knecht, A. Pike-Tay and R. White, pp. 117–135. Boca Raton: CRC Press.

Gilead, I. (1991). The Upper Palaeolithic period in the Levant. *Journal of World Prehistory* **5**: 105–153.

Goring-Morris, N. (1995). Complex hunter–gatherers at the end of the Palaeolithic (20,000–10,000 BP). In *The Archaeology of Society in the Holy Land* ed. T. Levy, pp. 141–168. London: Leicester University Press.

Goring-Morris, N. and Belfer-Cohen, A. (1998). The articulation of cultural processes and late Quaternary environmental changes in Cisjordan. *Paléorient* **23**: 71–93.

Grigor'ev, G.P. (1993). The Aveedvo archaeological culture and the Willendorf–Pavlov–Kostenki–Aveedvo cultural unity. In *From Kostenki to Clovis: Paleonindian and Upper Paleolithic Adaptations*, ed. O. Soffer and N. Praslov, pp. 51–66. New York: Plenum Press.

Groube, L. 1996. The impact of diseases upon the emergence of agriculture. In *The Origins and Spread of Agriculture and Pastoralism in Eurasia*, ed. D. Harris, pp. 101–129. Washington, DC: Smithsonian Institution Press.

Hahn, J. (1972). Aurignacian signs, pendants, and art objects in Central and Eastern Europe. *World Archaeology* **3**: 252–266.

Hahn, J. (1977). *Aurignacien: das ältere Jungpäleolithikum in Mittel- und Osteuropa.* Köln: Fundamenta Reihe.

Hawkes, K. (1991). Showing off: tests of an hypothesis about men's foraging goals. *Ethology and Sociobiology* **12**: 29–54.

Hawkes, K. and O'Connell, J. (1985). Optimal foraging models and the case of the !Kung. *American Anthropologist* **87**: 401–405.

Hayden, B. (1981a). Subsistence and ecological adaptations of modern hunter/gatherers. In *Omnivorous Primates: Gathering and Hunting in Human Evolution*, ed. R. Harding and G. Teleki, pp. 344–421. New York: Columbia University Press.

Hayden, B. (1981b). Research and development in the Stone Age: technological transitions among hunter–gatherers. *Current Anthropology* **22**: 519–548.

Hayden, B. (1993). The cultural capacity of Neandertals: a review and reevaluation. *Journal of Human Evolution* **24**: 113–146.

Hayden, B., Chisholm, B. and Schwarcz, H.P. (1987). Fishing and foraging: marine resources in the Upper Palaeolithic of France. In *The Pleistocene Old World: Regional Perspectives*, ed. O. Soffer, pp. 279–291.

Henry, D. (1989). *The Levant at the End of the Ice Age.* Philadelphia: University of Pennsylvania Press.

Henry, D. (1995). *Prehistoric Cultural Ecology and Evolution.* New York: Plenum Press.

Hillman, G., Madeyska, E. and Hather, J. (1989). Wild plant-foods and diet in late Palaeolithic Wadi Kubbaniya: the evidence from charred remains. In *The Prehistory of Wadi Kubbaniya*, vol. 2, *Paleoenvironmental and Stratigraphic Studies*, ed. F. Wendorf, R. Schild and A. Close, pp. 162–242. Dallas: Southern Methodist University Press.

Hoffecker, J.F., Baryshnikov, G. and Potapova, O. (1991). Vertebrate remains from the Mousterian site of Il'skaya I (northern Caucasus, U.S.S.R.): new analysis and interpretation. *Journal of Archaeological Science* **18**: 113–147.

Holliday, T. (1998). The ecological context of trapping among recent hunter–gatherers: implications for subsistence in terminal Pleistocene Europe. *Current Anthropology* **39**: 711–720.

Hovers, E. (1998). The lithic assemblages of Amud cave: implications for understanding the end of the Mousterian in the Levant. In *Neandertals and Modern Humans in Western Asia*, ed. T. Akazawa, K. Akoi and O. Bar-Yosef, pp. 143–164. New York: Plenum Press.

Ingold, T., Riches, D. and Woodburn, J. (eds.). (1991). *Hunters and Gatherers*, vol. 1, *History, Evolution and Social Change*. New York: Berg.

Jaubert, J., Lorblanchet, M., Laville, H., Slott-Moller, R., Turq, A. and Brugal, J.-P. (1990). *Les Chasseurs d'Aurochs de La Borde*. Paris: Editions de la Maison des Sciences de L'Homme, Documents d'Archéologique Français 27.

Jochim, M. (1998). *A Hunter-Gatherer Landscape*. New York: Plenum Press.

Julien, M. (1982). *Les Harpons Magdaléniens. XVII Supplément à Gallia Préhistoire*. Paris: Editions du CNRS.

Keeley, L. (1995). Protoagricultural practices among hunter–gatherers: a cross-cultural survey. In *Last Hunters, First Farmers*, ed. T.D. Price and A.B. Gebauer, pp. 243–272. Santa Fe: School of American Research.

Kelly, R. (1983). Hunter–gatherer mobility strategies. *Journal of Anthropological Research* **39**: 277–306.

Kelly, R. (1995). *The Foraging Spectrum: Diversity in Hunter-Gatherer Lifeways*. Washington DC: Smithsonian Institution Press.

Kelly, R.L. and Todd, L.C. (1988). Coming into the country: early Paleoindian hunting and mobility. *American Antiquity* **53**: 231–244.

Kislev, M.E., Nadel, D. and Carmi, I. (1992). Epi-Palaeolithic (19,000 BP) cereal and fruit diet at Ohalo II, Sea of Galilee, Israel. *Review of Palaeobotany and Palynology* **71**: 161–166.

Klein, R.G. and Scott, K. (1986). Re-analysis of faunal assemblages from the Haua Fteah and other Late Quaternary archaeological sites in Cyrenaican Libya. *Journal of Archaeological Science* **13**: 515–542.

Knecht, H. (1997). Projectile points of bone, antler and stone: experimental explorations of manufacture and use. In *Projectile Tehcnology*, ed. H. Knecht, pp. 191–212. New York: Plenum Press.

Knecht, H. (ed.) (1997). *Projectile Technology*. New York: Plenum Press.

Knecht, H., Pike-Tay, A. and White, R. (eds.). (1993). *Before Lascaux: The Complex Record of the Early Upper Palaeolithic*. Boca Raton: CRC Press.

Krotovna, A.A., and Belan, N.G. (1993). Amvrosievka: a unique Upper Palaeolithic site in Eastern Europe. In *From Kostenki to Clovis: Paleoindian and Upper Paleolithic Adaptations*, ed. O. Soffer and N.D. Praslov, pp. 125–142.

Kuhn, S. (1992). On planning and curated technologies in the Middle Palaeolithic. *Journal of Anthropological Research* **48**: 185–214.

Kuhn, S. (1994). A formal approach to the design and assembly of transported toolkits. *American Antiquity* **59**: 426–442.

Kuhn, S. (1995). *Mousterian Lithic Technology: An Ecological Approach*. Princeton: Princeton University Press.

Kuhn, S. and Stiner, M.C. (1998*a*). Middle Palaeolithic creativity: reflections on an oxymoron? In *Creativity in Human Evolution and Prehistory*, ed. S. Mithen, pp. 146–164. London: Routledge.

Kuhn, S. and Stiner, M.C. (1998*b*). The earliest Aurignacian of Riparo Mochi (Liguria, Italy). *Current Anthropology* **39** (Supplement): S175–S189.

Laville, H., Rigaud, J.-P. and Sackett, J. (1980). *Rock-Shelters of the Périgord*. New York: Academic Press.

Lee, R. (1968). What hunters do for a living, or, how to make out on scarce resources. In *Man the Hunter*, ed. R. Lee and I. DeVore, pp. 30–48. New York: Aldine.

Legge, A.J. (1972). Prehistoric exploitation of the gazelle in Palestine. In *Papers in Economic Prehistory*, ed. E. Higgs, pp. 119–124. Cambridge: Cambridge University Press.

Lindly, J. (1988). Hominid and carnivore activity at Middle and Upper Palaeolithic cave sites in eastern Spain. *Munibe* **40**: 45–70.

Madeyska, T. (1990). The distribution of human settlement in the extra-tropical Old World, 24,000–15,000 BP. In *The World at 18,000 BP*, vol. 2, *Low Latitutdes*, ed. C. Gamble and O. Soffer, pp. 24–37.

Marks, A. and Monigal, K. (1995). Modeling the production of elongated blanks from the early Levantine Mousterian at Rosh Ein Mor. In *The Definition and Interpretation of Levallois Technology*, ed. H. Dibble and O. Bar-Yosef, ed. H. Dibble and O. Bar-Yosef, pp. 267–278. Madison: Prehistory Press.

McComb, P. (1989). *Upper Palaeolithic Osseous Artefacts from Britain and Belgium*. BAR International Series 481. Oxford: British Archaeological Reports.

Mellars, P.A. (1985). The ecological basis of social complexity in the Upper Palaeolithic of southwestern France. In *Prehistoric Hunter-Gatherers: The Emergence of Cultural Complexity*, ed. T.D. Price and J. Brown, pp. 271–297. New York: Academic Press.

Mellars, P. (1989*a*). Technological changes at the Middle to Upper Palaeolithic transition: economic, social, and cognitive perspectives. In *The Human Revolution: Behavioural and Biological Perspectives on the Origins of Modern Humans*, ed. P. Mellars and C. Stringer, pp. 338–365. Princeton: Princeton University Press.

Mellars, P. (1989*b*). Major issues in the emergence of modern humans. *Current Anthropology* **30**: 349–385.

Mellars, P. (1996). *The Neanderthal Legacy*. Princeton: Princeton University Press.

Mercier, N., Valladas, H., Valladas, G., Reyss, J.-L., Jelinek, A., Meignen, L. and Joron, J.-L. (1995). TL dates of burnt flints from Jelinek's excavations at Tabun and their implications. *Journal of Archaeological Science* **22**: 495: 509.

Müller-Beck, H. (1988). The ecosystem of the 'Middle Palaeolithic' (Late Lower Palaeolithic) in the Danube region: a stepping-stone to the Upper Palaeolithic. In *The Upper Pleistocene Prehistory of Western Eurasia*, ed.

H. Dibble and A. Montet-White, pp. 233–254. Philadelphia: University Museum Monograph 54.

Munro, N.D. (1999). An investigation of occupation duration through population modeling in the Natufian period in the Levant. In *High Resolution Faunas of the Holocene Boundary*, ed. J. Driver, BAR International Series 800, pp. 37–45. Oxford: British Archaeological Reports.

Mussi, M. (1990). Continuity and change in Italy at the Last Glacial Maximum. In *The World at 18,000 BP*, vol. 1, *High Latitudes*, ed. O. Soffer and C. Gamble, pp. 126–147. New York: Plenum Press.

Nadel, D. (1991). Ohalo II – the third season (1991). *Journal of the Israel Prehistoric Society* **24**: 158–163.

Nadel, D. and Hershkovitz, I. (1991). New subsistence data and human remains from the earliest Levantine Epipalaeolithic. *Current Anthropology* **32**: 631–635.

Newcomer, M. (1974). Study and replication of bone artefacts from Ksar Akil. *World Archaeology* **6**: 138–154.

Newcomer, M. (1977). Experiments in Upper Palaeolithic bone work. In *Méthodologie Appliquée à l'Industrie de l'Os Préhistorique*, ed. H. Camps-Febrer, pp. 293–301. Paris: Editions du CNRS.

Oswalt, W. (1976). *An Anthropological Analysis of Food-Getting Technology*. New York: John Wiley.

Pennington, L. (1989). *Bowes and Church's Food Values of Portions Commonly Used*. New York: Harper and Row.

Peterson, J. (1978). Hunter–gatherer/farmer exchange. *American Anthropologist* **80**: 335–351.

Peterson, N. (1975). Hunter–gatherer territoriality: the perspective from Australia. *American Anthropologist* **77**: 53–68.

Pianka, E. (1978). *Evolutionary Ecology*. 2nd edn. New York: Harper and Row.

Pokines, J. and Krupa, M. (1997). Self-barbed antler spearpoints and evidence of fishing in the late Upper Palaeolithic of Cantabrian Spain. In *Projectile Technology*, ed. H. Knecht, pp. 241–262. New York: Plenum Press.

Rabinovich, R. and Tchernov, E. (1995). Chronological, paleoecological and taphonomical aspects of the Middle Palaeolithic site of Qafzeh, Israel. In *Archaeozoology of the Near East*, vol. 2, ed. H. Buitenhuis and H.-P. Uerpmann, pp. 5–44. Leiden: Backhuys Publishers.

Révillion, S. (1995). Technologie du débitage laminaire au Paléolithique moyen en Europe Septentrionale: état de la question. *Bulletin de la Société Préhistorique Française* **92**: 425–441.

Rigaud, J.-P. (ed.) (1989). *La Grotte Vaufrey: Paléoenvironnement, Chronologie, Activités Humaines*, Mémoires de la Société Préhistorique Française 19. Paris: Editions due CNRS.

Roebroeks, W., Kolen, J. and Rensink, E. (1988). Planning depth, anticipation, and the organisation of Middle Palaeolithic technology: the 'archaic natives' meet Eve's descendants. *Helinium* **28**: 17–34.

Ronen, A. (1984). *Sefunim Prehistoric Sites, Mount Carmel, Israel*, vol. 1, BAR International Series 230i. Oxford: British Archaeological Reports.

Rosenzweig, M. (1996). *Species Diversity in Time and Space*, 2nd imp. Cambridge: Cambridge University Press.

Rust, A. (1950). *Die Höhlenfunde von Jabrud (Syrien)*. Neumünster: Karl Wacholtz.

Schild, R. (1976). The Final Palaeolithic settlements of the European plain. *Scientific American* **234**: 88–99.

Schyle, D. (1992). *Near Eastern Upper Palaeolithic Cultural Stratigraphy*, Biehefte zum Thbinger Atlas des Vorderen Orients, Reihe B (Geisteswissenschaften) 59. Wiesbaden: Dr Ludwig Reichert.

Shea, J. (1989). A functional study of the lithic industries associated with the hominid fossils in the Kebara and Qafzeh caves, Israel. In *The Human Revolution: Behavioural and Biological Perspectives on the Origins of Modern Humans*, ed. P. Mellars and C. Stringer, pp. 598–610. Princeton: Princeton University Press.

Shea, J. (1998). A regional-scale approach to lithic evidence for hunting in the Levantine Mousterian. *Current Anthropology* **39** (Supplement): S45–S78.

Shott, M. (1986). Settlement mobility and technological organisation: an ethnographic examination. *Journal of Anthropological Research* **42**: 15–51.

Simek, J.F. and Snyder, L.M. (1988). Changing assemblage diversity in Perigord archaeofaunas. In *Upper Pleistocene Prehistory of Western Eurasia*, ed. H. Dibble and A. Montet-White, pp. 321–332. Philadelphia: University Museum Monograph 54.

Simms, S. (1987). *Behavioural Ecology and Hunter-Gatherer Foraging: An Example from the Great Basin*. BAR International Series 381. Oxford: British Archaeological Reports.

Smith, A. (1998). Intensification and transformation processes towards food production in Africa. In *Before Food Production in North Africa*, ed. S. di Lernia and G. Manzi, pp. 19–33. UISPP, XIII World Congress. Forlì: A.B.A.C.O.

Smith, E. (1988). Risk and uncertainty in the 'original affluent society': evolutionary ecology of resource-sharing and land tenure. In *Hunters and Gatheres*, vol. 1, *History, Evolution and Social Change*, ed. T. Ingold, D. Riches and J. Woodburn, pp. 222–251. New York: Berg.

Soffer, O. (1985). *The Upper Palaeolithic of the Central Russian Plain*. New York: Academic Press.

Soffer, O. (ed.) (1987). *The Pleistocene Old World: Regional Perspectives*. Plenum Press: New York.

Soffer, O. (1990). The Central Russian Plain at the Last Glacial Maximum. In *The World at 18,000 BP*, vol. 1, *High Latitudes*, ed. O. Soffer and C. Gamble, pp. 228–252. New York: Plenum Press.

Soffer, O. (1993). Upper Palaeolithic adaptations in Central and Eastern Europe and man-mammoth interactions. In *From Kostenki to Clovis: Paleoin-*

dian and Upper Paleolithic Adaptations, ed. O. Soffer and N.D. Praslov, pp. 31–49. New York: Plenum Press.

Soffer, O. and Gamble, C. (eds.). (1990). *The World at 18,000 BP*, vol. 1, *High Latitudes*. New York: Plenum Press.

Soffer, O. and Praslov, N. (eds.). (1993). *From Kostenki to Clovis: Paleoindian and Upper Palaeolithic Adaptations*. New York: Plenum Press.

Speth, J.D. and Spielmann, K.A. (1983). Energy source, protein metabolism, and hunter–gatherer subsistence strategies. *Journal of Anthropological Archaeology* **2**: 1–31.

Speth, J.D. and Tchernov, E. (1998). The role of hunting and scavenging in Neanderthal procurement strategies: new evidence from Kebara Cave (Israel). In *Neanderthals and Modern Humans in West Asia*, ed. T. Akazawa, K. Aoki and O. Bar-Yosef, pp. 223–240. New York: Plenum Press.

Spielmann, K. and Eder, J. (1994). Hunters and farmers: now and then. *Annual Review of Anthropology* **23**: 203–223.

Stahl, A. (1989). Plant-food processing: implications for dietary quality. In *Foraging and Farming: The Evolution of Plant Exploitation*, ed. D. Harris and G. Hillman, pp. 171–194. London: Unwin Hyman.

Stiner, M.C. (1990). The use of mortality patterns in archaeological studies of hominid predatory adaptations. *Journal of Anthropological Archaeology* **9**: 305–351.

Stiner, M.C. (1993). Small animal exploitation and its relation to hunting, scavenging, and gathering in the Italian Mousterian. In *Hunting and Animal Exploitation in the Later Palaeolithic and Mesolithic of Eurasia*, ed. G.L. Peterkin, H. Bricker, and P. Mellars, pp. 101–119. Archaeological Papers of the American Anthropological Association 4.

Stiner, M.C. (1994). *Honor Among Thieves: A Zooarchaeological Study of Neandertal Foraging Ecology*. Princeton: Princeton University Press.

Stiner, M.C. and Tchernov, E. (1998). Pleistocene species trends at Hayonim Cave: changes in climate versus human behaviour. In *Neanderthals and Modern Humans in West Asia*, ed. T. Akazawa, K. Aoki, and O. Bar-Yosef, pp. 241–262. New York: Plenum Press.

Stiner, M.C., Arsebuk, G. and Howell, F.C. (1996). Cave bears and Palaeolithic artefacts in Yarimburgaz Cave, Turkey: dissecting a palimpsest. *Geoarchaeology* **11**: 279–327.

Stiner, M.C., Munro, N.D., Surovell, T.A., Tchernov, E. and Bar-Yosef, O. (1999). Palaeolithic population growth pulses evidenced by small game use. *Science* **283**: 190–4.

Stiner, M.C., Munro, N.D. and Surovell, T.A. (2000). The tortoise and the hare: small game use, the Broad Spectrum Revolution and Paleolithic demography. *Current Anthropology* **41**: 39–73.

Straus, L. (1990*b*). The Last Glacial Maximum in Cantabrian Spain: the Solutrean. In *The World at 18,000 BP*, vol. 1, *High Latitudes*, ed. O. Soffer and C. Gamble, pp. 89–108. New York: Plenum Press.

Straus, L. (1993). Upper Palaeolithic hunting tactics and weapons in western Europe. In *Hunting and Animal Exploitation in the later Palaeolithic and Mesolithic of Eurasia*, ed. G.L. Peterkin, H. Bricker and P. Mellars, pp. 83–94. Archaeological Papers of the American Anthropological Association 4.

Straus, L. (1996). Continuity or rupture; convergence or invasion; adaptation or catastrophe; mosaic or monolith: views of the Middle to Upper Palaeolithic transition in Iberia. In *The Last Neandertals, The First Anatomically Modern Humans*, ed. E. Carbonell and M. Vaquero, pp. 203–218.Tarragona: Universitat Rovira I Virgili.

Straus, L. and Clark, G. (eds.) (1986). *La Riera Cave: Stone Age Hunter-Gatherer Adaptations in Northern Spain*. Anthropological Research Papers 36. Tempe: Arizona State University.

Svoboda, J. (1990). Moravia during the Upper Pleniglacia. In *The World at 18,000 BP*, vol. 1, *High Latitudes*, ed. O. Soffer and C. Gamble, pp. 193–203. New York: Plenum Press.

Svoboda, J., Ložek, V. and Vlček, E. (1996). *Hunters between East and West: The Palaeolithic of Moravia*. New York: Plenum Press.

Taborin, Y. (1993a). *La Parure en Coquillage au Paléolithique*, Supplement à Gallia Prehistoire 29. Paris: Editions du CNRS.

Taborin, Y. (1993b). Shells of the French Aurignacian and Périgordian. In *Before Lascaux: The Complex Record of the Early Upper Paleolithic*, ed. H. Knecht, A. Pike-Tay and R. White, pp. 211–228. Boca Raton: CRC Press.

Thieme, H. (1997). Lower Palaeolithic hunting spears from Germany. *Nature* **385**: 807–810.

Torrence, R. (1983). Time budgeting and hunter–gatherer technology. In *Hunter-Gatherer Economy in Prehistory: A European Perspective*, ed. G. Bailey, pp. 11–22. Cambridge: Cambridge University Press.

Torrence, R. (1989). Re-tooling: towards a behavioural theory of stone tools. In *Time, Energy and Stone Tools*, ed. R. Torrence, pp. 57–66. Cambridge: Cambridge University Press.

Tuffreau, A. (1984). Les Industries moustéeriennes et castelperroniennes de La Ferrassie. In *Le Grand Abri de la Ferrassie*, ed. H. Delporte, Études Quaternaires Mémoire 7, pp. 111–144. Paris: Editions du Laboratoire de Paléontologie Humaine et Préhistoire, Institut de Paléontologie Humaine.

Turq, A. (1996). L'Approvisionnement en matière première lithique au Moustérien et au début du Paléolithique supérieur dans le nord est du bassin Aquitain: continuité ou discontinuité? In *The Last Neandertals, The First Anatomically Modern Humans*, ed. E. Carbonell and M. Vaquero, pp. 355–362. Tarragona: Universitat Rovira I Virgili.

Van Andel, T. and Tzedakis, P. (1996). Palaeolithic landscapes of Europe and Environs, 150,000–25,000 years ago: an overview. *Quaternary Science Reviews* **115**: 481–500.

Vandermeersch, B. (1981). *Les Hommes Fossiles de Qafzeh (Israèl)*. Paris: Editions du CNRS.

Vincent, A. (1989). Remarques préliminaires concernant l'outillage osseux de la Grotte Vaufrey. In *La Grotte Vaufrey: Paléoenvironnement, Chronologie, Activités Humaines*, ed. J.-P. Rigaud, Mémoires de la Société Préhistorique Française 19, pp. 529–533. Paris: Editions du CNRS.

Wendorf, F. and Schild, R. (1990). *Prehistory of the Eastern Sahara*. New York: Academic Press.

Wengler, L. (1990). Economie des matières premières et territoires dans le Moustérien et l'Atérien maghrébiens: exemples du Maroc oriental. *l'Anthropologie* **94**: 335–360.

Weniger, G.-C. (1987). Magdalenian settlement pattern and subsistence in central Europe: the southwestern and central German cases. In *The Pleistocene Old World: Regional Perspectives*, ed. O. Soffer, pp. 201–215. New York: Plenum Press.

Weniger, G.-C. (1990). Germany at 18,000 BP In *The World at 18,000 BP*, vol. 1, *High Latitudes*, ed. O. Soffer and C. Gamble, pp. 171–192. New York: Plenum Press.

White, R. (1989). Production complexity and standardisation of early Aurignacian bead and pendent manufacture: evolutionary implications. In *The Human Revolution: Behavioural and Biological Perspectives on the Origins of Modern Humans*, ed. P. Mellars and C. Stringer, pp. 366–90. Princeton: Princeton University Press.

White, R. (1993). 'Technological and social dimensions of "Aurignacian-age" body ornaments across Europe.' In *Before Lascaux: The Complex Record of the Early Upper Paleolithic*, ed. H. Knecht, A. Pike-Tay and R. White, pp. 277–300. Boca Raton: CRC Press.

Wiessner, P. (1982). Risk, reciprocity, and social influences on !Kung San economics. In *Politics and History in Band Societies*, ed. E. Leacock and R. Lee, pp. 61–84. Cambridge: Cambridge University Press.

Wobst, H.M. (1978). The archaeo-ethnology of hunter–gatherers and the tyranny of the ethnographic record in archaeology. *American Antiquity* **43**: 303–309.

Woodburn, J. 1991. African hunter–gatherer social organisation: is it best understood as a product of encapsulation. In *Hunters and Gatherers*, vol. 1, *History, Evolution and Social Change*, ed. T. Ingold, D. Riches and J. Woodburn, pp. 31–64. New York: Berg.

Wright, K. (1994). Ground-stone tools and hunter–gatherer subsistence in southwest Asia: implications for the transition to farming. *American Antiquity* **59**: 238–263.

Zilhão, J. (1990). The Portuguese Estremadura at 18000 BP: the Solutrean. In *The World at 18,000 BP*, vol. 1, *High Latitudes*, ed. O. Soffer and C. Gamble, pp. 109–125. New York: Plenum Press.

6

Language shift and language spread among hunter–gatherers

PATRICK McCONVELL

Introduction

The last two centuries have seen an unprecedented decimation of languages around the world; many predictions forecast that this process will soon reach its culmination, leaving only a small number of languages to survive the next century. The aim of this chapter is to focus on how general principles in the study of language shift and language spread apply to the languages of hunter–gatherers in prehistory, rather than to describe present-day language endangerment, language shift and language maintenance in detail (see e.g. McConvell 1991, Robins and Uhlenbeck 1991; Grenoble and Whaley 1998).

While demographic decline and deliberate annihilation of groups speaking small languages has played its part, the primary mechanism for this loss of languages has been *language shift* – the adoption by populations of new languages and the giving up of their old languages. The new languages being adopted are in the process of *language spread* (or language expansion); in the recent era many of them are languages which were already widely used as lingua francas, and some of them are varieties of major world languages.

A disproportionate number of the populations undergoing language shift in the recent period have been hunter–gatherers. While the languages of hunter–gatherers would be, generally speaking, the most endangered of the world's languages, this is not particularly due to the nature of the languages nor to any peculiarity of the social organisation of language in hunter–gatherer groups. Rather it is the small size of language groups and their socio-economic vulnerability, compounded by the ideological low status of the hunter–gatherer lifestyle and, by association, their language (represented by dominant groups as 'old-fashioned', 'primitive', etc.), that lead to language shift (Kulick 1992). Similar processes are at work where new and old modes of production interface with each other, as for instance in modern-day Austria (Gal 1979). The picture of hunter–gatherers in modern times is one in which their languages are almost universally embattled and receding in the face of the oncoming tide of languages of farmers, pastoralists and colonising countries. Much the same picture is evident in most discussions of prehistory.

However it seems clear that not all major language spreads were led by agriculturalists and/or pastoralists. Many were in fact expansions of hunter–gatherer languages to produce widespread language families. Moreover these spreads did not always take place as initial colonisations of unoccupied or sparsely occupied areas, but across areas where other languages were already spoken, causing language shift to the newly incoming language in the resident populations.

This reconstruction of hunter–gatherer language shift and language spread is little discussed (Evans and McConvell 1998: 190) but tends to be controversial when it is. On the one hand, this is because the driving force of language spread is less clear-cut in the case of hunter–gatherers than it appears to be in the models where food production is the motor of expansion. On the other hand, various scenarios have been suggested in which the hunter–gatherer language families in question are much older than mid Holocene. These scenarios usually embody challenges to conventional wisdom in historical linguistics. Linguists are taken to task for greatly overestimating the rate of change in these families, or the classical historical linguistic model of languages diverging as they spread out is challenged, and similarities within language families are attributed to processes of convergence. Were the spreads of languages pushed back to the time of the initial colonisation of continents like Australia and the Americas, language shift would no longer need to be invoked to account for the widespread distribution of the resulting language families: the present-day language groupings have supposedly been 'in place' virtually from the time that the respective continents were occupied.

Contrary to these objections, the evidence indicates that hunter–gatherer languages did expand over wide areas during the Holocene; the expansions entailed divergence between the languages; and the languages involved were, at least in part, replacing other earlier languages by language shift. One aim of this chapter is to begin to build models of how these hunter–gatherer language spreads might have occurred. In what follows, language shift among hunter–gatherers in recent history in Africa is discussed, showing that change in mode of production and language shift do not always go hand in hand. Turning to prehistory, models are described which do postulate large-scale language expansions but link them to the spread of agriculture; and models which emphasise equilibrium and lack of dramatic language spread among hunter–gatherers. These two views can be combined in scenarios like those proposed by Robb (1993) and Nettle (1999), which, however, fail to capture the reality of hunter–gatherer language spread. A contrasting approach is that of Nichols (1992, 1998) which does not draw strong distinctions between hunter–gatherers and others, but distinguishes between the types of zones in which languages spread widely (spread zones) and those in which they do not. The final part of the chapter applies and refines Nichols's model in the context of Australian prehistory, in which hunter–gatherer languages spread widely both through migration and through language shift.

Language shift among hunter–gatherers in recent history

On all continents except Australia, hunter–gatherers lived together with farmers and/or pastoralists, often as neighbours with intertwined economies, and the general trend has been for the hunter–gatherer economies to decline over the last several millennia (see Layton, this volume). Their languages have generally lost ground correspondingly.

It would be a mistake, however, to see language shift as linked too closely with change in mode of production: Brenzinger, *et al.* (1991: 31) state that 'change in economy in itself does not induce language shift and language death'. They regard a change of economy as one of the major factors in language shift in Africa, and cite several examples of hunter–gatherer groups in Kenya which have switched to 'cattle languages' recently, as they adopted pastoralism. The shift seems often to be mediated by the intermarriage and the introduction of cattle as bridewealth: more specifically the marrying in of pastoralist women who continue to speak their language to their children (Brenzinger 1992: 299). However, some large groups of hunter–gatherers (like the Central African forest dwellers) have clearly shifted to neighbouring farmer/cattle languages without giving up their own hunter–gatherer mode of production, but rather entering into various forms of symbiosis with farmers and cattle-herders. This process of language shift among the Pygmies has been estimated to have been going on in stages for up to 5000 years (Nurse 1997: 373, citing Klieman 1996).

Conversely, other hunter–gatherers like the Waata (Brenzinger et al 1991: 31) and the Sandawe (Brenzinger 1992: 293) have gone over to farming, without shifting language. The Waata have not only changed economy but also live in small communities dispersed amid speakers of another language, normally a further factor leading to language shift. Brenzinger (1992: 293, 295) gives more weight to the adoption or rejection of new value systems than to the economy as such, and in the Waata case, while they are treated as inferior by the Giryama and polluted by the Gabbra (Kassam 1986), they are themselves proud of their own tradition and call the Giryama 'slaves'. Their maintenance of ethnic endogamy, contrasting with other groups discussed above, may be another factor in their language maintenance.

Prehistoric language shift: the agricultural expansion model

The model which takes the economy as the driving force of language replacement is also the most prominent in studies of

African prehistory, where a number of spreads are linked to the introduction of food production, and in the case of Bantu, with the beginning of the 'Iron Age'. Little corresponding effort has been dedicated to hunter–gatherer language spreads such as Khoisan, whose surviving languages are spoken by hunter–gatherers to this day, which occupied all of southern and probably eastern Africa, and the early spreads of other language phyla such as Niger–Congo which predate agriculture or pastoralism (Evans and McConvell 1998: 189).

More generally on a world scale, the agricultural-expansion model seeks to explain the spread of language families which occurred in the early to mid Holocene, before the existence of large-scale polities, by reference to a revolutionary change in mode of production which produces, in turn, expanding populations and expanding languages. The mechanism for this expansion is usually thought to be some combination of migration with social integration of the immigrants, resulting in language shift on the part of the indigenes. One model for such spread is wave-of-advance or demic diffusion, exemplified by the occupation of Europe by Neolithic farmers in the early to mid Holocene (Wijsman and Cavalli-Sforza 1984, Cavalli-Sforza 1997).

In this model, farming generates population increase, which causes some people to move short distances to new areas, where they intermarry with the indigenous population, and the cycle repeats itself. The bio-genetic result is gene flow in which the proportion of the genetic contribution of the initiators of the new mode of production is diluted the further it gets from the origin point. The newcomers' language expands as successive waves instigate language shift in the new population. Intermarriage is potentially an important factor, as in the more recent African cases above, but for all children to end up adopting the language of the parent who is a newcomer/farmer some other factor (sometimes vaguely labelled 'prestige') must be implicated.

Some writers have attempted to link the expansion of the Indo-European languages across Europe to the Neolithic revolution and spread of agriculture (Renfrew 1987). Making this fit chronologically is more troublesome, since the spread of farming precedes well-accepted dates for Proto-Indo-European and *a fortiori* of the spread of Indo-European languages through Europe (Mallory 1989). The link between the spread of agriculture and the spread of extensive language families has been proposed for all continents except Australia in some form or other, but problems beset many of the models – most commonly some form of agriculture existed before the new language arrived (e.g. Austronesian); or, in some cases (e.g. Finno-Ugric: Campbell 1997, Anttila 2001) the early phases of the expansion preceded agriculture or pastoralism.

Equilibrium approaches to linguistic prehistory

A common generalisation about hunter–gatherer and other small-scale 'tribal' societies (Weiss 1988: 142) is that

> Foci of [demic] expansion would continually ebb and flow across an area in a more or less stochastic fashion. No one focus would dominate except temporarily.

The bio-genetic result, Weiss adds, is usually one of 'patchiness'. If language accompanies demic expansion, then one would expect areas dominated by hunter–gatherers – Australia *par excellence* in recent times – to be 'patchy' in their language distribution. This is not the case, for reasons to be discussed later.

Ehret (1988) argues, in a somewhat parallel fashion, that small-scale societies throughout much of world history have been quite unstable in their language allegiances, tending to shift languages because of local perturbations of power and population. This model predicts random expansions and contractions of languages on a local scale, producing a patchwork of language families. It is undeniable that such localised shifts occur but this does not predict, in itself, any major language spreads. Most of the examples of widespread lingua francas currently in these areas are related to historical events of the recent colonial period. Lingua francas and trade languages played some role in earlier times, but they seem to be localised and relatively infrequent developments.

Dixon (1997) proposes a 'punctuated equilibrium' model, rejecting both the standard models of language divergence in historical linguistics, and the migration scenarios that frequently accompany them, as inapplicable to the great majority of linguistic prehistory on all continents, including Australia. Rather, he argues, throughout linguistic prehistory, languages and their speakers tend to remain static geographically and are affected much more by processes of contact-influenced change and convergence than by divergence. The divergence model of languages splitting and moving away from each other is applicable only to short bursts of rapid change (punctuations), such as when a region is initially colonised, according to this view. Thus, for Australia, the model pictures divergence of languages at about the time of first entry of humans (50–60 000 years ago perhaps) followed by little change except for convergence.

This model is clearly radically different from the view of most historical linguists. In the standard *Stammbaum* or 'family-tree' model, as developed in the nineteenth century and adopted in anthropology by Boas and Sapir (1916), the similarities of Pama-Nyungan languages are explained by the fact that the time-depth separating the modern languages from Proto-Pama-Nyungan is less than that separating non-Pama-Nyungan languages and Pama-Nyungan languages, taken together, from Proto-Australian. Dixon turns this on its head: because of the primacy given to convergence, greater similarity would tend to indicate *greater* time-depth of existence and contact rather than less time-depth since separation from a common ancestor.

Other writers who do not necessarily embrace the ultra-diffusionist 'punctuated equilibrium' model of Dixon nevertheless find reason to dispute the relatively 'short' time-depths attributed to some language families by linguists following models which typically locate proto-language origins in the mid Holocene, and some go on to question the basis of the methods used by standard historical linguistics (e.g. Gruhn 1997).

Apart from these radical challenges, there is a more general recognition in linguistics and anthropology, stemming largely from the advances made by sociolinguistics, that multilingualism and language contact phenomena are extremely important and should be fully integrated with historical linguistics. For most practitioners, however, this recognition does not mean abandoning the classical model of divergence but attempting to integrate linguistic separation and linguistic diffusion within a single framework, without reducing the two factors to one (Ross 1996). The fact that linguo-genetic relatedness of languages and the paths of linguistic diffusion are separate and 'orthogonal' (Nichols 1998: 228) provides a crucial source of evidence in the reconstruction of linguistic and cultural history.

It is important also not to overemphasise either migration or language shift as the means of language spread (McConvell 1996). Language spreads, among hunter–gatherers as well as others, can be driven by either mechanism or a combination of both. The important question is how to recognise the distinctive signature of each in the development of languages, the bio-genetic structure of populations and the archaeological record.

A social evolutionary approach to prehistoric language spread

Approaches to language spread among hunter–gatherers may be divided into those which see something distinctive about the way language is distributed in social and geographical space in hunter–gatherer society, *vis-à-vis* other types of society; and those which search for general principles which underpin language spread in all or most societies and which see continuity between patterns in both hunter–gatherer and other societies.

Two authors who spell out theories of the social prehistory of languages in which there is a major divide between the spread and distribution of languages among hunter–gatherers, on the one hand, and farmers/herders, on the other, are Robb (1993) and Nettle (1999). The general framework for both authors is one of social evolution in which the Neolithic revolution and its demographic effects play a strong role.

Although Robb's article (1993) relates to Europe, it proposes a more general theory of hunter–gatherer language distribution:

The low population densities of Palaeolithic and Mesolithic hunter–gatherers probably featured few language families, with each language spoken over wide regions. Although individual languages and language families expanded and contracted, the overall distribution remained constant. The onset of agriculture during the Neolithic and the later Neolithic Bronze Age could have induced the formation of languages.

In some ways the argument is similar to that of Ehret (1988) in highlighting stochastic variation and downplaying ethnicity and language loyalty in pre-Neolithic times. A difference is the role attributed to language extinction, another 'undirected' stochastic process, which, according to Robb, is the reason why widespread languages or language families are found among hunter–gatherers. Hunter–gatherer language spread is presented as essentially different from the expansion of languages following the Neolithic, in which distinct social processes supposedly drove major language spreads. Neolithic food-producer language spreads begin with the development of economically and demographically self-sufficient groups and develop into ethnogenesis and 'language formation' in which language develops as a strong marker of ethnic boundaries.

There are several difficulties with this picture. It is hard to see 'language extinction' attributed to hunter–gatherers as a very different process from language shift with an intermediate phase of bilingualism which seems to occur in all places and all eras (McConvell 1990). It is also clear that use of language as a stylistic marker or emblem of ethnic identity is found among modern hunter–gatherers and plays a strong role in communication among them, as it does among most people in all types of economy (Nettle 1999: 30). The fact that people in general, including hunter–gatherers, are commonly multilingual and use different languages to express different aspects of their identity does not detract at all from the point that language as mark of social identity is unlikely to have been a 'Neolithic' innovation. I have shown how Australian Aboriginal people code-switch between different languages to add messages about social identities to their discourse (McConvell 1988) and that this pattern occurs between traditional languages as well as between traditional languages and recently adopted English-based pidgins and creoles. It is not at all likely that this use of language as an identity marker arose only in the post-colonial situation in Australia, or only after hunter–gatherers contacted food producers on other continents.

Robb draws from recent hunter–gatherer language distributions to back up his argument. His main examples come from high-latitude hunter–gatherers in North America: Inuit and Athapaskans. There are indeed widespread languages and language families here, but it is incorrect to represent them as in any way 'typical' of hunter–gatherers in general. Even in the north of North America, there are isolates and pockets of very distantly related languages spoken by hunter–gatherers to the present, as for instance on the northwest Pacific coast; and around the world there are many examples of hunter–gatherer languages occupying quite small territories which are quite linguo-genetically distant from their neighbours. The similarity of Eskimo dialects is explained by their quite recent language spread, still extending their territory even in the last few hundred years (Fortescue 1997). As for the extreme dispersal of the Athapaskan family though the subarctic north and through the Plains to pockets in the arid southwestern United States, migration would appear to provide a better account of this distribution than some notion of an 'original' wide territory for hunter–gatherer groups.

Robb also cites the linguistic homogeneity of the bulk of Australia – i.e. the existence of the Pama-Nyungan family – as further evidence of the wide territories of languages and language families among hunter–gatherers. Yet the numerous non-Pama-Nyungan language families clustering in the north of the continent provide overwhelming contrary evidence, with deep linguo-genetic divisions, and often quite small language territories.

Nettle (1999) adopts the 'punctuated equilibrium' theory from Dixon (1997, discussed above). Apart from the first 'punctuation' of perhaps a few thousand years which occurred following the initial occupation of continents by hunter–gatherers, the second is identified as the 'Neolithic punctuation', in which major language families spread as a result of the spread of agriculture. This model thus brings together the 'equilibrium' and 'agricultural expansion' models, and denies the existence of major hunter–gatherer language spreads apart from initial colonisation.

Nettle explains the extent of language territories and the numbers of language speakers as responses to the level of ecological risk. He argues that hunter–gatherers in general are more likely to respond to ecological risk by using mobility strategies than exchange networks, and cites Australia as confirmation of this (Nettle 1999: 92–3). This means that a single hunter–gatherer language may occupy a wider territory than a farmer language in the same ecological zone, although the number of speakers may not be as great. Figures from Australia (based on disputed pre-colonial population estimates) indicate a much larger number of languages relative to population than for other 'post-Neolithic' regions of the world. Using the Australian figures (whose typicality must be open to question) leads Nettle to the conclusion that 'there would have been more language diversity in the world, certainly in relative terms, and perhaps absolutely, before the origin of agriculture' (1999: 93). The potential for difference between relative and absolute numbers here is related to the fact that he assumes, like most other writers, a much lower world population when it was populated only by hunter–gatherers (1999: 102).

This appears to be at odds with Robb's contention that Palaeolithic hunter–gatherer languages occupied much wider territories, and therefore that there would have been fewer languages. But larger language territories are also an aspect of Nettle's model, at least for those hunter–gatherers exposed to higher levels of ecological risk. When wider territories and lower populations are combined, Nettle estimates that the number of languages before the Neolithic was of the same order as today – around 6 500 (1999: 102).

According to Nettle's model (1999: 121–2), the number of linguo-genetic lineages (stocks and families) declines steadily through pre-Neolithic prehistory after the rapid increase at the time of initial colonisation of continents. Like Robb, he attributes this effect to extinction, one cause of which is that 'some groups might rise to local dominance . . . and subsume other groups' (1999: 122), but, like Robb, avoids putting this process among hunter–gatherers in the same category as 'post-Neolithic' language spread and shift, presumably by the addition of the word 'local'. The other cause of lineage extinction is said to be areal convergence. In the standard historical linguistic model, areal convergence does not lead to lineage extinction, although it may make the task of separating inheritance from diffusion arduous in some cases. Nettle's position has been influenced strongly by Dixon's (1997) controversial claim that standard historical linguistics has proved impossible in Australia, the continent of hunter–gatherers, because of long-term convergence (Nettle 1999: 9).

In the final sections of the chapter we shall consider Pama-Nyungan, a hunter–gatherer language family in Australia which does have a good tree-like structure discoverable by standard methods, and which spread not locally, but across most of a continent, much later than initial colonisation. But first let us look at an alternative theoretical framework which can account better for such phenomena than the social evolutionist approach.

A geographical approach

Johanna Nichols (1992) has written of 'spread zones' of languages, contrasting them with 'residual zones' in which language diversity accumulates and little language spread occurs. She has applied this approach to all continents and has not differentiated between hunter–gatherers and others in developing the framework. It seems to fit the dichotomous language distribution in Australia quite well: the Pama-Nyungan area, covering most of Australia, is a 'spread zone', whereas the non-Pama-Nyungan area, in about one-eighth of the continent in the central north, is a 'residual zone' of high diversity where language territories are relatively small and do not spread significantly. The actual formation processes of residual zones may include in-migration as well as development of diversity in place. It is possible that some of the diversity in Northern Australia was caused as language groups crowded into the region following the loss of extensive territory between Australia and New Guinea to the sea around 10 000–8000 BP (McConvell 1990).

What makes this a residual zone is the fact that the diversity remains in place rather than being overlaid with extensive subsequent spreads.

In a recent formulation of the concept of spread zone (Nichols 1998: 260) new proposals are advanced: (a) the notions of locus, range and trajectory, including the difference between language trajectories and loanword trajectories; (b) language shift as an important mechanism of language spreading in spread zones; (c) the dynamic of spread zones, including the accumulation of diversity at the periphery rather than near the locus.

Nichols's paper (1998) is on the 'Eurasian Spread Zone' and deals primarily with pastoralists and farmers, not with hunter–gatherers. However the general principles governing the geographical shape and process of language spreads is relevant to spread zones in general, including those involving hunter–gatherers, such as the Pama-Nyungan zone in Australia. Nichols's evolving model of spread zones is very valuable, but it is necessary to deal with issues arising from each of the above three points.

First, the notion of trajectory – the direction of language spread through a spread zone which is followed by successive spreads – is one of great relevance to the Pama-Nyungan and other hunter–gatherer spread zones. One of the ideas in Nichols's work is that we may be misguided in seeking very localised 'homelands' for proto-languages, but that within spread zones there were extensive territories in which a language was spoken, which she calls 'ranges'. In this respect, her ideas are somewhat reminiscent of those of Robb (1993) and Nettle (1999), who apply the idea of an extensive territory more specifically to hunter–gatherer languages. I would identify such 'ranges' with the initial expansions of populations and would not rule out the possibility of pinpointing a localised homeland within them.

Second, language shift may be emphasised as a mechanism because of the strong presumed association between migration and the spreads of Indo-European and other language families in historical linguistics and earlier archaeology. We are currently recovering from an anti-migrationist phase in archaeology and beginning to recognise once again migration as a reality in prehistory. It can now be more adequately theorised, although the analysis of migration among hunter–gatherers is not yet well developed (Anthony 1990).

What is worrying about Nichols's approach to language shift in spread zones is not the recognition of its role but the statement that other mechanisms are so insignificant as to be disregarded (1998: 224). As we shall see with Pama-Nyungan expansion in Australia, language spreads not only combine migration and language shift, but more significantly, one or other mechanism is dominant in different phases, and these differences yield different linguistic, archaeological and biological signatures. As the input of 'pure' language shift decreases and the input of migration across unpopulated or sparsely populated areas increases, the biological evidence becomes more significant, because migration produces sharp disjunctures in bio-genetic markers between the immigrant and earlier resident populations.

Third, the stress on accumulation of diversity on the periphery of spread zones appears to contradict Sapir's (1916) classic formulation locating the homeland where the greatest linguistic diversity is to be found, subsequently elaborated as 'migration theory' by Dyen (1956). But a contradiction only emerges when we consider languages only within the 'spread zone', in which case there may be little diversity immediately around her 'locus'. However if languages in the same linguo-genetic group *outside* the spread zone near the locus are also examined, the typical 'homeland' diversity may be found. This is important when we consider, as we will below, how a language moves out from a residual zone into a spread zone and then elongates out.

Spread zones of languages are often to be found in the more arid and less hospitable parts of continents, although this does not exhaust the list of spread zones – some sea, coastal and island routes of language spread could fall into this category, as well as the arctic and subarctic distributions of some language families. An ecological interpretation comes immediately to mind here: once in a poorly resourced zone a group would tend to be more mobile; more prone to fission and migration; and more prone to forging long-distance links, than in a more well-resourced area. Although Nettle (1999) does not recognise major hunter–gatherer language spreads, the way he uses the concept of 'ecological risk' could be adapted to account for such language spread events, rather than just to explain correlations between climate and language group size such as those noted by Birdsell (1953).

How the language originally entered the spread zone is a different question. A group from the residual zone could adapt to marginal areas, or the spread zone could come to the group, as in the case of environmental change. The type of social structures developed by people in spread zones can enable them to overcome those on the periphery of the zones, and this process of developing 'expansionist' systems would also be applicable to hunter–gatherer situations. I differ from Nichols (1998) in seeing a greater role for migration as the vehicle for moving languages through spread zones, particularly those regions which do not have the resources to support large populations. In my view, language shift comes into its own when the peoples and languages of the spread zone begin to push back into the periphery towards 'residual zones'.

Nichols sees a broad picture of improving land and water resources as we look from east to west across Central Asia. This is one of the major reasons adduced for the language spread trajectories occurring in this direction. She postulates a slow wave-of-advance by means of language shift towards better pasture or farming land, but there seems to me no reason in principle why long-distance migration or 'leap-frogging' could not have occurred also. A number of the hunter–gatherer expansions pursue marginal ecological gains along an inland corridor without necessarily seeking maximal gains in competition with dense resident populations by re-entering residual zones of higher linguistic diversity.

The Pama-Nyungan trajectory across Central Australia also moves from east to west in several successive phases. Initial movements out of the riverine or coastal zones would have been in search of an environment with a lower population density, rather than one with richer resources. Subsequently I see the trajectory as a vector between a return to a rich but highly populated peripheral area and moving to unpopulated or sparsely populated regions within the spread zone. Choices between these two options could be the basis of language splits, as in the standard cladistic model. The branch that stays in the spread zone expands more by migration than language shift: this would tend to be the more conservative, linguistically speaking. The other branch which heads into the residual zone would expand more by language shift than by migration, and would tend be more innovative because of the strong influence of the substratum – the language of the peoples of the residual zone who adopt the new language arriving from the spread zone. In the following section these ideas are illustrated from the Pama-Nyungan spread zone.

Pama-Nyungan expansion in Australia

There is strong evidence for the linguo-genetic unity of Pama-Nyungan drawn from lexical comparison and shared innovation in grammar and phonology (Evans and McConvell 1998). There is also a striking correlation between the distribution of small tool types, particularly backed blades, and the distribution of Pama-Nyungan languages. What is more, the earliest datings on these artefacts follow an east to west chronology with dates of 7000–6000 BP on the east coast and possibly older in the extreme northeast, 5000–4000 BP inland, and 3000 BP and less on the west coast (Figure 6.1). This pattern shows great similarity to east-to-west language spread patterns and tentative chronologies (McConvell 1996). It has been argued (Hiscock 1994) that the decisive advantage of such tools was to provide mobility in arid inland environments – precisely the situation of people embarking on life in the spread zone and combating a higher level of ecological risk.

There is also a correlation between Aboriginal bio-genetic markers and the linguistic Pama-Nyungan/non-Pama-Nyungan division. This pattern was evident in earlier studies of blood (Balakrishnan *et al.* 1975, Kirk 1981) and has been confirmed by more recent work using other markers (White 1997) and antibody studies (Evans and McConvell 1998). Such a pattern is consistent with language inheritance and migration playing a substantial role

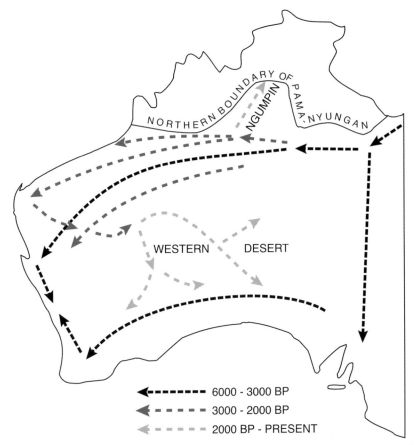

WESTERN   DESERT

◄-------- 6000 - 3000 BP
◄ - - - - - 3000 - 2000 BP
◄ - - - - - 2000 BP - PRESENT

Figure 6.1. Central and western Australia showing possible movements of Pama-Nyungan languages and their dates. (After McConvell 1996.)

in Pama-Nyungan spread, not simply language diffusion by language shift, contrary to the views of Nichols elaborated for Eurasia.

The model being developed here predicts that the bio-genetic distinctiveness of Pama-Nyungan will be greatest in the central part of of the spread zone, but will virtually disappear in some peripheral regions where the mechanism of language spread was predominantly language shift. Indeed, the central arid zone area is relatively homogeneous bio-genetically, much more so than one would expect if it had consisted of long-established isolated populations. Biological evidence has been interpreted as supporting archaeological models

of a Holocene recolonisation of large areas following partial or total
abandonment:

> It may be the case that the visible pattern of [biological] morphological
> variation presented here reflects a stable pattern that arose only
> recently and has overlaid or obliterated previous patterns. The
> increasingly well documented archaeological evidence for Holocene
> expansion of populations in the arid zone should provide a good basis
> for interpretation of the evolutionary history of arid zone peoples.
> (Pardoe 1994: 186)

Tasmania, joined to continental Sahul during the Pleistocene, was
severed 9000–6000 years ago. If the mid Holocene dates for Pama-
Nyungan expansion are correct, it occurred after the separation of
Tasmania, and one would predict that the languages of Tasmania
not to be Pama-Nyungan and to be related to the languages of
South-Eastern Australia very distantly if at all. While data on
Tasmanian languages are relatively meagre, they are sufficient to
bear out this prediction.

Biological evidence shows that Tasmanians were closer to Pleistocene inhabitants of Victoria than to any of the contemporary
Aboriginal people of South-Eastern Australia (Pardoe 1994: 185).
This would tend to support the idea that the Pama-Nyungan influx
into southeastern Australia in the early to mid Holocene was at least
partially a result of new genes entering the area via new populations
immigrating from the north. The relatively great biological diversity
found in southeastern Australia as compared with other areas may
reflect retention of a relatively greater proportion of an original
diverse population.

As well as the broad pattern of Pama-Nyungan occupation of
most of the continent, it is useful to pay attention to the various
waves of spread which occurred. In addition to moving across the
spread zone of inland Australia, languages also move into the
spread zone away from peripheral residual zone (riverine or coastal
areas) – the *upstream* phase; and also move out of the spread zone
back into the peripheral residual zone – the *downstream* phase. Peter
Sutton (1990) has written of similar fluctuations in terms of the
'pulsating heart'. Some of these movements may be triggered by

climatic fluctuations which either render the arid inland more attractive or virtually uninhabitable.

Pama-Nyungan languages spread in successive waves from the area of the Gulf of Carpentaria in North Queensland. Among the most recent of the spreads in this trajectory was that which brought the proposed Ngumpin–Yapa–Marrngu and Kartu/Wati sub-groups of Pama-Nyungan languages into northern Central Australia and Western Australia (McConvell 1996). The origin of this grouping may have been around the Queensland–Northern Territory border near the Barkly Tablelands. Subsequently the northern-most languages of this group (Eastern Ngumpin) moved further north into the territory of non-Pama-Nyungan language families out of the desert and into the riverine belt, intruding into the middle of the Mind family of languages and dividing it into two discontinuous branches. The proto-Kartu/Wati group moved much further west, and after reaching the northwest coast of Western Australia, the Western Desert branch of Kartu/Wati doubled back and spread east and then south, occupying the Western Desert.

The northward expansion of Eastern Ngumpin illustrates the more general phenomenon of 'downstream' language spread back into a residual zone primarily by means of language shift, creating a branch of a sub-group which innovates linguistically under substratum influence. The eastern Western Desert spread on the other hand is one in which language is spread primarily by migration 'upstream'. Biological evidence of the distinctiveness of the Western Desert population and a sharp bio-genetic break between this group and its eastern neighbours clearly supports this view of its spread.

The northward movement of Ngumpin may have been triggered by environmental conditions in the northern Tanami Desert about 2000 years ago, where it is likely that fairly abrupt loss of vegetation and water sources occurred. It is recorded in myth that people from the Tanami Desert arrived at the headwaters of rivers in the Victoria River District and instructed locals (speakers of non-Pama-Nyungan languages) in new ceremonies. A phase of bilingualism would have ensued, after which the population shifted to speaking the Pama-Nyungan language of the newcomers. While the modern languages which descended from this proto-language remain distinctly Pama-Nyungan in grammatical structure, they have borrowed many words from the non-Pama-Nyungan languages, especially for riverine flora and fauna. They have adapted the structure of their verbs to the two part structure found in the local non-Pama-Nyungan languages and absorbed a number of other grammatical and phonological characteristics of the northern languages. The details of this adaptation are typical effects of pervasive bilingualism, in particular pervasive code-switching (Myers-Scotton 1993).

The Western Desert expansion provides a different and contrasting case. Here, contrary to Gould's (1969) view of essential stability and continuity of the Western Desert population over the last 10 000 years, many archaeologists are now seeing a striking break in continuity between the occupation of the Desert in the Pleistocene and the occupation in the late Holocene, beginning around 3000 BP but intensifying markedly in the eastern Desert around 1500–1000 BP. Consequently the later occupation is now often referred to as a 'reoccupation' (Veth 1989, Smith 1996) with opinion leaning towards the hypothesis of near-complete abandonment of large areas for several thousand years of the early Holocene.

Linguistic evidence tends to support this scenario. The Western Desert language is indeed a single language divided into very similar dialects stretching over a vast area. The conventional opinion of historical linguistics is that such a pattern represents a shallow time depth – a spread in the last 1000 years or so would produce just such a pattern. It is not necessary to characterise such patterns as typical of hunter–gatherers, nor to construct special social or ideological features of Western Desert people stimulating linguistic convergence. It is simply that this language results from the most recent spread of Pama-Nyungan languages through this area.

The dialects around the southern and southeastern peripheries of the desert are partially losing, or have lost entirely, their system of pronominal clitics (bound pronoun elements) attached to the first word of the sentence, and have added full free pronouns instead. These are the dialects which are in touch with languages on the periphery which have no pronominal clitics. It seems likely that these changes are the result of bilingualism and code-switching –

this kind of change is predicted by the theories of Myers-Scotton (1993) and a degree of language shift may be implicated.

The field of bio-genetics also provides supportive evidence for the contention that Western Desert speakers are a new population which moved west to east across the desert in recent times. Birdsell (1993: 442) notes the particularly steep cline of a number of bio-genetic measures on the eastern edge of the desert where the Western Desert language abuts onto the Arandic languages of Central Australia, which he names the 'Aranda scarp', and attributes to a recent meeting up of populations not much more than 1000 years ago. The recent arrival of the Western Desert language along with its speakers and their western genes explains this pattern best. As well as the 'scarp' itself, the 'bow-wave' shape of the clines (e.g. of the 'Tawny Hair' gene, Birdsell 1993: 442), tapering towards the 'scarp' in the east surely captures graphically the history of a migration with gene flow accumulating with time of contact with peripheral populations.

Expansionist systems

These two examples have illustrated what may be typical cases: in the case of Eastern Ngumpin, language shift accompanying a 'downstream' phase of spread out of a spread zone; and, in the case of Western Desert expansion, migration with little or no language shift through a spread zone where population is sparse. Extensive language spreads typically involve long-distance movement through a spread zone and re-entry into the periphery by branches of the spreading sub-group of languages, as they are adopted on the edge of the residual zone. This model has been illustrated from the Pama-Nyungan language family in Australia, but has potential to explain a number of other hunter–gatherer language spreads in prehistory.

What is required is the modelling of the initial 'upstream' phase during which languages move into the spread zone and develop an extensive 'range'. A specific type of social organisation develops which not only fits the conditions of the spread zone but also allows the languages of spread zone groups to penetrate the periphery when they enter a 'downstream' phase. While 'downstream' phases involving movement of people out of the spread zone, language shift, and cultural influence from regions such as deserts are common in the recent history of Australia and other continents, the opposite phenomenon is not. It seems hard for archaeology, at its present stage in Australia for instance, to identify and track 'upstream' movements into spread zones in prehistory in a detailed fashion.

Groups moving into spread zones acquire some of the characteristics of an expansionist system, as identified in the context of nomadic pastoralists in Africa. The Nuer moved from being a subgroup of Dinka a few hundred years ago and began to expand and take over large parts of Dinka territory. A key difference in the initial conditions is the fact that the Dinka tended to stay in stationary villages whereas the proto-Nuer were more radically seasonally transhumant, assembling at large camps near the river in the dry season and scattering to more outlying cattle camps in the wet season (Newcomer 1972, Kelly 1985: 81). This conferred several advantages on the Nuer in terms of economic flexibility, mobility and political organisation, which enabled them to overtake their Dinka neighbours.

Hunter–gatherers in peripheral positions between a resource-rich area and a relatively poor area will also tend to be more mobile, both seasonally and opportunistically, than their better-favoured neighbours. This will translate into a willingness and ability to spread out further into the less-favoured area, and send out 'scouts' and outlying camps to further extend their range, while maintaining longer lines of communication and larger congregations in favourable spots at favourable times. If and when the situation demands (perhaps during a drought) groups organised in this way for the life of the less-favoured zone will also be able to 'move in on' peripheral groups in richer country and take advantage of their resources. The typical case of this involves raiding and military engagement, and this is certainly an important aspect of Nuer domination and the excursions of 'warlike' desert people into the periphery in Australia. However other advantages, both material and ideological, can supplement fighting force. In Australia this might include the ability to access very long 'dreaming tracks' or 'song lines' for ritual, or very distant trading partners, which will be seen as superior to the localized rituals and exchanges available to the more sedentary inhabitants in richer areas.

As noted in the case of language shift among hunter–gatherers in Africa in recent history, marriage systems and patterns are important mechanisms for penetration into residual zones, too. Ethnic exogamy can bring mothers who speak a prestige language and who practise asymmetrical bilingualism into a position where they ensure that their language is the primary one transmitted to their children in a new location, thus becoming agents of language spread.

Conclusions

It is often assumed that language shift is something that happens to hunter–gatherers, with the spread of languages of farmers and pastoralists, either in modern times or in prehistory. This is a common occurrence, but not the only scenario. Language shift does not always accompany a change of mode of production. In prehistory, there are many examples of hunter–gatherer languages spreading to replace other hunter–gatherer languages over extensive areas. Attempts to explain away such occurrences by overturning historical linguistic theory, or proposing that hunter–gatherer language distributions are peculiar to that type of economy, are inadequate. Most of the aspects of language shift and language spread among hunter–gatherers are amenable to treatment using general theories validated on other populations.

This chapter has focused on the theory of 'spread zones' (Nichols 1992, 1998). In particular, the characterisation of 'spread zone' fits the Pama-Nyungan language family in Australia well. Pama-Nyungan language spread also correlates with important developments in the archaeological record in the mid Holocene, and with biological differences in the human population.

Examination of different waves and phases of spread enables us to refine the 'spread zone' model. Spread of a language can result from migration through a sparsely populated belt without language shift, contrary to Nichols's (1998) model, and such 'upstream' phases of spread are linked to the development of a distinctive expansionist form of social organisation. The 'downstream' phase, in which such a language re-emerges into a more densely populated and resource-rich residual zone may be accomplished largely by language shift, on the other hand. These different phases of the process leave different signatures in linguistic change and the biological anthropology of the populations concerned, which are still apparent today.

Acknowledgements

Presentation of this paper at Durham and revision at the Institute of Social and Cultural Anthropology, University of Oxford, was carried out as part of an Australian Bicentennial Fellowship in 1999. I wish to thank Griffith University, the Robert Menzies Centre for Australian Studies, London, and the Biosocial Society for the support that made this possible. Thanks go also to Johanna Nichols, David Parkin, Bruce Connell, Lyle Campbell and participants at the Biosocial Society symposium for their advice and comments.

References

Anthony, D.W. (1990). Migration in archeology: the baby and the bathwater. *American Anthropologist* **92**: 895–914.

Anttila, R. (2001). The Indo-European and Baltic-Finnic interface: time against the ice. In *Time Depth in Historical Linguistics*, ed. C. Renfrew, A. McMahon and L. Trask (eds.) pp. 481–528. Cambridge: McDonald Institute for Archaeological Research (in press).

Balakrishnan, V., Sanghvi, L.D. and Kirk, R. (eds.) (1975). *Genetic Diversity among Australian Aborigines*. Canberra: Australian Institute of Aboriginal Studies.

Birdsell, J. (1953). Some environmental and cultural factors influencing the structuring of Australian aboriginal populations. *American Naturalist* **87**: 171–207.

Birdsell, J. (1993). *Microevolutionary Patterns in Aboriginal Australia: A Gradient Analysis of Clines*. New York: Oxford University Press.

Blench, R. and Spriggs, M. (eds.) (1998). *Archaeology and Language II*. London: Routledge.

Brenzinger, M. (1992). Patterns of language shift in East Africa. In *Language and Society in Africa: The Theory and Practice of Sociolinguistics*, ed. Robert K. Herbert, pp. 287–304. Wits: Witwatersrand University Press.

Brenzinger, M., Heine, B. and Sommer, G. (1991). Language death in Africa. In *Endangered Languages*, ed. R.H. Robins and E.M. Uhlenbeck, pp. 19–44. Oxford: Berg.

Campbell, L. (1997). On the linguistic prehistory of Finno-Ugric. In *Language History and Linguistic Modelling*, ed. R.Hickey and S.Puppuk, p. 829–61. Berlin: Mouton de Gruyter.

Cavalli-Sforza, L.L. (1997). Genetic and cultural diversity in Europe. *Journal of Anthropological Research* **53**: 383–404.

Dixon, R.M.W. (1997). *The Rise and Fall of Languages*. Cambridge: Cambridge University Press.

Dyen, I. (1956). Language distribution and migration theory. *Language* **32**: 611–636.

Ehret, C. (1988). Language change and the material correlates of language and ethnic shift. *Antiquity* **62**: 564–74.

Evans, N. and McConvell, P. (1998). The enigma of Pama-Nyungan expansion in Australia. In *Archaeology and Language*, ed. R. Blench and M. Spriggs, pp. 174–192. London: Routledge.

Fortescue, M. (1997). Dialect distribution and small group interaction in Greenlandic Eskimo. In *Archaeology and Linguistics: Australia in Global Perspective*, ed. P. McConvell and N. Evans, pp. 111–122. Melbourne: Oxford University Press.

Gal, S. (1979). *Language Shift: The Social Determinants of Language Change in Bilingual Austria*. New York: Academic Press.

Gould, R.A. (1969). *Yiwara: Foragers of the Australian Desert*. Glasgow: Collins.

Grenoble, L.A. and Whaley, L.J. (eds). (1998). *Endangered Languages: Language Loss and Community Response*. Cambridge: Cambridge University Press.

Gruhn, R. (1997) Language classification and models of the peopling of the Americas. In *Archaeology and Linguistics: Australia in Global Perspective*, ed. P. McConvell and N. Evans, pp. 99–110. Melbourne: Oxford University Press.

Hiscock, P. (1994). Technological responses to risk in Holocene Australia. *Journal of World Prehistory* **8**: 267–292.

Kassam, A. (1986). The Gabbra pastoralist/Waata hunter–gatherer symbiosis: a symbolic interpretation. *Sprache und Geschichte in Afrika* **7**: 189–204.

Kelly, R. (1983). *The Nuer Conquest: Structure and Development of an Expansionist System*. Ann Arbor: University of Michigan Press.

Kirk, R.L. (1981). *Aboriginal Man Adapting.* Melbourne: Oxford University Press.

Klieman, K. (1996). Fishers, farmers and food collectors. Unpublished PhD. thesis, University of California – Los Angeles.

Kulick, D. (1992). *Language Shift and Cultural Reproduction.* Cambridge: Cambridge University Press.

McConvell, P. (1988). Mix-im-up: Aboriginal code-switching, old and new. In *Codeswitching: Anthropological and Sociolinguistic Perspectives,* ed. Monica Heller, pp. 97–124. Berlin: Mouton de Gruyter.

McConvell, P. (1990). The linguistic prehistory of Australia: opportunities for dialogue with archaeology. *Australian Archaeology* **3**: 3–27.

McConvell, P. (1991). Understanding language shift: a step towards language maintenance. In *Language in Australia,* ed. Suzanne Romaine, pp. 143–156. Cambridge: Cambridge University Press.

McConvell, P. (1996). Backtracking to Babel: the chronology of Pama-Nyungan expansion in Australia. *Archaeology in Oceania* **31**: 125–144.

McConvell, P. and Evans, N. (eds.) (1997). *Archaeology and Linguistics: Australia in Global Perspective.* Melbourne: Oxford University Press.

Mallory, J.P. (1989). *In Search of the Indo-Europeans.* New York: Thames and Hudson.

Myers-Scotton, C. (1993). *Duelling Languages: Grammatical Structure in Codeswitching.* Oxford: Clarendon Press.

Nettle, D. (1999). *Linguistic Diversity.* Oxford: Oxford University Press.

Newcomer, P.J. (1972). The Nuer are Dinka: an essay on origins and environmental determinism. *Man* (n.s.) **7**: 5–11.

Nichols, J. (1992). *Linguistic Diversity in Space and Time.* Chicago: University of Chicago Press.

Nichols, J. (1998). The Eurasian spread zone and the Indo-European dispersal. In *Archaeology and Language,* ed. R. Blench and M. Spriggs, pp. 220–266. London: Routledge.

Nurse, D. (1997). The contributions of linguistics to the study of history in Africa. *Journal of African History* **18**: 359–392.

Pardoe, C. (1994). Bioscapes: the evolutionary landscape of Australia. *Archaeology in Oceania* **29**: 182–190.

Renfrew, C. (1987). *Archaeology and Language: The Puzzle of Indo-European Origins.* London: Jonathan Cape.

Robb, J. (1993). A social prehistory of European languages. *Antiquity* **64**: 747–791.

Robins, R.H. and Uhlenbeck, E.M. (eds.) (1991). *Endangered Languages.* Oxford: Berg.

Ross, M. (1996). Contact induced change and the comparative method: cases from Papua New Guinea. In *The Comparative Method Reviewed: Regularity and Irregularity in Language Change,* ed. M. Durie and M. Ross, pp. 180–217. Oxford: Oxford University Press.

Sapir, E. (1916). Time perspective in Aboriginal American culture. Reprinted in D. Mandelbaum (ed.) (1949). *Edward Sapir: Selected Writings in Language, Culture and Personality,* pp. 389–462. Berkeley: University of California Press.

Smith, M. (1996). Prehistoric and human ecology in Central Australia. In *Exploring Central Australia: Society, the Environment and the 1894 Horn Expedition.* ed. S.R.Morton and D.J.Mulvaney, pp. 61–73. Chipping Norton: Surrey Beatty.

Sutton, P. (1990). The Pulsating Heart: large-scale cultural and demographic processes in Aboriginal Australia. In. *Hunter–Gatherer Demography: Past and Present,* ed. Betty Meehan and Neville White, pp. 71–80. Sydney: Oceania Monographs 39.

Veth, P. (1989). Islands in the interior: a model for the colonisation of Australia's arid zone. *Archeology in Oceania* **24**: 81–91.

Weiss, K.M. (1988). In search of times past: gene flow and invasion in the generation of human diversity. In *Biological Aspects of Human Migration,* ed. C.G.N. Mascie-Taylor and G.W. Lasker, pp. 130–166. Cambridge: Cambridge University Press.

White, N. (1997). Genes, languages and landscapes in Australia. In *Archaeology and Linguistics: Australia in Global Perspective,* ed. P. McConvell and N. Evans, 45–81. Melbourne: Oxford University Press.

Wijsman, E.M. and Cavalli-Sforza, L.L. (1984). Migration and genetic population structure with special reference to humans. *Annual Review of Ecology and Systematics* **15**: 279–301.

7

Hunter–gatherer demography

RENEE PENNINGTON

Introduction

Demography is ultimately about sex, but never so much fun in its details. It describes numerically how members of populations use space, marry, reproduce and die. Since every human action depends on life and death, these seemingly mundane details are fundamental to understanding everything about our species. In these pages I focus on birth and death rates among hunter–gatherers and their relevance to human population history in the last 100 000 years or so. Despite modern concerns about overpopulation, it seems that imperceptibly slow population growth has characterised our species for many millennia. I consider the age-old question of how this occurred in light of new data and methods of analysis.

In this paper, I do not consider the biology or behaviour under-lying the rates reported or the earlier literature addressing my question as they recently have been reviewed elsewhere. In parti-cular Ellison *et al.* (1993), Ellison (1995), Wood (1994*b*), Bentley (1985), Vitzthum (1994) and Panter-Brick and Pollard (1999) con-sider the effects of activity levels, age, and breastfeeding patterns on ovarian function, while Wood (1994*a*) details the biology of human reproduction in general. Regarding variation in demographic rates among groups by subsistence pattern, see Hewlett (1991), Cohen (1989), Bentley *et al.* (1993), Campbell and Wood (1988) and Sellen and Mace (1997, 1999). The relevance of infanticide to human evolution is examined by Daly and Wilson (1984) and Hill and Ball (1996). The problem of population regulation addressed here, dating at least to the time of Malthus, has been reviewed by Wood

(1998) and Howell (1986). Applications of biodemographic models to the life history patterns of humans and other primates are found in Gage (1998).

My goal is to illustrate what is known about hunter–gatherer demography based on reported birth and death rates and what can be inferred from them about the past. My question is not new, and to some extent neither is my approach (cf. Weiss 1973). However, the puzzle of how we remained small in number in our history persists (Wood 1998), and I point to new directions of inquiry regarding demographic constraints on our species.

The big picture

Three decades ago there was a great deal of interest in anthropology concerning the mechanisms of human population regulation (cf. Birdsell 1968, Polgar 1970, Hayden 1972, Hassan 1973, Dumond 1974, Ward and Weiss 1976, Zubrow 1976). Even a small founding population of a few thousand near the origin of modern humans 100 000 years ago, increasing by just 0.015% per year, could produce the nearly 6 billion people on earth today. It would take more than 5 000 years for a population with this growth rate to double in size. A small community of 500 hunter–gatherers would require more than a decade to increase by just one soul.

Table 7.1 lists estimates of population at several points in history and the average growth rates implied by the population sizes between points. Much of the world population is the product of rapid growth in historical times, particularly since World War II (Cohen 1995). The estimates for 1998, 1950, and 1900, from the United Nations (1966, 2000), imply that annual growth rates in the last 50 years have averaged nearly 2% per year, about 30% higher than during the first 50 years of the twentieth century. As we go further back in time estimates are hardly better than educated guesses. For size at the beginning of the Neolithic, the time of the earliest plant and animal domestication, I supply the figure of 5 million people compiled by Cohen (1995) from his review of several sources.

Table 7.1. *Estimated size of population and implied exponential growth rates*

Date	Size[a]	Growth rate between dates[b]				
		1998	1950	1900	10 000 BC	100 000 BC
1998	5 901 000 000	—				
1950	2 521 000 000	0.01772	—			
1900	1 650 000 000	0.01300	0.00848	—		
10 000 BC	5 000 000	0.00071	0.00063	0.00059	—	
100 000 BC	4 000	0.00014	0.00013	0.00013	0.00008	—

[a] See text for sources.

[b] Growth rate computed from $N_0 e^{rt} = N_t$, where N_0 is the initial population size, e is the base of the natural logarithm, r is the growth rate, t is unit of time, and N_t is population size at time t.

The most widely cited source is Deevey (1960), who argues that our numbers have been increasing in a logarithmic, staircase fashion – growth is rather slow and steady until the advent of agriculture about 10 000 years ago, stepping again about 300 years ago as a result of the scientific–industrial revolution. He derives estimates of size from population densities of known groups, and by extrapolating these densities to human land-use patterns he estimates that there were 0.125 million people 1 million years ago, 1 million people 300 000 years ago, and 5.32 million people 10 000 years ago. These estimates imply an annual average growth rate of less than 0.004%. Other authors have made similar speculations (see Cohen 1995). Most agree that there were 2 or 3 million of us 100 000 years ago, and several more million at the origin of agriculture.

In contrast, recent interpretations of genetic data, summarised by Harpending *et al.* (1998), suggest that there has been just one major human population expansion. They date the time of the expansion to 50 000 to 100 000 years ago. These authors report that genetic differences in modern humans at a number of loci imply an effective population size of about 10 000. Effective size is the number of breeding adults in a population, roughly half the census size. The small effective size and pattern of genetic differences among humans indicate a large expansion in the distant past. The dates of the expansion (50 000 to 100 000 years ago) are based on estimates of mitochondrial DNA (mtDNA) mutation rates, which are not well known, and should be taken as uncertain. Their estimate of effective size averages over the span so that the number of breeding adults prior to the expansion was even fewer.

The genetic signatures of population expansion first identified in mtDNA have subsequently been identified in Y-chromosome genes, *Alu* insertions, and an increasing number of microsatellite loci (see sources in Harpending *et al.* 1998). Other markers, such as part of the beta-globin gene studied by Harding and colleagues (see Harpending *et al.* 1998), indicate that the effective population size of humans was about 10 000 during the last million years.

The historical and genetic information both indicate that there were very few of us for most of our history. If the interpretation of the genetic data is correct, the effective size of our species has been on the order of 10 000 for the last million years. The precise timing and scale of the large expansion of humanity recorded in our genes 50 000 to 100 000 years ago is not known. The genetic data suggest that a several-fold expansion of humanity occurred over several thousand years from a few thousand individuals. However, if the pattern of past growth was slow and steady, a population of a few thousand growing at about 0.008% per year in the 90 000 years prior to the advent of agriculture could produce the 6 billion people on earth today.

Given what we know about our reproductive capacity and survival under the worst conditions, it is puzzling that there were so few of us for so much of our history. Below I review such data in modern hunter–gatherers and suggest possible reasons for this apparent paradox.

Fertility

Age-pattern of fertility

The age-specific fertility rate (ASFR; see glossary) of women is their expected number of births at each age of the reproductive span.

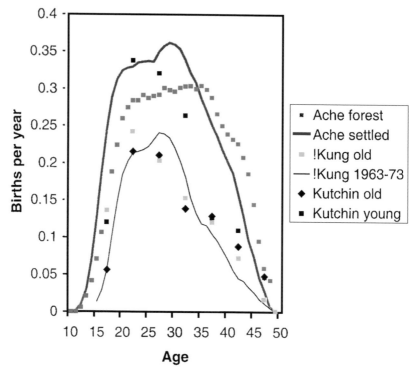

Figure 7.1. Hunter–gatherer age-specific fertility rates; Ache of Paraguay, !Kung of Botswana, and Kutchin of North America. The !Kung rates for 1963–73 and both Ache rates were reported by year. I smoothed them using 5-year running averages and resmoothed them with 3-year running averages to dampen noise caused by stochastic variation. The data for the Kutchin and older !Kung women were smoothed using traditonal 5-year age classes by Roth (1981) and Howell (1979). Either method of smoothing results in a similar pattern of fertility across the reproductive span. However, the customary practice of smoothing using 5-year-age classes removes much more of the intrinsic pattern of age variation.

Unlike other measures of fertility, such as the crude birth rate, the ASFR is not affected by age structure so meaningful comparisons between groups can be made.

In non-contracepting populations that do not attempt to limit family size, the age-pattern of fertility is remarkably consistent. Figure 7.1 is a plot of age-specific fertility rates for three nomadic hunter–gatherer populations before and after they adopted more sedentary lifestyles. The Ache began settling on reservations in the second half of this century (Hill and Hurtado 1996), the !Kung associated themselves with sedentary Bantu cattle people at increasing rates from the 1950s (Howell 1979), and the Kutchin became settled in towns in the early 1900s (Roth 1981).

Both groups of Kutchin and the older !Kung women show the typical human age-pattern of marital fertility. Rates increase from the teens, peaking in the late 20s, and decline to zero by age 50. The rates for these populations all have the same general shape but vary in the overall level of fertility at each age. Both settled and forest Ache differ from this characteristic pattern; their risk of birth is highest in the early 30s and declines more slowly. Whether this deviation is due to delayed sexual maturity, error in age estimation, stochastic variation, or some unspecified factor has not been determined. The reproductive rates for older !Kung women also peak later but the ages of some women in the sample may have been overestimated (see Pennington and Harpending 1993).

Hunter–gatherer fertility

Table 7.2 lists the total fertility rate (TFR; see glossary) of most of the hunter–gatherer populations for which this type of data is available on minimally large samples of people still living as hunter–gatherers. The TFR is the sum of the ASFR and reflects the average number of births a woman will bear if she survives the entire reproductive span. Only studies which reported sample size and data collection methods are included. The cohort TFRs in the table are the average number of births to post-reproductive women. The age ending the reproductive period is usually taken to be 50, when most women are menopausal. Where data were sparse, age 40 was used as the end of the reproductive span since few births occur among women older than 40 in most populations. The period TFRs are usually estimated from a cross-sectional sample of women of all ages during the defined years. These data are subject to various types of reporting and estimation errors. The most serious of these is probably the tendency for women everywhere to omit deceased children when reporting birth histories. Consequently the overall

Table 7.2. *Hunter-gatherer total fertility rates*

Group	Location	Date	Number of women	Number of births	Person-years	TFR[a]	Source
Africa							
Hadza	Tanzania	1966–7	12	100		5.9, 6.2[b]	Dyson 1977
Hadza	Tanzania	1980s ff.	36			5.5, 6.4[c]	Blurton Jones pers. comm.
Aka Pygmy	Central African Republic	1974–84	34			6.2	Hewlett 1988
Mbuti Pygmy	Zaïre	1971	9	45		5.0	Cavalli-Sforza 1986
Efe Pygmy	Zaïre	1980–	89	228		2.6	Bailey and Aunger 1995
!Kung	Botswana	1968	62	291		4.7	Howell 1979
!Kung	Botswana	1968	82			4.1	Harpending and Wandsnider 1982
Asia							
Birhor	India	1961–2	10	55		5.5	Williams 1974
Chenchu	India	1977, 1981	53	305		5.8	Sirajuddin 1984
Pahira	India	1963–4	36	228		6.3	Basu 1969
Australasia							
Sanio	New Guinea	1966–7	25	132		5.3	Townsend 1971
Asmat	Papua New Guinea	1973–4	71			6.9	Van Arsdale 1978
Au	Papua New Guinea	1988	21			6.1	Tracer 1991
Agta	Philippine	1980–2	26			6.5	Goodman *et al.* 1985
Agta	Philippine	1950–64		149		7.0	Early and Headland 1998
Batak	Philippine	1980–1	71	280		3.9	Eder 1987

Group	Location	Period/Year				TFR[a]	Reference
Pitjandjara	Australia	1966–7	19			4.1	Yengoyan 1970
Tiwi	Australia	1952–6		152		4.6[c]	Jones 1963
North America							
Nunamiut	Yukon	1950–70		139	699	6.4[c]	Binford and Chasko 1976
Kutchin	Yukon	1900	39	171		4.4	Roth 1981
South America							
Ache	Paraguay	born <1959	167	587	3309	8.0[c]	Hill and Hurtado 1996
Ayoreo	Paraguay/Bolivia	1968–75	55			6.2	Perez Diez and Salzano 1978
Macá	Paraguay	1965	51	182		3.6	Salzano *et al.* 1970
Cuiva (Hiwi)	Venezuela	1985	16			5.1	Hurtado and Hill 1987
Cayapo	Brazil	1965	49	192		3.9	Salzano 1971
Xavante	Brazil	1963–4	35			5.7	Salzano *et al.* 1967
Cashinahua	Peru	1966	24	125		5.2	Johnston and Kensinger 1971

[a] Cohort total fertility rate unless noted.
[b] Corrected TFR (see text).
[c] Period total fertility rate.

rate of reproduction is, if anything, most likely underestimated in these data.

Virtually all hunter–gatherers, at least those for whom we have demographic data, are involved economically in one way or another with non-foraging peoples. I included information from any study from which it could be determined that the group was still largely subsisting on foraged food either when the data were collected or when the women were reproducing. For example, the !Kung TFR reported by Howell (1979) is based on birth histories of post-reproductive women collected in 1963–73 when some !Kung were somewhat dependent on cultivated foods. Most of these women lived their reproductive years as foragers many years before. I included information about some forager–horticulturalists such as the Au (Tracer 1991) if their economy appeared primarily driven by foraging activities. I omitted groups like the Yanamamo and the Gainj whose main diet and way of life appeared to be based on cultivated crops. I could not assess the degree to which Tiwi still hunted and gathered. Although they were settling on reservations at increasing rates throughout the twentieth century, many Tiwi returned to the bush frequently. Because they represent the only complete demographic study from Australia I include them here.

There are multiple entries in the table for some groups reported by different authors or for different periods. For the Hadza, the rate reported by Dyson (1977) is based on only 12 women, but he adjusted this rate upward after fitting other demographic data to model life tables. Blurton Jones (personal communication) believes that women have more births than they reported to him, so Dyson's upward adjustment of his estimate is justified (Blurton Jones et al. 1992). The cohort TFR from Blurton Jones's Hadza work is probably biased by underreporting of children (Blurton Jones, personal communication); the period TFR is his estimate based on interviews conducted in 1992. The higher TFR reported by Howell (1979) compared to Harpending and Wandsnider (1982) is probably due to Howell's apparent omission of women with no births (Harpending and Wandsnider 1982).

Binford and Chasko (1976) reported Nunamiut fertility rates for three periods. They believed that rates increased when this group initially became sedentary and then declined as women began using contraceptives. Because these rates were based on fertility histories of a small number of women, I used the average of all three in Table 7.2 to give greater weight to the sample.

The TFRs in this sample of hunter–gatherers range from 2.6 to 8.0. The highest birth rate occurs among the Ache women of Paraguay in South America who have an average of 8 live births. Post-reproductive Efe Pygmy women in Zaïre give birth to only 2.6 children in their lifetimes. Most of the rates centre around 6, which is typical of women in any traditional society (Campbell and Wood 1988). Although it is widely believed that hunter–gatherers have lower fertility than groups with other subsistence economies, differences caused by subsistence economy cannot account for the wide variation evident in this table. Mode of subsistence is just one of many variables affecting reproductive output, and I show below that its effect, if any, is swamped by other factors.

Sedentarisation

Table 7.3 lists TFRs for five groups in Table 7.2 who became settled. The birth rates of the Agta, Kutchin, and Ache increased after they became sedentary. The Tiwi birth rate also increased as they become increasingly settled during the study period, although the increase is not statistically significant (Jones 1963). The TFR for all Aborigines in the Northern Territory of Australia, within which the Tiwi reside, was 4.2. It appears that partially settled Tiwi had higher fertility than other Aborigines in this region. The !Kung birth rate declined (Howell 1979) or remained steady (Harpending and Wandsnider 1982). A higher birth rate was also reported by Binford and Chasko (1976) coincident with settlement of the Nunamiut caribou hunters (see above), but the number of women in the study was small. The Agta differences may also be due to stochastic variation, although this study included many more women than Binford and Chasko's.

At first glance the data in Table 7.3 appear to support the widely held belief that hunter–gatherers have lower fertility than their sedentary counterparts due to the constraints of foraging. The

Table 7.3. *Fertility in transitional hunter–gatherers*

Group	Lifestyle	Date	Number of women	Number of births	Person–years	TFR[a]	Source
Botswana							
!Kung	Nomadic	1968	62	291		4.7	Howell 1979
!Kung	Sedentary	1963–73	166	179	1434	4.3[b]	Howell 1979
!Kung	Nomadic (Ngamiland)	1968	82			4.1	Harpending and Wandsnider 1982
!Kung	Sedentary (Ghanzi)	1968	104			4.0	Harpending and Wandsnider 1982
Australia							
Tiwi	Earlier sedentary	1952–6		152		4.6[b]	Jones 1963
Tiwi	Later sedentary	1957–62		186		5.8[b]	Jones 1963
All Aborigines (Northern Territory)		1958–60		481		4.2[b,c]	Jones 1963
Philippines							
Agta	Foragers	1950–64		149		7.0[b]	Early and Headland 1998
Agta	Transition	1965–79		137		6.5[b]	Early and Headland 1998
Agta	Peasants	1980–94		169		7.6[b]	Early and Headland 1998
Yukon							
Kutchin	Nomadic	born <1900	39	171		4.4	Roth 1981
Kutchin	Sedentary	born >1900	35	231		6.6	Roth 1981
Paraguay							
Ache	Nomadic	born <1959	167	587	3309	8.0[b]	Hill and Hurtado 1996
Ache	Reservation	1977–89		291	1257	8.5	Hill and Hurtado 1996

[a] Cohort total fertility rate unless noted. [b] Period total fertility rate. [c] Adjusted from 3.7.

relaxation of these constraints is expected to lower the age of reproduction, reduce birth spacing, and increase overall fertility. However, inspection of these and other variables shows that the rise in fertility is not associated with changes in the timing of births as predicted. Instead reproductive patterns in many of the groups considered here that have low fertility are best explained by the effects of sexually transmitted diseases (STDs) such as gonorrhoea and chlamidia. STDs appear to be the cause of pathologically low levels of fertility across Africa and the Pacific in this century (cf. Caldwell and Caldwell 1983). In these subfertile areas primary sterility rates of 40% are not uncommon, and many women have only one or two births. Birth rates in these regions have increased following the introduction of antibiotics (Frank 1983). In populations apparently not affected by these diseases, primary sterility rates are about 3% and women reproduce until age 40.

Numerous causes for low fertility have been considered, but only the sterilising effects and the epidemiology of STDs like gonorrhoea and chlamidia appear consistent with the patterns observed. These diseases can permanently damage the reproductive tracts of women when they are not treated, reducing the likelihood of pregnancy. Much of the demographic data on hunter–gatherers was collected before these effects were noted by demographers (e.g. Brass *et al.* 1968) and became mainstream only much more recently. The attribution of cause must be made from patterns apparent in population level demographic data as it is difficult to attribute cause of infertility in individual women, even if it can be determined that they are cycling, and there are few such data on hunter–gatherers. Because of the epidemiology of many STDs, surveys of their frequency may not even correspond to regions of infertility (Caldwell and Caldwell 1983).

The length of the reproductive span

Table 7.4 lists a few key variables that affect TFRs for 6 groups listed in Tables 7.2 and 7.3. These statistics are from women who are past menopause. From this table it is clear that low fertility in at

Table 7.4. *Variables of fertility in hunter-gatherers*

Group	Total fertility rate	Percent sterile[a]	Age at first birth	Age at last birth	Interbirth interval, months	Source
Ache	8.0	3[b]	20	42	37.6	Hill and Hurtado 1996
Australian Aborigines	4.2	22[b]				Jones 1965
Batek	3.8	10	18	26	(28)	Eder 1987
Efe	2.6	28				Bailey and Aunger 1995
!Kung–Dobe	4.7	0	19	34	49.4	Howell 1979
!Kung–Ngamiland	4.0	8				Harpending and Wandsnider 1982
Kutchin nomads	4.4	15	23	35	41.6	Roth 1981
Kutchin settled	6.6	9	20	39	41.1	Roth 1981

[a] Primary sterility rate.
[b] From premenopausal women so the true rate may be lower.

least a few forager populations is associated with high levels of primary and early secondary sterility (see glossary).

Harpending and Wandsnider (1982) found a primary sterility rate of about 8% among the !Kung. It is zero in the Dobe area because Howell apparently excluded women with no births. Post-menopausal !Kung women had their first birth at age 19, their last birth at 34, and averaged 49 months between births. It is widely believed that the !Kung's low fertility is due to their long birth intervals. However, if more !Kung women reproduced throughout the entire reproductive span the TFR would increase to more than 6 births.

Elsewhere, I have attributed the early termination of !Kung reproductive spans to epidemics of infectious infertility intensified by the migration of Herero and other pastoralists to the region (Pennington and Harpending 1993). !Kung fertility rates declined following the migrations. Despite the perception that the !Kung fertility rate is low, from a regional perspective the !Kung birth rate was high. In the Ngamiland district of Botswana, within which the !Kung reside, the TFR of post-reproductive women was 4 (Central Statistics Office 1972). The cohort TFR of neighbouring Herero pastoralists was 2.7 (Pennington and Harpending 1993). The fertility rates in the region began to increase following the introduction of health posts in this remote region of Botswana.

Like the !Kung, the Efe Pygmies, sedentary Kutchin, Batek, and Australian Aborigines have high primary sterility rates and low total fertility rates (Table 7.4). By contrast, the Ache have a low primary sterility rate and a high total fertility rate. Bailey and Aunger (1995) have already attributed the high primary sterility rate of 28% they observed in Efe to infectious infertility. The Australian Aborigine primary sterility rate is from women aged 30, overestimating the true rate since some may still have a first birth. However, the primary sterility rate was even higher among older women, indicating that primary sterility had been declining in this population.

Unfortunately, Jones (1963) could not calculate the primary sterility rate of Tiwi women. Since they are part of the larger population of Aborigines of the Northern Territory of Australia, it seems inevitable that they were afflicted by infectious infertility as well. Historical records summarised by Jones indicate centuries of contact between Tiwi and explorers. They were periodically harvested as slaves until the late eighteenth century and in the 1920s he reports (p. 21) that Japanese pearling lugger crews 'paid well for access to Tiwi women'.

Among the Kutchin, the interbirth interval (IBI; see glossary) is the same in both cohorts so the rise in fertility rates following sedentarisation can be largely attributed to differences in primary and early secondary sterility rates. The later age at first birth among the older women contributes only slightly. The later age at first birth is consistent with the prediction that nomadic foragers have later ages at sexual maturity, but it is also consistent with the hypothesis that first births occurred later due to infectious infertility as well as stochastic variation.

The statistics in Table 7.4 for the Batek were from a sub-sample of the post-reproductive aged women Eder (1987) ascertained. These data are from a smaller group of women whose years of birth he was able to determine. Overall they had a slightly lower fertility rate than the average of all post-reproductive women. The average reproductive span of fertile women is a mere 8 years; 10% of all post-reproductive women had no live births. The Batek IBI is suspiciously low – it implies a total fertility rate of 4.6; a mean IBI of 38 months is consistent with the other parameters.

Except for the Kutchin, where there are data on two sets of post-reproductive women, it is impossible to compare directly the kind of statistics presented in Table 7.4 with similar calculations on women who have not completed reproduction. The birth histories of reproductive aged women are censored – that is, they are not completed – and estimates based on censored events will be biased. Women who have not had a first birth may have one in the future, and the last birth of fertile women may occur in the future. Because of censoring bias, estimates of the proportions having no births will be higher than the true rate because many will give birth in the future. The true age of first birth is underestimated because it cannot include birth information about the less fertile women who have a first birth at later ages. The IBI is also underestimated because data are likely to exclude more long than short IBIs. Such statistics on women with censored birth histories are often reported by authors, but they are meaningless and should be ignored unless appropriate statistic methods, such as survival analysis, are used.

If the increases in births following sedentarisation in the Kutchin and Tiwi are real (i.e. not due to stochastic variation) they are more likely caused by improved access to antibiotics and a subsequent reduction in infectious fertility than by sedentariness. The cause of the rise in the Ache is less clear. Using a logistic regression model, Hill and Hurtado (1996) report that the ASFR curves of forest and settled Ache are significantly different. They attribute the rise to better health but also raise the possibility that they may have missed more births among older women whose children died. The change in the Agta rates of a half birth may be due to stochastic variation and the higher frequency of underreported births of children born in the more distant past. If these factors can be ruled out then further analysis identifying more specific mechanisms contributing to the differences need to be identified.

There are few data useful for identifying causes of low fertility in the other populations. The remarkably low rates for the Macá (3.6) and the Cayapo (3.9) do not appear to be due to primary sterility. The low Pitjandjara TFR is unaccountably low, although they, along with the Tiwi, are likely afflicted by high infectious infertility. The TFR of 5.0 for the Mbuti pygmies is based only on nine women.

From examination of these data it appears that STDs have suppressed the TFRs of many foraging communities by several births. The increases in fertility following settlement are probably caused by improvements in infectious disease control. While differences in diet, activity levels and lactation patterns may alter fecundity (see glossary) in individual women, the broad assumption that fertility increased because of sedentarisation is not well supported by these data.

Why !Kung have long birth intervals

The !Kung Bushmen are perhaps the best studied of all foraging populations. Although I have argued that infectious infertility is

responsible for their low fertility rates, three studies indicate that
their low TFR is adaptive. The idea that 4-year birth intervals
optimise the fitness of !Kung has become entrenched, and I take
care here to examine the actual findings of these studies. The first is
Blurton Jones's 1986 backload model in which he concluded that
!Kung women with 4-year IBIs had higher reproductive success (see
glossary) than women with shorter or longer IBIs. The second is
Konner and Worthman's 1980 study in which they found suppressed reproductive function in lactating !Kung women. The third
is the report by Lee that !Kung women living on cattleposts have
higher fertility than bush-living women. I argue that Blurton Jones's
conclusions are based on a misinterpretation of the data and that
Konner and Worthman's study has been misused. Lee's claim is
subject to alternative explanations. The hypotheses proposed by
Blurton Jones and Lee therefore need to be retested.

The backload model

Bleek (1928) proposed that Bushman women had wide birth
intervals because they cannot care for more than one small child
at a time due to the constraints of foraging activities and lack of
weaning foods. Children under age 2 are carried by mothers on
foraging trips. Lee (1979) provided quantitative data supporting
the suggestion that the demands of carrying more children, the
weights of foods collected, and the distances travelled were indeed
high. Blurton Jones and Sibly (1978) developed a model that
explicitly predicted the point at which the increased cost of the
additional backload weight caused by shorter IBIs became greater
than the gain in reproductive success from larger families. Their
model showed that the weight mothers had to carry on foraging
trips increased dramatically as intervals decreased from 4 years.
From this model they predicted that 4-year IBIs produced more
surviving offspring among !Kung women than either shorter or
longer IBIs – mothers who spaced their births more than 4 years
would produce too few births while those producing more children
due to shorter IBIs would lose too many of them to pre-reproductive mortality.

This prediction was tested in a subsequent paper by Blurton Jones (1986) using data provided by Howell. He examined the probability that pairs of !Kung children born to bush-living mothers survived by IBI length. IBIs in which both children survived to age 10 are classified as 'successes' while those in which either child died before age 10 were classified as 'failures.' (Intervals in which the first child died before the second was conceived were not considered because in these cases the cause of the death cannot be attributed to another birth.) He found that short IBIs had lower success rates than longer IBIs. From the proportion of successes by IBIs, Blurton Jones inferred expected offspring yields for given IBIs. This interpretation of the survival data indicated that yield increased as IBIs increased from 2 to 4 years, then declined for IBIs of 5 years, then peaked again for IBIs of 6 years, and then declined thereafter. Because of the fit of the data to regression models, Blurton Jones concluded that IBIs of about 4 years optimise the fitness of these women, validating the backload model (Blurton Jones and Sibly 1978) and the widely held notion that !Kung are a naturally low fertility population.

In a test of Blurton Jones's model, Henry Harpending and I (in Pennington and Harpending 1988) examined actual numbers of surviving offspring in two similar samples of !Kung – nomadic post-reproductive !Kung living throughout Ngamiland district (which includes Dobe) and settled post-reproductive !Kung living on cattle ranches in Ghanzi district. Based on our own model we expected child mortality rates to increase as family sizes of women increased and that women with an excessively high number of births would have fewer surviving offspring than women with fewer births. If Blurton Jones's model was correct, we expected reproductive success to peak among women giving birth to a total of four children in their lifetime. There was no support for any of these predictions. Children born into large families survived as well as children born into small families. Consequently, the number of offspring reaching reproductive age in both populations increased as the completed family size of women increased. Our study suggested that long interbirth intervals are not adaptive.

Given these findings, what accounts for Blurton Jones's conclusions? The problem most likely lies in the way Blurton Jones calculated yield from the proportion of successes by IBIs. He assumed that the increase in survival associated with longer inter-birth intervals was primarily due to the effect of birth spacing. However, it is easy to show[1] that the proportion of successes will increase as IBI increases, even if birth spacing has no effect on child survival. This is because a child bracketing the begining of a short IBI is at risk of dying longer than a child bracketing the beginning of a long IBI. For example, if the IBI is 2 years, the first child has to survive from age 2 to age 10, but if the IBI is 4 years the child has only to survive from age 4 to age 10. Because of the shorter risk period associated with the long IBI, fewer deaths will occur, and the proportion of successes will increase as the length of the IBI increases. For this reason, the data table presented by Blurton Jones does not provide any information about the effect of IBIs on child survival. Rather, it simply confirms that !Kung children, like everyone, die as they age.

The conclusions that backload limited family sizes and that 4-year interbirth intervals are adaptive for !Kung women are untested. It is my hope that this criticism will inspire reevaluation of the backload model. It is likely that the length of IBIs is related to child survival, especially for short intervals, but the optimal length is undetermined.

[1] Let x be the length of the IBI in years so that $x \leq 10$. x is then the age of the child when his birth interval is closed by the birth of a sibling. The probability that this child survives to age 10 is the conditional probability that a child alive at age x survives to age 10 and is given by l_{10}/l_x; the probability the child closing the interval survives is simply l_{10} (see Elandt-Johnson and Johnson 1980). A 'success' requires that both these events occur and so is the product $\frac{l_{10}*l_{10}}{l_x}$. Since the probability of being alive decreases as one grows old, it is easy to see from this product that the probability of success increases as x (and therefore the IBI) increases. The proportion of successes will be highest for IBIs of 10 years when it should be equal to l_{10}. Howell (1979: 81, Table 4.1) reports survival rates of $l_5 = 0.66$ and $l_{10} = 0.61$ for !Kung children recorded in reproductive histories. From these rates the proportion of successes for 5-year IBIs should be 0.56, which is identical to Blurton Jones's figure of 0.56. For 9-year IBIs the actual success rate of 0.42 he reports is probably lower than expected since it should be very close to $l_{10} = 0.61$. Although Blurton Jones's sample is a subset of Howell's birth-history data, this latter difference indicates error in the success-rate data, most likely due to stochastic variation. The success rate of IBIs of 5 and 6 years was 100% in the data.

Lactation and suppressed fecundity

In their landmark study on !Kung Bushmen women, Konner and Worthman (1980) reported correlations between women's nursing patterns (frequent and on-demand) and suppression of reproductive function. Although the study is often cited as explaining long IBIs in !Kung, this claim overstretches its actual findings.

The study examined nursing patterns of 17 nursing women and measured levels of estradiol (E_2) and progesterone (P) hormones of 16 of these women (12 amenorrhoeic and 4 non-amenorrhoeic). The age of nurselings averaged 64 weeks, ranging from 12 to 139 weeks. This sample of !Kung women nursed about four times an hour with intervals between nursing bouts increasing with the age of the child. E_2 and P levels increased with age of child, indicating that mothers gradually resumed menstrual cycles.

Konner and Worthman did not report the ages of children by amenorrhoeic status of mothers, and the duration of lactational suppression of fertility in !Kung was not explicitly examined. At best, the study correlated nursing behaviour with about 2 years of lactational infertility. The causes of further impaired reproductive functioning and 4-year IBIs are not explained.

Fertility of nomadic vs. sedentary women

Lee (1979) presented data on interbirth intervals of !Kung women reproducing in 1963–73 and classified them by degree of dependence on bush versus cattlepost foods. He then measured mean time between births among the women who had at least one completed birth interval in 1963–73. He found that 'more nomadic' women had IBIs of 44 months compared to IBIs of 36 months among 'less nomadic' women (Lee 1979: 322, Table 11.8).

Because this comparison omitted women with censored birth intervals (i.e. those that were open at the time of the study's conclusion), it effectively excluded women with long IBIs and underestimated the true IBI of both groups. Differences in mean IBI lengths cannot be determined when censored intervals are omitted so it is unknown whether bush-living or cattlepost !Kung have different IBIs. This problem of bias was not widely recognised when Lee published his findings.

Howell (1979) performed an analysis similar to Lee's but also plotted survival curves. She classified women as either 'bush thin,' 'bush fat,' 'cattlepost thin' or 'cattlepost fat' and compared the probabilities of closing birth intervals in the months following a birth. Her plot of the birth-interval survivor curves shows that the proportions of women having had a second birth 50 months later was about the same (70%) in all four groups of women. This hints that differences, if any, between bush and cattlepost women are not large.

Re-evaluation of Lee's data using alternative statistical methods could clarify the true relationship between the length of !Kung birth intervals and subsistence pattern, but the causal direction of any link may still be questionable. While Lee expected to find higher birth rates among sedentary women due to relaxed constraints on repro-duction at the cattleposts, Howell (1979) raised the possibility that he had the cause–effect relationship backward – women with higher fertility maybe drawn to the cattleposts because it is easier to rear many children there. Both interpretations are plausible.

Survival

There is but a handful of hunter–gatherer studies in which risk of death at all ages has been calculated. I compare mortality in three of them (sexes combined) in Figure 7.2, which shows the probability l_a of surviving to each age a. By definition, l_0 – the probability of surviving to birth – is 1.0. As one ages, the probability of survival decreases so l_a always declines. Figure 7.2 shows that the settled Ache and !Kung survive at similar rates, and that there is a better than 50% chance of surviving to age 60. The survival rates of nomadic !Kung and modern Hadza are dramatically lower – only about 50% of newborns survive to age 15.

Survival data for a few key ages are given in Table 7.5 for the few hunter–gatherers for whom we have any reliable figures. The best

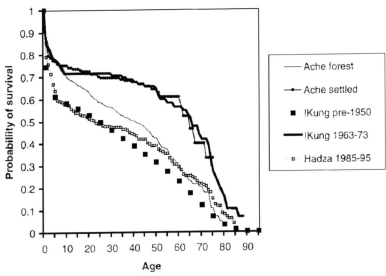

Figure 7.2. Hunter–gatherer survivor curves (sexes combined).

data come from the Ache and the Hadza because they are complemented by so much other demographically relevant information. The rates reported for the nomadic !Kung are taken from the Coale and Demeny (1983) model life table chosen by Nancy Howell (1979) to depict the mortality experience of the most traditional of !Kung. She computed a life table from reproductive histories and concluded that the Coale and Demeny West level 5 was a good fit to these rates. It must be emphasised that there was very little information in the reproductive histories about adult survival. The extrapolation from the young to the old may not be accurate. The other set of life table calculations for the Dobe !Kung were computed by Howell from deaths observed during 1963–73.

The Tiwi data are from the same study by Jones (1963) from which the fertility data were taken so they must be interpreted cautiously. It is unclear whether the rates are those of hunter–gatherers or a people experiencing rapid culture change associated with an increasingly settled reservation life. I interpret the Agta data from Early and Headland (1998) with caution as well because their computation methods were not well described. The table also includes rates from several studies reporting only on mortality during childhood.

Table 7.5. *Survival rates in hunter–gatherers*

Group	$1q_0$	$4q_1$	l_{15}	l_{50}	e_0	Adult survival	Source
Hadza (Tanzania)	0.21	0.19	0.54	0.46	33	0.85	Blurton Jones, personal communication
!Kung (Botswana)							
Nomadic (Dobe)[a]	0.26	0.18	0.56	0.31	30	0.55	Howell 1979, Pennington and Harpending 1993
Sedentary (Dobe)	0.15	0.08	0.71	0.64	50	0.90	Howell 1979, Pennington and Harpending 1993
Nomadic (Ngamiland)	0.12		0.58				Harpending and Wandsnider 1982
Sedentary (Ghanzi)	0.06		0.83				Harpending and Wandsnider 1982
Agta (Philippines)							
Forager	0.37	0.13	0.51[b]	0.21	24	0.41	Early and Headland 1998
Transition	0.24	0.23	0.54[b]	0.33	29	0.61	Early and Headland 1998
Peasant	0.27	0.34	0.42[b]	0.20	22	0.48	Early and Headland 1998
Asmat nomads (Papua New Guinea)	0.34						Van Arsdale 1978
Sanio nomads (New Guinea)		0.48					Townsend 1971

Australia (N. Territory)
Tiwi[d]

Earlier sedentary	0.08	0.08	0.80	0.64[e]		0.80	Jones 1963, 1965
Later sedentary	0.10	0.19	0.72	0.62		0.86	Jones 1963, 1965
Aborigines (mixed)[d]	0.14	0.08	0.77	0.62[d]	53	0.81	Jones 1963, 1965
Gidjingali (sedentary)	0.28	0.15					Hamilton 1981
Kutchin (Yukon)							
Nomadic	0.17	0.12	0.65				Roth 1981
Sedentary	0.09	0.07	0.83				Roth 1981
South America							
Ache (Paraguay)							
Forest	0.12	0.12	0.66	0.42	37	0.64	Hill and Hurtado 1996
Reservation	0.14	0.10	0.73	0.64	48	0.88	Hill and Hurtado 1996
Cuiva nomads (Venezuela)			0.52				Hurtado and Hill 1987

[a] From Coale and Demeny (1983) female model life table chosen by Howell (1979). Estimate of $_1q_0$ from her data is 0.22; $_4q_1 = 0.22$.

[b] Estimated this from l_{10} and l_{20}.

[c] Proportion of newborns who die by age 5 ($_5q_0$).

[d] Computed from the reported age-specific mortality rates.

[e] Proportion surviving to age 45 (l_{45}).

The best single summary of lifetime survival is e_0, the average number of years newborns live given the survival schedule. It is of course very sensitive to rates of death during infancy and early childhood but provides a feel for conditions in these groups. Among groups still foraging, the worst death rates occur among the Agta ($e_0=24$) and the best among the Ache ($e_0=37$). Proportions surviving to reproductive age – l_{15} – is a proxy for measuring parenting success. Approximately 55% of foraging !Kung, Hadza, Agta, and Cuiva children survive to age 15. About 65% of Ache and Kutchin survive to this age. The high rate of survival for Tiwi children (0.80 to 0.72) rather confirms the suspicion that they have benefited from settlement when compared with rates among children in the nearby Gidjingali. The proportion of Gidjingali children dying in the first year of life nearly exceeds the proportions of Tiwi dying during all of childhood.

Adult survival is the proportion of 15-year-olds that survive to age 50—l_{50}/l_{15}. These rates range from 0.41 (Agta) to 0.85 (Hadza). From the high proportion of survivors during the adult years it is apparent that most 15-year-olds have a better chance of surviving the next 35 years than they did getting through the first 15. This immediately contradicts a widely held notion that the prolonged human post-reproductive life span is an artefact of recent demographic changes (e.g. Olshansky *et al.* 1998). It is clear that adults living under the worst conditions (such as the Agta) have a good chance of surviving the reproductive span.

Examining changes in survival rates in populations undergoing change (Figure 7.2 and Table 7.2) suggests death rates are highly sensitive to ecological changes. With the exception of the Agta, all appear to have better survival after changes occurred. For the !Kung it is clear from infant and early childhood death rates that survival increased; the extent of change in adult survival cannot truly be assessed from Howell's data (see above). Survival among the Ache also increased substantially, largely due to improvements during adulthood. Similar improvements are evident in the Kutchin data. If the Gidjingali at all represent the rates of Australian Aborigines still living as hunter–gatherers, than the survival of Tiwi has increased by a great deal.

The Agta data indicate that things got better, then worse, when the Agta way of life changed. The differences in survival among children are large and indicate that infant mortality declined dramatically at the expense of very high early childhood mortality. As a result, many fewer children survive to reproductive age in the 'peasant' population. The differences in adult survival at later ages may be based on too few deaths to describe real differences, but, like the Ache, indicate improved adult survival.

I have suggested elsewhere (Pennington 1992, 1996) that positive improvements in child survival rates in traditional populations were due to improvements in weaning diets of children. In the case of the settled !Kung, pastoralists provided an abundance of cow's milk and fine cultivated grains. It is interesting that today's Hadza have the same poor survival prospects as the nomadic !Kung of decades past. Food is abundant among the Hadza but its quality is poor (Hawkes *et al.* 1989). If access to dairy and other high-quality weaning foods is indeed the the cause of better child survival among !Kung, similar rises in child survival should occur among Hadza in the future.

Putting it together

Throughout most of our species' history births and deaths must on a global scale have been closely balanced. If the recent interpretation of the genetic data is correct, then our population has grown an average 0.014% per year. The dramatic increase in population recorded in the signature of our genes suggests a growth rate of 0.008% per year in the 90 000 years prior to the beginning of plant and animal domestication.

The range of fertility rates of hunter–gatherers is between 2.6 and 8.0. Few data support the assumption that birth spacing is longer in nomadic hunter–gatherers than in their sedentary counterparts. Instead infectious diseases appear to be an important cause of low fertility. These diseases prematurely terminate the reproductive span of women and can increase birth spacing by reducing fecundity and increasing fetal loss. Healthy hunter–gatherer women will bear from 6 to 8 births in their lifetimes.

Table 7.6. *Simulation results[a]*

Model	e_0	l_{15}	l_{50}	Adult survival	Total fertility rate	Growth rate
Ache forest fertility						
Ache forest survival	37	0.61	0.42	0.69	8.00	0.02600
Lower survival all ages[b]	19	0.31	0.17	0.55	8.00	0.00000
Lower juvenile survival[b]	19	0.28	0.20	0.71	8.00	0.00000
Lower adult survival[b]	22	0.61	0.02	0.03	8.00	0.00000
Lower Ache fertility[c]						
Ache forest survival	37	0.61	0.42	0.69	3.70	0.00000
Lower juvenile survival[b]	24	0.40	0.24	0.60	6.00	0.00000

[a] Simulations are results of finding a population growth rate (r), maternity schedule (m_a), or survival schedule (p_a) that satisfied the equation $\int_0^\omega e^{-ra} p_a m_a \, da = 1$, where e is the base of the natural logarithm and w is the end of the life span (Coale 1972).

[b] Survival is relative to forest Ache survival schedule. The new survival schedule was generated from the Brass (1975) two-parameter method using the female forest Ache as the standard. The method takes one survival schedule (here the Ache's) and produces another by modifying the parameters. One parameter increases or decreases survival at all ages, the other shifts the relationship between juvenile and adult mortality. The two parameters can be used to generate any number of life tables that share general characteristics with the original. Other human life tables with similar expectations of life at birth produced the same results.

[c] Generated using the Coale and Trussell (1974) fertility function from fitted female forest Ache fertility rates. The method assumes a universal underlying natural fertility schedule. Its parameters capture deviations by allowing for different levels of fertility at every age in the population, different ages at marriage, and so forth. A fertility schedule with an earlier age peak slightly increases (in the fourth decimal place) the growth rate.

The expectation of life at birth in hunter–gatherers ranges between 24 and 37 years. At worst, half of all newborns die by age 15, and 4 out of 10 that survive to age 15 reach age 50. These are people living in the harshest of conditions.

These data show that our species is capable of a wide range of fertility and survival rates, and Table 7.6 gives an idea how this range effects population growth. The table lists demographic rates for the forest Ache and the results of simulations modifying their survival and fertility to levels that would produce non-growing populations. Although the simulation results are based on alterations of fertility and survival schedules unique to Ache, any human life table and set of fertility rates would produce similar results. I used the Ache data because they were reported by single year.

The first three simulations use the forest Ache ASFRs and modified forest Ache survival schedules. Compared to the Ache survival schedule, the new survival schedules (1) decrease overall survival, (2) decrease childhood survival but approximate Ache adult survival, and (3) approximate Ache childhood survival and decrease adult survival. All three produced life tables with expectations of life at birth between 19 and 22 years. To achieve the near-zero growth rate experienced by our species in the last 100 000 years or more, these life tables indicate that survival must have been much worse than anything we have observed among modern hunter–gatherers if TFRs of 8 prevailed.

Of the three life tables, the pattern of survival associated with the 22-year life expectancy seems least plausible. In it, pre-reproductive survival is about average, but virtually no adults survive the reproductive period. It is unlikely that children would continue to survive well without parents to help feed and protect them. Many palaeodemographic studies have indicated such an implausible pattern.

The fourth simulation uses the forest Ache survival rates and a modified forest Ache fertility schedule. The simulation shows that total fertility must be about 3.7 to produce a zero growth rate when populations survive like the Ache. Fertility rates as low as this are commonly observed in groups afflicted with infectious infertility. If we assume a TFR of 6 as typical of hunter–gatherers, the last simulation shows that a life table with an expectation of life of about 24 years is necessary to produce a non-growing population. Survival rates are typically higher than this in observed hunter–gatherers.

Conclusions

The best hunter–gatherer survival has been documented among the Ache, where newborns live about 37 years. The worst conditions were found among the Agta where newborns live only 24 years. The highest total fertility rates (7 to 8) are also observed in these groups. The lowest are found in populations such as the Efe (2.6) who were apparently severely affected by diseases such as gonorrhoea. Although lactational infertility has a powerful contraceptive effect, its effect lasts only about 2 years and it alone cannot account for the widely varying fertility rates observed among hunter–gatherers.

If the demographic rates evident in these data characterise hunter–gatherers past and present, the idea that we have been a slowly growing species throughout the millennium is not plausible. It seems more likely that periods of rapid growth and decline are characteristics of our species' history. The growth rate implied by the demographic rates of the forest Ache is nearly 3% per annum. A population growing at this rate doubles in size about every 25 years. The simulations confirm that the observed ranges of hunter–gatherer fertility and survival rates often produce rapidly growing populations and indicate that either we had death rates much higher than any observed or we continually experienced episodes of fertility-impairing diseases evident in the data. Since most modern hunter–gatherers live on the fringes of land-development plots or in the territory of economically more successful agricultural people, it is easy to imagine that the hunter–gatherers who once occupied these territories experienced better survival than we observe today and perhaps were capable of even higher growth rates.

These boom times were probably balanced by periods of epidemics and famine that periodically reduced survival to the worst levels (e.g. e_0 was 22 in the 'Peasant Agta'). Groups with this level of survival will begin declining as the TFR declines from 8. Since birth rates in today's hunter–gatherers are typically well below this, such poor survival is probably not typical of our species.

Inferences based on fertility rates probably provide the best information about average survival. A TFR of 6, which is typical of healthy women, implies a life table with an expectation of life at birth of about 25 years. Since the best available data implies much higher survival, this means that much lower fertility rates must have periodically plagued our species, and we have seen that such low fertility is consistently achieved through disease. I showed in the simulations that the growth rate of a population with an Ache-like survival schedule will begin declining when the TFR falls much below 4, and diseases such as gonorrhoea have the potential to reduce birth rates even more. These kinds of diseases may have episodically afflicted dispersed populations or were perhaps endemic in them. Modern theories of epidemiology now indicate that pathogens with low virulence and long infectivity periods or that use intermediate hosts may persist in small populations (Ewald 1994; Froment, this volume). Indeed sexually transmitted diseases are widespread in the animal kingdom, and, as they are in humans, may have long infectivity periods, cause low mortality, and impair fertility (Lockhart *et al.* 1996).

Many authors believe the diseases affecting fertility are too new to have greatly affected reproduction in our species history. But even using the lowest hunter–gatherer survival rates, we cannot account for low growth rates without them.

Acknowledgements

I am indebted to Nicholas Blurton Jones for kindly supplying me with unpublished Hadza demographic data. The life table estimates came from an unpublished manuscript of his and the fertility rates came from correspondence from him. I also thank Henry Harpending, Kim Hill and Nicholas Blurton Jones for extensive comments on an early draft of this manuscript. Thanks also to Catherine Panter-Brick, Elisabeth Cashdan, Jeffrey Kurland, Mark Jenike, Gillian Bentley, Kenneth Weiss, Kathryn Oths, Pauline Wiessner, and Kristen Hawkes for comments.

References

Bailey, R.C. and Aunger, R.V. (1995). Sexuality, infertility and sexually transmitted disease among farmers and foragers in Central Africa. In *Sexual Nature, Sexual Culture*, ed. P.R. Abramson and S.D. Pinkerton, pp. 195–222. Chicago: University of Chicago Press.

Basu, A. (1969). The Pahira: a population genetical study. *American Journal of Physical Anthropology* **31**: 399–416.

Bentley, G. (1985). Hunter–gatherer energetics and fertility: a reassessment of the !Kung San. *Human Ecology* **13**: 79–109.

Bentley, G.R., Goldberg, T. and Jasieńska, G. (1993). The fertility of agricultural and nonagricultural traditional societies. *Population Studies* **47**: 269–281.

Binford, L.R. and Chasko, W.J.C. Jr. (1976). Nunamiut demographic history: a provocative case, In *Demographic Anthropology: Quantitative Approaches*, ed., E.B.W. Zubrow, pp. 63–143. Albuquerque: University of New Mexico Press.

Birdsell, J.B. (1968). Some predictions for the Pleistocene based on equilibrium systems among recent hunter–gatherers. In *Man the Hunter*, ed., R.B. Lee and I. DeVore, pp. 229–240. Chicago: Aldine.

Bleek, D. (1928). *The Naron: A Bushman Tribe of the Central Kalahari*. Cambridge: Cambridge University Press.

Blurton Jones, N. (1986). Bushman birth spacing: a test for optimal interbirth intervals. *Ethology and Sociobiology* **7**: 91–105.

Blurton Jones, N. and Sibly, R. (1978). Testing adaptiveness of culturally determined behaviour: do Bushman women maximise their reproductive success by spacing births widely and foraging seldom? In *Human Behaviour and Adaptation*, ed. N. Blurton Jones and V. Reynolds, pp. 135–155. London: Taylor and Francis.

Blurton Jones, N.G., Smith, L.C., O'Connell, J.F., Hawkes, K. and Kamuzora, C. (1992). Demography of the Hadza, an increasing and high density population of savanna foragers. *American Journal of Physical Anthropology* **89**: 159–181.

Brass, W. (1975). *Methods for Estimating Fertility and Mortality from Limited and Defective Data*. Chapel Hill NC: International Program of Laboratories of Population Statistics, University of North Carolina.

Brass, W., Coale, A.J., Demeny, P., Heisel, D.F., Lorimer, F., Romaniuk, A. and van de Walle, E. (1968). *The Demography of Tropical Africa*. Princeton: Princeton University Press.

Caldwell, J. and Caldwell, P. (1983). The demographic evidence for the incidence and cause of abnormally low fertility in tropical Africa. *World Health Statistics Quarterly* **36**: 2–34.

Campbell, K.L. and Wood, J.W. (1988). Fertility in traditional societies: social and biological determinants. In *Natural Human Fertility*, ed. P. Diggory, M. Potts and S. Teper, pp. 39–69, London: Macmillan Press.

Cavalli-Sforza, L.L. (1986). Demographic data. In *African Pygmies*, ed. L.L. Cavalli-Sforza, pp. 23–44. New York: Academic Press.

Central Statistics Office (1972). *Report on the Population Census 1971*. Gaborone, Botswana.

Coale, A.J. (1972). *The Growth and Structure of Human Populations: A Mathematical Investigation*. Princeton: Princeton University Press.

Coale, A.J. and Demeny, P. (1983). *Regional Model Life Tables and Stable Populations*. New York: Academic Press.

Coale, A.J. and Trussell, T.J. (1974). Model fertility schedules: variations in the age structure of childbearing in human populations. *Population Index* **40**: 185–258.

Cohen, J.E. (1995). *How Many People Can the Earth Support?* New York: Norton.

Cohen, M.N. (1989). *Health and the Rise of Civilization*. New Haven: Yale University Press.

Daly, M. and Wilson, M. (1984). Sociobiological analysis of human infanticide. In *Infanticide: Comparative and Evolutionary Perspectives*, ed. G. Hausfater and S.B. Hrdy, pp. 487–502. New York: Aldine.

Deevey, E.S. Jr. (1960). The human population. *Scientific American* **203**: 195–204.

Dumond, D.E. (1974). The limitation of human population: a natural history. *Science* **187**: 713–721.

Dyson, T. (1977). *African Historical Demography*, Proceedings of a seminar held in the Centre of African Studies, University of Edinburgh, April, 1977.

Early, J.D. and Headland, T.N. (1998). *Population Dynamics of a Philippine Rain Forest People*. Gainesville: University Press of Florida.

Eder, J.F. (1987). *On the Road to Tribal Extinction: Depopulation, Deculturation, and Adaptive Well-Being Among the Batak of the Philippines*. Berkeley: University of California Press.

Elandt-Johnson, R.C. and Johnson, N.L. (1980). *Survival Models and Data Analysis*. New York: Wiley.

Ellison, P.T. (1995). Breastfeeding, fertility, and maternal condition. In *Breast-feeding, Biocultural Perspectives*, ed. P. Stuart-Macadam and K.A. Dettwyler, pp. 305–345. Hawthorne NY: Aldine de Gruyter.

Ellison, P.T., Panter-Brick, C., Lipson, S.F. and O'Rourke, M.T. (1993). The ecological context of human ovarian function. *Human Reproduction* **8**: 2248–2258.

Ewald, P.W. (1994). *Evolution of Infectious Disease*. Oxford: Oxford University Press.

Frank, O. (1983). Infertility in sub-Saharan Africa: estimates and implications. *Population and Development Review* **9**: 137–144.

202   RENEE PENNINGTON

Gage, T.B. (1998). The comparative demography of primates: with some comments on the evolution of life histories. *Annual Review of Anthropology* **27**: 197–221.

Goodman, M.J., Estioko-Griffin, A. and Grove, J.S. (1985). Menarche, pregnancy, birth spacing and menopause among the Agta women of northeastern Luzon, Philippines. In *The Agta of Northeastern Luzon*, ed. P.B. Griffin and A. Estioko-Griffin, pp. 147–156. Cebu City, Philippines: University of San Carlos.

Hamilton, A. (1981). *Nature and Nurture: Aboriginal Child-Rearing in North-Central Arnhem Land.* Canberra: Australian Institute of Aboriginal Studies.

Harpending, H. and Wandsnider, L. (1982). Population structures of Ghanzi and Ngamiland !Kung. In *Current Developments in Anthropological Genetics*, ed. M. Crawford and J. Mielke, pp. 29–50. New York: Plenum Press.

Harpending, H.C., Batzer, M.A., Gurven, M., Jorde, L.B., Rogers, A.R. and Sherry, S.T. (1998). Genetic traces of ancient demography. *Proceedings of the National Academy of Sciences USA* **95**: 1961–1967.

Hassan, F.A. (1973). On mechanisms of population growth during the Neolithic. *Current Anthropology* **14**: 535–542.

Hawkes, K., O'Connell, J.F. and Blurton Jones, N.G. (1989). Hardworking Hadza grandmothers. In *Comparative Socioecology, The Behavioural Ecology of Humans and Other Mammals*, ed. V. Sanden and R.A. Foley, pp. 341–366. Oxford: Blackwell Scientific Publications.

Hayden, B. (1972). Population control among hunter/gatherers. *World Archaeology* **4**: 205–221.

Hewlett, B.S. (1988). Sexual selection and paternal investment among Aka pygmies. In *Human Reproductive Behaviour, A Darwinian Perspective*, ed. L. Betzig, M. Borgerhoff Mulder and P. Turke, pp. 263–267. Cambridge: Cambridge University Press.

Hewlett, B.S. (1991). Demography and childcare in preindustrial societies. *Journal of Anthropological Research* **47**: 1–37.

Hill, C.M. and Ball, H.L. (1996). Abnormal births and other 'ill omens': the adaptive case for infanticide. *Human Nature* **7**: 381–401.

Hill, K.R. and Hurtado, A.M. (1996). *Ache Life History: The Ecology and Demography of a Foraging People.* Hawthorne NY: Aldine de Gruyter.

Howell, N. (1979). *Demography of the Dobe !Kung.* New York: Academic Press.

Howell, N. (1986). Demographic anthropology. *Annual Review of Anthropology* **15**: 219–246.

Hurtado, A.M. and Hill, K.R. (1987). Early dry season subsistence ecology of Cuiva (Hiwi) foragers of Venezuela. *Human Ecology* **15**: 163–187.

Johnston, F.E. and Kensinger, K.M. (1971). Fertility and mortality differentials and their implications for microevolutionary change among the Cashinahua. *Human Biology* **43**: 356–364.

Jones, F.L. (1963). *A Demographic Survey of the Aboriginal Population of the Northern*

Territory, with Special Reference to the Bathurst Island Mission, Occasional Papers in Aboriginal Studies 1. Canberra: Australian Institute of Aboriginal Studies.

Jones, F.L. (1965). The demography of the Australian Aborigines. *International Social Science Journal* **17**: 232–245.

Konner, M. and Worthman, C. (1980). Nursing frequency, gonadal function, and birth spacing among !Kung hunter–gatherers. *Science* **207**: 788–791.

Lee, R.B. (1979). *The !Kung San.* Cambridge: Cambridge University Press.

Lockhart, A.B., Thrall, P.H. and Antonovics, J. (1996). Sexually transmitted diseases in animals: ecological and evolutionary implications. *Biological Reviews of the Cambridge Philosophical Society* **71**: 415–471.

Olshansky, S.J., Carnes, B.A. and Grahn, D. (1998). Confronting the boundaries of human longevity. *American Scientist* **86**: 52–61.

Panter-Brick, C. and Pollard, T.M. (1999). Work and hormonal variation in subsistence and industrial contexts. In *Hormones, Health, and Behaviour: A Socioecological and Lifespan Perspective*, ed. C Panter-Brick and CM Worthman, pp. 139–183. Cambridge: Cambridge University Press.

Pennington, R. (1992). Did food increase fertility? An evaluation of !Kung and Herero history. *Human Biology* **64**: 497–521.

Pennington, R. (1996). The causes of human population growth. *American Journal of Physical Anthropology* **99**: 259–274.

Pennington, R. and Harpending, H. (1988). Fitness and fertility in Kalahari !Kung. *American Journal of Physical Anthropology* **77**: 303–319.

Pennington, R. and Harpending, H. (1993). *The Structure of an African Pastoralist Community: Demography, History, and Ecology of Ngamiland Herero*, Research Monographs on Human Population Biology. Oxford: Clarendon Press.

Perez Diez, A.A. and Salzano, F.M. (1978). Evolutionary implications of the ethnography and demography of Ayoreo Indians. *Journal of Human Evolution* **7**: 253–268.

Polgar, S. (ed.) (1970). *Culture and Population: A Collection of Current Studies.* Cambridge MA: Schenkman.

Roth, E.A. (1981). Sedentism and changing fertility patterns in a northern Athapascan isolate. *Journal of Human Evolution* **10**: 413–425.

Salzano, F.M. (1971). Demographic and genetic interrelationships among the Cayapo Indians of Brazil. *Social Biology* **18**: 148–157.

Salzano, F.M., Neel, J.V. and Maybury-Lewis, D. (1967). Further studies on the Xavante Indians. I. Demographic data on two additional villages: genetic structure of the tribe. *American Journal of Human Genetics* **19**: 463–489.

Salzano, F.M., Moreno, R., Palatnik, M. and Gershowitz, H. (1970). Demography and H-Le[a] salivary secretion of the Macá Indians of Paraguay. *American Journal of Physical Anthropology* **33**: 383–388.

Sellen, D.W. and Mace, R. (1997). Fertility and mode of subsistence: a phylogenetic analysis. *Current Anthropology* **38**: 878–889.

Sellen, D.W. and Mace, R. (1999). A phylogenetic analysis of the relationship between sub-adult mortality and mode of subsistence. *Journal of Biosocial Science* **31**: 1–16.

Sirajuddin, S.M. (1984). Reproduction and consanguinity among Chenchus of Andhra Pradesh. *Man In India* **64**: 181–192.

Townsend, P.K. (1971). New Guinea sago gatherers: a study of demography in relation to subsistence. *Ecology of Food and Nutrition* **1**: 19–24.

Tracer, D.P. (1991). Fertility-related changes in maternal body composition among the Au of Papua New Guinea. *American Journal of Physical Anthropology* **85**: 393–405.

United Nations (1966). *The Determinants and Consequences of Population Trends*, vol. 1. New York: United Nations.

United Nations (2000). *World Population Prospects: The 1998 Revision*. New York: United Nations.

Van Arsdale, P.W. (1978). Population dynamics among Asmat hunter–gatherers of New Guinea: data, methods, comparisons. *Human Ecology* **6**: 435–467.

Vitzthum, V.J. (1994). Comparative study of breastfeeding structure and its relation to human reproductive ecology. *Yearbook of Physical Anthropology* **37**: 307–349.

Ward, R.H. and Weiss, K.M. (eds.) (1976). *The Demographic Evolution of Human Populations*. New York: Academic Press.

Weiss, K.M. (1973). *Demographic Models for Anthropology*. Washington DC: Memoirs of the Society for American Archaeology 27.

Williams, B.J. (1974). *A Model of a Band Society*. Washington DC: Memoirs of the Society for American Archaeology 29.

Wood, J.W. (1994a), *Dynamics of Human Reproduction, Biology: Biology, Biometry, Demography*. Hawthorne NY: Aldine de Gruyter.

Wood, J.W. (1994b), Maternal nutrition and reproduction: why demographers and physiologists disagree about a fundamental relationship. *Annals of New York Academy of Sciences* **709**: 101–116.

Wood, J.W. (1998). A theory of preindustrical population dynamics. *Current Anthropology* **39**: 99–135.

Yengoyan, A.A. (1970). Demographic factors in Pitjandjara social organisation. In *Australian Aborigine Anthropology*, ed. R.M. Berndt, pp. 70–91. Nedlands: University of Western Australia Press.

Zubrow, E.B.W. (ed.) (1976). *Demographic Anthropology: Quantitative Approaches*. Albuquerque: University of New Mexico Press.

8

Nutritional ecology: diet, physical activity and body size

MARK R. JENIKE

Introduction

Subsistence ecology has held a central place in theories of the biological and cultural evolution of our species and played a prominent role in the proceedings of the seminal 'Man the Hunter' conference (Lee and DeVore 1968). As a result, diet and foraging behaviour have been a primary focus of hunter–gatherer studies during the past three decades. Several of the most well-used (and over-used) designations for hunter–gatherers derive from ideas about subsistence regime. These include 'Man the Hunter', 'Woman the Gatherer' (Dahlberg 1981) and the 'Original Affluent Society' (Sahlins 1972), in addition to hunter–gatherer, gatherer–hunter, and forager. With this focus on subsistence has come an interest in nutrition. Nutritional requirements shape subsistence behaviour, while nutritional adequacy is an indicator of quality of life.

Despite substantial efforts to document the characteristics of hunter–gatherer subsistence ecology and nutrition, cross-cultural and comparative research often identifies hunter–gatherers by what their diet and subsistence activities are not (e.g. Bailey *et al.* 1989), rather than by a widely accepted definition of what they are. Hunter–gatherers are *not* primarily farmers, herders, wage-earners, or exploiters of capital. In the introduction to this volume, Panter-Brick, Layton and Rowley-Conwy argue more precisely that hunter–gatherers are those who *do not* exercise direct control over the reproduction of a restricted population of a resource species in the manner of farmers and herders. These negative definitions of hunter–gatherers are necessary because of the great diversity among the peoples grouped together as hunter–gatherers, but they sometimes contribute to masking that diversity. While the archetypal hunter–gatherer subsists by foraging for wild animal and vegetable resources, many populations ethnographically described as hunter–gatherers engage in a much wider variety of subsistence activities. These include wage labour, the conscious or unconscious management of wild vegetable resources, animal husbandry, and horticulture; though it is usually assumed that these must play only a minor role in the overall subsistence regime, if a population is to be called 'hunter–gatherer'.

As with subsistence regimes, any simple and widely applicable definition of hunter–gatherer nutrition will necessarily focus on what hunter–gatherer nutrition is not, rather than on what it is, because of the enormous variability in nutrition that exists under the hunter–gatherer 'hut'. The diversity in dietary composition, energy budgets, pathogen loads and growth among the peoples grouped together as hunter–gatherers is at once a reflection of our species' successful colonisation of the very diverse terrestrial biomes available on our planet and testament to the adaptability of human nutritional physiology. This chapter will focus on that diversity, drawing on the dedicated field and laboratory research of a group of nutritionally oriented ethnographers during the past three decades. Inspired by the quantitative research on diet and activity patterns of the Dobe !Kung by Lee and colleagues and by parallel work among other animals, a generation of researchers devoted substantial time and effort to the observation of food intake and work effort. The resulting studies of the Ache, Aka, Batak, Efe, Hadza, Hiwi (Cuiva), Inuit, !Kung, Penan, Twa, and other modern hunter–gatherers have created a sizeable corpus of quantitative descriptions of hunter–gatherer nutrition. This chapter also builds upon the excellent work of others who have reviewed and synthesised the available information on diet, physical activity, health, and growth of hunter–gatherers (e.g. Lee 1968, Hayden 1981, Cohen and Armelagos 1984, Cohen 1989, Kelly 1995, Sackett 1996, Eaton *et al.* 1997).

Nutritional ecology

Nutritional ecology is defined here as the interaction of diet, somatic maintenance, physical activity, and pathogenic agents as they relate to growth, body composition, development, and function in a constraining social, political, and natural environment. Observed patterns of food intake, physical activity, growth, and health are viewed as the result of behaviourally and physiologically mediated trade-offs imposed by a constraining environment, and shaped by cultural and biological evolutionary forces (see Winterhalder and Smith 1992 for a description of the wider field of evolutionary ecology). Among the important environmental constraints on nutrition are the efficiency with which nutrients can be gathered, the level of parasitic and infectious disease, environmental seasonality, and thermoregulatory needs. When nutrients can be procured more efficiently, when fewer are lost to parasites, and when fewer are needed for thermoregulation, then the marginal costs in time and energy of additional growth, physical activity, somatic maintenance, and reproduction are reduced.

Past and present hunter–gatherers are characterised by very different nutritional ecologies. In the tropics, parasitic infection is more widespread and severe (see Froment, this volume). In arctic regions, more energy is needed for thermoregulation and for the elevated specific dynamic action of a diet high in protein (Rode and Shephard 1995). The marginal habitats in which most contemporary hunter–gatherers reside may be significantly less productive than aboriginal hunter–gatherer habitats. For all these reasons and many others, the marginal costs of growth, physical activity, somatic maintenance, and reproduction vary among populations and individuals. Because both foraging efficiency and disease have feedback relationships with population density (see Winterhalder, this volume, and Froment, this volume), changing population densities will reduce variation among populations over the long term. However, because of environmental differences some variation should remain (Winterhalder, this volume).

Diet

Though the diets of many modern hunter–gatherer populations contain substantial portions of domesticated plants and animals, this was not the case for any hunter–gatherer populations prior to 10 000 years ago in most parts of the world and probably did not describe most hunter–gatherers until quite recently. Domesticated plants and animals differ from their wild counterparts in that they are often more energy-dense because of selection for higher concentrations of fats and carbohydrates. As a consequence wild plants generally have higher concentrations of fibre, vitamins, minerals, and phytochemicals of potential nutritional significance than do their domesticated counterparts (Eaton and Konner 1985, Whitten 1999). Wild animals, in addition to being lower in fat than domesticated species also have a higher concentration of ω3 fatty acids[1] and a lower ratio of saturated to unsaturated fat in their tissue (Eaton 1992).

In a series of papers, S. Boyd Eaton and colleagues (Eaton and Konner 1985, Eaton *et al.* 1988*a*, 1996, 1997, Eaton and Eaton 1999) have developed a model hunter–gatherer diet which they argue is a valid description of the *central tendency* of Palaeolithic hunter–gatherer diets. Following work by Hayden (1981) and Lee (1968) they propose a diet of 35% animal food by weight and 65% plant food. Using these dietary proportions, an assumed energy budget of 12.56 MJ (3000 kcal)/day, and nutrient densities derived from analyses of 236 vegetable and 85 animal foods, as well as ethnographic and archaeological reports of hunter–gatherer diets, they conclude that the diet of humans during the Palaeolithic must have been relatively high in protein (>30% of energy consumed), high in fibre (~100 g/day), especially soluble fibre, and low in fat (20–25% of energy consumed), especially saturated fat (6% of

---

[1] A family of fatty acids that includes the essential fatty acid linolenic acid and that plays important roles in normal growth and development, as well as other physiological processes. They have been implicated in the prevention and treatment of heart disease, hypertension, arthritis, and cancer. ω3 fatty acids are identified chemically as those fatty acids whose first point of unsaturation is next to the third carbon atom when counting from the methyl ($CH3$) end of the carbon chain.

energy consumed), with nearly equal amounts of ω3 and ω6[2] polyunsaturated fatty acids. In addition, Palaeolithic humans would have obtained significantly higher levels of all of the major micronutrients, except sodium, than do modern Americans (Eaton *et al.* 1997). The higher micronutrient intake derives from the combination of the higher micronutrient content of wild foods and higher energy intake (corrected for body size). In the absence of energy-rich and micronutrient-poor refined foods, a high level of physical activity (and hence high food intake) leads to increased micronutrient intakes.

Eaton and colleagues effectively demonstrate that hunter–gatherer diets are unlikely to have been anything like the low fibre, high fat, high carbohydrate, high sodium and low micronutrient diets of late twentieth-century North America. However, they do not attempt to describe the diversity within known hunter–gatherer diets (though they acknowledge that this diversity exists). The few published, detailed quantitative studies of modern hunter–gatherer diet show enormous dispersion around a diet of 65% plant and 35% animal derived foods (Table 8.1). In the circumpolar regions, hunter–gatherer diets are reported to have been derived almost completely from animal sources, particularly during the period beginning in the late fall and lasting through the early spring (Draper 1976, 1977, 1978, Speth 1989, 1990). In the neotropics, Ache and Hiwi foragers also derive a majority of energy from animal sources (Hill *et al.* 1984, Hurtado and Hill 1990). In Africa, by contrast, meat seems to account for less than half of the food eaten among the !Kung (Lee 1979) and the Efe (Bailey and Peacock 1988). A consideration of less exacting (and hence less reliable) ethnographic reports compiled from the ethnographic atlas by Kelly (1995) yields even greater diversity. He reports hunter–gatherer

---

[2] A family of fatty acids that includes the essential fatty acid linoleic acid. ω6 fatty acids are identified chemically as those fatty acids whose first point of unsaturation is next to the sixth carbon atom when counting from the methyl (CH_3) end of the carbon chain. Research suggests that the ratio of ω3 to ω6 fatty acids in the diet has implications for heart disease risk, as well as inflammatory and immunological responses, though there is disagreement over which ratio is optimal (Mann and Skeaff 1998, Whitney and Rolfes 1999).

Table 8.1. *Composition of hunter–gatherer diets*

| Population | Dietary makeup (% of total) | | | Source |
	Animal products	Vegetable products and honey	Agricultural and store-bought foods	
Model Palaeolithic diet	35	65	0	Eaton *et al.* 1996
Dobe !Kung, 1964 (Namibia and Botswana)	31	69	0	Lee 1979
Ache[a] (Paraguay)	56	44	0	Hill *et al.* 1984
Hiwi (Venezuela)	68	27	5	Hurtado and Hill 1990
Efe (Congo)	9	28	64	Bailey and Peacock 1988
Ethnographic Atlas[b]	15–100	0–85		Kelly 1995

[a] Average of values for yearly quarters presented in Hill *et al.* (1984: Table III).
[b] Murdoch (1967).

diets whose 'gathered' portion (including small mammals and fish, and expressed in terms of weight, calories, or unspecified units) ranges from 0% to 85%, hunted portion from 10% to 90% and fished portion from 0% to 80%. Per capita energy consumption is also quite variable (Table 8.2).

Though most studies do not attempt to translate observations of gross dietary intake into nutrient composition, published data for macronutrient composition show substantial variation. Protein as a percentage of dietary energy exceeded Eaton *et al.*'s central tendency among those populations deriving a majority of their energy from animal products – 39% among the Ache (Hill 1988) and 44% among hunters of northwest Greenland (Krogh and Krogh 1913 as cited in Bang *et al.* 1976). In contrast, the Efe consumed only 13% of energy from protein during a 12-month period in 1981 and 1982 (Bailey and Peacock 1988) and the !Kung 16 % during July and August of 1964 (Lee 1979). There are few published reports of the fat content of actual hunter–gatherer diets, though the data with which to estimate them certainly exist. Draper (1976, 1977) reports that among arctic populations, fat content ranged between 35% and 47% of total energy (see also Bang *et al.* 1980). Fat-bearing, cold-adapted animals play a prominent role in arctic diets, whereas tropical and temperate animals can be relatively lean. Therefore, this high fat intake is unlikely to be typical of tropical or temperate hunter–gatherer diets, even if they relied substantially on animal products. In addition to lean animals, there are numerous very low or zero fat foods that play important roles in hunter–gatherer diets, including most fruits, vegetables, roots, and tubers. However, these are often consumed in combination with fat-containing items such as nuts, beans, and animal products when such are available.

Because temperature, rainfall, and therefore plant and animal productivity vary seasonally in virtually all environments inhabited by humans, hunter–gatherer diets also vary seasonally. Only a subset of those studies reporting quantitatively on the diet of hunter–gatherers include an estimate of seasonal variation (e.g. Hill *et al.* 1984, Bailey and Peacock 1988, Hurtado and Hill 1990), but seasonality is also well known from numerous qualitative or partially quantitative reports (e.g. Woodburn 1968, Wilmsen 1978, Bahuchet

Table 8.2. *Energy intake of hunter-gatherers*

Population[a]	MJ/person/day	(kcal/person/day)	Source
Anbarra (Australia)	6.69–10.46	(1600–2500)	Jones 1980, Meehan 1977
San (Botswana)	8.37–9.20	(2000–2200)	Tanaka 1980, Wilmsen 1978
Hiwi (Venezuela)	8.55	(2043)	Hurtado and Hill 1990
Mbuti (Congo)	9.54	(2280)	Ichikawa 1981
Onge (Andaman Islands)	10.96	(2620)	Sen Gupta 1980
Efe (Congo)	11.58	(2767)	Bailey and Peacock 1988
Hadza (Tanzania)	12.13–15.48	(2900–3700)	Hawkes, pers. comm.[b]
Alywara (Australia)	12.55	(3000)	O'Connell and Hawkes 1981
Ache (Paraguay)	16.01	(3827)	Hill et al 1984[c]

[a] In order of increasing intake.
[b] As cited in Cohen 1989, endnote 78, on which this table is based in part.
[c] Average of values for yearly quarters presented in Table III.

1988, Venkatesan 1993). In the tropics, insects and insect products are among the most seasonal of resources. Honey, for example, is known to comprise up to 80% of energy consumed during brief periods of superabundance, but disappears from the diet at other times (Ichikawa 1981, Hill *et al.* 1984, Bailey and Peacock 1988). Caterpillars and termites play analogous intermittently important roles in the diets of some tropical hunter–gatherers (Bahuchet 1988, Pagezy 1988). Seasonally available fruits and nuts, such as the palm fruits and oranges that can provide up to one-third of energy consumed by the Ache (Hill *et al.* 1984), also contribute to seasonality. Likewise, the roots on which the Hiwi rely for 54% of their energy during the late wet season are relatively minor constituents of the diet during the rest of the year (Hurtado and Hill 1990). Seasonal variation of plant food availability for temperate-zone hunter–gatherers may have been even more extreme, because of shortened growing seasons. Modern hunter–gatherers, such as the Efe who rely on trade for agricultural foods for a substantial portion of their diet, are affected by the seasonality of the local agricultural cycle.

Hunting and fishing conditions also change seasonally. In the tropics, fluctuating hunting conditions do not seem to translate into a pattern of pronounced seasonality of animal consumption among the Ache, Hiwi, and Efe (Hill *et al.* 1984, Bailey and Peacock 1988, Hurtado and Hill 1990), though this may have been the case for some San communities (Wilmsen 1978). However, even if animal consumption is steady through the seasons, the mix of macronutrients derived from these animal products may vary quite considerably as a result of changes in the fatness of animals. Seasonal variation in animal fat is rarely accounted for in analyses of the nutrient content of hunter–gatherer diets, though its importance is discussed (Hill *et al.* 1984). Seasonally increased fat stores in game animals can boost the energy content of meat by up to 50% and double or triple the percentage of energy derived from fat.[3] Greater efforts are needed to

---

[3] Large ungulate game animals range seasonally from a little as 1–2% body fat in the lean season to 12% or more in the fat season (Speth and Spielman 1983) translating into a significant nutrient difference for the human consumer. To illustrate this difference, consider the North American moose. At only 1.6% body fat it is the leanest animal listed in Eaton's (1992) review and provides about 12% of calories

measure the seasonal variation in the fatness of game animals and to correct for this in analyses of hunter–gatherer diet.

While those hunter–gatherer diets for which good information on seasonal variation is available seem to feature adequate or excessive protein content during all seasons, many are likely to be seasonally impoverished in dietary fats, carbohydrates, and energy because of the low availability of plant foods and the leanness of game. Seasons in which game animals are fat-poor are often also the seasons in which the reproductive, and hence nutrient-rich, parts of plants are least widely available (Hart and Hart 1986). During these seasons human foragers would have been forced to rely on carbohydrate-rich fat-poor plant storage organs or fibre-rich foliage, in combination with game for their sustenance. In temperate, subarctic, and arctic regions where even starchy plant foods may be unavailable in some seasons, diets may also have been low in carbohydrates. A diet low in both fats and carbohydrates, even if rich in high-protein animal flesh, would necessitate either exceeding tolerable upper limits for protein or subsisting on a very low-energy diet, with risk of micronutrient deficiencies (Speth 1990). Nutritional stress would be exacerbated by the elevated metabolic costs that accompany very high protein diets (Speth and Spielmann 1983). The relative absence of fat and carbohydrate to complement abundant lean meat has been proposed as an important seasonal nutritional constraint for hunter–gatherers in diverse environments (Speth and Spielmann 1983, Headland and Bailey 1991).

Seasonal variations in macronutrient availability and per capita energy consumption (Table 8.3) result in significant fluctuations of body weight. Among both the Hiwi and the Ache, the quarter of heaviest energy consumption follows immediately the quarter of lowest consumption, providing an opportunity to quickly replenish

from fat, 87% of calories from protein, and only negligible amounts of carbohydrate from corporeal glycogen stores. An average 100-g portion would contain 1.6 g of fat and 523 kJ (125 kcal). Adding 9 g of fat to this hypothetical 100-g portion would yield a 109-g portion with 10.6 g of fat (10% fat by weight). The caloric value of this added fat is approximately 339 kJ (81 kcal) yielding 862 kJ/109 g or 791 kJ/100 g, an increase of 51% over the caloric value of the lean moose. Additionally, the macronutrient mix (assuming no change in the small glycogen stores) would change from 12% fat and 87% protein to 46% fat and 53% protein.

Table 8.3. Seasonal variation in hunter–gatherer energy intake

Population	High season MJ/person/day (kcal/person/day)	Low season MJ/person/day (kcal/person/day)	% of high season	Source
Ache (Paraguay)	21.28 (5087)	11.95 (2856)	56	Hill et al 1984
Efe (Congo)	11.98 (2864)	8.86 (2117)	74	Bailey and Peacock 1988
Hadza (Tanzania)	15.48 (3700)[a]	7.95 (1900)	51	Hawkes, personal communication as cited in Cohen 1989
Hiwi (Venezuela)	11.53 (2756)	5.65 (1350)	49	Hurtado and Hill 1990

[a] High end of annual average.

body stores that may have become depleted during the season of lower food availability. In each case, the rate of consumption during the low season is only about half of the rate during the high season. Among the Efe, 64% of whose diet consists of cultivated foods, energy consumption during the lean season is 74% of the diet during the season of relative plenty and there is little variation in the energy intake during the three quarters (Jul–Mar) that are not within the hungry season.

Other hunter–gatherer populations have also been described as seasonally hungry, sometimes to the point of significant weight loss (Wilmsen 1978, Lee 1979, Eder 1987) and archaeological data are also consistent with seasonal food shortage. Though their interpretation is contested (Goodman 1994, Holland and O'Brien 1997), the widespread occurrence of Harris lines, often in combination with other skeletal indicators of nutritional stress (porotic hyperostosis, i.e. skull lesions linked to episodes of anaemia; enamel hypoplasias, i.e. growth arrest lines in tooth enamel; reduced stature) in archaeological populations is thought to be an indicator of seasonal nutrient deprivation (Sobolik 1994a,b). A substantial seasonal variation in energy intake, not unlike that experienced by farmers living on marginal lands (de Garine and Harrison 1988, Jenike 1995) or even some regular dieters in industrial societies (Prentice et al. 1991), may have been a near-universal characteristic of hunter–gatherer societies. Seasonal reductions in food availability probably resulted in periodic shortages of energy, but sufficient levels of most other micro- and macronutrients, including protein.

Widespread seasonal variation in energy intake and variation in the nutrient content of dietary items among human hunter–gatherers is reflected in our nutritional biology. Humans are extreme among mammals in the ability to store and mobilise large quantities of body fat (Prentice et al. 1996). Not surprisingly, therefore, many populations cope with seasonal fluctuations in energy availability through seasonal fluctuation in body weight and especially body fat (Lee 1979, Eder 1987, Ferro-Luzzi and Branca 1993, Jenike 1995, Panter-Brick 1995). Seasonal energy deprivation is also known to affect growth (Eveleth and Tanner 1976, Panter-Brick 1997) and physical activity (Jenike 1996, Panter-Brick 1996a,b) and there are indications of plasticity of human digestive organs in response to differing dietary composition (Milton 1987, Eaton *et al.* 1997). In addition, the efficiency with which we absorb micronutrients from the gut is known to be responsive to levels of circulating and stored nutrients, allowing for adaptive responses to temporary reductions in intake (Whitney and Rolfes 1999).

Recording age, gender, or other individual differences in dietary intake is difficult because it requires observation of individual, not aggregate, food intake for a family, camp, or community (Ulijaszek 1995). In addition, poorly fed individuals can adopt compensatory strategies that are not always apparent to the ethnographer (Bentley *et al.* 1999). Hence, there are very few reliable data with which to document age, gender, or other individual differences in dietary intake, though they undoubtedly exist (Speth 1990, Walker and Helwett 1990). Despite the formidable challenges inherent in investigating individual variation in nutrient intake, it should be a research priority because of the important role food sharing is thought to have played in human evolution (Isaac 1978, Hill 1982, Hawkes 1991, Stanford 1999), because variation in food intake among individual foragers might reflect power differentials within populations and households, and because individual variation in food intake may affect reproductive success, particularly among women.

The seasonal and cross-population variability of hunter–gatherer diets suggests that normative models of hunter–gatherer diets, whether quantitative (e.g. Eaton *et al.* 1997), or qualitative (e.g. the emphasis on either animal or plant foods implied by 'Man the Hunter' or 'Woman the Gatherer'), obscure rather than inform our understanding (Lieberman 1987, Kelly 1995). In addition, since nutritional requirements at both the population and individual level vary substantially and since hunter–gatherers have lived in widely varying environments, there is no a priori reason to believe that nutritional requirements would not also have varied substantially among hunter–gatherers in the historic and prehistoric past (Lieberman 1987, Sutton 1994). The hunter–gatherer dietary adaptation is therefore best characterised as flexible, both seasonally and over longer time spans. Energy, but not protein, is likely to have been the most significant limiting resource for most hunter–gatherer populations most of the time. For some populations, fatty-acid deficiency may also have been important during some periods of the year. As hunter–gatherers moved into harsher environments (arctic, arid deserts), the risk of seasonal hunger and starvation probably increased, even where dietary sufficiency was the rule (Cohen 1989).

Energy expenditure

As with energy intake, studies reporting direct measurement of energy expenditure among foraging populations are few (see Sackett 1996). Only Godin and Shephard (Godin and Shephard 1974, Shephard and Godin 1976) attempted a comprehensive and direct measurement of total daily energy expenditure (TDEE) of hunter–gatherers. Their study used respirometry and heart-rate monitoring to measure the energetic costs of activity among Igloolik Inuit as a part of the human adaptability studies of the International Biological Programme. The estimated mean daily energy expenditure was 10.04 MJ (2400 kcal) for women and 12.62 MJ (3016 kcal) for men (after the assumptions of the footnote in Table 8.4). The considerable physical and other challenges associated with the collection of these data are described in their paper. The difficulty of carrying out indirect calorimetry with free-living subjects is undoubtedly one reason why more such studies have not been attempted among hunter–gatherers (Sackett 1996).

When direct measurements are unavailable, TDEE can be estimated by (1) assuming that populations are in approximate energy balance over time and using intake as a proxy for expenditure and (2) combining observations of time allocation with estimates of the energetic cost of activities and of resting or basal metabolism to yield TDEE (the factorial method). Each of these methods involves potential error. Food intake data are notoriously difficult to obtain and often underestimate actual food consumption for a variety of reasons (Ulijaszek 1992, 1995). In the case of the factorial method, estimates of the energetic cost of activities are often derived from measurements taken on distant, unrelated

Table 8.4. *Physical Activity Level (PAL) of hunter-gatherers*

Population	Method of estimation	PAL[a]			Source
		Male	Female	Combined	
Ache	Factorial method	2.15[b]	1.88[b]		Hill et al. 1984, 1985, Leslie et al. 1984, Hurtado et al. 1985, Leonard and Robertson 1992
Hiwi (Cuiva)	Dietary intake			1.68	Hurtado and Hill 1986, 1987, Sackett 1996
Gunwinggu (Australia)	Dietary intake			1.47	McCarthy and MacArthur 1960, Sackett 1996
Groote Islanders (Australia)	Dietary intake			1.88	McCarthy and MacArthur 1960, Sackett 1996
Igloolik Inuit[c]	Field calorimetry	1.80	1.84		Godin and Shephard 1974
Dobe !Kung	Dietary intake			2.09	Sackett 1996, Lee 1979
!Kung	Factorial method	1.71[b]	1.51[b]		Leonard and Robertson 1992, Lee 1979, Leslie et al. 1984
Central Kalahari San	Dietary intake			1.77	Tanaka 1980, Sackett 1996
Forager composite	Factorial method	1.78	1.72		Sackett 1996
Horticulturalist composite	Factorial method	1.87	1.79		Sackett 1996
Agriculturalist composite	Factorial method	2.28	2.31		Sackett 1996
Industrialist composite	Factorial method	2.38	2.20		Sackett 1996

[a] According to the FAO/WHO/UNU Expert Consultation (1985) PAL of 1.55–1.77 for men and 1.56–1.63 for women is classified as light, 1.78–2.09 for men and 1.64–1.81 for women as moderate, and >2.09 for men and >1.81 for women as heavy.

[b] Leonard and Robertson (1992) define PAL as 24-h EE/resting metabolic rate (RMR). The use of RMR in place of basal metabolic rate (BMR) to calculate PAL results in a slight underestimation of PAL.

[c] BMR was calculated from FAO/WHO/UNU (1985) equations for a 65-kg man and a 55-kg woman. TDEE for men is based on annual activity budgets presented in Godin and Shephard (1974: Table 8); for hunter (as opposed to labourer and sedentary) men and married (as opposed to single or elderly) women, under the assumption of normal (as opposed to increased) BMR.

populations and it is impossible to account for either between- or within-individual variation in the intensity of activity. The factorial method also may underestimate TDEE (Leonard *et al.* 1997, Spurr *et al.* 1997). Finally, it is important to account for both daily and seasonal variation in activity level (Ulijaszek 1992, 1995). In spite of these weaknesses, these methods provide the best available estimates of the activity budgets of foraging peoples.

With these caveats in mind, Leonard and Robertson (1992) estimated TDEE using published anthropometric and time allocation data for !Kung and Ache, a published study of resting metabolic rate (Benedict 1938), an assumed allometric relationship between resting metabolic rate and bodyweight, and Leslie *et al.*'s (1984) estimates of the energetic costs of activity. They conclude that the TDEE of the !Kung is 9.113 MJ (2178 kcal) for men and 7.406 MJ (1770 kcal) for women. Their estimates for the Ache are 13.92 MJ (3327 kcal) for men and 10.99 MJ (2626 kcal) for women. For comparison with other populations, TDEE can be re-expressed as the physical activity level (PAL), defined as 24 hour energy expenditure expressed as a multiple of basal metabolic rate (TDEE/BMR). !Kung PAL is 1.71 for men and 1.51 for women (Table 8.4). The estimated PAL for the Ache is 2.15 for men and 1.88 for women. The !Kung PAL would fall into the light-to-moderate category, while the Ache PAL would fall into the heavy category according to FAO/WHO/UNU Expert Consultation (1985).

Sackett (1996) calculated a composite forager TDEE from published energy expenditure and time allocation data from multiple populations.[4] From these data he calculated a physical activity ratio

---

[4] He derived estimates of time spent each day in work (W_t), non-work (NW_t), and sleep (S_t) from time allocation data, and estimated the rate of energy expenditure during work (W_e) and non-work (NW_e) from published rates during similar activities in other populations and sleep (S_e) from a predictive equation. He then calculated TDEE as (W_t)(W_e) + (NW_t)(NW_e) + (S_t)(S_e). W_t is estimated to be 5.7 $\pm$ 1.8 h/d (mean $\pm$ sd, $n = 11$ populations) for men, and 6.1 $\pm$ 2.2 h/d ($n = 11$) for women. The estimate of W_e, expressed in units of physical activity ratio (PAR, the energy cost of individual activities maintained on a minute-by-minute basis as a ratio of basal metabolic rate, James and Schofield 1990) is 3.7 $\pm$ 0.1 ($n = 8$) for men and 3.1 $\pm$ 0.3 ($n = 7$) for women. S_t is 8.8 h/d ($n = 1$) for both men and women and S_e is assumed to be equivalent to BMR, calculated from the equations of Schofield (1985). $NW_t = 24h -$

(PAL) of 1.78 for adult male foragers and 1.72 for adult female foragers[5], within the range reported by Leonard and Robertson. These results are contrasted with male/female average PAL (derived using identical methodology) for horticulturalists of 1.87/ 1.79, for agriculturalists of 2.28/2.31, and for industrialists of 2.38/ 2.20. The sample for industrialists is biased toward occupations with heavy manual labour. Other studies have shown much lower PAL for residents of more developed nations engaged in sedentary occupations (Black *et al.* 1996). A review of PAL in populations with varying economic bases is given in Panter-Brick and Pollard (1999). Sackett also estimated variation in PAL from published dietary intake of two San communities, two Aboriginal Australian communities, and a Hiwi community (Table 8.4). Working from the assumption that energy intake and energy expenditure are balanced, he calculated the mean PAL (male and female combined) for these populations as 1.74 (SD 0.23), with a range of 1.47–2.09, in good agreement with the other estimates.

The results summarised in Table 8.4 reveal that most hunter–gatherer populations are at least moderately active, with forager men slightly more active than forager women, and that there is significant cross-population variability in PAL. It is also likely that there is significant seasonal variation in PAL among hunter–gatherers, but quantitative demonstration of this awaits future research. Sackett's (1996) composite analysis suggests that foragers are slightly less active than horticulturists who are in turn less active than agriculturists. Activity levels of farmers are, however, highly

---

$(S_t + W_t)$ and NW_e is 1.5 $\pm$ 0.2 PAR $(n=3)$ for men and 1.6 $\pm$ 0.1 PAR $(n=3)$ for women.

[5] The populations included in the data used to calculate W_t for foragers include two Yanomami communities, Shipibo and Mekranoti Kayapo, who engage in horticulture in addition to hunting and gathering and are therefore not widely considered to be hunter–gatherer populations. The Efe, who spend considerable time in agricultural labour (for non-Efe), but who are widely considered to be hunter–gatherers, are also included. However, removing these populations does not change W_t for either men or for women. The estimate of S_t though drawn from only one population, is in line with that for horticulturalists (8.8 $\pm$ 0.4 h/d, $n=9$ for men; 9.0 $\pm$ 0.6 h/d, $n=10$ for women) and exceeds that for agriculturalists and industrialists. An upward bias in S_t for foragers would result in a downward bias for PAL, since $S_e < NW_e < W_e$.

variable, both across seasons and across populations, indicating significant overlap between the distribution of population PALs for foragers and farmers (Sackett 1996, Panter-Brick and Pollard 1999). The forager PAL of about 1.75 indicates that resting metabolism accounts for, on average, about 57% of the energy budget. The energetic demands of pregnancy, lactation, immune function, growth, digestion, and thermoregulation, which contribute to resting metabolism, are all quite variable though the life cycle, as well as seasonally in most environments. These elements can combine to substantially elevate the resting requirements of hunter–gatherers and possibly constrain physical activity under certain ecological conditions and at certain stages of life history.

Body size

We might expect differences in energy budget to be reflected in differing patterns of growth and maturation. Numerous anthropometric studies of hunter–gatherer populations have been published, but few focus on growth, either longitudinally or cross-sectionally, and most use estimated rather than known birthdates or describe highly acculturated populations (see Bailey 1991, Hill and Hurtado 1996 for exceptions). The anthropometric studies demonstrate a wide range of adult hunter–gatherer body sizes. The so-called 'pygmy' populations from Central Africa are at the low end of adult stature (Table 8.5). They are followed by other tropical forest-dwelling populations – the Hiwi, Aka, Batak, and Agta who exceed the Efe and Mbuti by 8–9 cm. The Ache, Hadza, Dobe !Kung and G/wi San exceed the tropical forest group by 5–8 cm, though the Ache are themselves forest dwellers; and the Australian Aborigines are at the high end, exceeding the Hadza and Ache by a further 8 cm. Inuit fall midway between the Australian Aborigines and the Kalahari desert hunter–gatherers in stature, but are significantly heavier than any other hunter–gatherer population. This is by no means an exhaustive list, but is broadly representative of the range of extant hunter–gatherers. The extinct hunter–gatherer populations from temperate habitats reported in Cohen and Armelagos

Table 5. *Body size of hunter–gatherers*

Population	Males Stature n	cm	Weight n	kg	Females Stature n	cm	Weight n	kg	Source
Ethnographic samples[a]									
Efe (Democratic Republic of Congo)[b]	114	143	26	43	110	136	22	38	Bailey and Peacock 1988, Bailey 1991
Mbuti (Democratic Republic of Congo)	71	144			38	136	38	38	Cavalli-Sforza 1986
Batak (Phillippines)	44	153	44	47	40	143	40	41	Eder 1987
Aka (Central African Republic)	427	153	405	48	392	144	319	42	Pennetti et al. 1986
Agta (Philippines)	76	153	76	45	68	144	68	38	Headland 1989
Hiwi (Venezuela)	62	154	62	56	65	145	65	48	Hurtado and Hill 1987
G/wi San (Botswana)	36	159	36	55	17	149	17	50	Tanaka 1980
Dobe !Kung (Botswana and Namibia)	170	160	128	49	183	150	134	41	Lee 1979
Hadza (Tanzania)	125	161	126	54	110	150	110	48	Hiernaux and Hartono 1980
Ache (Paraguay)	19	161	41	60	16	150	32	52	Hill et al. 1984
Foxe Basin Inuit (Eastern Canada)	134	164	132	66	114	153	113	56	Auger et al 1980
Australian Aborigines (Rembarranga)	38	169	38	59	30	158	30	46	Prokopec 1977
Archaeological samples[c]									
Santa. Elena, Ecuador, 6000 BC	8	161			14	149			Ubelaker 1984
Westen Europe, Early Upper Palaeolithic	10	174			5	161			Meiklejohn et al. 1984
Westen Europe, Late Upper Palaeolithic	19	170			10	157			Meiklejohn et al. 1984
Westen Europe Mesolithic	46	168			36	156			Meiklejohn et al. 1984

Table 5. *Continued*

Population	Males				Females				Source
	Stature		Weight		Stature		Weight		
	n	cm	n	kg	n	cm	n	kg	
Georgia Coast, pre-1150 AD[d]	12	168			21	162			Larsen 1984
Levant, Natufian, 10 500–8700 BC	10	167			3	158			Smith et al. 1984
Mediterranean, Middle Palaeolithic	35	177			28	167			Angel 1984
Mediterranean, Mesolithic	61	173			35	160			Angel 1984
DuPont (US midwest), Late Archaic	5	170			5	160			Perzigan et al. 1984
Hopewell (US midwest)	20	168			13	160			Perzigan et al. 1984
Todd's Mound (US midwest), Middle Woodland	3	174			4	163			Perzigan et al. 1984

[*] In order of ascending stature.

[b] Average of June and December weights.

[c] These estimates may be biased upward because of the use of regression equations from a taller populations, however the magnitude of the bias is unlikely to be significant relative to the gulf between these populations and the ethnographic sample. In a test of the performance of the classical calibration method of stature estimation (regression of long-bone length on stature followed by solving for stature), Konigsberg et al. (1998) found that estimates of the stature of 199 individuals using a regression equation based on 1873 taller individuals resulted in a bias of 2 mm. One other method tested (regression of stature on long-bone length), however, returned an upward bias of 68 mm. Thank you to Andrew Millard for pointing out this source of error.

[d] Average of measurements based on right and left femur, n = minimum number of individuals.

(1984) are taller still and approach the mean height of 30-year-old Americans in the early 1980s – 176 cm for males, 163 cm for females (Frisancho 1990). Genetic differences account for some of the variation in height between populations of hunter–gatherers (e.g. see Merimee and Rimion 1986, Bailey 1991, Birdsell 1993, Shea and Bailey 1996). However, stature is also known to respond strongly to diet and disease exposure (Bogin 1988), suggesting that the archaeological populations of hunter–gatherers represented in Cohen and Armelagos (1984) were more advantaged in either or both of these respects than were present-day hunter–gatherers; moreover, the Ache appear more advantaged than other contemporary tropical forest hunter–gatherers.

Body mass index (BMI, kg/m^2), widely used as an indicator of nutritional condition (Cole 1991, Ferro-Luzzi *et al.* 1992), has a very low correlation with height and so facilitates meaningful comparison of the body weights of populations with different statures. A BMI of 18.5 kg/m^2 is a recognised indicator of chronic energy deficiency (James *et al.* 1988, Ferro-Luzzi *et al.* 1992). Figure 8.1 plots the mean body weight of hunter–gatherers vs. the square of their mean stature, with a reference line for BMI of 18.5. Inuit, Ache, and Hiwi, along with G/wi San women stand out as the most well-nourished populations, while Agta women, Dobe !Kung women, and the Australian Aborigine women stand out as the most poorly nourished. None would qualify as overweight by current Western standards. Though this sample is limited, it is striking that, at the population level, it is only women who appear to be at risk of undernutrition. This result reinforces the need for further investigation of individual variation in nutrient intake and energy expenditure.

Skinfold thicknesses of hunter–gatherer populations suggest that they are as a group very lean (Shephard and Rode 1976, Prokopec 1977, Jamison 1978, Ducros and Ducros 1979, Lee 1979, Hiernaux and Hartono 1980, Eder 1987, Dietz *et al.* 1989). Eaton *et al.* (1988) conclude that body fat is typically 5–15% for forager men and 20–25% for forager women.

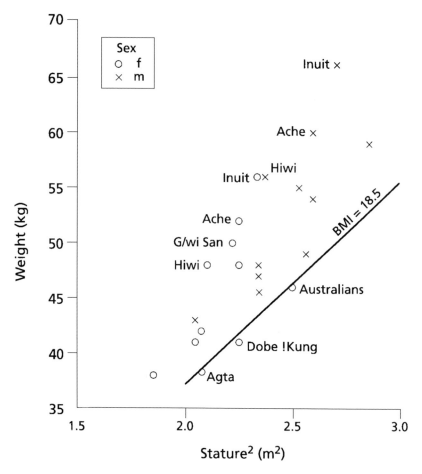

Figure 8.1. Body size of ethnographically studied hunter–gatherers. See Table 8.5 for additional labels and references.

Variation in nutritional ecologies

Variation in the energy budgets of hunter–gatherers is a reflection, in part, of differences in the opportunity costs of hunting and gathering and in the energetic efficiency with which food can be obtained in different environments. Each of these, in turn, is responsive to other social and biological variables, including population density and composition, mating competition, and the risk of mortality to both foragers and those remaining in camp. The energy budget then constrains total investment in reproduction, growth, and physical activity, with the pattern of allocation between these competing objectives determined by the interaction of genes, environment, and developmental history of individuals (Figure 8.2).

The !Kung, Efe, and most other modern hunter–gatherers represent a low-energy hunting and gathering adaptation with slower growth, less physical activity, slower reproduction, and lower energy budgets than populations such as the Ache. The Ache seem to have lived in a rich environment relative to population density for most of this century. This richness may result, in part, from the introduction of exotic food resources, including oranges and honeybees, from the Old World and possibly also from the elimination of competing groups from present-day Ache territory in the seventeenth and eighteenth centuries (Hill and Hurtado 1996). In the Ache, we see a much higher energy budget than among the !Kung with high levels of physical activity, higher energy intake, a much higher reproductive rate (see Pennington, this volume), and larger body size. This pattern of energy balance, made possible by their recently enriched environment, has allowed the Ache population to grow rapidly during the twentieth century, while the Efe and !Kung have been more stable (Howell 1979, Bailey 1989). Inuit represent an intermediate case, with higher growth and higher energy expenditure for thermoregulation, but slow reproduction, in part because of periodic severe food shortages (So 1980).

One of the challenges for hunter–gatherer studies is to integrate these and other data and to provide an explanation for variation in nutritional ecology between populations. Understanding the sources of variability in the nutritional ecology of extant hunter–gatherers will sharpen inference concerning the energy balance of archaeological populations of hunter–gatherers. Because their diets and activity patterns cannot be observed directly, we know much less about the nutritional ecology of archaeological populations. However, many of them were taller and seem to have lived in richer environments. Further data collection and model building incorporating variability in environmental productivity and parasite activity, combining a life history theory approach (Hill and Hurtado 1996) and a dynamic population–resource interaction approach (Winter-

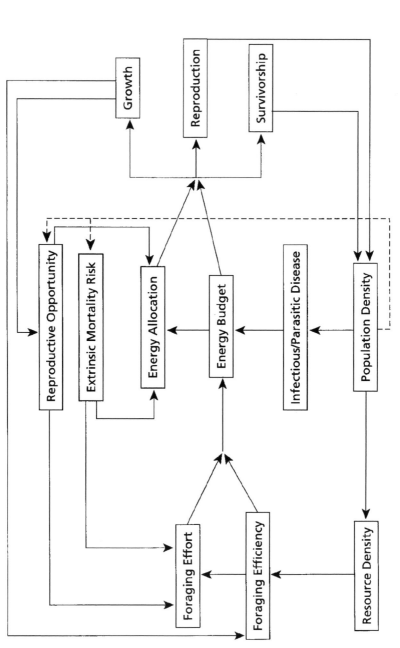

Figure 8.2. A model of the nutritional ecology of hunter–gatherer populations.

halder, this volume) will be needed to advance our understanding of those extinct populations. If our species has been selected to be an efficient coloniser, then a model of stable, slow-growth hunter–gatherer populations may not reflect the reality of much of hunter–gather population history (Hill and Hurtado 1996, Pennington, this volume).

Conclusion

The variability and flexibility in nutritional ecologies described here suggest a view of hunter–gatherers not as original affluents or as Hobbesian destitutes, but rather as nutritional strategists who balance the extrinsic constraints of variable food availability against the demands on energy for somatic maintenance, growth, reproduction, and physical activity. In spite of compelling evidence of adaptive responses to environmental constraints, hunter–gatherer nutritional adaptation is almost certainly not cost-free. Modern populations, whether hunter–gatherers or not, respond adaptively to food shortages or nutrient deficiencies, but also suffer functional, reproductive, growth, and health deficits relative to those with greater dietary sufficiency (Martorell 1989, Scrimshaw and Young 1989, Hill and Hurtado 1996, Froment, this volume). Because potentially deleterious responses to nutritional stress occur prior to tissue deformation and other visible clinical indications, mild to moderate nutritional stress is and has been almost certainly more widespread than is apparent from ethnographic and archaeological data (Armelagos 1994).

Acknowledgements

I thank Lynn Thomas for assistance with the figures and Catherine Panter-Brick for her extensive comments on the manuscript.

References

Angel, J.L. (1984). Health as a crucial factor in the changes from hunting to developed farming in the eastern Mediterranean. In *Paleopathology at the Origins of Agriculture*, ed. M.N. Cohen and G.J. Armelagos, pp. 51–74. Orlando: Academic Press.

Armelagos, G.J. (1994). 'You Are What You Eat'. In *Paleonutrition: The Diet and Health of Prehistoric Americans*, ed. K.D. Sobolik, pp. 235–246. Carbondale IL: Center for Archaeological Investigations, Southern Illinois University.

Auger, F., Jamison, P.L., Balslev-Jorgensen, J., Lewin, T., de Pena, J.F. and Skrobak-Kaczynski, J. (1980). Anthropometry of circumpolar populations. In *The Human Biology of Circumpolar Populations*, ed. F.A. Milan, pp. 213–255. Cambridge: Cambridge University Press.

Bahuchet, S. (1988). Food supply uncertainty among the Aka pygmies (Lobaye, Central African Republic). In *Coping with Uncertainty in Food Supply*, ed. I. de Garine and G.A. Harrison, pp. 118–149. Oxford: Clarendon Press.

Bailey, R.C. (1989). The comparative demography of Efe foragers and Lese horticulturalists in the Ituri Forest, Zaïre. In *Proceedings of the 88th Annual Meeting of the American Anthropological Association*. Washington DC: American Anthropological Association.

Bailey, R.C. (1991). The comparative growth of Efe pygmies and African farmers from birth to age 5 years. *Annals of Human Biology* **18**: 113–120.

Bailey, R.C. and Peacock, N.R. (1988). Efe pygmies of northeast Zaïre: subsistence strategies in the Ituri forest. In *Coping with Uncertainty in Food Supply*, ed. I. de Garine and G.A. Harrison, pp. 88–117. Oxford: Clarendon Press.

Bailey, R.C., Head, G., Jenike, M.R., Owen, B., Rechtman, R. and Zechenter, E. (1989). Hunters and gatherers in tropical rain forest: Is it possible? *American Anthropologist* **91**: 59–82.

Bang, H.O., Dyerberg, J. and Hjorne, N. (1976). The composition of food consumed by Greenland Eskimos. *Acta Medice Scandinavica* **200**: 69–73.

Bang, H.O., Dyerberg, J. and Sinclair, H.M. (1980). The composotion of the Eskimo food in northwestern Greenland. *American Journal of Clinical Nutrition* **33**: 2657–2661.

Benedict, F.G. (1938). *Vital Energetics*. Washington DC: Carnegie Institution.

Bentley, G.R., Aunger, R., Harrigan, A.M., Jenike, M., Bailey, R.C. and Ellison, P.T. (1999). Women's strategies to alleviate nutritional stress in a rural African society. *Social Science and Medicine* **48**: 149–162.

Birdsell, J.B. (1993). *Microevolutionary Patterns in Aboriginal Australia: A Gradient Analysis of Clines*. New York: Oxford University Press.

Black, A.E., Coward, W.A., Cole, T.J. and Prentice, A.M. (1996). Human energy measurements. *European Journal of Clinical Nutrition* **50**: 72–92.

Bogin, B. (1988). *Patterns of Human Growth*. Cambridge: Cambridge University Press.

Cavalli-Sforza, L. (1986). Anthropometric data. In *African Pygmies*, ed. L.L. Cavalli-Sforza, pp. 81–94. Orlando: Academic Press.

Cohen, M.N. (1989). *Health and the Rise of Civilisation*. New Haven: Yale University Press.

Cohen, M.N. and Armelagos, G.J. (1984). *Paleopathology at the Origins of Agriculture*. New York: Academic Press.

Cole, T.J. (1991). Weight–stature indices to measure underweight, overweight, and obesity. In *Anthropometric Assessment of Nutritional Status*, ed. J.H. Himes, pp. 83–114. New York: Wiley-Liss.

Dahlberg, F. (ed.) (1981). *Woman the Gatherer*. New Haven: Yale University Press.

de Garine, I. and Harrison, G.A. (1988). *Coping with Uncertainty in the Food Supply*. Oxford: Clarendon Press.

Dietz, W.H., Marino, B., Peacock, N.R. and Bailey, R.C. (1989). Nutritional status of Efe Pygmies and Lese horticulturists. *American Journal of Physical Anthropology* **78**: 509–518.

Draper, H.H. (1976). A review of recent nutritional research in the arctic. In *Circumpolar Health*, ed. R.J. Shephard and S. Itoh, pp. 120–129. Toronto: University of Toronto Press.

Draper, H.H. (1977). The aboriginal Eskimo diet in modern perspective. *American Anthropologist* **79**: 309–316.

Draper, H.H. (1978). Nutrition studies: the aboriginal Eskimo diet – a modern perspective. In *Eskimos of Northwestern Alaska: A Biological Perspective*, ed. P.L. Jamison, S.L. Zegura and F.A. Milan, pp. 139–144. Stroudsburg, PA: Dowden, Hutchinson and Ross.

Ducros, A. and Ducros, J. (1979). Recent anthropological data on the Ammassalimiut Eskimo of East Greenland: comparative studies. In *Physiological and Morphological Adaptation and Evolution*, ed. W. Stini, pp. 55–67. The Hague: Mouton.

Eaton, S.Boyd. (1992). Humans, lipids, and evolution. *Lipids* **27**: 814–820.

Eaton, S.Boyd and Eaton, Stanley B. (1999). Hunter–gatherers and human health. In *The Cambridge Encyclopedia of Hunters and Gatherers*, ed. R.B. Lee and R. Daly. Cambridge: Cambridge University Press.

Eaton, S. Boyd and Konner, J. (1985). Palaeolithic nutrition: a consideration of its nature and current implications. *New England Journal of Medicine* **312**: 283–289.

Eaton, S. Boyd, Konner, M. and Shostak, M. (1988*a*). Stone Agers in the fast lane: chronic degenerative diseases in evolutionary perspective. *American Journal of Medicine* **84**: 739–749.

Eaton, S. Boyd, Shostak, M. and Konner, M. (1988*b*). *The Palaeolithic Prescription*. New York: Harper and Row.

Eaton, S. Boyd, Eaton, Stanley B., Konner, M.J. and Shostak, M. (1996). An evolutionary perspective enhances understanding of human nutritional requirements. *Journal of Nutrition* **126**: 1732–1740.

Eaton, S. Boyd, Eaton, Stanley B. and Konner, M.J. (1997). Palaeolithic nutrition revisited: a twelve-year retrospective on its nature and implications. *European Journal of Clinical Nutrition* **51**: 207–216.

Eder, J.F. 1987. *On the Road to Tribal Extinction*. Berkeley: University of California Press.

Eveleth, P.B. and Tanner, J.M. (1976). *Worldwide Variation in Human Growth*. New York: Cambridge University Press.

FAO/WHO/UNU Expert Consultation (1985). *Energy and Protein Requirements*. Geneva: World Health Organisation.

Ferro-Luzzi, A. and Branca, F. (1993). Nutritional seasonality: the dimensions of the problem. In *Seasonality and Human Ecology*, ed. S.J. Ulijaszek and S.S. Strickland, pp. 149–165. Cambridge: Cambridge University Press.

Ferro-Luzzi, A., Franklin, M. and James, W.P.T. (1992). A simplified approach of assessing adult chronic energy deficiency. *European Journal of Clinical Nutrition* **46**: 173–186.

Frisancho, A.R. (1990). *Anthropometric Standards for the Assessment of Growth and Nutritional Status*. Ann Arbor: University of Michigan Press.

Godin, G. and Shephard, R.J. (1974). Activity patterns of the Canadian Eskimo. In *Polar Human Biology*, ed. O.G. Edholm and E.K.E. Gunderson, pp. 193–214. Chicago: Heinemann.

Goodman, A.H. (1994). Cartesian reductionism and vulgar adaptationism: issues in the interpretation of nutritional status in prehistory. In *Paleonutrition: The Diet and Health of Prehistoric Americans*, ed. K.D. Sobolik, pp. 163–177. Carbondale, IL: Center for Archaeological Investigations, Southern Illinois University.

Hart, T.B. and Hart, J.A. (1986). The ecological basis of hunter–gatherer subsistence in African rain forests: the Mbuti of eastern Zaïre. *Human Ecology* **14**: 29–56.

Hawkes, K. (1991). Showing off: tests of an hypothesis about men's foraging goals. *Ethology and Sociobiology* **12**: 29–54.

Hayden, B. (1981). Subsistence and ecological adaptations of modern hunter/gatherers. In *Omnivorous Primates: Gathering and Hunting in Human Evolution*, ed. R.S.O. Harding and G. Teleki, pp. 344–421. New York: Columbia University Press.

Headland, T.N. (1989). Population decline in a Philippine negrito hunter–gatherer society. *American Journal of Human Biology* **1**: 59–72.

Headland, T.N. and Bailey, R.C. (1991). Introduction: Have hunter–gatherers ever lived in tropical rain forest independently of agriculture? *Human Ecology* **19**: 115–122.

Hiernaux, J. and Hartono, D.B. (1980). Physical measurements of the adult Hadza of Tanzania. *Annals of Human Biology* **7**: 339–346.

Hill, K.R. (1982). Hunting and human evolution. *Journal of Human Evolution* **11**: 521–544.

Hill, K.R. (1988). Macronutrient modifications of optimal foraging theory: an approach using indifference curves applied to some modern foragers. *Human Ecology* **16**: 157–97.

Hill, K.R. and Hurtado, A.M. (1996). *Ache Life History: The Ecology and Demography of a Foraging People.* New York: Aldine de Gruyter.

Hill, K.R., Hawkes, K., Hurtado, M. and Kaplan, H. (1984). Seasonal variance in the diet of Ache hunter–gatherers in Eastern Paraguay. *Human Ecology* **12**: 101–135.

Hill, K.R., Kaplan, H., Hawkes, K. and Hurtado, A.M. (1985). Men's time allocation to subsistence work among the Ache of Eastern Paraguay. *Human Ecology* **13**: 29–47.

Holland, T.D. and O'Brien, M.J. (1997). Parasites, porotic hyperostosis, and the implications of changing perspectives. *American Antiquity* **62**: 183–193.

Howell, N. (1979). *Demography of the Dobe !Kung.* New York: Academic Press.

Hurtado, A.M. and Hill, K.R. (1986). The Cuiva: hunter–gatherers of western Venezuela. *AnthroQuest* **36**: 1–23.

Hurtado, A.M. and Hill, K.R. (1987). Early dry season subsistence ecology of Cuiva (Hiwi) foragers of Venezuela. *Human Ecology* **15**: 163–187.

Hurtado, A.M. and Hill, K.R. (1990). Seasonality in a foraging society: variation in diet, work effort, fertility, and sexual division of labour among the Hiwi of Venezuela. *Journal of Anthropological Research* **46**: 293–346.

Hurtado, A.M., Hawkes, K., Hill, K.R. and Kaplan, H. (1985). Female subsistence strategies among Ache hunter–gatherers of Eastern Paraguay. *Human Ecology* **13**: 1–28.

Ichikawa, M. (1981). Ecological and sociobiological importance of honey to the Mbuti Net Hunters, Eastern Zaïre. *African Study Monographs* **1**: 55–68.

Isaac, G. (1978). The food-sharing behavior of protohuman hominids. *Scientific American* **238**: 90–108.

James, W.P.T. and Schofield, E.C. (1990). *Human Energy Requirements: A Manual for Planners and Nutritionists.* New York: Oxford University Press.

James, W.P.T., Ferro-Luzzi, A. and Waterlow, J.C. (1988). Definition of chronic energy deficiency in adults. *European Journal of Clinical Nutrition* **42**: 969–981.

Jamison, P.L. (1978). Anthropometric variation. In *Eskimos of Northwestern Alaska*, ed. P.L. Jamison, S.L. Zegura and F.A. Milan, pp. 40–78. Stroudsburg PA: Dowden, Hutchinson and Ross.

Jenike, M.R. (1995). Variation in body fat and muscle mass: responses to seasonal hunger among tropical horticulturists, Zaïre. *Ecology of Food and Nutrition* **34**: 227–249.

Jenike, M.R. (1996). Activity reduction as an adaptive response to seasonal hunger. *American Journal of Human Biology* **8**: 517–534.

Jones, R. (1980). Hunters in the Australian coastal savanna. In *Human Ecology in Savanna Environments*, ed. D. Harris, pp. 107–147. New York: Academic Press.

Kelly, R.L. (1995). *The Foraging Spectrum: Diversity in Hunter-Gatherer Lifeways*. Washington DC: Smithsonian Institution Press.

Konigsberg, L.W., Hens, S.M., Jantz, L.M. and Jungers, W.L. (1998). Stature estimation and calibration: Bayesian and maximum likelihood perspectives in physical anthropology. *Yearbook of Physical Anthropology* **41**: 65–92.

Krogh, A. and Krogh, M. (1913). A study of the diet and metabolism of Eskimos undertaken in 1908 on an expedition to Greenland. *Medd. Gronland* **51**: 2.

Larsen, C.S. (1984). Health and disease in prehistoric Georgia: the transition to agriculture. In *Paleopathology at the Origins of Agriculture*, ed. M.N. Cohen and G.J. Armelagos, pp. 367–392. Orlando: Academic Press.

Lee, R.B. (1968). What hunters do for a living, or, how to make out on scarce resources. In *Man the Hunter*, ed. R.B. Lee and I. DeVore, pp. 30–48. New York: Aldine de Gruyter.

Lee, R.B. (1979). *The !Kung San*. Cambridge: Cambridge University Press.

Lee, R.B. and DeVore, I. (eds.) (1968). *Man the Hunter*. New York: Aldine de Gruyter.

Leonard, W.R. and Robertson, M.L. (1992). Nutritional requirements and human evolution: a bioenergetics model. *American Journal of Human Biology* **4**: 179–195.

Leonard, W.R., Galloway, V.A. and Ivakine, E. (1997). Underestimation of daily energy expenditure with the factorial method: implications for anthopological research. *American Journal of Physical Anthropology* **103**: 443–454.

Leslie, P.W., Bindon, J.R. and Baker, P.T. (1984). Caloric requirements of human populations: a model. *Human Ecology* **12**: 137–162.

Lieberman, L.S. (1987). Biocultural consequences of animals versus plants as sources of fats, proteins, and other nutrients. In *Food and Evolution*, ed. M. Harris and E.B. Ross, pp. 225–260. Philadelphia: Temple University Press.

Mann, J. and Skeaff, M. (1998). Lipids. In *Essentials of Human Nutrition*, ed. J. Mann and S. Truswell, pp. 29–50. Oxford: Oxford University Press.

Martorell, R. (1989). Body size, adaptation and function. *Human Organisation* **48**: 15–20.

McCarthy, F.D. and McArthur, M. (1960). The food quest and time factor in aboriginal economic life. In *Records of the American–Australian Scientific Expedi-*

tion to Arnhem Land, vol. 2, *Anthropology and Nutrition*, ed. C.P. Mountford, pp. 145–195. Parkville, Victoria: Melbourne University Press.

Meehan, B. (1977). Hunters by the seashore. *Journal of Human Evolution* **6**: 363–370.

Meiklejohn, C., Schentag, C., Venema, A. and Key, P. (1984). Socioeconomic change and patterns of pathology and variation in the Mesolithic of Western Europe: some suggestions. In *Paleopathology at the Origins of Agriculture*, ed. M.N. Cohen and G.J. Armelagos, pp. 75–100. Orlando: Academic Press.

Merimee, T.J. and Rimion, D.L. (1986). Growth hormone and insulin-like growth factors in the western pygmy. In *African Pygmies*, ed. L.L. Cavalli-Sforza, pp. 167–180. Orlando: Academic Press.

Milton, K. (1987). Primate diets and gut morphology: implications for hominid evolution. In *Food and Evolution*, ed. M. Harris and E.B. Ross, pp. 93–116. Philadelphia: Temple University Press.

Murdoch, G.P. (1967). *Ethnographic Atlas*. Pittsburgh: University of Pittsburgh Press.

O'Connell, J.F. and Hawkes, K. (1981). Alywara plant use and optimal foraging theory. In *Hunter-Gatherer Foraging Strategies*, ed. B. Winterhalder and E.A. Smith, pp. 91–125. Chicago: University of Chicago Press.

Pagezy, H. (1988). Coping with uncertainty in food supply among the Oto and the Twa living in the equatorial flooded forest near Lake Tumba, Zaïre. In *Coping with Uncertainty in Food Supply*, ed. I.de Garine and G.A. Harrison, pp. 175–209. Oxford: Clarendon Press.

Panter-Brick, C. (1995). Inter-individual and seasonal weight variation in rural Nepali women. *Journal of Biosocial Science* **27**: 215–233.

Panter-Brick, C. (1996*a*). Physical activity, energy stores and seasonal energy balance among men and women in Nepali households. *American Journal of Human Biology* **8**: 263–274.

Panter-Brick, C. (1996*b*). Seasonal and sex variation and physical activity levels among agro-patoralists in Nepal. *American Journal of Physical Anthropology* **100**: 7–21.

Panter-Brick, C. (1997). Seasonal growth patterns in rural Nepali children. *Annals of Human Biology* **24**: 1–18.

Panter-Brick, C. and Pollard, T.M. (1999). Work and hormonal variation in subsistence and industrial contexts. In *Hormones, Health, and Behavior: A Socioecological and Lifespan Perspective*, ed. C. Panter-Brick and C.M. Worthman, pp. 139–183. New York: Cambridge University Press.

Pennetti, V., Sgaramella-Zonta, L. and Astolfi, P. (1986). General health of the African pygmies of the Central African Republic. In *African Pygmies*, ed. L.L. Cavalli-Sforza, pp. 128–138. Orlando: Academic Press.

Perzigian, A.J., Tench, P.A. and Braun, D.J. (1984). Prehistoric health in the

Ohio River Valley. In *Paleopathology at the Origins of Agriculture*, ed. M.N. Cohen and G.J. Armelagos, pp. 347–366. Orlando: Academic Press.

Prentice, A.M., Goldberg, G.R.,. Jebb, S.A., Black, A.E., Murgatroyd, P.R. and Diaz, E.O. (1991). Physiological responses to slimming. *Proceedings of the Nutrition Society* **50**: 441–448.

Prentice, A.M., Goldberg, G.R. and Poppitt, S.D. (1996). Reproductive stresses in undernourished and well-nourished women. *Bibliotheca Nutrition et Dieta* **53**: 1–10.

Prokopec, M. (1977). An anthropometric study of the Rembarranga: comparison with other populations. *Journal of Human Evolution* **6**: 371–391.

Rode, A. and Shephard, R.J. (1995). Basal metabolic rate of Inuit. *American Journal of Clinical Nutrition* **7**: 723–729.

Sackett, R.D. (1996). Time, energy, and the indolent savage. Unpublished PhD thesis, University of California, Los Angeles.

Sahlins, M. (1972). *Stone Age Economics*. New York: Aldine de Gruyter.

Schofield, W.N. (1985). Predicting basal metabolic rate, new standards and review of previous work. *Human Nutrition: Clinical Nutrition* **39C**: 5–41.

Scrimshaw, N.S. and Young, V.R. (1989). Adaptation to low protein and energy intakes. *Human Organisation* **48**: 20–30.

Sen Gupta, P.N. (1980). Food consumption, and nutrition of regional tribes of India. *Ecology of Food and Nutrition* **9**: 93–108.

Shea, B.T. and Bailey, R.C. (1996). Allometry and adaptation of body proportions and stature in African pygmies. *American Journal of Physical Anthropology* **100**: 311–340.

Shephard, R.J. and Godin, G. (1976). Energy balance of an Eskimo community. In *Circumpolar Health*, ed. R.J. Shephard and S. Itoh, pp. 106–112. Toronto: University of Toronto Press.

Shephard, R.J. and Rode, A. (1976). On the body composition of the Eskimo. In *Circumpolar Health*, ed. R.J. Shephard and S. Itoh, pp. 91–97. Toronto: University of Toronto Press.

Sinclair, H.M. (1952). The diet of the Canadian Indians and Eskimos. *Proceedings of the Nutrition Society* **12**: 69–82.

Smith, P., Bar-Yosef, O. and Sillen, A. (1984). Archaeological and skeletal evidence for dietary change during the late Pleistocene/early Holocene in the Levant. In *Paleopathology at the Origins of Agriculture*, ed. M.N. Cohen and G.J. Armelagos, pp. 101–136. Orlando: Academic Press.

So, J.K. (1980). Human biological adaptation to arctic and subarctic zones. *Annual Review of Anthropology* **9**: 63–82.

Sobolik, K.D. (1994*a*). Introduction. In *Paleonutrition: The Diet and Health of Prehistoric Americans*, ed. K.D. Sobolik, pp. 1–20. Carbondale IL: Center for Archaeological Investigations, Southern Illinois University.

Sobolik, K.D. (1994*b*). Paleonutrition of the Lower Pecos Region of the Chihuahuan Desert. In *Paleonutrition: The Diet and Health of Prehistoric Amer-*

icans, ed. K.D. Sobolik, pp. 247–264. Carbondale IL: Center for Archaeological Investigations, Southern Illinois University.

Speth, J.D. (1989). Early hominid hunting and scavenging: the role of meat as an energy source. *Journal of Human Evolution* **18**: 329–343.

Speth, J.D. (1990). Seasonality, resource stress, and food sharing in so-called 'egalitarian' foraging societies. *Journal of Anthropological Archaeology* **9**: 148–188.

Speth, J.D. and Spielmann, K.A. (1983). Energy source, protein metabolism, and hunter–gatherer subsistence strategies. *Journal of Anthropological Archaeology* **2**: 1–31.

Spurr, G.B., Dufour, D.L, Reina, J.C. and Haught, T.A. (1997) Daily energy expenditure of women by factorial and heart rate methods. *Medicine and Science in Sports and Exercise* **29**: 1255–1262.

Stanford, C.B. (1999). *The Hunting Apes: Meat Eating and the Origins of Human Behavior.* Princeton: Princeton University Press.

Sutton, M.Q. (1994). Indirect evidence in paleonutrition studies. In *Paleonutrition: The Diet and Health of Prehistoric Americans*, ed. K.D. Sobolik, pp. 98–114. Carbondale IL: Center for Archaeological Investigations, Southern Illinois University.

Tanaka, J. (1980). *The San, Hunter-Gatherers of the Kalahari*, translated by D.W. Hughes. Tokyo: University of Tokyo Press.

Ubelaker, D.H. (1984). Prehistoric human biology of Ecuador: possible temporal trends and cultural correlations. In *Paleopathology at the Origins of Agriculture*, ed. M.N. Cohen and G.J. Armelagos, pp. 491–514. Orlando: Academic Press.

Ulijaszek, S.J. (1992). Human energetics methods in biological anthropology. *Yearbook of Physical Anthropology* **35**: 215–42.

Ulijaszek, S.J. (1995). *Human Energetics in Biological Anthropology.* Cambridge: Cambridge University Press.

Venkatesan, D. (1993). Ecology, food and nutrition: the Onge foragers of the Andaman tropical forest. In *Tropical Forests, People and Food: Biocultural Interactions and Applications to Development*, ed. C.M. Hladik, A. Hladik, O.M. Linares, H. Pagezy, A. Semple and M. Hadley, pp. 505–514. Paris: UNESCO.

Walker, P.L. and Helwett, B.S. (1990). Dental health, diet and social status among central African foragers and farmers. *American Anthropologist* **92**: 383–398.

Whitney, E.N. and Rolfes, S.R. (1999). *Understanding Nutrition.* 8th edn. Belmont CA: Wadsworth.

Whitten, P.L. (1999). Diet, hormones, and health: an evolutionary-ecological perspective. In *Hormones, Health, and Behavior: A Socio-Ecological and Lifespan Perspective*, ed. C. Panter-Brick and C.M. Worthman, pp. 210–243. Cambridge: Cambridge University Press.

Wilmsen, E.N. (1978). Seasonal effects of dietary intake on Kalahari San. *Federation Proceedings* **37**: 65–71.

Winterhalder, B. and Smith, E.A. (1992). Evolutionary ecology and the social sciences. In *Evolutionary Ecology and Human Behavior*, ed. E.A. Smith and B. Winterhalder, pp. 5–23. New York: Aldine De Gruyter.

Woodburn, J. (1968). An introduction to Hazda economy. In *Man the Hunter*, ed. R.B. Lee and I. DeVore, pp. 40–55. New York: Aldine de Gruyter.

9

Evolutionary biology and health of hunter–gatherer populations

ALAIN FROMENT

Introduction

Hunter–gatherers display a wide variety of morphological and physiological characteristics, and should provide a good model for the evolution of human biological characters across a considerable range of environments in presumably isolated situations. This chapter examines both ecological and genetic aspects of the evolution of present-day hunter–gatherers and also comments on what the future will hold for those who now face or soon will face cultural and technological transition through contact with dominant groups. Hunter–gatherers are not recognisable by their biological characteristics – they are defined by their way of life, namely their relation to nature, which is a cultural, not a biological, definition (see Panter-Brick, Layton and Rowley-Conwy, this volume). However their close interaction with the physical and animal environment, their small and mobile groups, their dietary and work patterns, did create ecological and evolutionary characteristics which shaped biological outcomes. Existing variation in biological traits will be examined as evolutionary responses to climate, diet and disease.

Some partially unanswered questions related to evolution and transition can be listed. Concerning morphology, is small stature an adaptation to hunting and gathering? What is the genetic basis for anatomical characteristics and what room is there for modulation by nutritional and infectious variables? Is there a secular trend modifying these characters? Concerning physiology, is the diet of foragers (poor in fat, rich in protein and fibre) an evolutionary optimum? What was gained, or lost, with the adoption of agriculture and herding? Are there lessons, of health, well-being and wisdom, to be derived from knowledge of these societies? Above all, what is the future of marginal groups, who are not well equipped to survive an unprecedented social and ecological upheaval?

Adaptations to ecological constraints

Climate and adaptation

Climate modulates biodiversity and food availability. Thus, the variety of edible plants is wider in the rainforest than in savannah, and wider in savannah than in the cold desert. Most hunters now live in tropical areas but some who live in arctic conditions, like the Inuit and other populations from Siberia to Greenland, and Ala-caluf and others in Tierra del Fuego, have no other choice than to rely mainly upon game and fish, in a near-absence of edible plants and carbohydrates. Despite their dark skin and low sunlight exposure, these populations avoid rickets by the intake of fresh fish liver. There are thermoregulatory adaptations to cold such as vascular shunts, which allow Inuit to keep their hands in cold water for longer than other peoples; the Australian Aborigines and the Alacaluf, who are able to sleep naked at a temperature of 0 °C, also display physiological adaptations to cold (Bittel 1992).

A correlation between climate and anatomy is difficult to assess. Pygmies who live in a very moist climate have as wide noses as do Australians and San[1], who live in dry environments. Newman

---

[1] San, who are hunter–gatherers, and Khoikhoi, who are herders, are usually united in a conglomerate of culturally different but linguistically related groups, called Khoisan or Koesaan. For political reasons, the picture of hunter–gatherers has been constantly manipulated, for worse, during colonial times, or for the better, since the emergence of ecological lobbying by ideologically inspired groups (churches, activists, etc.). Some ethnonyms widely used in the past like 'Bushman' (San), 'Pygmies', 'Eskimo', are offensive and it is certainly not by chance that most of these deprecatory terms have been used, by Europeans and also by sedentary neighbours, to qualify 'primitiveness' of hunters. The term 'Pygmies' confounds under the same label different populations (for instance the Baka, BaBongo, BaKola or Bagyeli, BaAka, BaSua, Efe, Asua, BaMbuti, BaBinga, Twa or BaTwa, Bedzan, and many other so-called Pygmies) with different histories

(1953) and Stinson (1990) reported some correlations between body size/shape and climatic variables in America, but conclusions are difficult to draw. In cold environments the stature of hunters is sometimes tall (males 176 ± 2 cm), as in the Aonikenk of Patagonia (Hernandez *et al.* 1998) and many North American hunters, and sometimes short (males 158 ± 2 cm) as in most Inuit or related arctic peoples (So 1980). Some authors (Holmes 1993) think that a reduction of body size is an adaptation to adverse ecological conditions, while for others (Spurr 1987), it is a pathologic impairment of development potential.

Small size is observed in all African hunter–gatherer populations (Twa Pygmies, San, Hadza) and in some other tropical groups like Andaman Islanders or Negritos (see Table 9.5 in Jenike, this volume). If nutritional deficiencies are excluded, several explanatory hypotheses have been advanced, all of which are disputed:

Thermoregulation needs (Ruff 1994). A smaller body in moist and warm areas like tropical rainforests is a well-known zoological law (Bergmann's rule, stated in 1847), but is also observed among Papua highlanders living in a fairly cold environment (Diamond 1991). By contrast, Australians living in a mainly dry environment have a very lean body with the most elongated lower limbs found in humankind (Norgan 1994), a morphology which fits with physiological adaptation to hot and dry savannah (Ruff 1994, Katzmarzyk and Leonard 1998). Conversely, San hunters are very short in a comparable climate. Comparing Bantu and Twa Pygmoids, Austin and Ghesquiere (1976) showed that larger bodied populations had a better heat tolerance, when exposed to a walk under the sun or to the immersion of an arm and a leg in warm water, than smaller-bodied populations. Thus no clear results support the thermoregulatory advantage of a smaller body.

Easier mobility, at least in rainforest (Hiernaux 1974). Holliday and Falsetti (1995), in a sample of 19 recent hunter–gatherer groups,

and cultures. The term 'Pygmoid' is sometimes used for forager peoples living like the Pygmies, but whose stature is higher than the conventional threshold of 150 cm. Its use, as the use of terms like 'Negritos' or 'Aborigines', is only justified by convenience.

failed to demonstrate any relation between relative lower-limb length and spatial mobility. Diamond (1991) notes that the short-statured San of the Kalahari live in an open landscape, where the argument of mobility according to density of trees is not relevant. So, unless the San first adapted to a forest ecosystem and kept a related morphology despite a drastic change in their environment, the hypothesis is not valid.

Economy of energetic requirements. A smaller body permits survival with less food: basal metabolism is 5.0 MJ (1200 kcal) for a Pygmy of 37 kg and 142 cm, as compared to 6.9 MJoules (1647 kcal) for a US citizen of 65 kg and 172 cm (Mann *et al.* 1962). In a context of limited resources, this reduction may allow more individuals to survive.

An optimal adequacy between body shape and weapon (Brues 1959), or a more efficient behaviour. Lee (1979) showed a better yield of hunting among short than tall !Kung men, a difference very apparent after the age of 35. In the same group, Winkler and Kirchengast (1994) found that slender men had a lower social position, fewer children with a higher offspring mortality and a higher ratio of daughters, than robust men. If shorter men can feed more children, a spread of genes conferring short stature can be expected.

Diet and adaptation

Many traditional societies which use a combination of swidden horticulture, hunting, fishing and foraging cannot be easily classified as hunters or agriculturists. For example, the Ok people of Papua New Guinea rely on game for 64% to 75% of their animal protein supply (Hyndman *et al.* 1989). Conversely, groups considered as 'pristine' hunter–gatherers, like Pygmies or San, who had long decided to live without agriculture – despite a close symbiosis, common language and long proximity to agriculturists – have now turned to some food production. Cassava, a crop introduced by colonisation from America, allows absence from the fields for several months, which fits in well with the seasonal movements of semi-nomadic 'Pygmy' communities; in drier environments, maize, another American crop, has been grown by the Hadza hunters of Tanzania since the mid-1960s (Bennett *et al.* 1970: 858). Symmetrically, the Hukwe ('black Boschimans') are a group of former herders said to have taken up hunting and gathering (Nurse *et al.* 1985: 67, see Layton this volume.).

The diet of hunter–gatherers used to be much more varied, and richer in animal protein, than the diet available to farmers. However, the small proportion of foods actually used from the edible wild species available argues for a recent change of the diet in favour of the security and ease of cultivated products, away from the uncertainty and difficulties involved in obtaining wild products. The dependency of hunters-gatherers *vis-à-vis* cultivated starchy food (cassava, plantain banana, or domesticated cereals) is a political issue, discussed by Bahuchet *et al.* (1991) in the case of Pygmies. Due to demographic increase, Pygmies will either be dominated by Bantu societies, through food dependency, or will have to abandon their way of life and become farmers. Cavalli-Sforza (1986: 424) noted that the Aka Pygmies of Central African Republic in the 1970s obtained 50% (in fresh weight) of their food from working 20% of their time in Bantu plantations, a good strategy. Cultivated food sources contribute around 20% of the diet among the Bakola of Cameroon (Koppert *et al.* 1993) and 65% among the Mbuti Efe of the Ituri forest (Bailey and Peacock 1988).

Nutritional issues are extensively developed by Jenike (this volume), and only some aspects relevant to human biology will be discussed here. Acute protein-energy malnutrition and anaemias have been reported in many foraging groups (Kent and Dunn 1996), mainly among sedentarised populations who are easier to monitor; reliable statistics on mobile bands are rare. It is also difficult to compare growth status in populations where children's age cannot be determined accurately. In Bakola Pygmies from Cameroon, the current nutritional status of men is reasonably good, but less satisfactory among women, who are very physically active, and have an adiposity of only 19% in contrast to 25% among Bantu women. This makes the Bakola women's health a little precarious, especially during pregnancy and breastfeeding (Froment *et al.* 1993). In the Ituri forest (Dietz *et al.* 1989), Pygmies' skinfolds, fat mass and lean mass are also significantly smaller, in both sexes, relative to Bantu neighbours. However, muscular development and fitness, determined by physical tests, are good in both men (Ghesquiere and Karvonen 1981, Ferretti *et al.* 1993) and women (Pagezy 1978).

Most hunters, in either cold or tropical areas, have a deficiency of intestinal lactase, which makes them unable to digest milk; the persistence of the enzyme in adults is found among herders and their modern descendants. The domestication of animals and dairying practices appeared only a few millennia ago, and favoured a genetic ability to use milk as an important source of energy and nutrients (Simoons 1978).

Taste thresholds, probably under genetic control, vary according to populations, and food environment may have played a significant selective role in that differentiation (Hladik and Simmen 1996). In arctic environments, Inuit have a remarkable sensitivity to salt, which is traditionally considered to be dangerous. Living on a very rich protein diet, they have to drink large amounts of water to prevent urea excess, and the use of small melted icebergs as drinking water could dangerously increase their salt intake. All rainforest populations, including Bakola and Twa Pygmoids, have a low sensitivity for salt and for glucose, which may be related to an abundance of sweet fruits in forests, as compared to savannahs. Despite a close resemblance in diet, prevalence of endemic goitre in Efe foragers is far less than observed among their Lese farmer neighbours (9% versus 43%), even for Efe people living in Lese villages; a genetic mechanism has been suspected, as an intermediate frequency of 29% has been reported in a small sample of 14 subjects of mixed Lese–Efe descent (Dormitzer *et al.* 1989).

The very developed adipose buttocks (steatopygia) displayed in San women, but also in Khoi herders, could be a genetic adaptation to food shortage, though there is no convincing demonstration of this hypothesis. If nutritional conditions were poor, a secular trend on stature would then be predicted with better access to food or Westernisation of diet. This trend has not been observed among aboriginal South Australians (Pretty *et al.* 1998) nor in Bakola Pygmies (Pasquet *et al.* 1995), but changes of 1 cm per decade have been noticed in Canadian Inuit (Rode and Shephard 1994).

Genetic issues

Hunter–gatherers genetics and plasticity

Some anatomical evolution has occurred, towards gracilisation (a structural reduction of the skeleton or of skull robustness), since modern human appeared: Henneberg (1988) notes that there is a general decrease of skull size and robustness since the Mesolithic. Have changes in food consistency between the Palaeolithic and the Neolithic induced this lighter skull morphology? In fact San, and even Pygmies, have a light, paedomorphic skull, while Australians, Inuit and Fuegians have a very robust one, with no dietary correlations. San gracile morphology is not explained by sex hormones levels, though there is a deficit in testosterone when compared to their Bantu neighbours and Efe Pygmies (Christiansen 1991); no elevation of estrogen hormones could be found in males, when compared to European and South African Bantu (Van Der Walt *et al.* 1978). Bribiescas (1996) proposed that a low testosterone level, also observed among Aché hunters of Paraguay, may be advantageous under conditions of chronic energy shortage.

Present-day hunter–gatherers reproduce some of the genetic characteristics of human ancestors such as endogamy (spouse choice within the group), with consequent genetic diversity lowered within groups and enhanced between groups. Australian Aborigines arrived some 40 000 to 60 000 years ago, probably through several waves of migration. Since then they have remained virtually isolated, scattered in a very wide territory where genetic clines can be observed (Birdsell 1993). They therefore provide a good model for the study of genetic evolution of small communities since the Palaeolithic. A difficulty in the study of the genetic structure of hunter–gatherers groups is related to their usually very small size, which causes strong genetic drift with important and recurrent founder effects (i.e. the small number of founders of a new group can lead to a large drift). There is debate regarding the smallest size of a group required for its survival, and bottlenecks experienced by humankind in the past are closely related to the group size of reproductive foragers (Hassan 1975). Cavalli-Sforza and Bodmer

(1971: 431), discussing the demographic data relevant to the analysis of such drift, mention densities of 0.2 humans per km^2 for the Pygmies, 0.6 per km^2 for Aleuts, 0.03 per km^2 for Australians, 0.04 per km^2 for Caribou Inuit and 0.06 h per km^2 for Greenland Inuit.

The wide range of environmental adaptations, dating from earliest anatomically modern humans, has generated wide genetic diversity. No common genetic characters are to be expected for this large group of foraging populations occupying the most extreme terrestrial ecosystems. Far more realistic is the study of genetic affinities between present-day hunter–gatherers and their sedentary neighbours. Gene flow between the two communities is subjected to strong social barriers related to the prejudices that most nomadic societies suffer from villagers. Such prejudices favour endogamy and genetic drift. In rainforest Bantu villages, Pygmies are often considered as half-apes, both feared and despised (Kazadi 1981, Vansina 1990: 57). In the Democratic Republic of Congo, Oto villagers despise the Twa but describe in a myth a common kinship which justifies a strong prohibition of intermarriage. The genetic exchanges between San and their Kavango (Bantu) neighbours are also very limited (Nurse et al. 1985). Thus selective pressures are associated with both environmental and social constraints.

The short stature of African Pygmies, evident early in life, has been attributed to a genetic mutation on the receptor to growth hormone. Insulin-like growth factor I (IGF-I), present at low concentrations in the blood level of African Pygmies, is normal in a short statured population of Papua New Guinea (adult male stature 151 ± 3 cm, weight 50 ± 3 kg), while the level of growth hormone transport protein is diminished (Baumann et al. 1991). Baka Pygmies of Cameroon do not differ from Europeans or Bantus in average serum IGF-I concentrations, nor in the relationship between serum IGF-I and its major binding protein (IGFBP-3), which Dulloo et al. (1996) attributed the low levels observed in some individuals to infections rather than to any inherited defect in the growth-hormone–IGF-I axis. However, Cortez et al. (1996) showed that cells from Mbuti cultivated in vitro have a genuine and unique resistance to IGF-I. The hormonal status of Pygmoid groups of intermediate stature, and the genetic mechanism involved (its penetrance and expressivity), are still unclear.

With a short stature (155 ± 6 cm), an elongated skull and marked prognathism, wide flat nose, dark skin and woolly hair, some Kainantu horticulturists groups of eastern Papua New Guinea (Littlewood 1972) look very similar to African Pygmies (more than Philippine Negrito hunters do). One can wonder if some adaptive convergence, arising from an uneven chain of mutations, is the only explanation for such a resemblance. Blood groups are too different to suggest any common recent origin between African and Asiatic short-statured peoples, but one cannot exclude the resurgence of a very old tropical morphotype interpreted, in the absence of fossil evidence, as a plesiomorphic heritage, i.e. the conservation of an ancestral pattern.

Differentiation and affinities

The quest for the primordial modern humans is a major agenda in palaeontology. According to an hypothetical 'African Eve', Khoisan and some Pygmy groups would have diverged from the root of anatomically modern humans' root earlier than other Africans (Maddison *et al.* 1992, Ruvolo *et al.* 1993) and would even represent the very stem of humankind. Genetic comparisons with other primates, such as the haplotype XIII of the Y-chromosome (Lucotte 1990), lead to the very suspect conclusion that some human groups could be a little more 'ape-like' and 'primitive' than others. In fact, Pygmies display genetic configurations which are closer to West Africans for Gm (specific antigens), to Bantus for HLA (human leukocyte antigens) and to Nilotes for Rhesus blood sub-groups (Excoffier *et al.* 1987) as if they belonged to an earlier, undifferentiated African group. They are African, and even 'hyper-Africans' for some traits; they also share (especially Mbuti, who are the most peculiar, with respect to both morphology and genetics) some traits with the San (erythrocyte acid phosphatase and phosphoglucomutase in particular). On this basis, Cavalli-Sforza (1986: 409) postulated a 'proto-African' stock (including San) diverging from non-

Pygmies at around 15 000 BP. Hiernaux (1974) thought that populations ancestral to present Pygmies and Pygmoids might have
significantly differed in the past and converged later, due to adaptation to a similar environment and to gene flow. Genetic relations
between San and Tanzanian (Sandawe and Hadza) click-speaking
hunters are not established.

In many cases, forager groups have been geographically isolated
(e.g. Inuit, Australians), receiving no gene flow. Elsewhere, cultural
contacts existed, but there is no close parallel between language
shift and gene admixture. Measuring hybridisation between
hunting and farming populations presupposes the preexistence of
two clear-cut separate gene pools; this assumption is probably
untrue, as in many cases the groups under consideration share a
common descent. From the few genetic surveys available (Cavalli-
Sforza 1986: 404–17), it appears that, as in most small foraging
bands, Pygmies display important genetic inter-group heterogeneity; for instance Aka (Babinga) from Central African Republic
are much closer to their farmer neighbours than to Ituri Mbuti,
which are classically considered 'true' Pygmies. They also have a
few genetic peculiarities concerning some rare markers, which
correspond to mutations which occurred, at very low frequencies,
after their differentiation from other populations. One of the aims
of the Human Genome Project (Cavalli-Sforza et al. 1991) is to
explore the specificities of such small groups, before they disappear
or become admixed.

In order to test the physical resemblances between different
groups of hunter–gatherers, from North America, the Arctic, Asia,
Australia and Africa, six of their cephalic measurements were
compared to those of African farmers, in a multivariate analysis
(Figure 9.1). The populations differ mainly by their nose breadth
(horizontal axis) – narrow in North America, intermediate in Asian
Negritos, large in Africa, very large in Australia – and also by head
shape (vertical axis) – rounder head for Pygmies, and a broader face
for native Americans and Australians. These differences in head
and face morphology are observed on a world-wide basis within the
human species (Froment 1992), and probably have a strong genetic
basis. Within Africa, the clusters of 'true' Pygmies and Khoisan do

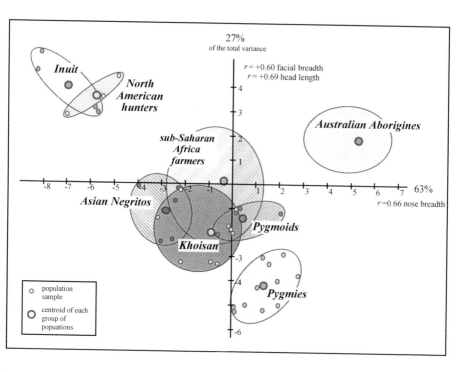

Figure 9.1. Multivariate discriminant analysis of head morphology for hunter-gatherers from North America, the Arctic, Asia (Negritos), Australia and Africa (San, Pygmies and Pygmoids), compared to the variation for farmers of sub-Saharan Africa. The six variables used are head length, head breadth, total face height, facial breadth (bizygomatic), nose breadth and nose height, for 215 populations (adult males only; the same pattern is obtained for females for a smaller sample). The two axes express 90% of the total variance; 83% of the populations are correctly classified in their group of origin by the analysis.

not overlap, while Khoisan and Pygmoids are closer to the observed biological variation of sub-Saharan farmer populations than are Pygmies. This could be attributed to a genetic heterogeneity between Pygmies and Pygmoids, possibly due, as Hiernaux (1974) proposed, to different histories of adaptation to the rainforest.

Medical constraints

Medical surveys are difficult to conduct in remote groups, as people are often reluctant to accept investigations, especially the sampling of urine, stools and blood. X-rays or refined biochemical investigations are technically complicated, and autopsy records are virtually unknown. With rapid acculturation, it will soon be too late to have a precise idea of the health of genuine foragers. Hence, the interesting question of knowing whether past populations had a better life than nowadays could remain partially unanswered: Webb (1995) was unable to conclude whether Australians had fewer diseases in pre-colonial times despite studying extensive skeletal material. The biology of living groups may not reflect the health status of past populations, and palaeopathological data must be handled with caution, because of many biases; for instance, one may hypothesise that the increase of visible diseases could be balanced by a decrease of diseases which do not leave lesions on bones. However, with methods in palaeopathology still limited to anatomical examinations, future improvements in DNA amplification may reveal evidence of microbial past infections.

Epidemiological transitions

Barrett *et al.* (1998) distinguished three major 'epidemiological transitions' with neolithisation, industrialisation and disease re-emergence. Transition to agriculture – associated with food crises, increase of workload, contact with cattle and bush clearing favouring the extension of transmissible diseases like malaria – was accompanied with an apparent deterioration of health and nutritional status (Larsen 1995), but also with extraordinary biological success exemplified by a demographic explosion.

The traditional way of life of foraging bands modulates exposure to diseases as follows. A very low density (less than one human per km^2) is under the critical threshold necessary for the transmission of some acute and destructive infections like smallpox, influenza, poliomyelitis or measles (Black 1975), a set of epidemics which probably did not affect early human evolution. Low density is also protective, by host 'dilution' in the environment, from vector-borne parasites (*Plasmodium* of malaria, *Onchocerca* of river blindness, *Trypanosoma* of sleeping sickness in Africa and of Chagas' disease in South America). Limited contacts with other nomadic groups, and remote situations, keep people away from sedentary habitats where the usual epidemics, including sexually transmissible diseases, circulate. Also, nomadic life prevents the accumulation of refuse and faecal pollution around the habitat. Fungal dermatoses, ectoparasites like lice and scabies and cutaneous fly larvae are dependent on limited hygiene and washing facilities. People in hot climates were less exposed when nearly naked, before missionaries urged them to wear clothes, which are often very dirty in places where water or soap are rare.

As well as such advantages, foraging societies experience specific epidemiological risks. A closer contact with wild animals exposes them to rare or new viruses (including emerging HIVs, HTLVs and filoviruses), and to more violent deaths from snake bites, hunting accidents or others hazards (not eliminated by technological progress, as in the case of snow motorbike accidents among Inuit). The overall result is, at least nowadays, a shorter life expectancy compared to other types of societies (see Pennington, this volume), usually in the context of great economic poverty. Even in countries where the standard of life is better than in Third World tropical areas, differences in life span are very marked; for instance, national Canadian statistics give a life expectancy of 59 years and 63 years for male and female Inuit versus 70.3 and 77.8, respectively, in the rest of the population.

The ecology of infectious diseases

Infections have been a major cause of mortality in the past. This strong pressure, however, did not select many genetic adaptations to viruses or bacteria, and these pathogens are still very harmful in poorly medicalised societies. Despite the variety of ailments affecting different hunter–gatherer populations in such diverse environments, some problems are common to many groups (Polunin 1979).

Epidemiological studies show that while the forest diet is rich and varied, people have a low life expectancy; the hot and humid environment is favourable to the transmission of numerous pathogens, notably infectious diarrhoeas and intestinal parasites (Froment *et al.* 1993). Hence malnutrition is no less frequent there than in the savannah where food availability is more precarious but the environment healthier (Nurse and Jenkins 1977). Dunn (1977) developed an opposition between complex (tropical rainforest) and simple (tundra, desert bush, thorn woodland) ecosystems; the main difference is climatic and modulates biodiversity. Consequently, the number of human parasitic diseases can range from 1 (central Australian desert) or 3 (San of Africa) to 20 (African Pygmies) or 22 (Semang of Malaya). In the wooded savannah of Mato Grosso, Brazil, Neel *et al.* (1968) conducted extensive biological studies among the Xavante Indians, and found them to have low rates of malaria, a disease of African origin, and virtually no sign of treponemal infections, but a high exposure to *Toxoplasma* and to many viruses (poliomyelitis, measles, arboviruses), indicating a wide variety of pathogenic contacts. Many foraging peoples, as do the Xavante, look very healthy but they experience very high childhood mortality.

Table 9.1 shows some key health indicators among Cameroon Pygmoids compared to their agriculturist neighbours, in two different ecosystems, in order to examine differences between foraging and farming ways of life. Haemoglobin levels indicate anaemia, gamma-globulin levels reflect antigenic contacts, malaria and blood filariae are linked to exposure to biting insects, and intestinal worms are indicators of faecal contamination. The Bedzan Pygmoids in the forest–savannah contact area are less healthy than the forest Bakola

Pygmoids, and less so than Tikar (Bantoid) farmers. Bakola score better than Mvae (Bantu) farmers for malaria and ascaris, but have higher immunoglobulin levels indicating cumulated infections, related to a lifestyle close to nature. The very significant difference between Pygmoids and farmers, especially marked in children, is confirmed by Dulloo *et al.* (1996), Constans (cited by Heymer 1992: 187) and Pagezy (personal communication). High exposure to infections is also noticed in drier areas, like the Kalahari (Brontë-Stewart *et al.* 1960), where !Kung had higher rates of gamma-globulins (27.4 g/l) than Okavango Bantus (23.4 g/l), and Cape Town Bantus (17.2 g/l). However, no such high levels are seen among Hadza (Bennett *et al.* 1970); it is interesting that, as noted by Pennington (this volume), survival in Hadza is better than in others foragers, probably because of a safer environment.

Common viruses and bacteria

The presence of viral infections, like smallpox, influenza, HIV or measles, which represent an enormous burden for humankind, is closely related to population size and density. Diarrhoeal diseases, the highest cause of childhood morbidity and mortality in developing countries, also show a relationship with the mode of settlement; in an Australian Aboriginal community, with an average of less than one episode per child per year, diarrhoea was less frequent in families living the traditional way than among those living in houses (Ratnaike and Ratnaike 1989). Hepatites follow the same rule and are common in any society where hygiene is deficient and promiscuity frequent, as in foraging bands; chronic infection by hepatitis B and hepatitis C leads to high incidence of liver cancer, long noticed among native Alaskans (Alberts *et al.* 1991) and in the tropics. HIV is rare among hunters-gatherers, because they have few sexual contacts with outside populations. Other retroviruses like HTLV-I (Yanagihara *et al.* 1995) and HTLV-II (Black 1997), transmitted from generation to generation through breast-feeding, and found at endemic level in Pygmies, hunters from Amazonia, Ne-

Table 9.1. Comparisons between semi-sedentarised Pygmoid foragers and neighbouring farmers in two ecological areas of Cameroon

Health indicators[a]	Rainforest (2°30′ N, 10° E)				Forest–savannah transition (5°30′ N, 11°30′ E)				Comparisons[b]			
	A. Kola Pygmoids foragers		B. Mvae Bantu farmers		C. Bedzan Pygmoids foragers		D. Tikar Bantoid farmers		A vs. B	C vs. D	A vs. C	B vs. D
Haematology												
Haemoglobin g/100 ml	76	11.8 ± 1.8	173	11.4 ± 1.6	174	10.7 ± 1.5	409	10.9 ± 1.8	ns	ns	ns	**
Gamma-globulins g/l	76	33.7 ± 9.2	173	24.2 ± 11.0	174	—	409	—	**	—	—	—
Blood parasites												
Malaria	84	2%	193	8%	153	45%	359	39%	*	ns	*	**
Filariae	84	8%	193	13%	153	7%	359	16%	ns	*	ns	ns
Stool parasites												
Ascaris	68	51%	213	69%	108	90%	227	63%	*	**	*	**
Trichuris	68	85%	213	89%	108	83%	227	68%	ns	**	ns	ns

[a] Results (*n*, mean ± standard deviation, or frequency) are for adults and children, male and female, pooled.
[b] The statistical tests have been paired by column: Kola vs. Mvae (A vs. B), Bedzan vs. Tikar (C vs. D) and the two pygmoid groups (A vs. C). ns: not significant, *: significant, **: highly significant.
Source: Surveys by Froment, Cameroon 1984–94.

gritos and Australian Aborigines, prove to be potential markers of past world-wide human migrations.

Yaws, the endemic (not venereal) form of syphilis, transmitted from person to person or by flies, can be used as a marker of poverty. In Africa, its incidence is more common among Pygmies than villagers: 55% among Bakola (and even 72 to 85% among East Cameroon and Ituri Pygmies (Cavalli-Sforza 1986: 160) versus 37% among Bantus in south-atlantic Cameroon (Froment *et al.* 1993). This difference has two main causes: lower corporeal hygiene, and the fact that Pygmies had more limited access to the campaigns of penicillin injections which attempted to eradicate yaws in central Africa in the 1960s. In the savannah where yaws is replaced by a less visible infection called bejel, only 6% of Hadza had a positive treponema serology (Bennett *et al.* 1973).

Lung diseases such as bronchitis are widespread in either cold or tropical climates, because hearth fires generate heavy pollution in small huts. Tuberculosis is now spreading among foragers, but most of cases observed would have come from their contacts with settled populations. Probably due to the severity of climate, otitis media, which impairs hearing, is remarkably frequent among Inuit (Reed *et al.* 1967). Eye diseases, which follow accidents or infections like trachoma, and which severely limit hunting abilities, often lead to blindness: among the Hadza, 29% of 484 people examined suffered from an eye disease, while two were blind (Bennett *et al.* 1973: 255).

Parasites

Blood parasites

Malaria, caused by an African parasite (*Plasmodium falciparum*) imported to Asia, America and the Pacific, is one of the highest causes of mortality in tropical countries. The percentage of children with enlarged spleens, an indirect symptom of chronic malaria, is two or three times higher among present-day Bakola foragers than among the rainforest villagers; conversely the frequency of sickle-cell anaemia, conferring genetic protection against malaria, is two times lower, a characteristic shared by all the Pygmy populations (Cavalli-

Sforza 1986). Coursey and Alexander (1968) described the relationships between agricultural systems, malaria and sickle-cell anaemia: deforestation during the Neolithic created the habitats for the malarial vector in agricultural areas. The Pygmy populations, formerly little exposed, would not have had time to develop the high frequency of protection provided by sickle-cell anaemia. Out of 256 Mbuti of all ages (Mann *et al.* 1962), 48% had an enlarged spleen and as many as 20% (51% between age 5 and 9 years) had blood smears positive for malaria. Moreover, between 55% and 100% of the sample were positive for *Dipetalonema perstans*, and more than 60% of adults suffered from onchocerciasis, two insect-borne filariae.

In savannah areas, malaria has an epidemic pattern with a peak during the rainy season. Among 885 !Kung examined (Brontë-Stewart *et al.* 1960), 52% had splenomegaly, attributed to malaria contamination around the Okavango River area, and also to some urinary bilharziasis. Bennett *et al.* (1970) found a rate varying from 10% (dry season) to 26% (wet season) of blood smears positive with malaria in the Hadza; the corresponding figures for enlarged spleens were 22% and 32%; no differences occurred between nomadic camps and settlements, and all the 132 sera tested were positive for *Plasmodium* malaria antibodies.

Intestinal parasites

Helminth transmission is related to the faecal pollution of the surrounding environment. The relatively high mobility of hunters used to protect them from high rates of infection, but most of the groups are now semi-sedentarised. Among Ituri Mbuti (Mann *et al.* 1962), as much as 85% of the population had hookworms (*Necator americanus* or *Ancylostoma duodenale*), 70% had *Trichuris* and 57% had *Ascaris*; 7% had intestinal bilharziasis, and 36% had pathogen amoebas (*Entamoeba histolytica*), while 13% of children under age 15 had *Giardia lamblia* infection, a cause of severe diarrhoea. Surveys in Australia showed high rates of infection with hookworm in the tropical northwest (Holt *et al.* 1980) or protozoa (*Giardia*, *Entamoeba*) in the Kimberley (Meloni *et al.* 1993); near-total absence of infection with *Ascaris*, *Trichuris* and *Entamoeba* species (all frequent in eastern

Australian Aboriginal communities) is noted in this western area (Jones 1980), probably for ecological reasons. Among the San of Namibia (Evans *et al.* 1990), stools examination revealed that out of 31 inhabitants of a camp, 63% had hookworms and 35% *Trichuris*; among 105 children 6–17 years of age attending schools in Bushmanland, 85% had hookworms, and 25% *Strongyloides*, one of the highest prevalences in South Africa. In Hadza figures are low (Bennett *et al.* 1970): only 14% of nomads had *Trichuris* and 4% *Ascaris*, and in settled villages, maybe due to medical treatments (Bennett *et al.* 1973: 249), prevalences were even lower or nill; serological tests for amoebiasis proved, however, that nomads had the lowest incidence.

In circumpolar areas, people in contact with wild animals (mammals and fish) are exposed to parasites via direct contamination (*Echinococcus*, *Taenia*, *Diphyllobothrium*, *Trichinella*) and human-to-human transmission (*Ascaris*, *Enterobius*, *Trichuris*, amoebas), but not to parasites which have an external cycle of maturation (*Ancylostoma*, *Necator*, *Strongyloides*) in the ground – a cycle unlikely to suceed when soils are frozen. In a comprehensive synthesis of Amerindians' epidemiology, Salzano and Callegari-Jacques (1988: 87–113) reported heavy rates (40% to 99%) of *Ascaris*, *Trichuris* or hookworms in most groups, but it was unclear whether foragers got these helminths from recent contacts with farmers or had been infected prior to contacts. More generally, as for HTLV viruses, molecular genetics of parasites found in remote living populations could provide some clues to human migrations.

Chronic diseases

Neel's fruitful hypothesis of a 'thrifty genotype' (Neel 1962) proposes that useful genes in adverse environments become harmful in a context of affluence, with the observed consequences on obesity and diabetes observed in American Indians (Barsh 1999) or Aboriginal Australians (O'Dea 1991). In South Cameroon, Pygmies are noticeably affected by arterial hypertension (15% of adults in the author's survey of Bakola); the explanation lies in high salt consumption, alcohol and tobacco, and perhaps stress, as their life is not one of leisure and affluence as famously claimed by some anthropologists such as Turnbull (1961) or Sahlins (see Winterhalder, and Rowley-Conwy, this volume). In Mbuti (Mann *et al.* 1962), only 5% of adults had excessive blood pressure, while Kesteloot *et al.* (1996) found no blood pressure difference between Bantus and Baka Pygmies, and observed a tendency for blood pressure to increase with age, a trend absent among the !Kung (Truswell 1979). Hunters are said to have remarkable powers of endurance in following game; however not many cardiac tests have been performed to check this claim, and the epidemiology of heart diseases is not well known; the same is true for cancers, but this type of affliction is dependent on life span, and cannot appear if people die early from other, mainly infectious, causes.

Beside heart pathology, other non-communicable diseases are to be considered. Osteoporosis is not only a disease of modernity and inactivity, as decalcification has been observed in Inuit (even in the pre-contact era) with ageing (Harper *et al.* 1984); arthritic inflammation is also common in most traditional societies. Tooth health is often poor and most hunter–gatherers show a high level of dental attrition, abrasion, tartar deposit and gingivitis (Kent 1991); however cavities are usually rare, in both present-day and Palaeolithic samples. Another category of diseases, psychiatric disorders, is not absent in non-acculturated foraging societies, but is very difficult to study (among Pygmies or San for example; Doob 1965). Adaptability to a changing world is strongly dependent on mental equilibrium, a crucial issue that foraging societies have now to face.

Conclusion: future changes

For most indigenous minorities, the transition to modernisation is synonym of impoverishment, racism, violence, alcoholism, drug addiction, suicide and social disintegration. In fact, the tendency to consume toxic substances can be symptomatic of an unconscious desire of self-destruction, and a mute protest against the collapse of the old values. For Pygmy, San, Negrito, Inuit and other economically marginal groups, ways of life have already changed or will soon do so, with modifications of the environment, such as game depletion and competition from other types of economies.

Coping with hazards and a heavy burden of diseases, hunter–gatherers do not live – and have never lived – in the Garden of Eden; they are not affluent, but poor, with limited needs and limited satisfaction, and little access to any facility. We cannot be sure, however, that more-or-less acculturated present-day hunter–gatherer populations are a true reflection of their past – perhaps this poverty is a consequence of contacts (yet in Africa, both Pygmies and Khoisan have been in contact with Bantus for thousands of years). The human species may well be more adapted to a hunter–gatherer diet, usually poor in fat and sugar and rich in fibres, than to what is ours today, and the price to pay will be the so-called 'diseases of civilisation' (Eaton and Eaton 1999), but the multiple infections, the uncertainty of survival and the demographic limitations imposed by a hunting way of life cast serious doubts on any nostalgia of a lost Paradise. Of course, as Eaton and Eaton argue, past foragers had a healthy way of life, a good diet and physical exercise, virtually no salt, alcohol or tobacco, no pollution, fewer cancers, and a life span and child mortality not so different of what was observed in Europe a few centuries ago. But this condition of isolated bands has vanished, and the present context is radically different.

The challenge, for present-day hunter–gatherers groups, is to adapt quickly to radical changes in lifestyle, a problem they already faced, to lesser extent, in the past, since they are not immobile cultures fossilised since the Palaeolithic. Among expected changes, some are positive, others negative or neutral. The quantifiable changes may include demographic expansion, due to improved sanitation and medical care, and to increased fertility. With the modification of ecosystems and game depletion, the growing importance of agriculture will modify, and probably mitigate, the exposure to transmissible diseases. However, nutritional disorders, like anaemias and other deficiencies, obesity, hypertension and diabetes, will appear because of dietary imbalance and alcoholism (O'Keefe and Lavender 1989), especially where people are regrouped in artificial villages or reserves. This new crowding favours the spread of acute and chronic diseases. In these mostly egalitarian communities, old social structures will vanish and the emergence of a hierarchical order can be predicted; possible psychiatric troubles, sometimes leading to homicidal tendencies (Headland 1989), are seen as the symptoms of refusal to change. The loss of knowledge of resources for food or medicine from the environment will be replaced, not necessarily for worse, by another – more scientific – corpus. An enhanced admixture will lead to a breakdown of genetic isolation, and plausibly to the appearance of secular trends such as increase in stature.

Hunter–gatherers have poorer access to schools and to medical assistance than sedentary populations, and the transition to modernity raises specific problems. Some hopes relate to a better access to land, a difficult matter for people believed to be nomadic, but this increased food security, together with a better access to schools and health services, will also precipitate the disappearance of their traditional life style. And despite such a cultural disappearance, physical differences based on different phenotypes will persists. Due to a persistent social segregation, the former hunter–gatherer, when becoming a farmer, an industry worker or a civil servant, will still be viewed as a 'Pygmy', a Negrito, a Bushman, an Aborigine, for as long as distinctive physical features are present.

Though hunting and gathering is a legacy for humankind, it is disappearing everywhere without much hope of revival. Considering the difficulties that the last hunter–gatherer societies are facing, especially in maintaining food resources and coping with diseases, we may wonder whether hunter–gatherers should themselves keep that way of life. The romantic myth of a Golden Age, revitalised by some ecological activists or by the paternalism of some religious institutions, is far from actual reality. In the end, the biological consequences of modernity for hunter–gatherer groups will be dictated by the evolution of social prejudice against them, their access to school, affluence and health facilities, the acknowledgement of traditional rights to land, as well as their own choices in the matter of development.

References

Alberts, S.R., Lanier, A.P., McMahon, B.J., Harpster, A., Bulkow, L.R., Heyward, W.L. and Murray, C. (1991). Clustering of hepatocellular carcinoma in Alaska native families, *Genetics Epidemiology* **8**: 127–139.

Austin, D.M. and Ghesquiere, J. (1976). Heat tolerance of Bantu and Pygmoid groups of the Zaïre. *Human Biology* **48**: 439–453.

Bahuchet, S., McKey, D. and Garine, I. de. (1991). Wild yams revisited: is independence from agriculture possible for rain-forest hunter–gatherers? *Human Ecology* **19**: 213–243.

Bailey, R.C. and Peacock, N.R. (1988). Efe Pygmies of northeast Zaïre: subsistence strategies in the Ituri forest. In *Coping with Uncertainty in Food Supply*, ed. I. de Garine and G.A. Harrison, pp. 88–117. Oxford: Clarendon Press.

Barrett, R., Kuzawa, C.W., McDade, T. and Armelagos, G.J. (1998). Emerging and re-emerging infectious diseases: the third epidemiologic transition. *Annual Review of Anthropology* **27**: 247–271.

Barsh, R.L. (1999). Chronic health effects of dispossession and dietary change: lessons from North American hunter–gatherers. *Medical Anthropology* **18**: 135–161.

Baumann, G., Shaw, M.A., Brumbaugh, R.C. and Schwartz, J. (1991). Short stature and decreased serum Growth Hormone-Binding Protein in the mountain Ok people of Papua New Guinea. *Journal of Clinical Endocrinology and Metabolism* **72**: 1346–1349.

Bennett, F.J., Kagan, I.G., Barnicot, N.A. and Woodburn, J.C. (1970). Helminth and protozoal parasites of the Hadza of Tanzania. *Transactions of the Royal Society of Tropical Medicine and Hygiene* **64**: 857–880.

Bennett, F.J., Barnicot, N.A., Woodburn, J.C., Pereira, M.S. and Henderson, B.E. (1973). Studies on viral, bacterial, rickettsial and treponemal diseases in the Hadza of Tanzania and a note on injuries. *Human Biology* **45**: 243–272.

Birdsell, J.B. (1993). *Microevolutionary Patterns in Aboriginal Australia: A Gradient Analysis of Clines*, Research Monographs on Human Population Biology. Oxford: Oxford University Press.

Bittel, J. (1992). The different types of general cold adaptation in man. *International Journal of Sports and Medicine* **13**: S172–S176.

Black, F.L. (1975). Infectious diseases in primitive societies. *Science* *187*: 515–518.

Black, F.L. (1997). Tracing prehistoric migrations by the viruses they carry: human T-cell lymphotropic viruses as markers of ethnic relationships. *Human Biology* **69**: 467–482.

Bribiescas, R.G. (1996). Testosterone levels among Aché hunter–gatherer men. A functional interpretation of population variation among adult males. *Human Nature* **7**: 163–188.

Brontë-Stewart, B., Budtz-Olsen, O.E., Hickley, J.M. and Brock, J.F. (1960). The health and nutritional status of the Kung bushmen of South West Africa. *South African Journal of Laboratory and Clinical Medicine* **6**: 187–216.

Brues, A. (1959). The spearman and the archer: an essay on selection on body build. *American Anthropologist* **61**: 457–459.

Cavalli-Sforza, L L. (ed.) (1986). *African Pygmies*. New York: Academic Press.

Cavalli-Sforza, L.L. and Bodmer, W.F. (1971). *The Genetics of Human Populations*. San Francisco: W.H. Freeman .

Cavalli-Sforza, L.L., Wilson, A.C., Cantor, C.R., Cook Deegan, R.M. and King, M.C. (1991). Call for a worldwide survey of human genetic diversity: a vanishing opportunity for the Human Genome Project. *Genomics* **11**: 490–491.

Christiansen, K.H. (1991). Serum and saliva sex hormone levels in !Kung San Men. *American Journal of Physical Anthropology* **86**: 37–44.

Cortez, A.B., Van Dop, C., Bailey, R.C., Bersch, N., Scott, M., Golde, D.W. and Geffner, M.E. (1996). IGF-I resistance in virus-transformed B-lympho-cytes from African Efe Pygmies. *Biochemical and Molecular Medicine* **58**: 31–36.

Coursey, D.G. and Alexander, J. (1968). African agricultural patterns and the sickle cell. *Science* **160**: 1474–1475.

Diamond, J.M. (1991). Why are pygmies small?, *Nature* **354**: 111–112.

Dietz, W.H., Marino, B., Peacock, N.R. and Bailey, R.C. (1989). Nutritional status of Efe Pygmies and Lese horticulturists. *American Journal of Physical Anthropology* **78**: 509–518.

Doob, L.W. (1965). Psychology. In *The African World*, ed. R.A. Lystad, New York: Praeger.

Dormitzer, P.R., Ellison, P.T. and Bode, H.H. (1989). Anomalously low endemic goiter prevalence among Efe pygmies. *American Journal of Physical Anthropology* **78**: 527–531.

Dulloo, A.G., Shahkhalili, Y., Atchou, G., Mensi, N., Jacquet, J. and Girardier, L. (1996). Dissociation of systemic GH–IGF-I axis from a genetic basis for short stature in African Pygmies. *European Journal of Clinical Nutrition* **50**: 371–380.

Dunn, F.L. (1977). Health and disease in hunter–gatherers: epidemiological factors. In *Culture, Disease, and Healing*, ed. D. Landy, pp. 99–113. New York, Macmillan.

Eaton, S. Boyd and Eaton, Stanley B. (1999). Hunter–gatherers and human health. In *The Cambridge Encyclopedia of Hunters and Gatherers*, ed. R.B. Lee and R. Daly, pp. 449–455. Cambridge: Cambridge University Press.

Evans, A.C., Markus, M.B. and Steyn, E. (1990). A survey of the intestinal nematodes of Bushmen in Namibia. *American Journal of Tropical Medicine and Hygiene* **42**: 243–247.

Excoffier, L., Pellegrini, B., Sanchez-Mazas, A., Simon, C. and Langaney, A. (1987). Genetics and history of sub-saharan Africa. *Yearbook of Physical Anthropology* **30**: 151–194.

Ferretti, G., Atchou, G., Grassi, B., Marconi, C. and Cerretelli, P. (1993). Energetics of locomotion in African Pygmoids. *European Journal of Applied Physiology* **62**: 7–10.

Froment, A. (1992). La différenciation morphologique de l'Homme moderne: congruence entre forme du crâne et répartition géographique du peuplement. *Comptes-Rendus de l'Académie des Sciences (Paris)*, **315**, ser. III: 323–329.

Froment, A., Koppert, G. and Loung, J.F. (1993). Eat well, live well: nutritional status and health of forest populations in Southern Cameroon. In *Tropical Forests: People and Food*, MAB Series 13, ed. C.M. Hladik, A. Hladik, O. Linares, H. Pagezy, A. Semple M. and Hadley, pp. 357–364. London: Parthenon-UNESCO.

Ghesquiere, J.L. and Karvonen, M.J. (1981). Some anthropometric and functional dimensions of the pygmy (Kivu Twa). *Annals of Human Biology* **8**: 119–134.

Harper, A.B., Laughlin, W.S. and Mazess, R.B. (1984). Bone mineral content in St. Lawrence Island Eskimos. *Human Biology* **56**: 63–77.

Hassan, F.A. (1975). Determination of the size, density and growth rate of hunting-gathering populations. In *Population, Ecology and Social Evolution*, ed. S. Polgar, pp. 27–52. The Hague: Mouton.

Headland, T.L. (1989). Population decline in a Philippine Negrito hunter–gatherer society. *American Journal of Human Biology* **1**: 59–72.

Henneberg, M. (1988). Decrease of human skull size in the Holocene. *Human Biology* **60**: 395–405.

Hernandez, M., Garcia-Moro, C. and Lalueza-Fox, C. (1998). Stature estimation in extinct Aonikenk and the myth of Patagonian gigantism. *American Journal of Physical Anthropology* **105**: 545–551.

Heymer, A. (1992). Die physische Erscheinungsform der afrikanischen Pygmäen und Gedanken zur Evolution. *Mitteilungen der Anthropologischen Gesellschaft in Wien* **122**: S155–S190.

Hiernaux, J. (1974). *The People of Africa*. New York: Scribner's Sons.

Hladik, C.M. and Simmen, B. (1996). Taste perception and feeding behaviour in nonhuman primates and human populations. *Evolutionary Anthropology* **5**: 58–71.

Holliday, T.W. and Falsetti, A.B. (1995). Lower limb length of European early modern humans in relation to mobility and climate. *Journal of Human Evolution* **29**: 141–153.

Holmes, R. (1993). Nutritional anthropometry of South American indigenes: growth deficits in biocultural and development perspective. In *Tropical Forests: People and Food*, MAB Series 13, ed. C.M. Hladik, A. Hladik,

O. Linares, H. Pagezy, A. Semple and M. Hadley, pp. 349–356. London: Parthenon-UNESCO.

Holt, A.B., Spargo, R.M., Iveson, J.B., Faulkner, G.S. and Cheek, D.B. (1980). Serum and plasma zinc, copper and iron concentrations in Aboriginal communities of North Western Australia. *American Journal of Clinical Nutrition* **33**: 119–132.

Hyndman, D.C., Ulijaszek, S.J. and Lourie, J.A. (1989). Variability in body physique, ecology, and subsistence in the Fly River region of Papua New Guinea. *American Journal of Physical Anthropology* **79**: 89–101.

Jones, H.I. (1980). Intestinal parasite infections in Western Australian Aborigines. *Medical Journal of Australia* **2**: 375–380.

Katzmarzyk, P.T. and Leonard, W.R. (1998). Climatic influences on human body size and proportions: ecological adaptations and secular trends. *American Journal of Physical Anthropology* **106**: 483–503.

Kazadi, N. (1981). Méprisés et admirés: l'ambivalence des relations entre les Bacwa (Pygmées) et les Bahemba (Bantu). *Africa* **51**: 836–848.

Kent, S. (1991). Cause and effect of dental health, diet, and status among foragers. *American Anthropologist* **93**: 942–943.

Kent, S. and Dunn, D. (1996). Anemia and the transition of nomadic hunter–gatherers to a sedentary life-style: follow-up study of a Kalahari community. *American Journal of Physical Anthropology* **99**: 455–472.

Kesteloot, H., Ndam, N., Sasaki, S., Kowo, M. and Seghers, V. (1996). A survey of blood pressure distribution in Pygmy and Bantu populations in Cameroon. *Hypertension* **27**: 108–113.

Koppert, G., Dounias, E., Froment, A. and Pasquet, P. (1993). Food consumption in three forest populations of the Southern coastal Cameroon. In *Tropical Forests: People and Food*, MAB Series 13, ed. C.M. Hladik, A. Hladik, O. Linares, H. Pagezy, A. Semple and M. Hadley, pp. 295–311. London: Parthenon-UNESCO.

Larsen, C.S. (1995). Biological changes in human populations with agriculture. *Annual Review of Anthropology* **24**: 185–213.

Lee, R.B. (1979). *The !Kung San: Men, Women and Work in a Foraging Society.* Cambridge: Cambridge University Press.

Littlewood, R.A. (1972). *Physical Anthropology of the Eastern Highlands of New Guinea.* Seattle: University of Washington Press.

Lucotte, G. (1990). *Introduction à l'Anthropologie Moléculaire: Eve était noire.* Paris: Lavoisier.

Maddison, D.R., Ruvolo, M. and Swofford, D.L. (1992). Geographic origins of human mitochondrial DNA: phylogenetic evidence from control region sequences. *Systematic Biology* **41**: 111–124.

Mann, G.V., Roels, A., Price, D.L. and Merrill, J.M. (1962). Cardiovascular disease in African Pygmies: a survey of the health status, serum lipids, and diet of Pygmies in Congo. *Journal of Chronic Diseases* **15**: 341–371.

Meloni, B.P., Thompson, R.C., Hopkins, R.M., Reynoldson, J.A. and Gracey, M. (1993). The prevalence of *Giardia* and other intestinal parasites in children, dogs and cats from aboriginal communities in the Kimberley. *Medical Journal of Australia* **158**: 157–159.

Neel, J.V. (1962). Diabetes mellitus: a thrifty genotype rendered detrimental by 'progress'. *American Journal of Human Genetics* **14**: 353–361.

Neel, J.V., Andrade, A.H.P., Brown, G.E., Eveland, W.E., Goobar, J., Sodeman, W.A. Jr, Stollerman, G.H., Weinstein, E.D. and Wheeler, A.H. (1968). Further studies of the Xavante Indians. IX. Immunologic status with respect to various diseases and organisms. *American Journal of Tropical Medicine and Hygiene* **17**: 486–498.

Newman, M.T. (1953). The applications of ecological rules to the racial anthropology of the aboriginal New World. *American Anthropologist* **55**: 311–327.

Norgan, N.G. (1994). Interpretation of low body mass indices: Australian Aborigines. *American Journal of Physical Anthropology* **94**: 229–237.

Nurse, G.T. and Jenkins, T. (1977). *Health and the Hunter–gatherer: Biomedical Studies on the Hunting and Gathering Populations of Southern Africa*. Basel: Karger.

Nurse, G.T., Weiner, J.S. and Jenkins, T. (1985). *The Peoples of Southern Africa and their Affinities*. Oxford: Clarendon Press.

O'Dea K. (1991). Westernisation, insulin resistance and diabetes in Australian aborigines. *Medical Journal of Australia* **155**: 258–264.

O'Keefe, S.J. and Lavender, R. (1989). The plight of modern Bushmen. *Lancet* **334** (**8657**): 255–258.

Pagezy, H. (1978). Morphological, physical and ethoecological adaptation of Oto and Twa women living in the equatorial forest. *Journal of Human Evolution* **7**: 683–692.

Pasquet, P., Froment, A. and Koppert, G. (1995). Variations staturales liées à l'âge chez l'adulte en Afrique : étude semi-longitudinale de la sénescence et recherches de tendances séculaires en fonction du milieu au Cameroun. *Cahiers d'Anthropologie et Biométrie Humaine* **13**: 233–245.

Polunin, I. (1979). Some characteristics of tribal peoples. In *Health and Disease in Tribal Societies*, CIBA Foundation Symposium 49, pp. 5–24. Amsterdam: Excerpta Medica.

Pretty, G.L., Henneberg, M., Lambert, K.M. and Prokopec, M. (1998). Trends in stature in the South Australian Aboriginal Murraylands. *American Journal of Physical Anthropology* **106**: 505–514.

Ratnaike, R.N. and Ratnaike, S.K. (1989). Diarrhoeal disease in under five years olds: an epidemiological study in an Australian aboriginal community. *European Journal of Epidemiology*, **5**: 82–86.

Reed, D., Struve, S. and Maynard, J.E. (1967). Otitis media and hearing deficiency among Eskimo children: a cohort study. *American Journal of Public Health* **57**: 1657–1662.

Rode, A. and Shephard, R.J. (1994). Growth and fitness of Canadian Inuit: secular trends, 1970–1990. *American Journal of Human Biology* **6**: 525–541.

Ruff, C.B. (1994). Morphological adaptation to climate in modern and fossil hominids. *Yearbook of Physical Anthropology* **37**: 65–107.

Ruvolo, M., Zehr, S., von Dornum, M., Pan, D., Chang, B. and Lin, J. (1993). Mitochondrial COH sequences and modern human origins. *Molecular Biological Evolution* **10**: 1115–1135.

Salzano, F.M. and Callegari-Jacques S.M. (1988). *South American Indians. A case study in Evolution*. Oxford: Clarendon Press.

Simoons, F.J. (1978). The geographic hypothesis and lactose malabsorption: a weighing of the evidence. *Digestive Diseases* **23**: 963–980.

So, J.K. (1980). Human biological adaptation to arctic and subarctic zones. *Annual Review of Anthropology* **9**: 63–82.

Spurr, G.B. (1987). Effects of chronic energy deficiency on stature, work capacity and productivity. In *Chronic Energy Deficiency: Consequences and Related Issues*, ed. B. Schürch and N.S. Scrimshaw, pp. 95–134. Lausanne: Nestlé Foundation.

Stinson, S. (1990). Variation in body size and shape among South American Indians. *American Journal of Human Biology* **2**: 37–51.

Truswell, A.S. (1979). Diet and nutrition in hunter–gatherers. In *Health and Disease in Tribal Societies*, CIBA Foundation Symposium 49, pp. 213–226. Amsterdam: Excerpta Medica.

Turnbull C. (1961). *The Forest People*. New York: Simon and Schuster.

Van Der Walt, L., Wilmsen, L.A. and Jenkins, T. (1978). Unusual sex hormone pattern among desert-dwelling hunter–gatherers. *Journal of Clinical Endocrinology and Metabolism* **46**: 658–663.

Vansina,, J. (1990). *Paths in the Rainforests. Towards a History of Political Tradition in Equatorial Africa*. London: Currey.

Webb, S. (1995). *Palaeopathology of Aboriginal Australians. Health and Disease across a Hunter–Gatherer Continent*. Cambridge: Cambridge University Press.

Winkler, E.M. and Kirchengast, S. (1994). Body dimensions and differential fertility in !Kung San males from Namibia. *American Journal of Human Biology* **6**: 203–213.

Yanagihara, R., Saitou, N., Nerurkar, V.R., Song, K.J., Bastian, I., Franchini, G. and Gajdusek, D.C. (1995). Molecular phylogeny and dissemination of human T-cell lymphotropic virus type I viewed within the context of primate evolution and human migration. *Cellular and Molecular Biology* **4**: S145–S161.

10

Hunting for images, gathering up meanings: art for life in hunting–gathering societies

MARGARET W. CONKEY

Introduction

In 1879, the now-famous Ice Age cave paintings on the ceiling of the cave of Altamira in Cantabrian Spain were 'discovered'. As the story goes, it was the little daughter of the landowner who noticed them. The landowner, Sautuola, was already doing some archaeology in the cave, but, at that time, it was still not widely accepted or understood that humans had an ancestry earlier than 4004 BC, the date for Creation established by the Church. Excavations in archaeological sites in Europe had, however, already recovered pieces of bone and antler, often shaped into implements, with engraved animals and geometric shapes on them, and these could be attributed to very ancient cultures because they were found in stratigraphic layers. Engraved bones were considered to be more 'craft' products and tools, whereas the polychrome animals on the Altamira ceiling (mostly bison, already long extinct in the region, but also deer and horse) were not accepted, even by the leading thinkers in prehistory, as having been the work, the 'art', of ancient peoples.

The ancient peoples in question had left the traces of their lifestyle, especially their hunting activities, and the notions of the day held that those who lived by hunting and gathering were primitive indeed, and they certainly could not have been responsible for, or capable of, the creation of the lively, dynamic, even aesthetically powerful images of curled, perhaps charging or dying bison in browns, reds, and blacks painted upon and using the natural shapes and protruberances of the cave ceiling. As it happened, Sautuola had been sheltering an artist at his estate, and surely, it was said, the ceiling paintings had been his work, not that of the ancient peoples, whose midden and trash were encountered in the cave. There could not have been a 'hunter–gatherer art', especially an 'art' that was defined in the current terms of the late nineteenth century as painting, in a naturalistic, realistic fashion.

It took until 1902, some 25 years later, for even the major prehistorians of the day to accept that the Altamira paintings could have been the work of very ancient hunter–gatherers but, by then, the ethnographic work of Spencer and Gillen (1899) among Australian aboriginal groups (who were themselves making rock art) had provided some ways to 'explain' or at least account for this curious phenomenon of 'hunter–gatherer art'. Although it is a much longer story than can be told here, the scholars and researchers of the early twentieth century came to accept the painted images as the work of prehistoric hunter–gatherers, but as ritual acts focused on gaining successes in the hunt, as primitive hunting magic. More painted caves had been discovered since the one at Altamira, and it was assumed that prehistoric hunters had painted or engraved animal images on these cave walls because the animals were 'good to eat'; they were trying to 'capture' these animals by making images of them. Many other features of the cave art were accounted for as part of hunting magic. Painted geometric shapes were interpreted as traps, hunters' huts, weapons, or wounds.

These prehistoric peoples were seen as less advanced than modern civilisations that had well-developed religious systems and had long ago left magic behind. Despite the widespread acceptance of the idea that acts of sympathetic hunting magic lay behind the placing of images on cave and rock-shelter walls, it was still a dilemma to account for the 'realism' of many images: they must have merely been painting what they 'saw', as it was unlikely they could have been engaged in symbolic thought in which the images could have embodied abstract, culturally significant values, meanings, and signification.

A century later, it is perfectly acceptable to think that hunter–gatherers are and were capable of producing 'art'. Those people who painted at Altamira (perhaps 15 000 years ago or more) and elsewhere (going back now to at least 30 000 years ago in Europe and to comparatively early dates for art in South Africa and Australia) are known to have been modern humans, *Homo sapiens sapiens*, with the same cognitive capacities as ours. But it took many decades of research with both the ethnographic and pre-historic arts of hunting–gathering–foraging peoples to show the complexity of image-makings, the complexity of attributing mean-ings, and the rich symbolic and cultural worlds of meaning-making within which hunter–gatherers, like most other humans, create, perpetuate, and transform a visual culture, creating what we might often call 'art'.

Instead of debating the humanity of the makers, their cognitive sophistication, or the symbolic depth and richness of such hunter–gatherer 'arts', current concerns are more with what 'art' is or was, and, even more challenging, with how to interpret or under-stand the visual and material worlds of 'art'. And thus, in a review of what we might know about the art of hunter–gatherers, there are at least three aspects of the topic to address. First, we need to clarify what we mean by 'art', especially at a time when the anthropology of art has been undergoing a considerable redefini-tion. Second, we need to consider the range of cultural phe-nomena included in the category of 'hunter–gatherer art'. What becomes clear here is that we need to be aware of both ethno-graphically and ethnohistorically known and archaeologically re-corded hunter–gatherers, and this will have important implications, both in terms of what kinds of 'arts' we know about, and in how they are studied and interpreted. This leads to the third aspect, namely, the need to grapple with how we try to understand and interpret these 'arts'. What are the analytical and interpretive approaches and what have we learned from them? As we will see, there are also many political and ethical issues involved, as these 'arts' (whether made in the past or the present) exist in the present, where issues of conservation, preservation, and the globa-lised market economy loom large.

What do we mean by 'art'?

Most of us have our own ideas about what we mean by the term 'art', but it is important to appreciate that this concept has a history. We have held changing notions about what 'art' is, and these notions, not surprisingly, have influenced how we think about the images and material forms produced in other cultures. In the past century or so in the western world, we have come to think of 'art' as something that is aesthetically pleasing, that is usually produced by specialists who are often considered to be gifted individuals with admirable degrees of creativity, and who are often somehow separate from real-life activities. In the nineteenth century, for example, painting was considered to be the pinnacle of artistic activity and achievement, which is why, perhaps, it was difficult for people of the time to accept that the prehistoric peoples at Altamira could have made paintings on the ceilings.

Our present-day objects of art – paintings, sculptures, drawings – are to be viewed, held in awe, and are embedded in the capitalist economic system; these objects have cultural and therefore economic value. Art objects are considered to 'function' in their own domain, that of high culture and aesthetics (Bourdieu 1984). No one would think that a sculpture, for example, should be used to work the soil in a garden. It is not surprising that when we look at the images and materials made in other cultures, especially in those that are somehow part of what we call hunter–gatherer cultures, we have tended to look for phenomena that correspond to our notion of 'art'. As Sparshott (1997) has argued so provocatively, the word 'art', and everything that is implied or comes along with it, is 'so specifically framed within "our" civilisation that it is perhaps something native only to "us"'!

It is a well-known truism in anthropology that most cultures that have been studied ethnographically rarely have a word or even a concept equivalent to our word and concept, 'art'. As we will see with some examples below, to try to separate out 'art' from other aspects of cultural life is not really possible. The relation between the so-called artistic aspects of any culture and what we would sort out as other aspects, such as the social, the symbolic, the economic, the political, etc., is, at best, problematical to anthropologists, and certainly cannot be reduced to any generalisations.

However, there are images, material culture and cultural practices in other cultures that we readily acknowledge as 'art', such as the cave paintings or totem poles, because, as Sparshott would argue, 'if they'd been products of our civilisation, we would have found it second nature to class them as art' (1997: 240). While we find it a real challenge to consider and describe cultural phenomena such as paintings on rock surfaces without a label, such as rock art, it is none the less not so much the label itself that is the problem but that what we mean by it is often left unexamined and the analysis or interpretation of the phenomena is led in certain directions because of the label.

For example, if one approaches the rock art imagery made by some hunting–gathering peoples of southern Africa in literal terms as 'art', many of the social, economic, and symbolic issues that we now know to be implicated in and constituted by these images would not be addressed, much less understood. It is not surprising, for example, that the lively images of people and animals that appear as the subject matter of this rock art were long considered to have been done just for aesthetic pleasure, as 'art-for-art's sake'. As we will see when we consider below how some of the art of southern African hunter–gatherers is now understood, this aesthetic categorisation not only precludes learning about a very rich and complex world of meanings and social practices but also has led to deeply problematic, limited, if not negative characterisations of the people presumed to have made the art (cf. Lewis-Williams 1995).

While an aesthetic element, for example, must surely often be a part of what goes into the decisions and productions of 'art' in other cultures (see e.g. Child and Siroto 1965, Thompson 1968, Morphy 1992, Shelton 1992), we must not presume the aesthetic and certainly not 'our' aesthetics. While people hold the cave paintings of many millennia ago in a kind of breathless awe and rave over their dynamism and beauty, we, of course, do not know what kinds of aesthetic preferences were held by the makers and ancient viewers. Would the image of the painted horse from the Palaeolithic cave art site of Lascaux that is shown so extensively today be the 'favourite' image of people of that time? Is what is pleasing or accomplished to us necessarily what was pleasing or accomplished to them?

Some people might suggest that to agonise over the use of the term 'art' is indulgent and distracts from the more important issues of understanding the practices and meanings of the arts in question. However, in a review of the so-called 'art' of hunter–gatherers, it is crucial to be aware of the ways in which 'our' categories structure our anthropological enquiry, and structure what we think we find out. That the 'making' of art is somehow considered separate or autonomous from the 'rest' of social life and that it is a highly individualistic enterprise are only two of 'our' notions about art that have led to problems in interpreting and understanding other cultures and their arts. As Morphy (1999) has pointed out, we need to develop a concept of art that 'neither distances the objects of other societies from Western cultures nor appropriates the object to European categories'.

In this regard, the more recent trend in contemporary anthropology to study 'material culture', especially if defined as broadly as possible, has allowed a more value-neutral framework for the study of what we would consider to be decorated baskets or pots, beadwork, iron-working, textiles, and other forms and media that might not readily conform to some notions of 'art'. What has been so revealing about this turn to 'material culture' is that material culture is often now taken to be inseparable from the immaterial, and, quite powerfully, so much of this 'material culture' is intimately bound up with all sorts of social and cultural phenomena, such as the study of gender, power relations, exchange, colonialism, tourism, and more (e.g. Appadurai 1986, Strathern 1988, MacKenzie 1991, Thomas 1991, among many). If what we call 'art' is more appropriately taken in under the rubric of 'material culture' then perhaps all of the ways in which art 'works' and the ways in which art is more for life's sake (than merely art-for-art's-sake) will be more central.

How anthropologists study 'art'

A decade ago, it might have been relatively uncontroversial to outline what anthropological approaches to art would entail, and there was not much debate or discussion as to what is meant by 'art'. Textbooks on the topic were fairly straightforward (e.g. Layton 1981, Hatcher 1985, Anderson 1989), although many studies still had to show that the arts were more than marginal or optional to the more 'core' aspects of culture that anthropologists studied, such as social structure. Firth (1992) reviews how the field has changed during the 60 years in which he has been an important contributor, although Gell (1992) argues that perhaps there is not a separate intellectual enterprise that we can label 'the anthropology of art'.

None the less, after many decades of neglect by anthropologists, there was, by the 1970s and 1980s, a noticeable increase in the scholarship that undertook to analyze and interpret the 'arts' of ethnographic and prehistoric peoples (e.g. Jopling 1971, Otten 1971), and many different approaches were tried out. These ranged from structuralist approaches (e.g. Lévi-Strauss 1963, Holm 1965, Leroi-Gourhan 1965, Fernandez 1966, Munn 1973) and psychological approaches (Wallace 1950, Fischer 1961) to ethnoaesthetics (e.g. Salvador 1978, Hedlund 1992, O'Neale 1995).

Simply put, many studies tended to treat the arts in small-scale and/or prehistoric societies as fairly contained within the social and cultural system in which they were found. With the exception of the then-emergent literature on what was called 'tourist arts' (Graburn 1976), relatively little attention was paid to the historical trajectories within which the objects being studied were situated. Many, if not most, studies were synchronic or approached the art in question either as being somehow functionally integrated into a coherent cultural system or as being autonomous from the dynamics of cultural disruption, change, and transformation. As Graburn (1999: 345) has recently summarized:

> Past anthropological analyses of non-western arts were dominated by models of the symbolic, ritual and political embeddedness of these 'authentic and traditional' functional arts . . . yet practically all the

objects in our ethnographic collections were acquired in politically complex, multicultural colonial situations.

There has been what one might call a 'loss of innocence' as anthropologists have come to realise just how complex and multi-faceted these colonial situations were, even for the very 'first' people who collected the objects that came to fill Western museums and provide the primary corpus for many early studies of what was then unproblematically called 'primitive art'. Townsend-Gault (1998: 425) has called this realisation a 'profound disturbance in the epistemology that underlies the anthropological study of art'; 'the kind of art that anthropologists study is no longer a given'. There is widespread recognition, as Graburn (1999), among others, would argue, that most non-Western art forms have a considerable history, that there probably never were static unchanging arts, that there is not necessarily a distinction to be made between the pure arts (of some imagined static pre-contact time) and the hybrid arts (developed in and out of colonial and contact situations) (cf. Morphy 1991: 2). Furthermore, it is widely agreed that most past studies focused more on the 'objects' than on the 'agents', or on the agents (e.g. 'artists') as part of the social matrix; it was not often that studies took up the social production of art (e.g. Wolff 1981) or the idea of art as practice.

One particular situation in regard to the rock art of contemporary Australian Aboriginal people makes an illuminating example. There has been considerable debate and discussion (e.g. Mowaljarlai et al. 1988) over whether contemporary Aboriginal painters should be allowed (!) to retouch their art in the Kimberley region. Rather than accepting that retouching had long been a practice and was, in fact, apparently culturally required (Layton 1985: 446), these (western) rock art researchers presumed that there was some sort of 'original' or 'pure-bred' imagery that needed to be contained or held constant. Rather than understand image-making as an ongoing cultural process, the researchers, perhaps unwittingly, privileged a static notion of 'preservation' over the ongoing connectedness of Aboriginal people with their own traditions (Vinnicombe 1995: 91).

While all of these statements about the changing nature of the anthropology of art may characterise the study of the ethnographic arts more than the study of prehistoric arts, given the influences that ethnographic studies have on how to approach prehistoric arts, it is relevant to understand these trends. Errington (1998) has recently shown how the study of 'authentic primitive art' was embedded, for example, in long-standing and problematic notions of 'progress'. And Price (1989), among others, has discussed some of the ways in which so-called primitive art objects have taken on new and often problematic meanings and values as part of the international art market (see also Marcus and Myers 1995, Phillips and Steiner 1999).

It would take us in many directions away from the topic at hand, if we were to elaborate on the implications of these changes for the anthropological study of art. Suffice it to say, however, that in reviewing the literature that has taken up the study of the arts of hunter–gatherers, we must be aware of what these new perspectives imply. For example, in regard to such well-developed arts, especially the monumental (e.g. totem poles) and portable arts of the North-west Coast (North America) hunter–gatherers, it has been suggested that 'the arts we have thought of as traditional may have been invented, or at least stimulated, enlarged, and proliferated in response to the new contact-era functions of trade and tourism' (Graburn 1999: 346 summarizing Jonaitis 1999). As Layton (this volume) considers in some detail, there is much debate about our understandings of hunter–gatherers, in general, given the colonial and post-colonial contexts within which all ethnographic observations and studies took place.

Furthermore, since many of the art-making hunter–gatherers have themselves engaged in pastoralism or in some agriculture, or have been in trading relations with groups of varying subsistence practices (see Morphy 1999), the very notion of there being something readily delimited as 'hunter–gatherer art' gets to be more elusive. Often, it was through these trade relations or alternative subsistence practices that the so-called hunter–gatherers obtained some of the raw materials, such as beads, for their 'art'. Although the rest of this chapter will discuss some of the arts of some groups that we usually identify as being, or having been, hunter–gatherers, the main point is that there is no such clearly definable thing that we can readily call 'hunter–gatherer art'.

'Art' in hunter–gatherer context(s)

Now that we have recognised that the category of 'art' and the category of 'hunter–gatherer' are fluid and qualified, we can consider some of the many objects and images that we would most likely consider as hunter–gatherer art: carved boxes and implements in wood, ivory, antler, and other materials; sand drawings; baskets and textiles; pictographs and petrogylphs on rock surfaces all around the globe; statuettes of animals and humans; beadwork, decorated hides and clothing; and shell ornaments, to name just a few. Some of the more well-studied traditions and practices of art and image making would be those of the many tribes of the North-west Coast of North America (e.g. Holm 1965, Inverarity 1967); those of Australian Aboriginal peoples (e.g. Morphy 1991, Layton 1992); those of northern and arctic latitudes, such as the Inuit, the Aleut, and the Athapaskan peoples, (e.g. Black 1982, Fitzhugh and Crowell 1988); the basketry of native Californians (e.g. Bates and Lee 1990, O'Neale 1995); the rock art of southern Africa (e.g. Lewis-Williams 1981, Dowson 1992, Garlake 1995); and the cave art and portable arts of the late Ice Age peoples of Europe and Russia (e.g. Leroi-Gourhan 1965, Bahn and Vertut 1997). Rock art has been of particular interest and attention in the last decade (e.g. Whitley and Loendorf 1994, Chippindale and Taçon 1998), and although not all rock art is the work of past or present hunter–gatherers, much of it is. Some art-making traditions have been relatively neglected, such as those of some parts of Africa (but see Kratz 1994) or of southeast Asia (but see Endicott 1979).

What we can identify then as a corpus of hunter–gatherer art has come into existence and has been brought to our attention through a myriad of historical factors. The kinds of materials used and their relative preservation is one factor that influences what kinds of art and artefacts we have from archaeological contexts. If the Ice Age Upper Palaeolithic hunter–gatherers of Europe had made the kinds of baskets that native Californians did, often with feathers and shells, instead of the engraved bone and antler implements and sculpted objects that they did, we would certainly not have their basketry, and our ideas of their material and visual culture would be very different. Although rock art is not immune to fading and preservational problems, it is likely that we have as much of it as we do because of its having been made on more durable surfaces. The overwhelmingly rich material and visual culture of Northwest Coast groups, so much of it made in wood, is unlikely to be preserved in typical archaeological sites.

Furthermore, the history of culture contact, such as that of Europeans with the Northwest Coast groups, notably influenced the collections of 'primitive art' that often comprise much of the material culture left at hand in the aftermath of colonialisation. However, as many studies have shown (e.g. Phillips and Steiner 1999, Graburn 1976), many art-making traditions have continued, been re-worked, transformed, and given new meanings in new socio-political contexts, even if one can no longer claim that the makers are 'hunter–gatherers'. The particularities of anthropological attention have had the effect of highlighting some arts. For example, Boas's early (1897) and pioneering (Boas 1927) studies of Northwest Coast arts and Lévi-Strauss's (1963) use of some of these arts as a primary example in his (then) new structuralist approach did much to draw our attention to these materials.

In the nineteenth and early twentieth centuries, it was possible to make what we see today as rather sweeping generalisations about hunter–gatherer arts. For example, once established as the most compelling interpretation for Palaeolithic cave art, the interpretation of rock arts everywhere as being ritual and magic for the hunt was taken up in many different contexts (e.g. Heizer and Baumhoff 1962 for the Great Basin, USA). Today, it is clear that it is not possible to generalise about the purpose of certain kinds of imagery in hunter–gatherer societies. We cannot say, for example, that hunter–gatherers made art primarily for ritual purposes related to the food quest, or that they engaged in making some art in order to negotiate identity. Both of these 'reasons' for art might have been at work in some places, at some times, and according to some people's perspectives, but we have to inquire into each differing context to approach the 'why's. As we will see below, there are still some approaches to rock art, for example, that draw on some generalised notions of hunter–gatherer societies, but we are far beyond the simplistic ideas that early interpreters put forth. We cannot even say that there is any uniformity among hunter–gatherers about the making of 'art': there have always been dynamic, ever-changing contexts of production, contexts within which images, forms, shapes, materials, places, and practices have had multiple and varying meanings and manifestations. How then might we understand this?

Researching and interpreting hunter–gatherer arts

Robert Layton once wisely remarked that 'it is undesireable to construct too detailed interpretations of prehistoric rock art' (1991: 172), and, I might add, by extension, too detailed interpretations of any of the arts of the peoples we are studying. If we have learned anything from decades of thought and study, it is that there is not likely to be a single simple account for such things as rock art of a certain sort or for ivory statuettes or basketry designs. In other work on rock art, Layton (1985) shows how, none the less, we might get some general sense of what differing rock art traditions might have been about. That is, for example, he suggests that the rock art of the San peoples of southern Africa, in comparison to that of Australia, might have been 'about' different cultural issues. One starting point might be to show how rock art from Australia is 'about' the corporate totemic identity (e.g. Morphy 1991), while that from southern Africa is more 'about' interpersonal relationships, about animals as exemplars of interpersonal roles (e.g. Solomon 1992, Parkington 1994). Note that Layton is not suggesting that he knows what any specific painting 'means'; rather, he is trying to identify a general frame of social and cultural references within which the production of rock art (in this case) is carried out. How do we get to such initial understandings?

For both the Australian and southern African cases, there is a great deal of ethnography and ethnohistorical work that has allowed us to understand some general principles of life within which their 'art' comes into existence and is 'used'; these would be what Lewis-Williams (1990) has called 'the informing context'. For example, a core aspect of Australian Aboriginal life is the symbolic, semantic, ritual, and everyday relationships between people, the land, and ancestral beings. The making of rock art is the making of meaning; it is the evocation of meanings and cultural facts about specific connections – 'ancestral connections', Morphy (1991) calls them – among people, land, place, spirits, ancestors. In fact, art is integral and necessary, required and unquestioned as part of what it means to be an Aboriginal and to the reproduction of social life. This does not, however, mean that their 'art' is everywhere the same in amount, media, and signification.

Ethnographic and ethnohistoric information is, of course, problematic, for precisely the reasons noted above: much of it came out of specific and varying historic situations of what we call 'culture contact'. None the less, we have had our eyes opened to a wider range of possibilities as to how objects and images 'work' in different cultures and contexts. There is, moreover, no ethnohistory for the study of prehistoric arts, such as for the cave and portable art of some 20 000 years ago; there are no direct links to be made. How can anything be said about the 'informing contexts'? How can anything be said regarding what prehistoric arts might have been 'about'?

In such instances, researchers may take more formal approaches to the images and objects; that is, to work with style, colour, shape, designs, materials and techniques used, to try to infer aspects of context and signification (e.g. Clegg 1978, Conkey 1982, Lenssen-Erz 1989, Jacknis 1995, Hartley and Vawser 1998). Stylistic similarities may be shown to exist between different areas, suggesting some sorts of interaction (trade, gifting, travelling 'artists', actual movements and relocations of people) or mutual participation in similar cultural belief systems . Technological studies (of the different pigment mixes, the carving style, the ways in which baskets are woven, the sources of raw materials) may also provide a line of evidence about the social relations of production. For example, among native Californian Pomo basket-makers, different techniques are used for those baskets that are kept for use, and for those that are to be given away; twining for one, coiling for the other.

Researchers may also start from a set of generalised or even universalist premises. For example, as a result of the influence of structuralist approaches beginning in the 1960s, many researchers have worked from the assumption that there are underlying rules or 'grammars' for the making of objects and 'art', and that we can elucidate these (e.g. Holm 1965), gaining insight into the ways in which images and forms were brought into existence. The universalist assumption here is that cultural meanings among all cognitively modern humans are spawned from the 'deep structures' of the mind (for a review of these approaches in rock art research, see Conkey 2000).

Classic among this kind of work with the prehistoric arts of hunter–gatherers is that of Leroi-Gourhan (e.g. 1965, 1986) for the Palaeolithic cave art of southwest Europe. Leroi-Gourhan suggested there was an underlying 'mythogram', a set of unspecified mythological meanings that underlay the empirically observed fact that certain animals (especially horse and bison) were selected for depiction and that certain animals tend to be placed in certain parts of the cave, and/or in association with certain other animal species. While there have been significant challenges to this 'structuralist reading' of cave art (e.g. Ucko and Rosenfeld 1967, GRAPP 1993: 405), there are also on-going extensions of it (e.g. Sauvet and Wlodarczyk 1992). Even though there are now serious objections to structuralist approaches, we can say that, in this particular instance, the structuralist approach completely redefined the study of Palaeolithic art, if only because it did show that there was order and pattern to the imagery, and that it was not random accumulations as a result of hunting magic rituals, as interpreters thought for more than fifty years (Michelson 1986, Bahn and Vertut 1997).

Another set of universalist assumptions concern what we call 'altered states of consciousness' and the making of images that derive from and constitute 'visions'. After many years of work with the abundant corpus of rock art of southern Africa, Lewis-Williams (e.g. 1981) and his colleagues (e.g. Lewis-Williams and Dowson 1994) have revolutionized the study of rock art through challenging the simplistic, often degrading (to the Bushmen makers), and functionalist interpretations of the rock art that had prevailed well into the 1960s. To them, the making of much rock art can be shown to derive from the visions 'seen' by shamans in trance, in altered states of consciousness. These visions were then reproduced in varying culturally relevant forms on rock walls and shelters as part of the ways in which shamans mediated between the everyday world and the spirit worlds. Furthermore, as Lewis-Williams and Dowson (1990) suggest, the spirit world appears to 'exist' in or behind the rock wall on which the imagery is placed; images appear to emerge from 'behind and through the veil', and contact with the rock wall (with negative hand prints, for example) may be a means through which power (to heal, for example) may be accessed.

In this particular interpretive framework, the researchers draw on a combination of some universalist notions about the prevalence of some kind of shamanism in hunter–gatherer societies (Lewis-Williams 1994: 284) and about the way the human mind works in altered states of consciousness, coupled with specific analyses of the imagery – the eland antelope/human figures, the red line of potency connecting figures, etc. – ethnohistoric documentation about the mythology, and ethnographic studies of the trance aspects of the contemporary descendants of the painters. There is considerable debate about how inclusive this account for the rock art can be for the southern African imagery (e.g. Manhire, *et al.* 1985, Solomon 1994), and how readily the model can be applied to other ethnographic (e.g. the California Coso Range rock art, see Quinlan 2001 contra Whitley 1994) or even archaeological (e.g. the Palaeolithic cave art, see Hámayon 1997 contra Clottes and Lewis-Williams 1996) cases.

Given that there are so many diverse manifestations of what we might call hunter–gatherer art around the world, and from as early as 30 000 years ago right up into the present, it is only feasible here to identify just a few kinds of insights that the interpretive work has generated. Just two such insights can be mentioned here. One insight shows precisely how 'art' works at the level of overall social organisation and with core cultural myths. The second insight is how art 'works' as integral to some of the more internal social dynamics of hunter–gatherer life, how material culture is as much about such social relations as gender as it is about aesthetics.

Following on from the above critique of the term 'art', we must remember that, in many instances, the so-called decorated objects of hunter–gatherer (or other) art are not decorated objects in the Western sense. We will be completely misled if we try to sort out the function or utility from the decoration, from the symbolic, from the aesthetic form or structure. As Taylor (1974: 8) notes in regard to the boxes, bowls, and decorated containers of the nineteenth century Northwest Coast Indians, which we will use here as a specific example, it is not the point to decide if a given bowl was made to look like an animal or if the animal was distorted to become the 'proper' shape for a bowl; rather, 'they grow together: the bowl became animate and its animation gave reason for its becoming a being as well as a bowl'.

The art of the Northwest Coast is especially rich in regional and temporal variations, and there is a very great variety of objects and in many media: spoons, fish-hooks, bowls, shaman's charms, masks, tattooing, face-painting, blankets, basketry hats, painted buckskin garments, huge canoes, house posts, tall totem poles. While the materiality of their world is impressive and would often be lost in the studies of hunter–gatherer ecology and diet that all too often dominate hunter–gatherer research and literature, this materiality is, on the one hand, integral to a fuller understanding of these often overemphasised aspects of hunter–gatherer life. On the other hand, this materiality is so rooted in and constitutive of social and symbolic life that it is not possible to comprehend one without explicit reference to the other.

For example, among the Tlingit (Northwest Coast of North America), boxes and bowls that are incised, carved and, as we might say, 'decorated', are a rich and varied material culture or art. The functions, so to speak, of such boxes and bowls were social (Jacknis 1974): neither art-for-art's sake nor limited to utilitarian purposes. As Sturtevant (1974) illustrates, these boxes and bowls, as containers, are primary cultural symbols. There is a single Tlingit word that expresses the meanings of a whole range of things – box, coffin, bivalve shell, womb, outside, opposite moiety – and this word implicates a 'key central concept around which Tlingit life and thought can be seen to have been organized' (Sturtevant 1974: 12, following Stone 1971).

In fact, the notion of 'container' is essential to the Raven myth that explains the very creation of the present world order, in which the crucial distinctions were established between night and day, between humans and animals, and between a man and his mother's brother. The moiety was the social container. Artifactual containers – the lineage house, the boxes and other ceremonial objects inside the house, the grave house and its coffins – and who made, used, lived in and maintained them, can be said to make manifest, to bring into the social arena the very structure and enacting of Tlingit social groups and social–symbolic life and sensibilities.

At a somewhat more refined or micro scale than the level of the overall social formation or social structure, we can glimpse how what we call 'art' works in defining and producing social relations by and within factions or social sub-groups, such as gender. It is important to point out that some of the most interesting and important work in the anthropological understandings of gender have been advanced in reference to hunter–gatherer societies (e.g. Slocum 1975, Collier and Rosaldo 1982, Endicott 1999). Certain understandings of gender (such as the multiplicity of possible third and fourth genders beyond the bipolar notion of there being just men and women) have come from studies of hunter–gatherers (e.g. Hollimon 1997). Unfortunately, we cannot develop this further here, except to provide a few examples of how the study of art as material culture is as much about such central anthropological issues as gender, power, and politics, as it is about aesthetics, style, or the material world.

There are numerous cases where it matters who makes many heralded objects of 'art' in hunter–gatherer societies. For example, among native California groups, the rich basketry corpus is often exclusively the domain of women. These women basket-makers were the ones who developed and generated specific and multiple designs for the baskets, who keep the design names in circulation, and who teach their very young daughters the basket-making craft (e.g. O'Neale 1995). In the daily lives of many native California peoples (e.g. the Yurok, Karok, Hupa, Pomo), baskets were ubiqui-tous: they were for food collecting, processing, storage, and cooking; they were for ceremonies (e.g. the Jumping dance); given as gifts;

and included hats as well as containers. Thus, baskets and their designs were 'everywhere' in daily life: the work of women, attesting to the skills of women and their abilities to achieve and maintain remarkable standardisation (O'Neale 1995: 161). Men often provided many of the raw materials for basket-making, and, at least among some groups (e.g. the Klamath River tribes), they engaged in their own material culture making, especially carving (of spoons, 'purses', etc.) (Jacknis 1995). The carving traditions, however, seem to lack the well-developed system of named designs as in basketry, and it was often a basket design that was associated with individual houses, at least among the Klamath River groups.

In other hunter–gatherer groups, there are distinct traditions of 'women's' and 'men's' designs, as among the Walbiri of Australia (Munn 1973), especially in the domain of sand-drawings, which are integral to the telling of stories and myths that themselves are crucial to social reproduction. Elsewhere in Australia, it is documented that although men may be the primary painters of rock art, especially as part of their male ritual ceremonies, their abilities to obtain the needed ochres for painting may be dependent upon the women who are the only ones allowed the access to the ochre sources (Hamilton and Vachon 1985, Franklin 1998). Thus, the very maintenance and enactment of male rituals, including the making of rock art, is entangled with the nature of gender relations and gender negotiations. For some of the rock art of southern Africa, as presumably made by the recent ancestors of the San Bushmen, Solomon (1992, 1994) and Parkington (1994) have both argued that aspects of gender identity and gendered social relations are not just depicted in the rock art but, more actively, are played out and brought into a social dialogue through the visual manifestations of rock art imagery.

Some conclusions

In this chapter, I have tried to touch on a number of issues that arise if one is to broach the topic of 'hunter–gatherer art'. I have tried to show that what we mean by 'art' is contested and must only be applied to hunter–gatherer societies with care and with an explicit awareness of what assumptions we might be making in thinking about their visual and material worlds as 'art'. I have also noted that the very ways in which anthropologists have studied the arts of other cultures have been changing, and that many of the ethnographic studies must be understood in terms of the particular analytical and theoretical frameworks held by the investigators. The idea that there might have been a relatively static and 'pre-contact' world of art in non-Western societies, even in prehistoric times, must be replaced.

Today, much of what we might call 'art' can perhaps be better understood, anthropologically, under the rubric of 'material culture', especially if material culture is itself understood to be about both the immaterial as well as the material (e.g. Thomas 1991, Tilley 1999). I have tried to give some examples as to the ways in which the material and visual culture of some hunter–gatherers is just as much about the core cultural and social concepts of everything from daily life and gender relations to overarching understandings of how the world came to be, as they are about object shape, form, aesthetics, colour, or utilitarian function. These latter are the usual categories that we think of, perhaps, when faced with trying to study what we call 'art', but it is both more complex and richer than this.

It is because of this potential for us to gain much more inclusive understandings, given the more embedded meanings and functions of 'art' in hunter–gatherer (and other) societies, that I have suggested that 'art' in such societies may be as much art-for-life's sake as it is art-for-art's sake or art-as-'extra', something not necessary to the so-called food quest, to the need for extended mating networks or other 'needs' that are so often the framework for the study of hunter–gatherer peoples. Rather, I want readers to get a glimpse here of how the social and material worlds of hunter–gatherers are central to 'getting on'. To represent 'things' – animals, spirits, social facts, aesthetically pleasing shapes, and so forth, perhaps many of these simultaneously – in visual and material form is a mode of knowledge. To 'make' a Tlingit box is to 'make' Tlingit social life. Often the arts embody the conceptual interests of a particular culture or of particular factions within a culture. 'The act of representation [may well be seen as] the integration of [these] experiences into the social body, the social process, and also, most importantly, the act of extracting from the social process a set of informative, resonant symbols and narratives' (Davis 1984: 28).

References

Anderson, R. (1989). *Art in Primitive Societies*. Englewood Cliffs NJ: Prentice-Hall.

Appadurai, A. (1986). *The Social Life of Things*. Cambridge: Cambridge University Press.

Bahn, P.G. and Vertut, J. (1997). *Journey through the Ice Age*. Berkeley: University of California Press.

Bates, C. and Lee, M.J. (1990). *Tradition and Innovation : A Basket History of the Indians of the Yosemite-Mono Lake Area*. Yosemite National Park CA: Yosemite Association.

Black, L. (1982). *Aleut Art*. Anchorage: Aleutian/Pribilof Islands Association.

Boas, F. (1897) The decorative arts of the Indians of the Northwest Coast. *Bulletin of the American Museum of Natural History* **9**: 123–176.

Boas, F. (1927). *Primitive Art*. New York: Dover.

Bourdieu, P. (1984). *Distinction: A Social Critique of the Judgement of Taste*, translated by R. Nice. Cambridge MA: Harvard University Press.

Chippindale, C. and P.S.C. Taçon, (1998). *The Archaeology of Rock Art*. Cambridge: Cambridge University Press.

Child, I. and Siroto, L. (1965). Bakwele and American aesthetic evaluations compared. *Ethnology*. **4**: 349–360.

Clegg, J. (1978). Mathesis words, Mathesis pictures. Unpublished PhD thesis, University of Sydney.

Clottes, J. and Lewis-Williams, J.D. (1996). *Les Chamanes de la Préhistoire: Transe et Magie dans les Grottes Ornées*. Paris: Le Seuil.

Collier, J. and Rosaldo, M. (1982). Politics and gender in simple societies. In *Sexual Meanings: The Cultural Construction of Gender and Sexuality*, ed. S. Ortner and H. Whitehead, pp. 275–329. Cambridge: Cambridge University Press.

Conkey, M. (1982). Boundedness in art and society. In *Symbolic and Structural Archaeology*, ed. I. Hodder, pp. 115–128. Cambridge: Cambridge University Press.

Conkey, M. (2000). Structural and semiotic approaches. In *The Handbook of Rock Art Research*, ed. D. Whitley, pp. 273–310. Walnut Creek CA: Altamira Press.

Davis, W. (1984). Representation and knowledge in the prehistoric rock art of Africa. *African Archaeological Review.* **2**: 7–35.

Dowson, T. (1992). *Rock Engravings of Southern Africa.* Johannesburg: Witwatersrand University Press.

Endicott, Karen (1999). Gender relations in hunter–gatherer societies. In *The Cambridge Encyclopedia of Hunters and Gatherers*, ed. R.B. Lee and R. Daly, pp. 411–18. Cambridge: Cambridge University Press.

Endicott, Kirk (1979). *Batek Negrito Religion: The World View and Rituals of a Hunting and Gathering People of Peninsular Malaysia.* Oxford: Clarendon Press.

Errington, S. (1998). *The Death of Authentic Primitive Art and Other Tales of Progress.* Berkeley: University of California Press.

Fernandez, J. (1966). Principles of opposition and vitality in Fang aesthetics. *Journal of Aesthetics and Art Criticism* **1**: 53–64.

Firth, R. (1992). Art and anthropology. In *Anthropology, Art and Aesthetics*, ed. J. Coote and A. Shelton, pp. 15–39. Oxford: Clarendon Press.

Fischer, J. (1961). Art styles as cultural cognitive maps. *American Anthropologist* **63**: 79–93.

Fitzhugh, W. and Crowell, A. (1988). *Crossroads of Continents: Cultures of Siberia and Alaska.* Washington DC: Smithsonian Institution Press.

Franklin, U. (1998). Drawing in differences: changing social contexts of rock art production in Watarrka (Kings Canyon) National Park, Central Australia. Unpublished MA thesis, Australian National University.

Garlake, P. (1995). *The Hunter's Vision: The Prehistoric Art of Zimbabwe.* Seattle: University of Washington Press.

Gell, A. (1992). The technology of enchantment and the enchantment of technology. In *Anthropology, Art and Aesthetics*, ed. J. Coote and A. Shelton, pp. 40–66. Oxford: Clarendon Press.

Graburn, N. (1976). *Ethnic and Tourist Arts .* Berkeley: University of California Press.

Graburn, N. (1999). Epilogue: ethnic and tourist arts revisited. In *Unpacking Culture: Art and Commodity in Colonial and Postcolonial Worlds*, ed. R.B. Phillips and C. Steiner, pp. 335–354. Berkeley: University of California Press.

GRAPP (Groupe de Réflexions sur l'Art Pariétal Paléolithique) (1993). *L'Art Pariétal Paléolithique: Techniques et Méthodes d'Etude.* Paris: Comité des Travaux Historiques et Scientifiques.

Hámayon, R. (1997). Le Transe d'un préhistorien: à propos du livre de Jean Clottes et David Lewis-Williams. *Les Nouvelles de l'Archéologie* **67**: 65–67.

Hamilton, A. and Vachon, D. (1985). *Lake Amadeus/Luritja Land Claim Claim Book.* Central Land Council, Australia.

Hartley, R. and Vawser, A.M.W. (1998). Spatial behaviour and learning in the prehistoric environment of the Colorado River drainage (southeastern Utah), western North America. In *The Archaeology of Rock Art* , ed. C. Chippindale and P.S.C. Taçon, pp. 185–211. Cambridge: Cambridge University Press.

Hatcher, E.M. (1985). *Art as Culture: An Introduction to the Anthropology of Art.* Lanham MD: University Press of America.

Hedlund, A. (1992). *Reflections on a Weaver's World: The Gloria F. Ross Collection of Contemporary Navajo Weaving.* Denver: Denver Art Museum.

Heizer, R. and Baumhoff, M. (1962). *Prehistoric Rock Art of Nevada and Eastern California.* Berkeley: University of California Press.

Hollimon, S.E. (1997). The third gender in California: two-spirit undertakers among the Chumash and their neighbors. In *Women in Prehistory, North America and Mesoamerica,* ed. C. Claassen and R. Joyce, pp. 173–188. Philadelphia: University of Pennsylvania Press.

Holm, B. (1965). *Northwest Coast Indian Art.* Seattle: University of Washington Press.

Inverarity, R.B. (1967). *Art of the Northwest Coast Indians.* Berkeley: University of California Press.

Jacknis, I. (1974). Functions of the containers. In *Boxes and Bowls: Decorated Containers by Nineteenth Cenury Haida, Tlingit, Bella Bella, and Tsimshian Indians,* ed. W. Sturtevant, pp. 16–19. Washington DC: Smithsonian Institution Press.

Jacknis, I. (1995). *Carving Traditions of Northwest California.* Berkeley: Universiy of California Press.

Jonaitis, A. (1999). Northwest coast totem poles. In *Unpacking Culture: Art and Commodity in Colonial and Postcolonial Worlds* , ed. R.B. Phillips and C.B. Steiner, pp. 104–121. Berkeley: University of California Press.

Jopling, C. (1971). *Art and Aesthetics in Primitive Society.* New York: Dutton.

Kratz, C. (1994). *Affecting Performance: Meaning, Movement, and Experience in Okiek Women's Initiation.* Washington DC: Smithsonian Institution Press.

Layton, R. (1981). *The Anthropology of Art.* London: Granada.

Layton, R. (1985). The cultural context of hunter–gatherer art. *Man* (N.S) **20**: 434–453.

Layton, R. (1991). Trends in the hunter–gatherer rock art of western Europe. *Proceedings of the Prehistoric Society* **57**: 163–174.

Layton, R. (1992). *Australian Rock Art: A New Synthesis.* Cambridge: Cambridge University Press.

Lenssen-Erz, T. (1989). The conceptual framework for the analysis of the Brandberg Rock Paintings. In *The Rock Paintings of the Upper Brandberg,* Part I, *Amis Gorge,* ed. H. Pager, pp. 361–370. Cologne: Heinrich Barth Institute.

Leroi-Gourhan, A. (1965). *Treasures of Prehistoric Art.* New York: Harry Abrams.

Leroi-Gourhan, A. (1986). The religion of the caves: magic or metaphysics, translated A. Michelson. *October* **37**: 6–17.

Levi-Strauss, C. (1963). Split representation in the art of Asia and America. In *Structural Anthropology,* by C. Lévi-Strauss, pp. 245–268. New York: Basic Books.

Lewis-Williams, J.D. (1981). *Believing and Seeing: Symbolic Meanings in Southern San Rock Paintings*. London: Academic Press.

Lewis-Williams, J.D. (1990). Documentation, analysis, and interpretation: dilemmas in rock art research. A review of *The Rock Paintings of the Upper Brandberg*, Part I, *Amis Gorge*, by H. Pager (1989). *South African Archaeological Bulletin* **45**: 126–136.

Lewis-Williams, J.D. (1994). Rock art and ritual: Southern Africa and beyond. *Complutum* **5**: 277–289.

Lewis-Williams, J.D. (1995). Some aspects of rock art research in the politics of present-day South Africa. In *Perceiving Rock Art: Social and Political Perspectives*, ed. K. Helskog and B. Olsen, pp. 317–337. Oslo: Instituttet for Sammenlignende Kulturforskning.

Lewis-Williams, J.D. and T.A. Dowson (1990). Through the veil: San rock paintings and the rock face. *South African Archaeological Bulletin* **45**: 5–16.

Lewis-Williams, J.D. and T.A. Dowson (1994). Aspects of rock art research: a critical perspective. In *Contested Images: Diversity in Southern Africa Rock Art Research*, ed. T.A. Dowson and J.D. Lewis-Williams, pp. 201–222. Johannesburg: Witwatersrand University Press.

MacKenzie, M. (1991). *Androgynous Objects: String Bags and Gender in Central New Guinea*. Chur, Switzerland: Harwood Academic Publishers.

Manhire, T., J. Parkington and R. Yates (1985). Nets and fully-recurved bows: rock paintings and hunting methods in the Western Cape, South Africa. *World Archaeology* **17**: 161–174.

Marcus, G. and Myers, F. (1995). *The Traffic in Culture: Refiguring Art and Anthropology*. Berkeley: University of California Press.

Michelson, A. (1986). In praise of horizontality: André Leroi-Gourhan, 1911–1986. *October* **37**: 3–5.

Morphy, F. (1977). The social significance of schematisation in Northwest Coast American Indian art. In *Form in Indigenous Art: Schematisation in the Art of Aboriginal Australia and Prehistoric Europe*, ed. P.J. Ucko, pp. 73–76. Canberra: Australian Institute of Aboriginal Studies.

Morphy, H. (1991). *Ancestral Connections: Art and an Aboriginal System of Knowledge*. Chicago: University of Chicago Press.

Morphy, H. (1992). From dull to brilliant: the aesthetics of spiritual power among the Yolngu. In *Anthropology, Art and Aesthetics*, ed. J. Coote and A. Shelton, pp. 181–208. Oxford: Clarendon Press.

Morphy, H. (1999). Traditional and modern visual art of hunting and gathering peoples. In *The Cambridge Encyclopedia of Hunters and Gatherers*, ed. R.B. Lee and R. Daly, pp. 441–448. Cambridge: Cambridge University Press.

Mowaljarlai, D., Vinnicombe, P., Ward, G.K. and Chippindale, C. (1988). Repainting of images on rock art in Australia and the maintenance of Aboriginal culture. *Antiquity* **62**: 690–696.

Munn, N. (1973). *Walbiri Iconography.* Ithaca NY: Cornell University Press.

O'Neale, L. (1995). [orig. 1932] *Yurok-Karok Basket Weavers.* Berkeley: University of California Press.

Otten, C. (1971). *Anthropology and Art.* Garden City NJ: Natural History Press.

Parkington, J. (1994). What is an eland? N!ao and the politics of age and sex in the paintings of the Western Cape. In *Miscast: Negotiating the Presence of the Bushmen,* ed. P. Skotnes, pp. 281–289. Cape Town: University of Cape Town Press.

Phillips, R.B. and Steiner, C.B. (1999). *Unpacking Culture: Art and Commodity in Colonial and Postcolonial Worlds.* Berkeley: University of California Press.

Price, S. (1989). *Primitive Art in Civilized Places.* Chicago: University of Chicago Press.

Quinlan, A. (2001) The ventriloquist's dummy: a critical review of shamanism and rock art in far western North America. *Journal of California and Great Basin Anthropology.* (in press)

Salvador, M.L. (1978). *Yer Dailege! Kuna Women's Art.* Albuquerque: Maxwell Museum of Anthropology, University of New Mexico.

Sauvet, G. and A. Wlodarczyk (1992). Structural interpretation of statistical data from European palaeolithic cave art. In *Ancient Images, Ancient Thought: The Archaeology of Ideology,* ed. A.S. Goldsmith, S. Garvie, D. Selin and J. Smith, pp. 223–234. Calgary, Alberta: Archaeological Association, University of Calgary.

Shelton, A. (1992). Predicates of aesthetic judgement: ontology and value in Huichol material representations. In *Anthropology, Art and Aesthetics,* ed. J. Coote and A. Shelton, pp. 209–244. Oxford: Clarendon Press.

Slocum, S. (1975). Woman the gatherer: male bias in anthropology. In *Toward An Anthropology of Women,* ed. R.R. Reiter, pp. 36–50. New York: Monthly Review Press.

Solomon, A. (1992). Gender, representation and power in San ethnography and rock art. *Journal of Anthropological Archaeology* **11**: 291–329.

Solomon, A. (1994). 'Mythic women': a study in variability in San art. In *Contested Images: Diversity in Southern African Rock Art Research,* ed. T.A. Dowson and J.D. Lewis-Williams, pp. 331–371. Johannesburg: Witwatersrand University Press.

Sparshott, F. (1997). Art and anthropology. *Journal of Aesthetics and Art Criticism* **55**: 239–243.

Spencer, B. and Gillen, F. (1899). *The Native Tribes of Central Australia.* London: Macmillan.

Stone, P. (1971). Reciprocity: the gift of a trickster. Unpublished paper.

Strathern, M. (1988). *The Gender of the Gift.* Berkeley: University of California Press.

Sturtevant, W. (1974). Introduction. In *Boxes and Bowls: Decorated Containers by Nineteenth Century Haida, Tlingit, Bella Bella, and Tsimshian Indian Artists,* ed.

W.C. Sturtevant, pp. 10–15. Washington DC: Smithsonian Instituttion Press.

Taylor, J.C. (1974). Foreword: Form and spirit. In *Boxes and Bowls: Decorated Containers by Nineteenth Century Haida, Tlingit, Bella Bella, and Tsimshian Indian Artists*, ed. W.C. Sturtevant, pp. 7–9. Washington DC: Smithsonian Institution Press.

Thomas, N. (1991). *Entangled Objects: Exchange, Material Culture, and Colonialism in the Pacific*. Cambridge MA: Harvard University Press.

Thompson, R.F. (1968). Aesthetics in traditional Africa. *Art News* **66**: 44–45.

Tilley, C. (1999). *Metaphor and Material Culture*. Oxford: Basil Blackwell.

Townsend-Gault, C. (1998). At the margin or the centre? – The anthropological study of art. *Reviews in Anthropology* **27**: 425–439.

Ucko, P. and A. Rosenfeld (1967). *Palaeolithic Cave Art*. New York: McGraw-Hill.

Vinnicombe, P. (1995). Perspectives and traditions in Australian rock art research. In *Pereciving Rock Art: Social and Political Perspectives*, ed. K. Helskog and B. Olsen, pp. 87–103. Oslo: Instituttet for Sammenlignende Kulturforskning.

Wallace, A.F.C. (1950). A possible technique for recognizing psychological characteristics of the ancient Maya from an analysis of their art. *American Imago* **7**: 239–258.

Whitley, D. (1994). Shamanism, natural modelling and the rock art of far western North America. In *Shamanism and Rock Art in North America*, ed. S. Turpin, pp. 1–43. San Antonio TX: Rock Art Foundation.

Whitley, D. and Loendorf, L. (1994). *New Light on Old Art: Recent Advances in Hunter-Gatherer Rock Art Research*, UCLA Institute of Archaeology Monograph 36. Los Angeles.

Wolff, J. (1981). *The Social Production of Art*. London: MacMillan.

11

Hunter–gatherers, their neighbours and the Nation State

ROBERT H. LAYTON

Introduction

Considerable controversy surrounds the description of modern populations as hunter–gatherers, let alone the use of data from modern populations to reconstruct the social and material adaptations of our pre-agricultural ancestors. In their introduction to *Man the Hunter* Lee and DeVore wrote, 'nowhere today do we find hunters living in a world of hunters' (Lee and DeVore 1968: ix). Lee and his co-workers in the Kalahari have nonetheless been severely criticised by Schrire (1980) and Wilmsen (1989) for exaggerating the degree to which hunter–gatherers have been isolated from interaction with and influence by other peoples. Headland and Reid (1989), and Bailey *et al.* (1989) have made similar criticisms with regard to other hunter–gatherer populations. The most striking case of Western gullibility has been the willingness of some to accept claims that the 'Tasaday' of the Philippines were previously uncontacted hunter–gatherers who had no knowledge of farming, war or weapons. Berreman (1991, 1999) persuasively argues these claims were manufactured by President Marcos's assistant on national minorities and foisted on a group of impoverished farmers who may or may not have resorted at times to some hunting and gathering.

This chapter reviews the range and historical depth of hunter–gatherer interactions with non-foraging communities and assesses the ways in which such interaction affects the hunter–gatherer way of life, influencing the significance of data collected among contemporary hunter–gatherers (cf. Leacock 1982).

What is genuine hunting and gathering?

The debate concerning the status of recent hunter–gatherers in southern Africa highlights the difficulty of defining 'genuine' hunting and gathering. Solway and Lee's rejoinder to the arguments of Schrire and Wilmsen is titled 'Foragers: genuine or spurious?' (Solway and Lee 1990). They do not define what they mean by *genuine* and *spurious* hunter–gatherers, but two interpretations can be deduced from their discussion. In one sense, genuine foragers are those whose ancestors had a continuous history of hunting and gathering. Solway and Lee accept that many (San) Basarwa[1] have long been drawn into farming and herding, but point out that the Dobe area is surrounded by a waterless belt between 70 and 200 kilometres wide. The few archaeological finds of pottery and iron show that the !Kung have been intermittently trading desert products for other goods for centuries, perhaps since AD 500 but, they argue, pastoralists were unable to cross the waterless buffer zone with their livestock until shortly before the colonial era (Solway and Lee 1990: 115). However, Solway and Lee also argue that contemporary foragers are not to be understood only as a cultural residue degraded through their marginality to more powerful systems. In this second sense, genuine hunter–gatherers are those who are able to determine their own way of life, even if their history includes periods of reliance on other modes of subsistence. They consider that the Dobe !Kung, for example, were economically self-sufficient until the 1960s (Solway and Lee 1990: 110, 120). Genuine foragers are thus economically self-sufficient while spurious ones are marginalised dependants. Hunter–gatherers who had learnt to forage from others after abandoning farming or pastoralism could qualify, under this definition, as 'genuine'.

---

[1] The San or Bushmen hunter–gatherers of southern Africa have also been termed Basarwa. All three words San, Bushmen and Basarwa have derogatory connotations and their use in anthropology is problematic. The !Kung are a subset of the San and comprise three main ethno-linguistic groups, the Central, Northern and Southern !Kung. The central !Kung include those living in the Dobe area and are sometimes referred to by their own designation *Ju/* or *Zu/'hoansi* ('real people') (see Barnard 1992: 8–10, 39).

The Kalahari debate raises several general questions. Most importantly, do hunter–gatherers usually seek to remain isolated when they come into contact with farmers or pastoralists, or do they enter into relationships with their neighbours? Once they have become implicated in such relationships, can they retain their independence? Second, do all recent hunter–gatherers have a continuous history of hunting and gathering, or have they shifted between modes of subsistence in the past? Third, to what extent have anthropologists ever observed hunter–gatherers unaffected by Western colonisation? What circumstances allow hunter–gatherers to continue traditional practices once they have been incorporated into a nation state? How does the present condition of hunter–gatherers influence demography, foraging strategies, nutrition, territoriality or other aspects of behaviour of interest to evolutionary anthropology?

Comparative studies show that hunter–gatherers do normally interact with farmers or pastoralists when they come into contact. The interaction ranges from symbiosis to exploitation of hunter–gatherers by their neighbours. Moreover, hunter–gatherers can change their mode of subsistence and farmers or pastoralists can learn to become hunter–gatherers.

Change before the origins of agriculture

One of the dangers of searching for 'pure' hunter–gatherers is the assumption that change in hunter–gatherer society is always caused by contact with other peoples. Even when situated in a world of hunter–gatherers, hunter–gatherer cultures were not static. Environmental change and cultural creativity generated substantial modification in the behaviour of many hunter–gatherers over the past 60 000 years. Hunter–gatherers may have been obliged to abandon arid regions in Africa and Australia during the last glaciation (Lampert and Hughes 1987: 32–3, Bailey *et al.* 1989). After the last glaciation, further change occurred. In Europe, stone tools became simpler, more expedient and less task-specific as the climate warmed and woodland replaced tundra. On the Northwest coast of North

America the first human settlers probably arrived before 13 000 BP, at least 1000 years before the now-familiar forest cover returned. Rising sea levels rendered the estuarine environments along the coast unstable, preventing the accumulation of shellfish beds and making rivers and lakes unsuitable for spawning runs by fish. The earliest inhabitants of the Northwest Coast therefore probably lived in small, nomadic, relatively egalitarian bands. Cultures resembling those recorded in the eighteenth and nineteenth centuries emerged after the sea level stabilised at about 3500 BC, while the familiar art style developed after AD 500 (Maschner 1991, Ames 1994). At the height of the last glaciation Australia and New Guinea formed a single land mass. Arnhem Land lay far from the sea. Salt water invaded the rivers of what is now coastal Arnhem Land at around 8000 BP, enabling the growth of extensive mangrove swamps. The earliest surviving shell middens date to about 6000 BP (Schrire 1982: 230), while the subsequent accumulation of sediments washed downstream during the annual monsoon later gave rise to flood plains on which productive freshwater lagoons created what is probably 'the richest environment Arnhem Land has known for at least 20 000 years' (Lewis 1988: 63). Changes in rock art and camping patterns suggest that new exchange networks, ceremonial complexes and totemic clans developed during the last 5000 years (Schrire 1982: 249–252, Lewis 1988: 73–77, Layton 1992: 235–6, Taçon and Chippindale 1994). Even when unaffected by contact with outsiders, recent hunter–gatherers have an extensive history of change.

Processes of interaction

European hunter–gatherers and their neighbours

Interaction between hunter–gatherers and farmers has a long history. Despite the rapid spread of early agriculture through eastern and central Europe, the diffusion of farming came to a halt in what is now northern Germany. The first attempt to establish agriculture in lowland (northern) Poland at about 7000 BP failed.

Hunting and gathering continued, and it was not until the second half of the fifth millennium BC (calibrated[2]) that farming was successfully established in northern Poland (Marciniak, in press). Between 7000 and 5000 BP the Ertebølle Mesolithic hunter–gatherers of Denmark also coexisted with farmers to the south (cf. Zvelebil 1986). Danubian axes, probably made from rock quarried in upland Poland, have been found at later Ertebølle sites, suggesting these hunter–gatherers exchanged goods with farmers (Fischer 1982, see Verhart and Wansleeben 1997 for evidence of exchange between Mesolithic hunter–gatherers and farmers in the Netherlands). What did the Ertebølle people exchange for stone axes? Ringkloster was a seasonally occupied Ertebølle site, apparently mainly utilised during winter and spring. Many animal bones were thrown into the nearby lake. The evidence of the preserved bone shows the principal meat-bearing species hunted were wild boar and red deer, but there is also a high proportion of pine marten. The pine marten bones were frequently still articulated, indicating they had been thrown unbutchered into the lake. Some have transverse cut marks across the skull, characteristic of skinning. This suggests they were hunted for their pelts (Rowley-Conwy 1994: 95). The high number of pine marten raises the possibility some were obtained for fur trade (Rowley-Conwy personal communication).

Although the Ertebølle culture gave way to farming at around 3000 BC, Sognnes suggests a stable frontier between hunter–gatherers and Bronze Age farmers existed in the Trondheim region between about 1800 and 500 BC (Sognnes 1998: 156). Tacitus's description of the Fenni demonstrates hunting and gathering was still practised in the region around AD 100.[3] Eight hundred years later, Othere told King Alfred about the Finna who paid tribute, partly in furs to Norwegian chiefs on the Atlantic coast, and also traded in the pelts of squirrel, marten, beaver and fox eastward to Novgorod (Mulk and Bayliss-Smith 1999: 385). Parts of southwest Finland were

---

[2] Radiocarbon dates corrected to calendar years. By contrast, BP is Before Present.

[3] Tacitus (1955: 141) wrote: the Fenni 'eat wild herbs, dress in skins and sleep on the ground. Their only hope of getting better fare lies in their arrows, which, for want of iron they tip with bone . . . Yet they count their lot happier than that of others who groan over field labour.'

only settled by farmers in the late Iron Age, and at some sites there is no evidence of cultivation before AD 900 (Roeck Hansen 1996).

The Sámi (Lapps), presumed descendants of the Finna, were regularly trading in furs with Russians and Swedes during the fifteenth and sixteenth centuries, at a time when they lived variously by reindeer herding, fishing and hunting. Although Othere's account suggests tame reindeer were already used by the Finna as decoys in their hunting during the ninth century, intensive reindeer pastoralism did not replace hunting until the sixteenth or seventeenth centuries (Carpelan, cited in Aikio and Aikio 1989: 117, Mulk and Bayliss-Smith 1999: 359, 385). The Sámi were probably pushed into intensive reindeer husbandry by Swedish settlers, who depleted wildlife in traditional Sámi hunting areas and extracted pelts from the Sámi in tax as they colonised their land (Beach 1981: 66).

The Kalahari

The history of northern Europe gives good reason to anticipate coexistence and interaction between hunter–gatherers and their neighbours elsewhere. Wilmsen argues this was the case in the Kalahari. In his opinion, archaeological evidence suggests pre-Iron Age pastoralists occupied sites on the edge of the Kalahari between 200 BC and AD 400. Late first-century BC ceramics have been found close to Dobe, while ceramics, cattle and iron are present at /Xai/ Xai, in Lee's field research area, from the eighth to the eleventh century (Wilmsen 1989: 65, 72, but see Kent 1992: 57). During the seventh to twelfth centuries a large number of sites was established by pastoralists further to the east, in the hardveld Kalahari. Sheep, goats and cattle make up 80% of the faunal remains in some of the larger sites, but the smallest ones lack kraals, are dominated by Late Stone Age artefacts and remains of hunted animals usually outnumber those of domestic stock. It is clear a hunting and gathering mode of subsistence persisted alongside pastoralism. Wild plants, including mongongo nuts, 'indicate that foraging continued to be important' (Wilmsen 1989: 72). Between the twelfth and nineteenth centuries, archaeological evidence shows agropastoralists were present in the Sandveld zone where the !Kung live, alongside foragers.

Tropical forest zones

Headland and Reid (1989) argued that hunter–gatherers of the Philippines have lived in a symbiotic relationship with neighbouring farmers for 1000 years. Although communities such as the Agta obtain meat by hunting, they depend on farmers for almost all their rice. Wild plant foods only provide about 2% of their starch intake (Headland and Reid 1989: 45). Archaeological evidence suggests that the Pleistocene inhabitants of the Philippines lived in wooded savannah areas, not forest. Like Bailey *et al.* (1989), Headland and Reid argue that hunter–gatherers could only move into tropical forest when they had established a symbiotic relationship with cultivators. Headland and Reid (1989) concluded that hunter–gatherers had moved into forest zones in order to collect wild produce to trade with local farmers and overseas traders. Junker (1996: 390) agrees that 'Ethnohistoric, linguistic and archaeological evidence all point to a lengthy history of intense and frequent trade interactions between Philippine hunter–gatherer groups and adjacent agriculturists'. Upland swidden farmers and hunter–gatherers such as the Agta, Ata and Batak depended on iron implements, salt, fish and pottery which were produced on the coast, while lowland farmers obtained pelts and meat, swidden crops and wild tubers from the interior. Since all Philippine Negrito hunter–gatherers speak Austronesian languages related to those of adjacent non-Negrito farmers the two populations have probably long been in close association (cf. McConvell, this volume).

Agriculture was introduced to the Philippines during the second millennium BC. Archaeological evidence of rice cultivation in northern Luzon suggests foraging and farming have been linked for 3500 years, either through symbiosis between communities with different modes of subsistence, or a seasonal oscillation between hunting and cultivation. Sites at which hunter–gatherers and farmers may have exchanged produce have been identified from the sixth century AD, but become more numerous during the fifteenth and sixteenth centuries. Junker points out that while the lowland farmers of the Philippines provided inland hunter–gatherers with archaeologically visible products such as pottery and metal weapons, the ethnohistorically attested produce exchanged by the hunter–gatherers, including pelts, resins and beeswax, is perishable and leaves little or no archaeological residue (Junker 1996: 398).

The political organisation of lowland Philippine kingdoms became more complex as access was gained to prestige goods through trade with China after AD 1000. The greater number of sites where hunter–gatherers may have interacted with farmers suggests an increase in the intensity of exchange, raising the possibility that hunter–gatherers were coming under increasing domination as lowland chiefs extracted the wild produce on which they depended for trade with the Chinese.

The current condition of hunter–gatherers

Since close links between hunter–gatherers and their neighbours are very common, it is important to consider what effects these have on the 'genuineness' of hunting and gathering in the sense of economic self-sufficiency used by Solway and Lee.

Local adaptations

Australia is probably the best continent on which to study recent hunting and gathering as an adaptation to the physical environment. Population densities in Arnhem Land, protected from the devastation of intense colonisation, are as high as those sustained by farming or stock-raising in northern Australia (Jones 1981: 108). Jones and Meehan (1989) conclude that if farming did not spread into Arnhem Land, it is because hunting and gathering provides a more efficient subsistence strategy. Macassan (Indonesian) fishermen visited the Arnhem Land coast for several hundred years to harvest *bêche-de-mer*, which they sold to the Chinese as an aphrodisiac. The Macassans also planted wet rice in coastal swamps close to Aboriginal camps. There has, moreover, always been contact between New Guinea and northern Australia via the islands of the Torres Straits. Horticulture is practised on several of the islands, but intensive reliance on horticulture only occurs north of the zone subjected to a prolonged dry season, on the New Guinea mainland. Hunting and gathering in Arnhem Land was not a response to marginalisation.

It would be an oversimplification to argue that hunter–gatherers have been least affected by contact where they live in environments least suited to farming. None the less, where hunter–gatherers do survive, they are likely to show adaptations most different from farming, which may unduly accentuate the status of hunting and gathering as a pure category. The practices of gathering and stacking wild millet in the Darling Basin of southeast Australia, digging channels to extend the range of eels at the head of coastal rivers in Victoria, and replanting *Dioscorea* in artificially irrigated gardens in southwest Australia, were all wiped out during early colonisation due to the suitability of these areas for agriculture (Allen 1974, Lourandos 1980, Hallam 1989).

Symbiosis

Bailey *et al.* (1989) hypothesise that hunter–gatherers in tropical forests must always have relied on symbiotic relations with farmers. They argue many of the plants exploited by tropical forest foragers have been introduced, that yams, nuts, etc. require clearings in the forest to grow, and that animal biomass in such forests is low. The plant foods Mbuti obtain from farmers, principally manioc and bananas, are substitutes for the forest *itaba* root which is more difficult to dig up (Turnbull 1965: 34). Ellen, on the other hand, argues that among the Nuaulu of eastern Indonesia 'hunting and gathering not only supply most calories and all animal protein, but appear to be more productive than activities focused on gardens' (Ellen 1988: 119); 63% of Nuaulu energy intake comes from sago palm while virtually all animal protein is obtained by hunting, even if productivity is low (118). A critical variable, for hunter–gatherers exploiting tropical forest, will therefore be the accessibility of wild sources of starch. Froment (personal communication) reports that wild yams are sufficiently dense in some parts of the African tropical forest to support pure hunting and gathering, but not in others.

The Mbuti of central Africa supply neighbouring Bantu farmers with meat and honey, forest produce which typically rank highly in a optimal foraging series. Bantu farmers cannot prevent Mbuti raiding their gardens, but hunting within half a day's walk of Bantu villages is difficult, because game is scarce. The Mbuti have the double advantage of being able to live deeper in the forest and obtain intimate knowledge of the movements of local game (Turnbull 1965: 35–8). In this case it is plausible to argue that both farmers and hunter–gatherers enjoy a better diet through co-operation.

While the Batek De' of western peninsula Malaysia live by hunting small game and gathering wild yams and fruit, they also trade forest produce for rice, flour, tobacco, iron tools and other goods with Malay traders. In the past, the Batek sometimes planted small gardens with seed crops obtained from these traders and there was more intensive exchange of forest produce for cultivated crops with local Malay farmers until the farmers were removed by the Malaysian government (Endicott 1988: 112).

Dependence

Contrary to Turnbull's (1965) picture of the Mbuti living in a stable symbiotic relationship with Bantu farmers, other writers describe a downward spiral of increasing subordination in central Africa (e.g. Bahuchet and Guillaume 1982, Pederson and Wæhle 1988). Under such circumstances hunter–gatherers often seem to be driven toward the increasing exploitation of high-ranking resources (meat, honey, etc.) pushing them into inescapable dependence on neighbouring farmers once these high-ranking resources are over-exploited (see Layton, Foley *et al.* 1991: 257–8).

Wilmsen (1989) dates subordination of the Basarwa to their neighbours to the nineteenth century. Until 1826, Basarwa could raid and seize others' cattle successfully, but the Tswana and Europeans put an end to this, rendering the Basarwa dependent on dominant groups. Wilmsen believes that many !Kung remained economically and politically independent until the mid nineteenth century. Growth of the Tswana state and European colonial domination during the nineteenth century reduced the Basarwa from equal partners in exchange to a marginalised underclass, forced into hunting and gathering by their powerlessness. Between the 1850s and 1880s, European traders unleashed a booming trade in ivory and ostrich feathers from the Kalahari. Hunting became very lucrative, but by 1880 the elephants had been hunted out. German colonists in southwest Africa expropriated the cattle belonging to indigenous people, to sell them for beef and to deprive the native people of economic self-sufficiency (Wilmsen 1989: 140–7). Although a few Basarwa managed to keep hold of some cattle, many were forced ever deeper into the Kalahari, becoming increasingly dependent on hunting and gathering to survive.

The Kubu of Sumatra oscillate between foraging and cultivation (Sandbukt 1988). Until a few generations ago, the Kubu were at risk from slave-raiding and the main advantage of foraging, for the Kubu, was the capacity it gives to move freely through the forest. Most peoples of lowland South America combine horticulture with hunting and gathering. The Ache of Paraguay are an exception, well known in the literature on hunter–gatherers through studies on their foraging behaviour (Hawkes *et al.* 1982, Hill and Hurtado 1996). According to Clastres (1972: 145), the Ache of Paraguay were very mobile hunter–gatherers because they lived for many years on the run to escape slave-raiders.

Oscillations

Schrire (1980) argues the Kalahari Basarwa have moved repeatedly between herding and foraging, in response to climatic fluctuation between drought and periods of higher rainfall, as earlier proposed by Elphick (1975) for the Cape region. This argument confronts the 'genuiness' of recent hunter–gatherers in the first sense used by Solway and Lee, that is populations whose ancestors have a continuous history of hunting and gathering. The earliest pastoralists, who both Schrire (1980) and Wilmsen (1989) identify as Khoisan, reached the southern Cape about 2000 years ago. The 'strandlopers' of the Cape were gradually recognised by Dutch observers to be, not pure hunter–gatherers, but communities capable of shifting back and forth between foraging and herding according to the availability of livestock. Historical records also show Bushmen on the Orange River owned stock in the early nineteenth century, but that their stock was sometimes stolen by Hottentots, forcing them into dependence on hunting and gathering. While a similar process cannot be demonstrated among the ancestors of the !Kung, Schrire believes it probably occurred.

Like the nineteenth-century observer on the Orange River who left the cattle out of his illustration of a San camp when he prepared it for publication (Schrire 1980: 23), twentieth-century anthropologists have left descriptions of San interaction with Bantu-speakers out of their accounts because these conflicted with their model of 'pure' hunter–gatherers (Wilmsen 1989: xiv, and see Barnard 1999). Colonial administrators have been guilty of similar thinking, crystallising what were once fluid relations between flexible communities into rigid ethnic divisions defined by modes of subsistence.

Chang (1982) similarly argues for a 'revisionist' interpretation of the Dorobo (Okiek) hunter–gatherers of Kenya and Tanzania whom, she contends, may not have a continuous history of hunting and gathering. 'At least from the mid-1800s onwards, Rift Valley hunters and gatherers have consisted largely of disenfranchised pastoralists and farmers, rather than being descendants of ancient populations who have hunted since "time immemorial"' (Chang 1982: 271). Hodder (1982: 87) similarly concludes it is by no means certain an Aboriginal stock of 'true Dorobo' ever existed, while a recent study by Spencer underlines the versatility of East African hunter–gatherers in adapting their culture to suit current conditions (Spencer 1998: 131ff). Like Wilmsen, Chang regards the notion of a Dorobo tribe as the creation of colonial ethnography. Late nineteenth- and early twentieth-century explorers considered some groups of Dorobo had a distinct language and culture, while others were said to be Masai who had lost their cattle. Slave-raiding, smallpox and cattle disease devastated those Masai living close to trade routes, forcing them into hunting and gathering to survive (Chang 1982: 276–7). Hodder traces the history of a Masai group who lost their cattle around 1880, joined the Dorobo but after 1914 earned sufficient money to return to pastoralism (Hodder 1982: 97–8). Blackburn (1982), on the other hand, argues strongly for the existence of an Aboriginal Okiek/Dorobo people who have survived by establishing diverse exchange relationships with, or working for, Masai.

The two interpretations of the Dorobo are not necessarily incompatible. Nineteenth-century Europeans recorded cases of South African people who, having lost their cattle through raids, took up hunting and gathering. One told how he 'became a poor man, which obliged him for some time to live among the wild bushmen, to sustain sustenance' (Wilmsen 1989: 85). The Difaqane wars of the 1820s deprived Kgalagadi of their livestock and forced them into the desert. According to Kgalagadi oral tradition, Basarwa taught them the skills they needed to survive as hunter–gatherers until they earned sufficient money through producing furs, ostrich feathers and ivory to repurchase livestock. During the 1964 drought at Dobe, Herero women gathered wild foods along-side their Basarwa neighbours (Solway and Lee 1990: 112, 120). This raises the intriguing possibility that there could be a continuous cultural tradition of hunting and gathering in an area, but a complete turnover in the biological population practising it (this possibility would surely have appealed to Boas).

Current hunter–gatherer behaviour and academic theory

Foraging practices

Hunter–gatherers' reliance on their neighbours for elements of their diet has an important effect on foraging strategies. The observations from which Sahlins's notion of the 'original affluent society' were derived (Sahlins 1974: 14–24) were not representative of pre-contact conditions. Altman (1987) has reassessed the Australian data that contributed to Sahlins' conclusions. His detailed study of foraging at Momega outstation showed the mid wet season (January–March) was the leanest time of year. Even if women had worked all available hours, they would have only produced 6.69–7.53 MJ (1600–1800 kcal) per person per day. Imported flour has released women from this work (Altman 1987: 71–95). Grazing cattle have dramatically decreased the availability of plant foods on leases in central Australia (Layton 1986*a*: 62) and must have had a similar impact on the Kalahari. Access to firearms improves hunting efficiency. All of these factors will tend to diminish the importance of plant foods in observations of hunter–gatherer foraging, although they do not preclude calculations of pre-contact foraging efficiency.

The impact of foraging on demography

Movement between foraging and other modes of subsistence has important implications for anthropological studies of demography and territoriality among recent hunter–gatherers. Wilmsen found foraging !Kung suffered double the weight loss pastoral !Kung experienced during lean months. He concurred with other authors that foraging !Kung women averaged only 4.5 live births per woman, while women who had adopted agropastoralism and sedentary village life had an average of 7 live births (Wilmsen 1989: 303–313). Wilmsen's findings agree well with Jones's conclusion that Gidjingali birth spacing is half the 4–5 years it appears to have been before contact (Jones 1981: 134–5, but see Pennington's critique of such arguments in this volume). Current hunter–gatherer population densities may be doubly misleading. Up to 95% of the Aboriginal population in the Darwin hinterland and Victoria River district was killed during the early colonial era of the late nineteenth and early twentieth centuries and the survivors lived precariously attached to white buffalo shooters or on the fringes of towns and mining camps (Keen 1980*a*: 36–44, 1980*b*: 171, Rose 1992: 7–8).

Territoriality

Cree territoriality has been the subject of a classic debate in hunter–gatherer studies. Early ethnographers, working in the 1920s and 1930s, claimed that individual Cree owned their hunting territories. Leacock (1954, 1982) later argued individual hunters had developed exclusive trapping rights over certain areas in response to over-hunting by white trappers during the fur trade, and that hunting lands were previously communally owned. Subsequent research has supported Leacock's interpretation (Feit 1985, Scott 1988). The transition may also be a response to near extinction of large migratory game after the introduction of guns and traps, since hunting territories are only adaptive where the game is non-migratory (e.g. beaver, hare).

Lee described how !Kung move frequently between water-holes. Wilmsen argues the frequent movement emphasised by Lee is the strategy of marginal !Kung who have no ancestral right to the water-hole at which they live (Wilmsen 1989: 207–15, cf. Lee 1979: 42). Those !Kung at /Xai/Xai with secure entitlement to the group owning the local water-hole own the most cattle and favour marriage within the group, whereas those without secure rights preferred to maintain dispersed marriage networks (Wilmsen 1989: 181). The pastoral !Kung may have converged on what is an adaptive strategy for pastoralists in a semi-arid environment (cf. Barth 1967). Among Bedouin pastoralists, each lineage owns the summer wells, which lie at the centre of their grazing land. Impoverished families attach themselves as clients to wealthier ones. Marriage tends to be lineage endogamous, to keep livestock within the group (Bonte 1979, Lefébure 1979, Tapper 1979). Foraging !Kung rely on strategies similar to those of Aboriginal hunter–gatherers in the Western Desert of Australia (Layton 1986b).

State policy and hunter–gatherers

Anthropology and the colonial impact

Studies of living hunter–gatherers by anthropologists are doubly removed from the pristine world of hunters and gatherers, since such studies are not only typically made on populations who have long interacted with their neighbours, but also are all carried out in a colonial context (see Trigger 1999). The Western impact on hunter–gatherers had been uneven by the time they were first studied by anthropologists, but all had been affected to some degree (see Bodley 1999). Spencer and Gillen's influential field research in Australia (Spencer and Gillen 1899, 1904), for example, shaped the theories of totemism proposed by Frazer and Durkheim (see Layton 1997: 129–30). Many of the Aboriginal communities Spencer and Gillen visited were still living in their traditional territories, but had been engulfed by pastoral colonisation some 20 years earlier, suffering massacres, introduced diseases and substantial dependence on imported foods. Totemic rituals asserting traditional rights to land would have been performed in the face of colonial expropriation. In response to the damaging effect of colonisation, a number of Aboriginal communities were later settled on missions or government townships and a number of classic Australian ethnographies were based on fieldwork in such settlements (e.g. Warner 1937, Meggitt 1962). Since the 1970s, some Aboriginal groups have returned to their traditional countries and increased their reliance on foraging. Altman's more recent study, referred to above (Altman 1987), was carried out among such a group.

In 1923, the explorer and anthropologist Knud Rasmussen wrote that the Netsilik of the Arctic had been 'suffered to live their own life, entirely untrammelled by outside influence right up to the present time' (quoted in Savelle 1985: 206). Savelle shows, to the contrary, that when the Ross and Franklin expeditions abandoned their ships in 1832 and 1848, vast qualities of wood, copper and iron became available to the Netsilik and were extensively used to manufacture traditional artefacts. Equally dramatic, but more disruptive, were the effects on trade. Previously the Netsilik had depended on the Ukjulik for wood and on the Iglulik for iron. The Ukjulik depended on the Netsilik in turn for the right to camp and hunt with them if resources failed in their own country. For the next 30 years, material from both expeditions' ships circulated widely among Netsilik. The Ukjulik attempted to develop trade with their western neighbours the Copper Inuit, apparently without success. Balikci noted historical evidence that the Netsilik had expanded westward prior to Rasmussen's fieldwork, apparently replacing a community called the Ukjulingmiut [Ukjulik], many of whom had died during a severe winter, but Balicki did not appreciate the cause (Balikci 1970: xix, xxi). Savelle comments that, despite these upheavals, Rasmussen was perhaps describing a 'traditional' Inuit society. For the Netsilik (although not the Ukjulik) the changes were reversible and by the time Rasmussen had arrived they were again dependent on other Inuit groups for much of their wood and iron.

On the Northwest Coast of North America change arising from colonial contact had become irreversible by the time the earliest anthropological studies were made, but the indigenous culture was still active. Sea otter pelts obtained by Captain Cook in 1778 initiated the fur trade (Jonaitis 1988: 20). Furs obtained by the native people were traded for iron and copper. Within 20 years Northwest Coast society had all the iron and copper it needed. Indigenous people drove increasingly hard bargains. By 1830 the sea otter was virtually extinct. Land animals such as marten, otter, bear and mink were now hunted. Some native communities abandoned their traditional villages and settled at trading posts, where a new cycle of potlatching was required to establish the relative rank of leaders from different communities (Garfield and Wingert 1966: 7, 35, Jonaitis 1988: 40).

Few Europeans had settled on the Northwest Coast during the fur trade but the discovery of gold on Queen Charlotte Island and the Fraser River during the 1850s brought large numbers of settlers. White attitudes to the indigenous people changed; curiosity and even admiration turned to insult (Jonaitis 1988: 47). In 1862 a smallpox epidemic killed up to one-third of the Haida. Some villages were abandoned and some elite families were wiped out, causing more intensive potlatching, the construction of ever-greater numbers of totem poles and more impressive houses, even as the white American colonists were oppressing and decimating the native people. Potlatching was declared a punishable offence in 1884, two years before Boas arrived to carry out his first fieldwork, although the Kwakiutl whom he met told him they had no intention of abandoning the potlatch (Jonaitis 1988: 54).

Ranching

While the fur trade provided the principal means through which high-latitude hunter–gatherers were incorporated into the market economy, in lower latitudes cattle-ranching has often been the primary medium through which hunter–gatherers become incorporated into the nation state. The outcome has been variable, depending both on the density of European settlement and on state policy.

In California the Franciscan mission system based on the coerced labour of native Americans dominated livestock production at the time of the region's incorporation into the world market (Salvatore 1991: 445). Ironically, therefore, the first cowboys (*vaqueros*) were in fact Indians. Native Americans rebelled against living conditions during the 1820s and the mission system was abolished after 1833. Although secularisation was intended to return land to native people much was acquired by colonists (Silliman 1999). By the 1850s many native Americans had become itinerant workers and were suffering competition from European immigrants. Silliman's excavations at Alta California Ranch (Silliman 1999) suggest that during the 1840s native employees, probably coastal Miwok, were continuing both to hunt small game and fish and to manufacture stone tools from obsidian.

British colonists took the ranching economy to Australia. Work as cattle men and women enabled many Aboriginal people to continue living in their traditional country and provided continuity of practice crucial to contemporary anthropological study (Layton 1986*a*, 1999, Rose 1992, Strang 1997). Aboriginal labour was cheap and Aboriginal stockmen possessed vital knowledge of the country in which livestock was pastured. Until the 1960s, it was usual in the monsoon zone of northern Australia for employees to be paid off at the start of the wet season, allowing a return to hunting and gathering (Layton 1992: 110–12). During the 1960s, legislation compelled ranchers to pay award wages to Aboriginal employees. Many lost their jobs, but the government created excisions from pastoral leases, which enabled communities to remain on their own land.

Land in the Ghanzi district of Botswana was alienated from Basarwa in the 1890s when large areas were offered to prospective white settlers. As in Australia, indigenous labour has been increasingly displaced but, in contrast to Australia, there is no provision for unemployed Basarwa to live on their traditional country (see Hitch-cock 1999). The first settlers to take up holdings were impoverished Boers who had lost many of their cattle in the 1000-km trek across the Kalahari. Not only did they depend on Basarwa labour, many also 'came to depend to some degree on the San staple, the marama bean, collected each season by the wives of farmers' labourers and exchanged for meat, blankets and tobacco' (Guenther 1976: 126). Large antelope have now become very scarce, and contemporary hunting is confined to small antelope and rodents. The traditional pattern of seasonal aggregation, working on ranches during the dry season, and dispersal to small hunting camps during the wet season to some extent continues. The adjacent Central Kalahari Game Reserve is, in principle, open to any Basarwa but in practice only those who continue to subsist more or less entirely by hunting and gathering have the necessary skills to survive in that environment.

Conservationism and national parks

The relationship between hunter–gatherers and the management of national parks demonstrates particularly clearly the pernicious influence of Western ideology (cf. Barnard 1999, Trigger 1999). Here, however, it is not the assertion of hunting and gathering as the natural human condition, but that of the *wilderness* as a landscape unaffected by human occupation. This ideology arguably has its origin in the politics of the enclosures in eighteenth-century England. The very landlords who were dispossessing peasant farmers by enclosing village common land (asserting it was unowned because it was unfenced and unploughed) were seeking to create a 'natural', untamed landscape in their country parks (Cos-grove 1984). The same ideology was used to dispossess the native peoples of Australia and North America. The first US national parks owed their landscapes to indigenous management practices, but to the early proponents of national parks, 'the land seemed vacant, garden like, unspoiled, ripe for the taking – or saving' (Keller and Turek 1998: 20). Yosemite appeared virgin because gold miners had driven out or killed its Miwok inhabitants 12 years before it was declared a park. The indigenous inhabitants of Yellowstone were, on the other hand, evicted from the park in the late nineteenth century (Keller and Turek 1998: 23–4).

The US Wilderness Act of 1964 perpetuated these attitudes, defining a wilderness as 'an area where the earth and its community of life are untrammelled by man, where man himself is a visitor who does not remain' (in Pratt 1996: 337). Pratt documents the effect of declaring part of their traditional land a wilderness area on the Nunivak Inuit of Alaska. Although the Nunivak participate in the Western cash economy, the majority still carry out traditional subsistence activities throughout the year. Nunivak do not know Alaskan wilderness legislation allows indigenous people to use snowmobiles and set up temporary hunting and fishing encampments, and a cabin constructed by one man at his family's campsite was ordered to be pulled down. Most importantly, the Nunivak resent the idea that their own traditional land-management practices are deemed inadequate.

A similar process has taken place in southern Africa. Unlike other ethnic groups in Botswana, Basarwa can hunt freely throughout the year without a licence, provided they hunt on foot and use only bow and arrows or spear (Guenther 1976: 125). Rangers in the Central Kalahari Game Reserve have, however, reportedly applied a strict interpretation of hunting by traditional means. 'One game scout told me that he arrested any Basarwa who were wearing pants while hunting' (Hitchcock 1985: 59). As Lewis remarks of Euro-Australian staff in Kakadu National Park, there is a tendency to interpret Aboriginal culture 'in terms of the more visible and material aspects of life . . . they see that Aborigines have acculturated in lifestyles, transportation, tools, dress and so on, rather than the underlying knowledge and belief system' (Lewis 1989: 954).

Despite Lewis's criticisms, the federally managed national parks in Australia are notable for their enlightened approach to indigenous land management. Controlled burning is now known to be the traditional practice that had the greatest impact on Australia's ecology and it has been incorporated into park management at Uluru and Kakadu. Euro-Australian rangers initially had difficulty accepting that Kakadu's traditional owners had retained the necessary skills or applied them systematically, but a greater degree of cross-cultural understanding has developed over the years (Lewis 1989, Cordell 1993). In sharp contrast to the US national parks legislation, UNESCO recently created a new category of properties that could be inscribed on the World Heritage List, 'cultural land-scapes'. Demonstration that the landscape of the Uluru National Park had been created through controlled burning by its traditional owners was essential to success of the Park's nomination for inclusion on the World Heritage List as a cultural landscape.

Hunter–gatherers' encounters with conservationism show how important it is not to be misled by the superficial evidence for enculturation and thus succumb to the misleading idea that foragers are bound to lose their traditional knowledge when confronted with Western colonisation.

Land rights

Unlike conservationism, land rights seek to recognise customary rights that have been previously disregarded or denied by the colonial power (see Hitchcock 1999). Land rights depend on the maintenance of a separate cultural identity within a defined area of land. Mr. Viner, the Federal Minister introducing the second reading of Australia's Northern Territory Land Rights Bill to Parliament in 1976, said:

> Most of us now appreciate more sensitively than in the past that traditional Aboriginals think, feel and act about land according to a plan of life a world apart from ours.

The logic of Wilmsen's analysis of the Basarwa, that they share a common history and cultural institutions with neighbouring pastor-alists, is that land rights for hunting and gathering Basarwa are inappropriate. Rather, Wilmsen (1989) recommends they should be enabled to (re)enter the pastoral economy as stock-owners. Chang (1982: 274) is similarly sceptical of Dorobo land rights. The Central Kalahari Game Reserve was declared during the colonial period as a refuge for Basarwa, but since independence the Botswanan government has been relatively ineffective in securing land rights for Basarwa (Hitchcock 1985, Ikeya 1998).

One of the biggest difficulties land rights movements have had to face is the great disjunction between Western and hunter–gatherer concepts of land use and land tenure (see for example Williams 1987, Scott 1988, Siddle 1996). Australia was colonised on the legal premise that hunter–gatherers could not own land because they did not 'improve' it. This doctrine was not overturned until the 1992 Mabo case in the High Court of Australia (Attwood 1996).

There is no federal legislation in Canada that recognises aboriginal title (see Oakes *et al.* 1998). Although treaties signed between the Crown and native Canadian groups should confer sovereign status on the native groups under international law, recent legislation has declared that Canadian treaties were merely internal agreements. Native Canadian communities have usually had to surrender their claim to aboriginal title in exchange for negotiated rights. Deborah Webster, president of the Inuit Heritage Trust, explained they had agreed to this because they did not know how a court might adjudicate on the extent of aboriginal rights. An acknowledged right was better than an unknown one (Webster, personal communication).

The James Bay case demonstrates the potential economic impact of undetermined land rights. The Quebec State government announced the James Bay hydroelectric project in 1971. Cree and neighbouring Inuit who were also affected took the State government to court. They claimed flooding would damage hunting which still formed an 'essential and substantial portion of Cree diet' and a central element of their culture and social organisation (Feit 1983: 416). In 1973 the judge ruled that they had proven the existence of 'personal and usufructory rights over the territory and had possessed and occupied it since time immemorial' (Feit 1983: 420). The two parties agreed to negotiate. US investors said the native claim must be settled before the project could be considered 'a safe, economically-viable investment' (Feit 1983: 420). In 1994, stage two of the James Bay scheme was cancelled after protests at the environmental damage it would cause dissuaded the people in New York from buying the electricity.

In 1993, the Canadian government agreed to return *administration* of 903 000 km^2 of the Northwest Territories to the Inuit, one-fifth of the area over which the Inuit can demonstrate continuous use and occupancy. Ownership of mineral rights over small portions of this land and rights to all surface resources over slightly larger areas have also been returned to the Inuit. The remainder remains Crown (i.e. government) land, over which the Inuit have the right to 'hunt, fish and participate in management'. The Alaskan Native Claims Settlement Act of 1971 similarly granted Alaskan natives fee simple title to 16 million ha of land in Alaska, but extinguished aboriginal title to any additional lands (Pratt 1996: 342).

Conclusion

Hunter–gatherers clearly exist in a range of relationships with their neighbours and the nation state. As Kent argued for the Basarwa of Botswana, 'The question, then, is not whether Basarwa engage (even peripherally) in activities other than hunting and gathering . . . as do virtually all modern foragers . . . ; rather, the question is whether we can still learn about foraging behaviour by studying such people' (Kent 1992: 52). I have shown that foraging practices, demography and territoriality are all profoundly affected by interaction between hunter–gatherers and their neighbours, but that modern hunter–gatherers live in a variety of conditions. Any attempt to derive a model of 'genuine' hunting and gathering from ethnographic research must recognise the local impact of neighbouring peoples and colonial powers.

There are three possible histories for recent hunter–gatherers. They may possess a continuous cultural and genetic history inherited from pre-farming ancestors, albeit influenced by interaction with non-foraging peoples. They may possess a continuous cultural history, but have become genetically diverse as they are joined by former farmers or pastoralists and left by others. They may possess neither cultural nor genetic continuity with pre-farming ancestors, being refugees from farming or pastoral communities who have been forced to reinvent hunting and gathering. I consider the tendency for hunter–gatherers with very different histories to converge on particular solutions to living in certain environments more insightful, in understanding the role of hunting and gathering in human evolution, than the hypothetical conservation of an ancestral condition. It remains essential to establish whether hunters and gatherers are living independently of farmers or herders, symbiotically or under duress, in order to assess the significance of their behaviours.

Acknowledgements

The paper has benefited from discussions with David Anderson, Gerald Berreman, Kathy Fewster, Aneesa Kassam, Arek Marciniak, Peter Rowley-Conwy, Mayura Sato and Steven Silliman and I thank all of them for their advice.

References

Aikio, P. and Aikia, M. (1989). A chapter in the history of the colonisation of Sámi lands: the forced migration of Norwegian reindeer Sámi to Finland in the 1800s. In *Conflict in the Archaeology of Living Traditions*, ed. R. Layton, pp. 116–130. London: Routledge.

Allen, H. (1974). The Bagundji of the Darling Basin. *World Archaeology* **5**: 309–322.

Altman, J.C. (1987). *Hunter–Gatherers Today: An Aboriginal Economy in North Australia*. Canberra: Aboriginal Studies Press.

Ames, K.M. (1994). The Northwest Coast: complex hunter–gatherers, ecology, and social evolution. *Annual Review of Anthropology* **23**: 209–229.

Attwood, B. (ed) (1996). *In the Age of Mabo: History, Aborigines and Australia*. St. Leonard's, Australia: Allen and Unwin.

Bahuchet, S. and Guillaume, H. (1982). Aka–farmer relations in the Northwest Congo Basin. In *Politics and History in Band Societies*, ed. E. Leacock and R. Lee, pp. 189–211. Cambridge: Cambridge University Press.

Bailey, R.C., Head, G., Jenike, M., Owen, B., Rechtman, R. and Zechenter, E. (1989). Hunting and gathering in tropical rain forest: is it possible? *American Anthropologist* **91**: 59–82.

Balikci, A. (1970). *The Netsilik Eskimo*. New York: Natural History Press.

Barnard, A. (1992). *Hunters and Herders of Southern Africa: A Comparative Ethnography of the Khoisan Peoples*. Cambridge: Cambridge University Press.

Barnard, A. (1999). Images of hunters and gatherers in European social thought. In *The Cambridge Encyclopedia of Hunters and Gatherers*, ed. R.B. Lee and R. Daly, pp. 375–383. Cambridge: Cambridge University Press.

Barth, F. (1967). On the study of social change. *American Anthropologist* **69**: 661–669.

Beach, H. (1981). *Reindeer-Herd Management in Transition: The Case of Tuorpon Saameby in Northern Sweden*, Uppsala Studies in Cultural Anthropology 3. Stockholm: Almqvist and Wiksell.

Berreman, G.D. (1991). The incredible 'Tasaday': deconstructing the myth of a 'Stone-age' people. *Cultural Survival Quarterly* **15**: 3–45.

Berreman, G.D. (1999). The Tasaday controversy. In *The Cambridge Encyclopedia of Hunters and Gatherers*, ed. R.B. Lee and R. Daly, pp. 457–464. Cambridge: Cambridge University Press.

Blackburn, R. (1982). In the land of milk and honey: Okiek adaptations to their forests and neighbours. In *Politics and History in Band Societies*, ed. E. Leacock and R. Lee, pp. 283–305. Cambridge: Cambridge University Press.

Bodley, J. (1999). Hunter–gatherers and the colonial encounter. In *The Cambridge Encyclopedia of Hunters and Gatherers*, ed. R.B. Lee and R. Daly, pp.465–472. Cambridge: Cambridge University Press.

Bonte, P. (1979). Segmentarité et pouvoir chez les éléveurs nomades sahariens. In *Pastoral Production and Society*, ed. Equipe écologie et anthropologie des sociétés pastorales, pp. 171–199. Cambridge: Cambridge University Press.

Chang, C. (1982). Nomads without cattle: East African foragers in historical perspective. In *Politics and history in band societies*, ed. E. Leacock and R. Lee, pp. 269–282. Cambridge: Cambridge University Press.

Clastres, P. (1972). The Guayaki. In *Hunters and Gatherers today*, ed. M.G. Bicchieri, pp. 138–174. New York: Holt, Rinehart.

Cordell, J. (1993). Who owns the land? Indigenous involvement in Australian protected areas. In *Indigenous Peoples and Protected Areas*, ed. E. Kemf, pp. 104–113. London: Earthscan.

Cosgrove, D. (1984). *Social Formation and Symbolic Landscape*. London: Croom Helm.

Ellen, R. (1988). Foraging, starch extraction and the sedentary lifestyle in the lowland rain forest of central Seram. In *Hunters and Gatherers: History, Evolution and Social Change*, ed. T. Ingold, D. Riches and J. Woodburn, pp. 117–134. Oxford: Berg.

Elphick, R. (1975). *Khoikhoi and the Founding of White South Africa*. New Haven: Yale University Press.

Endicott, K. (1988). Property, power and conflict among the Batek of Malaysia. In *Hunters and Gatherers: Property, Power and Ideology*, ed. T. Ingold, D. Riches and J. Woodburn, pp. 110–127. Oxford: Berg.

Feit, H. (1983). Negotiating recognition of aboriginal rights: history, strategies and reactions to the James Bay and northern Quebec Agreement. In

Aborigines, Land and Land Rights, ed. N. Peterson and M. Langton, pp. 416–138. Canberra: Australian Institute of Aboriginal Studies.

Feit, H. (1985). Legitimation and autonomy in James Bay Cree responses to hydro-electric development. In *Indigenous Peoples and the Nation-State*, ed. N. Dyck, pp. 27–66. St. Johns: Institute of Social and Economic Research, Memorial University of Newfoundland.

Fischer, A. (1982). Trade in Danubian shaft-hole axes and the introduction of Neolithic economy in Denmark. *Journal of Danish Archaeology* **1**: 7–12.

Garfield, V. and Wingert, P. (1966). *The Tsimshian Indians and their Arts*. Seattle: University of Washington Press.

Guenther, M. (1976). From hunters to squatters: social and cultural change among the farm San of Ghanzi, Botswana. In *Kalahari Hunter–Gatherers: Studies of the !Kung San and their Neighbours*, ed. R. Lee and I. DeVore, pp. 120–133. Cambridge MA: Harvard University Press.

Hallam, S. (1989). Plant usage and management in Southwest Australian Aboriginal societies. In *Foraging and Farming: The Evolution of Plant Exploitation*, ed. D. Harris and G. Hillman, pp. 136–151. London: Unwin.

Hawkes, K, Hill, K. and O'Connell, J. (1982). Why hunters gather: optimal foraging and the Ache of eastern Paraguay. *American Ethnologist* **9**: 379–398.

Headland, T. and Reid, L. (1989). Hunter–gatherers and their neighbours from prehistory to the present. *Current Anthropology* **30**: 43–66.

Hill, K. and Hurtado, A.M. (1999). *Ache Life History: The Ecology and Demography of a Foraging People*. New York: Aldine de Gruyter.

Hitchcock, R. (1985). Development planning, government policy and the future of the Basarwa in Botswana. In *The Future of Former Foragers*, ed. C. Schrire and R, Gordon, pp. 55–62. London: Cultural Survival.

Hitchcock, R. (1999). Indigenous peoples' rights and the struggle for survival. In *The Cambridge Encyclopedia of Hunters and Gatherers*, ed. R.B. Lee and R. Daly, pp. 480–486. Cambridge: Cambridge University Press.

Hodder, I. (1982). *Symbols in Action*. Cambridge: Cambridge University Press.

Ikeya, K. (1998). Social changes among the San under the influence of the resettlement policy. Paper presented at the 8th International Conference on Hunting and Gathering Societies, Osaka.

Jonaitis, A. (1988). *From the Land of the Totem Poles: the Northwest Coast Indian Art Collection at the American Museum of Natural History*. New York: American Museum of Natural History.

Jones, R. (1981). Hunters in the Australian coastal savanna. In *Human Ecology in Savanna Evironments*, ed. D. Harris, pp. 107–146. London: Academic Press.

Jones, R. and Meehan, B. (1989). Plant foods of the Gidjingali: ethnographic and archaeological perspectives from northern Australia on tuber and seed exploitation. In *Foraging and Farming: The Evolution of Plant Exploitation*, ed. D. Harris and G. Hillman, pp. 120–135. London: Unwin.

Junker, L.L. (1996). Hunter–gatherer landscapes and lowland trade in the prehispanic Philippines. *World Archaeology* **27**: 389–410.

Keen, I. (1980*a*). *Alligator Rivers Stage II Land Claim*. Darwin: Northern Land Council.

Keen, I. (1980*b*) The Alligator Rivers Aborigines: retrospect and prospect. In *Northern Australia: options and implications*, ed. R. Jones, pp. 171–186. Canberra: Australian National University Research School of Pacific Studies.

Keller, R. and Turek, M. (1998). *American Indians and National Parks*. Tucson: University of Arizona Press.

Kent, S. (1992). The current forager controversy: real versus ideal views of hunter–gatherers. *Man* (N.S.) **27**: 45–70.

Lampert, R. and Hughes, P. (1987). The Flinders Ranges: a Pleistocene outpost in the arid zone? *Records of the South Australian Museum* **20**: 29–34.

Layton, R. (1986*a*). *Uluru: An Aboriginal History of Ayers Rock*. Canberra: Aboriginal Studies Press.

Layton, R. (1986*b*). Political and territorial structures among hunter–gatherers. *Man* (n.s.) **21**: 18–33.

Layton, R. (1992). *Australian Rock Art: A New Synthesis*. Cambridge: Cambridge University Press.

Layton, R. (1997). Representing and translating people's place in the landscape of northern Australia. In *After Writing Culture*, ed. A. James, J. Hockey and A. Dawson, pp. 122–143. London: Routledge.

Layton, R. (1999). The Alawa totemic landscape: economy, religion and politics. In *The Archaeology and Anthropology of Landscape*, ed. P. Ucko and R. Layton, pp. 219–239. London: Routledge.

Layton, R., Foley, R. and Williams, E. (1991). The transition between hunting and gathering and the specialised husbandry of resources: a socio-ecological approach. *Current Anthropology* **32**: 255–274.

Leacock, E. (1954). *The Montagnais 'Hunting Territory' and the Fur Trade*. American Anthropological Association Memoir 78. Arlington MA: American Anthropological Association.

Leacock, E. (1982). Relations of production in band society. In *Politics and History in Band Societies*, ed. E. Leacock and R. Lee, pp. 159–170. Cambridge: Cambridge University Press.

Lee, R.B. (1976). !Kung spatial organisation: an ecological and historical perspective. In, *Kalahari Hunter–Gatherers*, ed. R.B. Lee and I. DeVore, pp. 73–97. Cambridge, Mass.: Harvard University Press.

Lee, R.B. (1979). *The !Kung San: Men, Women and Work in a foraging society*. Cambridge: Cambridge University Press.

Lee, R.B. and DeVore, I. (eds.) (1968*)*. *Man the Hunter*. Chicago: Aldine.

Lefébure, C. (1979). Introduction: the specificity of nomadic pastoral societies. In *Pastoral Production and Society*, ed. Équipe écologie et anthropologie des sociétés pastorales, pp. 1–14. Cambridge: Cambridge University Press.

Lewis, D. (1988). *The Rock Paintings of Arnhem Land, Australia.* Oxford: BAR International Series 415. Oxford: British Archaeological Reports.

Lewis, H.T. (1989). Ecological and technical use of fire: Aborigines versus park rangers in northern Australia. *American Anthropologist* **91**: 940–961.

Lourandos, H. (1980). Change or stability? Hydraulics, hunter–gatherers and population in temperate Australia. *World Archaeology* **11**: 245–264.

Marciniak, A. (*in press*). Living space: the construction of social complexity in the European Neolithic. In *The Neolithic in Orkney and its European context*, ed. A. Richie. Cambridge: Cambridge University Press.

Maschner, H. (1991). Emergence of cultural complexity on the northern Northwest Coast. *Antiquity* **65**: 924–934.

Meggitt, M.J. (1962). *Desert People.* Sydney: Angus and Robertson.

Morphy, H. (1991). *Ancestral Connections: Art and an Aboriginal System of Knowledge.* Chicago: University of Chicago Press.

Mulk, I.-M. and Bayliss-Smith, T. (1999). The representation of Sámi cultural identity in the cultural landscapes of northern Sweden: the use and misuse of archaeological knowledge. In *The Archaeology and Anthropology of Landscape*, ed. P. Ucko and R. Layton, pp. 358–396. London: Routledge.

Oakes, J., Rewe, R., Kinew, K. and Maloney, E. (eds) (1998). *Sacred Lands: Aboriginal World Views, Claims and Conflicts*, Canadian Circumpolar Institute Occasional Publication 32. Edmonton: Canadian Circumpolar Institute and University of Manitoba Department of Native Studies.

Pederson, J. and Wæhle, E. (1988). The complexities of residential organisation among the Efe (Mbuti) and Bagombi (Baka): a critical view of the notion of flux in hunter–gatherer societies. In *Hunters and Gatherers: History, Evolution and Social Change*, ed. T. Ingold, D. Riches and J. Woodburn, pp. 75–90. Oxford: Berg.

Pratt, K.L. (1996). 'They never ask the people': native views about the Nunivak Wilderness. In *Key Issues in Hunter–Gatherer Research*, ed. E. Burch and L. Ellanna, pp. 333–356. Oxford: Berg.

Roeck Hansen, B. (1996). *The Agrarian Landscape in Finland Circa 1700, With Special Reference to Southwest Finland and Ostrobothnia.* Stockholm: Department of Human Geography, Stockholm University.

Rose, D.B. (1992). *Dingo Makes us Human: Life and Land in an Australian Aboriginal Culture.* Cambridge: Cambridge University Press.

Rowley-Conwy, P. (1994). Meat, furs and skins: Mesolithic animal bones from Ringkloster, a seasonal hunting camp in Jutland. *Journal of Danish Archaeology* **12**: 87–98.

Sahlins, M. (1974). *Stone Age Economics.* London: Tavistock.

Salvatore, R. (1991). Modes of labour control in cattle-ranching economies: California, southern Brazil and Argentina 1820–1860. *Journal of Economic History* **51**: 441–451.

Sandbukt, Ø. (1988). Tributary tradition and relations of affinity and gender among the Sumatran Kubu. In *Hunters and Gatherers: History, Evolution and Social Change*, ed. T. Ingold, D. Riches and J. Woodburn, pp. 107–116. Oxford: Berg.

Savelle, J.M. (1985). Effects of nineteenth century European exploration on the development of the Netsilik Inuit culture. In *The Franklin era in Canadian Arctic history. Mercury series Archaeological Survey of Canada paper 131*, ed. P.D. Sutherland, pp. 192–214. Ottawa: National Museums of Canada.

Schrire, C. (1980). An enquiry into the evolutionary status and apparent identity of San hunter–gatherers. *Human Ecology* **8**: 9–32.

Schrire, C. (1982). *The Alligator Rivers: Prehistory and Ecology in Western Arnhem Land, Terra Australis 7*. Canberra: Australian National University Research School of Pacific Studies.

Scott, C. (1988). Property, practice and aboriginal rights among Quebec Cree hunters. In *Hunters and Gatherers: Property, Power and Ideology*, ed. T. Ingold, J. Woodburn and D. Riches, pp. 35–51. Oxford: Berg.

Siddle, R. (1996). *Race, Resistance and the Ainu of Japan*. London: Routledge.

Silliman, S. (1999). A plurality of people, a plurality of data: investigating the 19th century Mexican–Californian rancho. Paper presented at the Society for Historical Archaeology 32nd Conference, Salt Lake City, January 1999.

Solway, J. and Lee, R. (1990). Foragers: genuine or spurious? Situating the Kalahari San in history. *Current Anthropology* **31**: 109–146.

Sognnes, K. (1998). Symbols in a changing world: rock art and the transition from hunting to farming in mid Norway. In *The Archaeology of Rock Art*, ed. C. Chippindale and P. Taçon, pp. 146–162. Cambridge: Cambridge University Press.

Spencer, B. and Gillen, F.J. (1899). *The Native Tribes of Central Australia*. London: Macmillan.

Spencer, B. and Gillen, F.J. (1904). *The Northern Tribes of Central Australia*. London: Macmillan.

Spencer, P. (1998). *The Pastoral Continuum: The Marginalisation of Tradition in East Africa*. Oxford: Oxford University Press.

Strang, V. (1997). *Uncommon Ground: Cultural Landscapes and Environmental Values*. Oxford: Berg.

Sutton, P. ed. (1988). *Dreamings: The Art of Aboriginal Australia*. New York: George Braziller.

Tacitus, C. (1985). *The Agricola and the Germania*, translated H. Mattingly and S.A. Hadford. Harmondsworth: Penguin.

Taçon, P. and Chippindale, C. (1994). Australia's ancient warriors. *Cambridge Archaeological Journal* **4**: 211–248.

Tapper, R. (1979). The organisation of nomadic communities in pastoral societies of the Middle East. In *Pastoral Production and Society*, ed. Équipe écologie et anthropologie des sociétés pastorales, pp. 43–65. Cambridge: Cambridge University Press.

Trigger, D. (1999). Hunter/gatherer peoples and nation states. In *The Cambridge Encyclopedia of Hunters and Gatherers*, ed. R.B. Lee and R. Daly, pp. 473–479. Cambridge: Cambridge University Press.

Turnbull, C.M. (1965). *Wayward Servants: The Two Worlds of African Pygmies*. Westport CT: Greenwood.

Verhart, L. and Wansleeben, M. (1997). Waste and prestige: the Mesolithic-Neolithic transition in the Netherlands from a social perspective. *Analecta Praehistorica Leidensia* **29**: 65–73.

Warner, W.L. (1937). *A Black Civilisation*. New York: Harper.

Williams, N. (1989). *Two Laws: Managing Disputes in a Contemporary Aboriginal Community*. Canberra: Aboriginal Studies Press.

Wilmsen, E.N. (1989). *Land Filled with Flies: A Political Economy of the Kalahari*. Chicago: University of Chicago Press.

Zvelebil, M. (ed.) (1986). *Hunters in Transition: Mesolithic Societies of Temperate Eurasia and their Transition to Farming*. Cambridge: Cambridge University Press.

GLOSSARY

Ahmarian A complex of Early Upper Palaeolithic assemblages found in the eastern Mediterranean area.

ASFR Age-specific fertility rate, the average number of births women in a population bear at each age. It can be computed by dividing the number of births that occur to women at each age by the number of women that are at each age. See also *TFR*.

assemblage In British usage, a group of associated contemporary artefact types. In American usage, collections of artefacts and other archaeological materials recovered from a single bounded unit, such as a geological layer or a spatial cluster (see also *Tool Assemblage*).

asymmetrical bilingualism The practice of a person who understands two languages but usually only speaks one (usually their first language) to others.

Aurignacian A very widespread form of Early Upper Palaeolithic stone tool industry.

Azilian A Late Upper Palaeolithic variant found around the French–Spanish border.

behavioural ecology The subfield of evolutionary ecology that applies natural selection theory and micro-economic conceptual tools to the study of behavioural adaptation in a socio-ecological setting.

bilingual/multilingual Of individuals, using two or more languages on a regular basis; of societies, comprising a large number of individuals who are bilingual/multilingual.

blade Elongated, narrow stone flake, frequently produced by one of several specialised techniques.

bladelet A very small, narrow stone blade.

blank Generic term for flaked-stone flakes or blade.

BMI Body mass index, calculated as weight in kg divided by square of height in metres (kg/m^2). A BMI less than 18.5 kg/m^2 indicates chronic energy deficiency.

BMR Basal metabolic rate, the body's energy expenditure under resting conditions.

BP Years before present.

Castelperronian A form of Early Upper Palaeolithic industry found in southern France and northern Spain. Also known as Chatelperronian.

central place foragers (CPF) A system in which individuals radiate out from a group living site or home base to hunt and gather resources which they return to the base for consumption.

chaîne opératoire All the stages in the history of a tool including the acquiring of raw materials, making, using, exchanging and discarding it. Includes an account of the physical materials, knowledge, skills, actions, personnel and social relationships between the various people involved.

cline A geographic gradient in the frequency of specific genetic, phenotypic or behavioural traits in organisms.

code-switching Switching frequently between two languages in speech.

constrained optimisation The premise that evolutionary processes tend toward behaviours that maximise the net adaptive benefits of an activity, subject to cognitive, technological, environmental and other constraints.

costly-signalling A model for the evolution of behaviours that unambiguously convey accurate information about the fitness of the individual performing them. For instance, a hunter may share large game widely because it benefits him and the recipients to have accurate information about his foraging prowess. A costly signal is one that is not easily faked; it thus conveys honest information about adaptive prowess.

creole The language resulting when a pidgin becomes the first language of a group and becomes more complex.

curation A form of risk-averse behaviour in technology in which tools are made and transported in anticipation of use. May also involve prolonging the longevity of tools.

demand sharing Sharing motivated by social pressures on the holder of a resource to distribute portions of it to others.

design systems In technology these include the choice and employment of behaviours for making, using, maintaining, moving and discarding tools and the materials employed in these behaviours. The following types are recognised: reliability, maintainability, flexibility (which includes versatility and portability) and longevity.

diffusion The spread of cultural items or features from one group to another; not necessarily accompanied by migration of people; linguistic diffusion (or 'borrowing') is the spread of linguistic items or features specifically.

encounter-contingent model A model predicting the optimal set of resources for a forager to harvest, from among those encountered during the course of a foraging expedition.

Epigravettian A variety of Late Upper Palaeolithic industry common in southern, central and eastern Europe.

Epipalaeolithic See *Palaeolithic*.

ethnogenesis The development of a new ethnic identity on the part of a population.

exchange A form of transfer, involving the two-way flow of goods or services between individuals according to some principle of equivalence of value.

expedient behaviour In technology, involves the making and using of tools at the same spot and the immediate discard of the tool.

fecundity The ability of women to bear children. Individuals may be fecund but infertile.

fertility The actual number of live births.

glacial/interglacial Respectively, cold and warm periods in the climatic history of high-latitude regions.

Gravettian A widespread Upper Palaeolithic industry, found throughout Europe.

habitat A zone characterised by a particular set of resources at a regional scale, that is, a scale large enough that foraging expeditions would regularly occur within the habitat (see also *patch*).

Holocene The current geological epoch, dating to after 10 000 years BP, in which world climate has been approximately that of the present day. Synonymous with postglacial.

ideal free distribution (IFD) A model that predicts the ideal population distribution of freely migrating foragers over habitats with differing resource characteristics.

industry A group of technologically and typologically similar artefacts confined to a limited area of time and space. Synonymous with complex or industrial complex.

intensification Increases in the focus of resource extraction efforts on one or a small range of resources.

Jomon The archaeological remains left by hunter–gatherers in Japan from the Late Pleistocene until the arrival of rice agriculture 3000 years ago.

Kebaran A group of early Epipalaeolithic industries found throughout the eastern Mediterranean. followed in the Levant by the Geometric Kebaran.

kJ/hr Kilojoules per hour (see also *MJ/hr*): kJ/kg is kilojoules per kilogram of body weight.

language death The loss of speakers by a language leading to the result that no one speaks the language.

language shift The replacement an old language by a new one as the main language of a population.

language spread The increase of geographical area in which a language is spoken, by means of language shift and/or by migration of speakers into new areas.

Last Glacial Maximum (LGM) The period approximately 16 000 and 22 000 years ago, witnessing the most recent major glacial advance.

leaf point A small, thin, symmetrical, bifacially flaked stone artefact with one sharp end.

Levallois A distinctive set of techniques for making stone flakes and blades, normally associated with the Middle Palaeolithic/Middle Stone Age.

Levallois point A unique type of triangular, pointed flake produced by a specific variant of the Levallois method.

lingua franca A language used as a second language by a number of groups for communication between groups.

linguo-genetic Indicates relationships of languages sharing a common ancestor like a language family, used to avoid confusion with 'bio-genetic', i.e. genetic in the biological sense. The general model is known as the Stammbaum ('family tree') model and family and genetic metaphors derived from it are common, e.g. 'daughter languages', 'inheritance' for features descended from the parent or proto-language, as opposed to 'diffusion' or borrowing of features from other languages.

macroscale approach Considers variability in the choice of, making and using of tools at a very large scale, as for example at a continent or global level or for changes through time within a region. Insights from evolutionary ecology are employed and there is often an emphasis on models based on optimality. (See also *microscale approach*.)

Magdalenian A widespread Late Upper Palaeolithic industrial complex in Europe.

maintainable designs, maintainability Of tools that are always ready for use and continue to work effectively until a task is completed. Tools are therefore made of modular parts for easy repair and contain backup parts which are arranged in a series. Manufacture and repair is continuous so tools are always ready. Within this design system are flexibility which involves the use of tools which change their form for different functions and versatility in which tools that are multipurpose are used.

marginal value The value, in fitness, utility or another currency, of the nth unit of a resource to an individual already in possession of $n-1$ units. Marginal value typically decreases (the fourth serving of potatoes at a meal is not as valuable as the first).

marginal value theorem (MVT) A micro-ecological model that predicts when a forager should abandon a patch that is declining in its yield.

Maritime Archaic The archaeological remains left by early postglacial hunter–gatherers in maritime regions of eastern Canada and the North-eastern United States, ending in some areas about 5000 years ago by the arrival of the Paleoeskimo tradition, believed to represent the first Inuit.

Mesolithic In Europe, the archaeological time period that started 11 000 years ago at the end of the *Palaeolithic* and ended when farming was adopted.

microliths Very small, intentionally shaped lithic artefacts, most often associated with the Late Upper Palaeolithic, Epipalaeolithic or Mesolithic.

microscale approach Concentrates on processes which relate to individuals, households, or local groups and considers how technology is meaningfully and socially constituted and how it can transform social life. (See also *macroscale approach*.)

MJ/hr Megajoules/hour, the international standard unit for measuring energy gain or expenditure. One MJ/hr equals 238.9 kcal/hr. (See also *kJ/hr*.)

mode of production Marx's concept for characterising different economic forms by forces (land, labour, knowledge and skill, technology) and relations (property rights, access to and distribution of resources) of production.

Mousterian Archaeological assemblages from Europe and western Asia dating to the middle and late Pleistocene, from roughly 250 000 to 35 000 years BP, sharing a preponderance of flake tools and the frequent use of Levallois method.

Mousterian point A stone flake or blade, generally thin, with two convergent retouched edges forming a point.

Mushabian A late Epipalaeolithic culture of the southern Levant.

Natufian The archaeological remains left by the final hunter–gatherers in the Near East, characterised by a high degree of sedentism and intensive use of wild-plant resources, lasting some 3 000 years and ending with the appearance of farming about 11 000 years ago.

Neanderthal Extinct form of hominid frequently associated with Mousterian and sometimes Early Upper Palaeolithic assemblages in Europe and the Near East. The taxonomic status of Neanderthals remains a topic of debate.

Neolithic Archaeological period associated with earliest evidence of domesticated plants and animals, agriculture and village life.

net acquisition rate (NAR) A commonly used measure of value in foraging studies: the gross energy gained by pursuing a particular set of resources, minus the energy costs, divided by the time required, expressed in terms such as MJ/hr.

opportunistic behaviour A response to unintended conditions.

opportunity cost The cost of a behaviour, measured by the benefits associated with the alternative activities that it precludes. For a forager, an opportunity cost of a mid-day nap is the food that could have been obtained by foraging during the same period.

optimality As defined by Torrence, the process of seeking the best solution to problems as perceived and defined by individuals and situated within a particular physical and social context. A wide range of responses can be expected including the reduction of costs, maximisation of benefits, or the preservation of *status quo*. Optimality of risk is defined as the avoidance of severe costs of not meeting dietary requirements.

Original Affluent Society (OAS) A term applied to hunter–gatherers in small nomadic groups to imply that they have few material needs and that these needs are easily satisfied.

oxygen isotope stages Division of recent geological history into climatic phases based on oxygen isotope evidence from deep-sea cores. Even-numbered stages represent cold periods; odd-numbered stages are warm intervals.

Physical activity level (PAL) the ratio of total daily energy expenditure and basal metabolic rate, correcting for body weight, age and sex, to enable cross-population comparisons. PAL values are used to indicate light, moderate and heavy workloads.

Palaeolithic (Paleolithic) The archaeological time period which ended 11 000 years ago. Middle Palaeolithic: stone tool assemblages from Europe and Asia dating to between approximately 250 000 and 35 000 BP, and virtually synonymous with Mousterian. Equivalent to Middle Stone Age in Africa, associated hominids include both Neanderthals and anatomically modern humans (*Homo sapiens sapiens*). Upper Palaeolithic: stone tool assemblages from Europe and Asia dating to between approximately 45 000 and 12 000 BP, characterised by frequent use of blade blanks for lithic artefacts and the presence of distinctive stone and bone or antler tool forms, ornamental objects and sometimes art; mostly associated with anatomically modern humans. Often divided into two phases, the Early Upper Palaeolithic (EUP), between roughly 45 000 and 20 000 BP, and the Late Upper Palaeolithic (LUP), between roughly 20 000 and 10 000 BP. Epipalaeolithic: late Pleistocene archaeological assemblages from western Asia generally characterised by an abundance of microlithic artefacts, roughly equivalent to the LUP in Europe.

Pama-Nyungan A language family which covers most of Australia except for the central North.

patch A localised concentration of a particular resource or set of resources, on a scale such that a hunter–gatherer would regularly encounter several such concentrations in the course of a foraging trip. (See also *Habitat.*)

pidgin A simplified form of a language or mixture of more than one languages used as a second language, often as a *lingua franca.*

Pleistocene Geological epoch dating between 1.8 million and 10 000 years ago, approximately. Conventionally divided into three intervals: lower/early (1.8 million to 730 000 years ago); middle (730 000 to 120 000 years ago); and upper/late (120 000 to 10 000 years ago).

postglacial Synonymous with *Holocene.*

reciprocity Behaviours in which an individual acts to significantly benefit another, at some smaller cost to itself, in the expectation that the other individual will reciprocate when their roles are reversed. Ethnographic studies of hunter–gatherers typically describe food sharing in terms of reciprocity.

reductionism Analysis which presumes that complex phenomena can be better understood by study of their constituent structures and processes. Thus, the foraging mode of production is profitably analysed in terms of elements such as resource selection, settlement relocation, within-group transfers, etc.

reliable designs, reliability Behaviours which prevent failure while a tool is being used. They result in the overdesign of tools by knowledgeable and skilled actors who make tools that are well constructed, sturdy and composed of numerous redundant parts. In addition, manufacture and repair is carefully scheduled to avoid periods of use.

reproductive success Number of children born that survive to reproductive age.

residual zone A region in which there are many diverse languages with relatively small territories which do not spread significantly. (See also *language spread, spread zone.*)

resource ranking Ordering of resources according to ratio of yield to cost, using a single currency (frequently energy).

risk Most ecologists and economists define risk as unpredictable variation in an outcome variable (e.g. rate of obtaining resources). Other scholars, such as Torrence, use a definition derived from the insurance industry and consider two components which include the probability of not meeting dietary requirements and the costs of this failure.

show-off model A model predicting when male hunters will be motivated to invest in the capture and wide distribution of large game or other valuable resources, in exchange for social benefits that enhance their fitness.

Solutrean A group of Upper Palaeolithic assemblages from southern France and northern Spain.

spread zone A term used to describe regions in which languages have spread widely in history and prehistory, contrasted with *residual zone.*

sterility Inability to reproduce. The primary sterility rate is the proportion of postmenopausal women who have had no live births. Secondary sterility is the inability to reproduce after having at least one live birth (early secondary sterility occurs when women lose the ability to reproduce before menopause; postmenopausal women either have primary or secondary sterility).

substratum The language which existed in an area before a new language spread into it. Often this substratum influences the development of the new language.

taphonomy The scientific study of how assemblages of skeletal elements are formed, and how chemical, geological and biological agents can modify buried skeletal tissues.

technology Physical actions by knowledgeable actors within a particular social, symbolic and historical context who employ selected materials to produce a desired outcome. Key elements include physical setting, social context, actors, knowledge, energy sources, raw materials, tools, actions and outcomes.

territorial behavior Perimeter defence of a bounded range in order to secure exclusive use of the resources it contains.

TFR Total fertility rate, the average number of births women who survive the reproductive span will bear. It is the sum of ASFRs. The cohort TFR is measured from women who have already completed the reproductive span. The period TFR is estimated from a cross sectional sample of women reproducing during the specified years. If fertility rates are unchanging through time, cohort and period TFRs will be equal.

tolerated theft A resource transfer occurring when the holder of a packet relinquishes portions that have low *marginal value* because they are being contested by an individual for whom they have higher marginal value.

tool assemblage The totality of tools used by an individual or a group (see also assemblage).

tool assemblage structure The various characteristics of a tool assemblage including assemblage composition (the various types of tools present), assemblage diversity (the number of different types of tools present) and assemblage complexity (the total or average number of parts for each tool).

tyransfers A neutral term for the movement of goods and services among the individuals in a group, which does not presuppose a particular causal mechanism (such as tolerated theft, costly-signalling or reciprocity).

Uluzzian A form of Early Upper Palaeolithic industry occurring exclusively in Italy.

Upper Palaeolithic See *Palaeolithic.*

Zarzian Late Upper Palaeolithic or Epipalaeolithic assemblages of the Zagros and Taurus regions of western Asia.

Index

Note: page numbers in *italics* refer to figures and tables